The MODERN GENTLEMAN

The MODERN GENTLEMAN

A GUIDE TO ESSENTIAL MANNERS, SAVVY & VICE

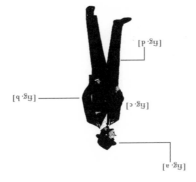

[fig. a]

[fig. b]

[fig. c]

[fig. d]

PHINEAS MOLLOD & JASON TESAURO

TEN SPEED PRESS

Berkeley • Toronto

A Kirsty Melville Book

Ten Speed Press
P.O. Box 7123 · Berkeley, California 94707
www.tenspeed.com

Permission granted to reprint material from the following publications:

p. 81. Henry Miller, *My Life and Times*. New York: Gemini Smith/Playboy Press, 1971.

p. 126. D.H. Lawrence, *Lady Chatterley's Lover*. New York: Penguin, 1962.

p. 198. Raymond Chandler, *The Long Goodbye*. New York: Random House, 1992.

p. 200. From *One-Upmanship* by Stephen Potter. © 1952 by Stephen Potter.
Reprinted by permission of Henry Holt & Co., LLC.

p. 211. Tom Robbins, *Fierce Invalids Home from Hot Climates*. New York: Bantam Books, 2001.

p 220. Excerpt from *Woman: An Intimate Geography*. Copyright (c) 1999 by Natalie Angier.
Reprinted by permission of Houghton Mifflin Company. All rights reserved.

p. 243. Jackie Stewart, Interview, *Playboy* June 1972.

p. 303. *Amy Vanderbilt's Complete Book of Etiquette*. New York: Random House, 1958.

Distributed in Australia by Simon and Schuster Australia; in Canada by Ten Speed Press Canada;
in New Zealand by Southern Publishers Group; in South Africa by Real Books; in Southeast Asia
by Berkeley Books; and in the United Kingdom and Europe by Airlift Book Company.

Design by Paul Kepple @ Headcase Design

Library of Congress Cataloging-in-Publication Data

Mollod, Phineas.
    The modern gentleman / Phineas Mollod and Jason Tesauro.
        p. cm.
    Includes bibliographical references and index.
    ISBN 1-58008-430-3 (paperback)
    ISBN 1-58008-478-8 (hardcover)
    1. Etiquette for men. I. Tesauro, Jason. II. Title.
    BJ1855 .M65 2002
    395.1'42—dc21
                                        2002001355

First printing 2002 · Printed in Canada · 2 3 4 5 6 7 8 9 10 — 06 05 04 03 02

To all the books that made me think and blush, and the hidden gems of life that begged my discovery.

—P. M.

For the two bewitching, dichotomous ladies who polished me— Momma and my Fairest E, who taught me vowels besides I.

—J. T.

A C K N O W L E D G M E N T S

♦ ♦ ♦ ♦ ♦ ♦ ♦ ♦

Thanks to Mom and Dad, who provided endless support during my tunnel out of the law and into the light. Thanks again, Mom, for teaching me the decorum of eating while seated; and Dad, for lessons on the finer points of drinking from the faucet. My bros, Mike and Dan, for rearing me in wrestling, wit, vice, and Red, White & Blue— especially Dan, who made the brilliance of Classical Music and the sublimity of Catsup what they are. My beaming grandmas, who instilled some old-world values into my rebellious frame and hopefully too, their dominant genes of longevity. Gracias, Vanderbilt buds who mentored me during my early twenties: Glen, Raj, and Fischer, who offered Beyond Bachelorhood counsel; Jones, Keough, and Ahrens for ushering in my Golf and meat-and-three education; and Keene, who was a gentlemanly paragon while residing in a dangerous hotel pantry, 3,000 miles away from his sweetheart, Margie. Merci, Gillian for loaning her alluring editing eyes, focus grouping the byline, and refining Phineas's Phavourites. And New York, the greatest city in the world and the ultimate proving ground for all gentlemanly pursuits.

—P. M.

Thank you, Aunt Georgia and the pack of wild women who groomed me, made me dress up for kindergarten, and stood in front of doors until I opened them. Uncle Vincent and his imperious sermons that rendered me too scared to fail. Dan and his dogma, love of bijous, and insights on Tenderness. Claire and Matt for clever Interlocution, Tantric floggings, and wicked wickets. Golf claps to Conal for long-hand Correspondence regarding Monogamy and midtown Skinny-Dips. Eleanor Brangan, Frederick Eckert, Frank Occhiogrosso, and Eli Kirk-Moffett . . . classroom stirrers of my logodaedaly. A penitent *sigh* to those who bore a roguish, pre-MG Tesauro: RO, MB, NL, BS, SF. Thomas Lux for inciting truth and curbing my magniloquence. Geri and Georgia Writers, Inc. for filling my pen with local support. Jacqueline and her loupe for masterpieces on E's and my fingers. Grazie, Veni Vidi Vici for edifying my Oenophilia and scheduling endless personal days, especially Ryuichi for an a design eye and an ever-full Riedel of Barbaresco. Chris and Kellette for sharing a splendid '94 Cabernet Sauvignon and a humidor's worth of cigar knowledge. Standing O to Atlanta, my Southern-fried metropolis, where the likes of Gentleman Jim and Stefan's stiffen a man's bow before a julep at 1848 House and a jounce at the Chamber.

—*J. T.*

Both authors express fond gratitude: HA Krewe for their Group Dynamics and Charcoal Briquetiquette; specifically McGrath, who provided inspiration for Cutting Back and the antimodel for the

Gentleman's Bedroom. Heartfelt shout-out to Jill for rooftop, darkroom, and cell phone inspirations on Intimate Gatherings, Photography, and Answering Machines. Namaste, Ninety-second Street Y, David, Nancy, and Michael for refining our Yoga, spines, and kundalini. Kudos to the elusive Karl for backstage antics Between the Sheets; and Heidi, Gordon, Kenny (the Three Little Pigs) for mowing our Leaves of Grass. All our former employers' (and Greer's) toner-filled office machines. Traci, for sharing her Wooing expertise and the finer points of Office Romance at an Internet start-up. Robbie and Mary Kay for exhibitions of Public Gaming and Yahtzee yelling. Thankful alohas to Atlanta Cheetah Club for demonstrating how naked has manners. James Bond for managing martinis, Miss Moneypenny, SPECTRE, and the baccarat shoe with equal éclat. A thunderous oink to KPIG 107.5, Freedom, California, the finest swine on the air, for providing via Internet the soundtrack for past-midnight creative sessions. Cindy Lou Who for the vintage volumes on kink, clothes, and etiquette. A secret handshake to the dapper designer, Paul, and the patient, sure-fire illustrator, Tony. Thanks to our sharp-eyed copyeditor, proofer, and indexer: Tamar, Clancy, and Ken. Our staunch supporters at Ten Speed Press, especially Aaron Wehner, a fellow gent, for wielding a mighty blue pencil. Brother Antoine and the Carthusian monks for deciphering the Elixir of Long Life. Lastly, to our velvety agent, Kimberley Cameron for believing in us—twice—and having an exquisite sweet tooth.

CONTENTS

INTRODUCTION I

PART ONE: THE GREGARIOUS GENTLEMAN 3

CHAPTER ONE: OUT & ABOUT **4**
Interlocution • Tipping • Jukeboxing • Flaskmanship • Photography • Elevator Etiquette • Eating Out • Skinny-Dipping • Gate-Crashing • Comings & Goings • Reunions

CHAPTER TWO: ENTERTAINING **38**
Group Dynamics • Hosting • Intimate Gatherings • The Active Table • Houseguests • Charcoal Briquetiquette • Bachelor Party • Best Manning

CHAPTER THREE: WOOING **67**
Flirtation • Dates • The Open Triangle • Do-It-Yourself • Long-Distance Runaround • Exes & Ohs • The Crack-Up

PART TWO: THE INNER GENTLEMAN 97

CHAPTER FOUR: GENTLEMANLY KNOWLEDGE **98**
Literature • Classical Music • Jazz • Fitness • Yoga • Flora • Soothsaying • Profanity & Vulgarity • Man Cycle • Fonzarelli Moves & Legerdemain

CHAPTER FIVE: APPEARANCE & STYLE **132**
Fashion • Business Attire • Accessories • Seasonal Toggery • Neckwear • Pyjamas • Eyewear • Men Without Hats • Umbrella Policy • Tattoos • Hygiene & Habits

CHAPTER SIX: DOMESTICITY **161**
Domestic Guidelines • The Kitchen • Cooking • Breaking Bread • The Gentleman's Bedroom • Heartifacts • Toiletiquette • Spitting, Hiccoughing & Other Expulsions

PART THREE: THE POTENT GENTLEMAN 181

CHAPTER SEVEN: VENERABLE VICES: ALCOHOL, TOBACCO
& FIREWORKS 182
*Spirits • Beyond & Tonic • Concocting • The Solitary Drink • Oenophilia • Bubbly •
Saké • Working with a Hangover • The Ethic of Alcohol • Tobacco • Drugs • Leaves
of Grass • Gaming • Golf • Card Playing • The Ponies*

CHAPTER EIGHT: BETWEEN THE SHEETS 233
*Prophyletiquette • XXX: Phineas's Phavourites & Tesauro's Titillations • Kink &
Fetish • To the Power of ³ • Gentleman's Club*

CHAPTER NINE: TROUBLE 251
*Sticky Situations & Solutions • How Many People Have You Slept With? • Your Lover
Finds Evidence of Old Flames • Your Girlfriend Says, "I'm Pregnant" • Conversational
Gaffes • Secrets, Lies & Confidences • Office Romance • Losing It • The Apology*

PART FOUR: THE WAYFARING GENTLEMAN 277

CHAPTER TEN: TRAVEL 278
*Motoring • Asking Directions • Bumper Stickers • Jet-Setting • Mile-High Club •
Sleeper Trains • Theorem de Valise • Guest Decorum*

PART FIVE: THE CEREMONIAL GENTLEMAN 301

CHAPTER ELEVEN: PUBLIC RELATIONS 302
Correspondence • Answering Machines • E-mail • Gifting • Handy Gifting Guide

CHAPTER TWELVE: BEYOND BACHELORHOOD 321
The Rock • Proposals • Vows • The Good Husband

AFTERWORD 331
BIBLIOGRAPHY 334
INDEX 337

INTRODUCTION

◆ ◆ ◆ ◆ ◆ ◆

A man may possess expensive duds, slick wheels, and a tongue to match, but these are not the prerequisites of a gentleman. A gentleman is defined by how he carries himself in fairways and stormy climes. A student of the classics and a pilot of the new, he recommends sizzling reads, pays his gambling debts, mans the grill, and curbs his dog. Reserved, flamboyant, or likely somewhere in between, a gentleman's charisma is cultivated, not canned. He fosters an infectious comfort in others as they quietly marvel at his manner and his hats, from the erudite bowler to the plucky fedora. Little charms performed thoughtfully ensure that inevitable faux pas are measured against a graceful reputation. He can be trusted with his word and your wife.

The Modern Gentleman is a visually stimulating, rib-tickling, thought-provoking sourcebook of manners and mischief. Enlightened and more than a little bit decadent, it's a pioneering slant on etiquette for gallery-openers and bar-closers alike. The book offers a panoramic snapshot of the gentleman: witty and poignant, traditional but spontaneous, flirtatious yet courtly. The contents are breadth-taking, ranging from classic ("Motoring," "Oenophilia") and serious ("Secrets, Lies & Confidences," "The Good Husband"), to racy ("Kink & Fetish," "To the Power of ³") and silly ("Bumper Stickers," "Spitting, Hiccoughing & Other Expulsions"). Brush up on skinny-dipping and jukebox etiquette, and then settle into comprehensive discussions on literature, jazz, and hosting large or intimate gatherings in pyjamas. And since it is inevitable that a gentleman will dabble in the friskier areas of excess, trouble, and chance, the book's naughty nucleus, "The Potent

Gentleman," explores leisure and dalliance, from alcohol and snuff to recreational botanicals and sex. "Trouble" delves into character-defining obstacles, conundrums, and gaffes; even when composure erodes, a gentleman keeps a few vital wits in reserve.

Long-forgotten cocktail recipes litter these pages, reminding us of the colorful life available in fine glassware, if one is armed with an open mind and shaker. *Incidentally*, in addition to "Working with a Hangover," all topics and activities were thoroughly researched and undertaken. "Gaming," "Flaskmanship," "Wooing," "Prophyletiquette," and all applicable stunts continue to be practiced by the authors.

The Modern Gentleman is not a cure-all for flaccid character (though readers will absorb knowledge and depth that vastly improves leisure and sexuality). Nor is it a pick-up guide for dummies, a fudge-your-way-through-life primer, or the "last word" on style or dress. We purposely avoid most topics blanketed in ordinary guy guides filled with ruler-rapping dictums about brown shoes and black belts. *Lover* and *bedmate* appear more frequently here than *girlfriend* or *lady*; the Modern Gentleman knows that kindness is not gender-specific, and that a gay gentleman practices most of the same considerations as his heterosexual counterpart.

The Modern Gentleman is an attainable character, not larger than life, but exactly the size of it. We all aspire to be perpetually dapper, fluent in three languages, and able to hit 300-yard drives off the blue tees, as well as quote poetry by the stanza and win a back-alley scrap. However, there is a plateau more desirable than Hollywood perfection, a level of gallantry that makes you stand out, even in the elevator. Perhaps it's as simple as remembering first names or including the shy in a conversation for a change. So knot up your ascot, pour a glass of sherry, and dim the lights: your Man Cycle is peaking.

PART ONE

The GREGARIOUS GENTLEMAN

Chapter One

OUT & ABOUT

◆ ◆ ◆ ◆ ◆ ◆ ◆ ◆

Interlocution 5

Tipping 9

Jukeboxing 12

Flaskmanship 15

Photography 17

Elevator Etiquette 19

Eating Out 21

Skinny-Dipping 24

Gate-Crashing 27

Comings & Goings 29

Reunions 32

INTERLOCUTION

Clever interlocution is a toss of salt on the ice of inhibition; know when to be bold (but not coarse). Don't be a loudmouth, but in the right moment, savor the occasional animated outburst that turns heads. Counterbalance the usual Q&A with pointed questions about alternate career yens, spirituality, current affairs, sexual proclivities, and after-hours pursuits. Ready these in the verbal arsenal even if they are not fired at the opening shot. Though, sometimes the best catalyst is a quiet listener who facilitates conversation with eye contact and interest in another's story. Like the aging hurler facing the cleanup hitter, nibble early in the count, and then throw your best curveballs for full effect. The best conversations blur time as those involved establish shared interests or spark healthy debate.

Eavesdropping would be a juicier sport if dialogue were more exciting than a litany of tired phrases:

"How are you?"

"Fine."

"What's happening with you?"

"Not much."

"Job's okay?"

"Same old, same old."

Every gentleman should banish this conversational game of chicken—waiting for the other to share. Scores of intelligent and discerning minds retreat to small talk and smatter when mixed with strangers. Good chat begins when one person pushes talk forward with personal news or current-events nuggets. Be a beacon. Make it your responsibility to wade through a crowd of shallow souls, looking for the deep end.

Clichés and hackneyed language are pollutants that belong in bad poetry, not daily discourse. Pet jargon spices diction, yet the hallmark of a good keynoter is freshness. To avoid being annoying, root out overused exclamations and superlatives.

Engage, don't disparage. Verbal interplay is not a strike of braggadocio upon those down on their luck or a haughty high-hat pounce on introverts. Ask about recent vacations or outings, not relationship woes. Better to break ice with hobbies than with how unemployment is going. The unthinking tighten the circle around lofty topics of singular specialty. Perhaps Argentinean fiscal policy isn't another's forte; sports and the holidays might be more accessible starters. Don't shy away from the perpetually shy, but refrain from needling with a smug and smarmy, "Having a good time?"

Hot topics are less a list of things to discuss and more a mandate to probe further. Delving into lesser-explored areas of interest leads to surprising discoveries and deepened connections. Limber the wit with trifling matters before steering talk to greater issues. Mine too soon and conversation sputters due to a premature leap into personal space.

Clever conversation includes the following, used in light rotation:

• **Witty Devices**: puns, hyperbole, double entendre, homophones.

• **Recitations**: literary quotations, movie lines, song lyrics, poetry.

• **Interjections**: trenchant asides, sound effects, exclamations.

• **Rehearsed Material**: jokes (very limited), stories, tall tales.

• **Interrogatives**: questions that get heads scratching.

- **Bullhorns**: large-group addresses (know when to pass the mic).

- **Proofreading**: corrections of fact, tactfully offered, that spur continued discussion.

- **Ref Whistles**: debate arbitration (throw the flag on low blows when necessary).

The gentleman is as comfortable trading esoteric talk with bow-tied theatregoers as he is regaling toweled locker-room buddies with the one about the Pope and the Seven Dwarves. Deft talk is not about grandiloquence, rather raising the comfort level of those around by sharing

BUTTING IN

Bouts of spirited wordplay in storytelling circles are soulful music, not henhouse cacophony. Sharp interjections pitch a story to greater heights, extracting juicy details and creating operatic tension. But beware the verbal blue jay: this predator lacks the originality to start meaningful conversation, but not the temerity to barge into your nest during a fulminating climax. Bland asides and chirping interruptions sully a hot retelling. Bleats of "ooh," "ahh," and "No foolin'!" are oxygen. Too often, the unthinking listener needlessly footnotes or fact-checks ("Well actually, Montpelier is the capital of Vermont"), or worse, prematurely follows up and murders the punch line ("The same thing happened to a friend of mine"). Only the plonking boor drains the conversational momentum with worthless tangents or untimely transitions.

knowledge and wit befitting the tenor of the moment. Adapt and employ conversational dexterity like a Swiss Army knife of the tongue: for most occasions, the three-inch blade will suffice; however, certain company may warrant the saw (cut through the thick of it), spoon (speak in small doses), toothpick (get in hard-to-reach places), or tweezers (be pointed and delicate). But cool the jaw—too much is overwhelming. A constant entertainer who is always "on" is like tiresome Labor Day telethon shtick. Some nights, be the group's emcee; on others, turn off the spotlight and enjoy friendly chat traded over a pint.

Despite your full quiver of anecdotes and accomplishments, curtail showboating and needless rodomontade. Ask questions and gain insight into others' character instead of trumpeting your own. Share reason and realizations, not résumés.

Some talking pointers:

+ When others are basking in a moment of grandeur, do not engage in one-upmanship simply to tout vast experience.

+ Stir energy into flailing circles. Instigate easy chat by finding a touchstone ("Dugan, haven't you just returned from Walla Walla?").

+ Never refer to yourself in the third person plural (we) or the first person proper (Tesauro), lest you sound like Sybil.

+ Know how to banter and sling slang. Not every word must be polished.

+ Keep your eyes out for these feckless perpetrators and discomfiting yakkers of nervous interlocution: shifty-eyed ceiling starers, closed-eyed pensives, obsessive nose scratchers, mouth watchers, snorting snits, slithering blatherers, tongue wetters, cheek clickers, ear cockers, gum smackers, hair twirlers, brow wrinklers, lobe pullers, lane shifters, beeper checkers, beard strokers, surprising crescendoers, and dorky guffawers—not to mention the warblers, mumblers, spittlers, ummers, and whistlers.

Incidentally, no tacking on two worthless cents. The fourth frustrating anecdote of airport delays and snowy travel snags is less than fresh.

TIPPING

Step up to the charge-card plate—former waiters shouldn't be the only decent tippers. Yet, don't be goaded into a gratuity unless a real service or extra consideration has been proffered. A to-go cup of java poured from a coffee shop carafe is not *service.* However, be kind to teenage girls who toil at beachside ice-cream/snack bar shops for minimum wage.

RESTAURANT

Fifteen percent is reasonable and appreciated. If the food is well prepared, and timely and professionally served, tip 20 percent. If special requests were honored without gripe or if service greatly enhanced your enjoyment, consider more. Leave extra when the difference between a good tip and a great tip is minimal. When using a coupon, or when a discount is applied, don't gyp the server—tip as if you paid full price. Whenever possible, leave the gratuity in cash; it's easier for the server and harder for the IRS.

Nice touch: When amidst tight-wadded guests, drop the Supplement: upon departure, surreptitiously slip a few extra dollars to compensate for a host's parsimony.

Two things people in the service industry remember: great tippers and cantankerous souls. If service was distinctly poor and it appears the kitchen was not at fault, tip minimally. Conversely, if fine service has ameliorated a poor meal, don't punish a waiter for the chef's blunders. If the entire experience was abominable, leave nothing but a note. In finer establishments, don't leave without first voicing complaints to a manager. If a concern is not spoken with vituperative spit, you may be invited back for another try. . .on their dime.

A tip chart? Do you also need a multiplication table and an alphabet schematic? Take 10 percent and double the amount, or simply double the sales tax for an approximation.

Maitre D'. If a restaurant is full, don't bother lying ("I'm sure there's a reservation"). Simply say, "I appreciate whatever you can do" as you discreetly palm a twenty. Use similar strategies when stuck for a last-minute hotel room.

Sommelier. Not sure what to tip the sommelier? Wouldn't a steward with shrewd recommendations also like a small taste?

Valet. Offer $1 to $2 for most domestic automobiles, more for luxury or exotic cars that have been well tended and quickly produced. Increase the gratuity in inclement weather.

Coatcheck. One dollar is standard, but double for additional coats, even if they are hung on a single hanger.

Hair Stylist. Give $5 or more to the stylist, more for complete coif renovation. Chip in at least $1 to the shampoo attendant, especially for foreign accents and deft neck-kneading skills.

Mechanic. An honest mechanic who resists the temptation to find fictitious transmission problems deserves a small sum along with your continued patronage. Off-the-main-drag repairmen who fix minor problems on the spot deserve at least a $10 tip.

Nice touch: Find yourself filling up on a cold holiday night? Slip the station attendant a few extra bucks just for working.

Food Delivery. Deliverymen are not well paid. Fork over an extra dollar and loose quarters to show appreciation. Tip handsomely for hot food delivered in gelid conditions.

Dry Cleaners. Drop-offs do not require a tip, but for customers wanting rushed service or kid-glove treatment of delicates, leave a few dollars to the launderer handling your duds.

Shoeshine. Give $1 to $2, possibly more with any extra services and snappy political or historical conversation. If the shoeblack provides a newspaper or does a fine re-dye of the outsoles, an extra tip is mandatory.

Hotel Staff. Reward a bellman for help with baggage and unexpected requests. No need to engage the staff to carry an attaché case, and never ask to borrow the luggage cart yourself—it's like asking a landscaper for his leaf blower. Leave a minimum $5 tip, $10 or more if you are with a rowdy crowd. A twenty will buy an inside accomplice. No change is no excuse; ask the bellman to break a bill. To ensure bag safety, tip again if the hotel safeguards your luggage after checkout.

As for chambermaids, tip for lengthy stays, inspired turndown service, and soaring levels of filth. Room service is already a decadent activity—don't run out of generosity when signing the bill. Leave at least 15 percent to the room-service waiter for your $14.95 cheeseburger.

Taxi Drivers. For a fare under $6, round up to the next dollar (fare is $5.20, leave $6). On longer rides or if the conversation is especially randy and fresh, increase your gratuity to 15 percent. An extra-generous tip is standard for drunken groups and late-night rides home. Leave more when the cabbie is quick on the gas or merciless with the horn toward sluggards.

Yearly Services. At year's end, certain service personnel deserve holiday tips. While a gift or tin of cookies is nice, cash is most appreciated. Despite regulations, post and parcel carriers graciously accept tips ($10 to $20 is sufficient). Try not to skimp on those caring for your dependents: regular babysitters and dog-walkers should be given at least a $30 to $50 tip. Newspaper deliverers often insert a holiday card and self-addressed envelope into the newspaper as a reminder (at least $10).

City dwellers are invariably faced with anxious doormen and building superintendents in December. Residents have two options for doormen. Tip $30 to $50 individually to the doorman and the super, or deposit one lump sum into the tip pool. As a ballpark figure, expect to contribute 1 to 2 percent of annual rent toward a large building's staff.

JUKEBOXING

Like Lou Gramm of Foreigner once crooned, be a jukebox hero. A jukebox affords a public opportunity to select moodful tunes and display an eclectic musical canon. In the right hands, greatest hits are tabled so that B-sides may shine.

Your dollar is a well-considered three-act passion play, not a heedless afterthought. Do not feel constrained by random shuffle play—put a set together. Range the emotions and forage deep. Do a "double-shot" and your genius will be noticed. Avoid the pitfalls of the vapid and eschew standards of heavy rotation. Can't you do better than "Brown-Eyed Girl" or "Margaritaville"? At every unenlightened venue, you will find *The Best of Blondie, Saturday Night Fever,* and Neil Diamond's favorites. These are a constant presence, like the flu. Be underground radio, not Casey Kasem. When in doubt or rushed to return for your pool shot, toss in a guaranteed crowd-pleaser. In the event of sudden dead air, make a quick choice from the current open page.

Before mashing final selections, tour the entire menu: don't squander a dollar before you've seen the merchandise (though, first-pitch fastball swinging is allowed for an especially tasty number). Don't be one-minded: mix it up and enhance the vibe of the room. Like at a railroad crossing, stop, look, and listen; perhaps a touch of the blues or the dive special (any Allman Brothers' song over twelve minutes) is in order. As long as Devo's "We're Through Being Cool" isn't your first selection, give the people what they want. In any case, the "no Kenny Loggins" lamp is always lit.

Exercise restraint before fulfilling some inner-alcoholic, inexplicable need for a tired favorite like "Start Me Up." However, the above guidelines are suspended when: "impairment" becomes an understatement, the waitress has joined your party, or you are a regular patron.

THE BIG SPENDER

When settled in for an evening's entertainment, go ahead and splurge on the eighteen-song super set. Your wrinkle-free Lincoln can provide the soundtrack for a solid, golden hour. Don't tarry—popular jukeboxes boast large backlogs, forcing a twenty-minute wait before your medley begins. Select early, so that "Superstition" won't be just starting as you settle the tab. If someone is already at the helm, offer a "settlement." For example, Tesauro steps up to the box and spies a young lass frustrated because the bill acceptor is spitting back her tattered buck:

> May I offer you some fresh currency? Why don't you give me your dollar, I'll put in a five, and qualify us for the extra songs . . . like the upper-section 35-point bonus in Yahtzee. The catch? I get to pick the first song; you can have the next three. As the benefactor, I retain veto power. Shall we dance?

TABLETOP DINER MODELS

Famished in a Jersey diner late one evening, you encounter a diminutive, tabletop, twenty-five-cent mono jukebox nestled behind the A-1 Sauce. Soak in the playlist: ne'er heard Billy Joel singles sit beside Elton John's "I'm Still Standing," just above Bobby Darin's "Mack the Knife," to the left of "That's Amore!" If you have at least a booth's-length from the nearest revelers, punch up the volume from LO to HI.

NINE INCH NAILING

After an especially horrible experience of poor service, repeated short pours, or unsavory clientele, it's clearly time to leave the bar. Even if you harbor enough resentment to piss in the corner pocket, stop and instead use your underdeveloped superego to produce a gift for everyone. Pure fury is much sweeter when spread out over the course of $5. This is the time for stuffing the jukebox with "Let's Get Physical." Put that dusty *Irish Drinking Songs* disc on repeat (after three or four plays, "The Rover" ceases to be pleasant). Perhaps you might go for the darker side—play the last four songs on Nine Inch Nails's *Downward Spiral,* repeatedly. If you are a victim of Nine Inch Nailing, simply yank the plug and start over.

FLASKMANSHIP

[cap]

[monogram]

The flask provides a gentleman with a dash of home-style comfort, a hint of luxurious élan, portable panache in less than nine ounces. It is essential clandestine equipment, favored during airplane travel, train trips, and motorcarring (for passengers).

While the gentleman's daily chapeau remains out of current favor, a flask is classic and need not connote whiskey-induced dipsomania . . . unless you carry one in the breast pocket of your three-buttoned, notched-lapel jacket, and swig during Tuesday's board meeting.

Purchase wisely and steer clear of downtown discount tobacco shops or delis that also peddle Graffix bongs and pipes under the glass counter to local teens. Select tastefully: no models redeemed via Camel Cash, molded from lightweight synthetics,* or stamped from flimsy alloys by the Franklin Mint. Select silver, pewter, leather-bound glass, or fine stainless steel styles, with that supple curve for easy portability. A small funnel aids in liquor transfer.

Carry a flask in a breast or coat pocket; if this is not possible, you are underdressed for flasking. The only exception to this rule is the ripped back pocket of your redheaded girlfriend's faded dungarees. A monogrammed flask makes an exceptional gift, especially for the clever lady.

---

* Though, employ a biodegradable or plastic flask when camping or tailgating, or when facing impending seizure or loss (customs, principal's office, skydiving).

Better: Relish these shining moments to display your guarded suavity, and to season an evening or solitary moment with a delicate sip.

Better Not: Do not unduly flaunt your flask. Certain instances do not warrant open consumption, lest you be perceived unfairly.

BETTER	*BETTER NOT*
Between acts at the theatre or when cinema houselights dim.	At school plays (though perfect for the Pinewood Derby winner's circle).
Before any special-teams play at a football game.	A flask is for intermittent sips, not collegiate gulps.
Anywhere you can see your breath, especially on a blustery platform awaiting a homebound commuter train.	Any place where there is already available liquor.
A fall day at the beach or a wetting of the lips for taxi cab trips.	Don't put bad booze in a good flask— just bring the plastic bottle.
At the track as your horse rounds the home stretch.	Inexcusable during a job interview (a callback interview for an Internet start-up, maybe).
In the guest bathroom after meeting your lover's puritanical parents.	During Lamaze class.

Advanced flaskmanship: Stow Italian liqueur in your vessel and top off your companion's cappuccino during an afternoon rendezvous.

PHOTOGRAPHY

[film advance]

[shutter]

[lens]

Photos tickle brain fibers, reminding us of the frozen moment. Click and shoot like an expert shutterbug, but don't refer to yourself as a "photographer" until you have demonstrated minimum darkroom skills, know the unique odor of fixer, or have been previously paid for your craft. Sprinkling terms such as "F-stop" or "400 speed applicability" means nothing in the face of a tasteless Mickey Mouse shoulder strap.

Capture the everyday, not just the holidays. Periodically, document your neighborhood and living space. Shoot your car once and your pet often, and click especially well-garnished entrées or cocktails. Frame some snowy days, nimbus skies, or historical curiosities to round out a roll. For a slight Freudian delight, preserve on film the angelic innocence of a sleeping lover. To protect your oeuvre, recycle the under-the-bed shoebox and pick up a $5 drugstore photo album.

Make a roll more than just a snap-happy bundle of throwaway prints. Structured photos are for weddings and police mug shots. Go beyond bottom-row-kneeling group photos or synchronized smiles. Honor the dearly departed Alan Funt: be candid with your glossies. Catalogue an evening by taking photos of friends in slightly compromising positions, and save them for good-humored threats of extortion or unexpected envelope stuffings. Maintain the arsenal by getting doubles.

Try your hand at slides, panoramas, or underwater photography. Pack a disposable for skiing and canoeing trips, or a cheap point-and-shoot for rougher venues. Polaroids are suitable for insurance documentation and affairs even the automated developer system shouldn't scan.

Sometimes the camera comes to you. Keep eyes peeled for curtained boardwalk photo booths that spit out wet strips of make-out sessions and evidence of your fabulous tan. In lieu of a daguerreotype, send these four frivolous frames to a pen pal. Best in black and white, tear in half and keep the naughtier ones.

PHOTO FAUX PAS

When the countdown begins, get ready to click. Don't leave subjects floundering in an awkward minute of jaw-numbing smiles. Also, no instant replays. Redramatization of candid moments is soulless and taints the spontaneity of the moment. Sometimes it's best to put down the camera and leave reality unrecorded. The intrusiveness of trigger snapping at formal affairs should be in direct proportion to your skills and your relation to the subjects; do not knock over the infant flower girl to get a picture of your boss's cousin at the altar. Lastly, unless you are in the Sears child photo department, grow up. If you must say "cheese" to compel grinning conformity, select a variety commonly sold by the finest purveyors ("One, two, say 'Havarti with Dill!'"). Never use this joke more than once per decade.

DIGITAL STILLS & VIDEO

With the advent of digital cameras, it's easy and inexpensive to be prolific and experimental. It's great fun to huddle around the viewscreen after a well-captured frame, or e-mail pix in the morning to the previous night's revelers. Video cameras should be left to cinematographers, action news telecasters, and those with young children. Nothing drags on like two hours of mundane vacation video or shaky party-panning around the keg. Nonconsensual voyeuristic videotaping is dishonorable and litigious.

ELEVATOR ETIQUETTE

Ah, the elevator: tarnished brass walls, clanking exhaust fan, and the ever-tempting red STOP button. Savvy urbanites quickly learn that an empty, uninterrupted elevator ride is a rare treat, the crème brûlée of your day. Thus, do not feel like a misanthrope as you "appear to" fumble with the DOOR OPEN button while shrill cries of "Hold the door" echo down the hall. Yet, if you are courteously "saved" by a Samaritan who kindly reopens the door, reciprocate accordingly within five business days.

Joy of solitude aside, certain conventions must be followed for a seamless trip. While it is not improper to stand impassively in the lift among disgruntled employees mesmerized by the lighted floor display, a friendly solicitation, climate comment, or witticism may enrich the lives of even the surliest riders. There is only a small window in which to proffer elevatorial banter—like the rodeo and that ne'er seen Luke Perry movie, about eight seconds. After this period, the pall of awkwardness has indelibly clouded the car. Your floor is next, anyway.

If the carriage is crowded, do not wantonly snake an arm for the controls. Rather, politely inquire of the lovely lady near the buttons: "Could you mash five please?" As when riding in a subway car, don't hold up transit with chivalry; promptly step in and out.

Reserve the elevator for trips over three floors, except when toting parcels or hobbling to podiatrist appointments. If lucky enough to ride a manual elevator, have a smile and salutation ready for the attendant.

Moreover, allow at least a fourteen-floor buffer for the retelling of a long, filthy joke. Don't be the Nervous Nelly twitching at the CLOSE DOOR control, foolishly thinking it will speed the doors shut. Similarly, must you press and re-press the lit call button in the lobby, demonstrating egotistical mistrust of another's push?

Note: The elevator is an ideal spot to exercise Flaskmanship, steal a quick snuff, or refresh your bow-tie knot.

SMALL TALK

When the elevator car stops or the DMV line stalls, ready the small talk.

THE WEATHER. A gentleman has relevant and meaty morsels of meteorological phenomena at the ready for elevator chat. Don't fret over Tropical Depression Liza off the Lesser Antilles or the location of the prevailing jet stream; but at the minimum, shouldn't a man be heard to offer, "Feels like rain today"?

CURRENT EVENTS. Keep apprised of the world and metro area. Subscribe to the daily paper; at least read the news digests online. Follow a few pet scandals and fugitives for mention in longer lines. Scan the obits daily for quirkier tidbits, and discover how many relatively obscure people contributed to this society.

SPORTS. A fair number of gentlemen can recite the starting lineups of the '76 Reds, '78 Yankees, or '81 Dodgers. Should lunchtime or party chatter turn to the NCAA tournament seedings, Derby favorites, or the old Hartford Whalers, hold your own. At least follow the prevailing sport of the season. At bare minimum, know what is happening in the post-season. Keep an eye on recent player suspensions and batting leaders, and always tune in to the second half of Monday Night Football and the first half-hour of ESPN's SportsCenter.

EATING OUT

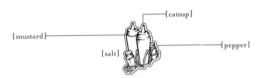

Lesser men are ogres at the kitchen table and little better when dining out. Politeness is a gentleman's constant, and he plays by the rules with fork and knife, especially on the road. If etiquette feels constricting, take latitude in the attitude, not the manners. Preserve outward decorum but maintain your inner maverick. Dessert conversation might make the maitre d' blush, but two tables over, they're marveling at your manners and wishing they could eavesdrop. Make Mom proud of your graceful grazing skills, but lift the ban on playing with your food when the clock strikes midnight.

Here are a few tips for the well-mannered man at the bistro:

- Whistling, snapping, or signaling unduly for a waiter's attention is unnecessary; good servers are trained to spot needy eye contact.

- When an escort rises from the table, exhibit a finger bowlful of punctilio and stand, if only into an acceptable three-quarter crouch where gravity hasn't yet tugged the napkin from your lap to the floor.

- Ordering meat well done is implicit permission for the chef to give you a less choice cut.

- Refrain from crude sawing, poking, or bowing a knife through the fork tines. Skip the precut woodpiles of meat and slice one tender forkful at a time. Cutting linguini into tatters insults all of Italy; twirl long noodles with a fork and pasta spoon.

- Enjoy the pampering: abstain from piling plates, self-crumbing your place mat, or bussing your own table.

- Play together = pay together: if a group is familiar enough to share a meal, split the check evenly rather than auditing it to save yourself three dollars. Expense accounts aside, separate checks are loathsome.

Incidentally, master chopsticks. A fork is an affront to the beauty of sushi and anything cooked in a wok. To hone dexterity, take two days of home-cooked meals exclusively with chopsticks, even slippery noodles.

DINER BEHAVIOR

A baseline of poise and refinement is never out of style, but monitor the atmosphere and measure formality against poshness, volume, and entrée prices. For homey establishments with napkin dispensers on tables sans linen, protocol and low cholesterol diets are relaxed. With less emphasis on posture and elbow position, diners and their vinyl booths are perfect for minor mischief.

No need to be prince of improv, but bring out a pocketful of gags to dish out like the curious corned beef hash you ordered. Be naughty at the diner without bothering the staff. Master a few tricks and sleights-of-hand involving spoons or nondairy creamers. Hatch behind-the-scenes waiter conspiracies to embarrass close friends. Become proficient in targeted, nonproliferating food volleys and inconspicuous lettuce placements. Above all, be silly with your garnish and your mouth.

Betcha can't eat six saltines in one minute—waiting in the diner is the optimal time for off-the-wall digestive wagering. Bet your comrade a sawbuck that he cannot eat his entire plate of silver-dollar pancakes in one bite; twenty to gulp the half-and-half pitcher; thirty if you mix in the entire bottle of A-1 Sauce. When pats of butter and onion halves are gobbled, everybody wins. This is a great venue for public gaming.

Don't dally with the menu or bask in the entrée selections. Despite any impairment, draw the first line in the sand: breakfast foods (eggi-wegs or French toast?) or not (pizza burger deluxe, moussaka), but never seafood, even if the bluefish blue-plate special is recommended. Never mind inquiring about toast types—order the rye for its optimal crunch and butter-soaking qualities.

Value the colorful waiter with the smart mouth and permanent-pressed pants. Feel free to politely use his first name, ask what's good tonight, and strike a sprightly dialogue. After all, it's 4 A.M. and you are eating Yankee pot roast with a side of chicken-fried something. Mildly raucous boothsmanship is encouraged, but it is unseemly for clumsy, noisy utensils to spoil a neighbor's Western omelette. Remember the

CATSUP

Easy with the Heinz. Give it a light rattle before tilting. If the viscosity or level does not allow for quick pouring, force a light rap on the bottle's sternum, the upper bulge where the neck meets the torso. As a last resort, use a fresh knife to coax the sauce forth. It is not ungentlemanly to offer catsup to a friend first; politeness notwithstanding, there is the wily avoidance of that first watery discharge out of a fallow bottle.

round of drinks you bought like a big shot an hour ago? After bouts of buffoonery, be nice to the chaperones—tip the babysitting server extra.

BUFFETIQUETTE

Reconnoiter the smorgasbord before ever ladling a dollop of country-style anything onto the plate. Lesser souls litter a disk with breads and filler foods before noticing the carving station and raw bar. Return serving utensils to a utility plate or hang them unsoiled upon the handles. Close a steaming chafer if an inconsiderate guest has allowed the trout almandine to cool or the biscuit gravy to skin over.

Nice touches: Offer fresh plates to your escort and the person immediately following. At the dessert station, swirl raspberry and chocolate sauces around brioche and flapjacks and make geometric shapes on plate rims for personal presentation.

SKINNY-DIPPING

What better end to an evening of group revelry, romantic frolic, or solitary mischief than a refreshing rinse and spin? Breaststroke sans a slap in the face, the skinny-dip is the most laudable of swims. Here, group or dual dynamics are fortified by liberating nakedness and a tinge of naughtiness. Like a night at sleep-away camp, once a small band has shared a bare splash, all bonds are reinforced. Besides, you've always wanted to see your pal's girlfriend naked anyway.

Even without drawers, the after-hours puddle plash is no time for a gentleman to lose his shirt.

Here are a few recommended scenarios:

- **Oceanfront Foray:** A moonlight jaunt is a must for any beach stay.

- **Disco Dip:** After bouts of the Hustle, sweaty friends assuage the heat by dodging into a local hotel water hole.

- **Lakeside Isolation:** Nobody's around, so it's a day or night treat (watch for snapping turtles).

- **Polar Drench:** Have a warm robe and a hot toddy waiting.

- **Post-Love Lave:** Beyond the bath . . . lagoons aren't just for Brooke Shields and seven stranded castaways.

- **Chlorine Nightcap:** Why don't we all go back to my place for a float?

- **Solo Soak:** Spiritual "me time" in quiet waters.

How does a gentleman maintain a polite personal space when the only thing between him and her is H_2O? Casting off clothing doesn't signal the loss of manners. Despite primal urges to take to the bleacher seats with binoculars and peanuts, glance but furtively upon disrobing others. A callipygian lady should be allowed to slip languidly into the water without probing eyeballs keeping her in the crosshairs like a turkey shoot. Likewise, while assessment of fellow men's equipment is generally more open here than at the local YMCA, refrain from applause-o-meter-like responses. Like savvy investors, some chaps retain hidden assets.

While a quorum is necessary to begin, sometimes not all parties are eager participants. In this case, excuses like "It's too cold," "I'm too tired," or "There might be jellyfish" should be left unmeddled, even if deeper issues are clearly at stake. A skinny-dip is no time to coercively purge someone's genuine fears of murky water, incarceration, or physical insecurity. Do not reprimand a swimmer who retains skivvies—all levels of daring are encouraged. On the other hand, a small mob of friends may overtake a noisy flapdoodler or oafish bore and toss him gleefully into the drink.

Skinny-dipping already carries a badge of rascality. However, the more experienced rabble-rouser may up the stakes. When choosing a site, do not rule out private pools. The exhilaration of backstrokes in the buff is nearly matched by the thrill of scaling a neighbor's fence or tiptoeing into the hotel whirlpool. Be wary of consequences, but do not eschew a titillating round of Marco Polo just because "your parents might catch us." A dripping posse of scampering nudes is more likely to elicit giggles and envy than actual litigation.

When necessary, keep it quiet, fun, and light on the libido; chicken fights are more efficient without the hydrodynamic drag of an uninvited erection.

Nice touch: It worked for securing that hot bistro table on a Saturday night, so slip an understanding security guard a ten spot to look the other way as the gang has a midnight swim.

Skinny-dipping etiquette translates to hot tubs, where the cloak of rising steam shouldn't cloud conduct. Normal rules of personal space are suspended when abutting another's nakedness. However, don't commit the post-tub flub of projected hot-water fantasies until a continued connection is proven on land.

GATE-CRASHING

*No person, with intent gratuitously to avail himself of the
entertainment or recreation furnished . . . shall enter any theater, stadium,
athletic club, ball park, golf course, golf club, tennis club,
beach club, bathing beach or other place of amusement, entertainment or
recreation, for admission to which an admission fee or membership fee is charged,
without first paying such admission fee or membership fee.*

—§ 4.08.300, CITY OF SANTA MONICA MUNICIPAL CODE,
ARTICLE 4 (PUBLIC WELFARE, MORALS AND POLICY)

It is impolite to intrude upon an affair where you are explicitly not welcome. The impetus for crashing a party, however, is the confidence that
had the host known you, he certainly would have issued you an invite.

There are two types of gate-crashing and neither one is for introverts: (1) The Sly Stopover, showing up to a known private party without
invitation; and (2) The Serendipitous Stumble-In, in which a pervasive
beat has sucked you in. Barging into bar mitzvahs and wedding recep-
tions might be done once for novelty.

THE SLY STOPOVER

In this scenario, you probably have a fringe relationship with either the
host or an attendee. The goal is not merely to say you were there, rather
to assimilate yourself and interact with fellow guests on equal footing.
Examples might include sneaking into a high-profile corporate event, a
charity ball at a manor, or a large, intra-neighborhood gazebo gathering you heard about through the grapevine. Arrive once the party is
underway, when most guests are loose with drink, and leave before the

party dilutes. Dress the part and fit in. Keep a keen eye out for discarded props such as name tags, wristbands, programs, and ticket stubs that might identify you as an invitee. If approached by the host, don't assume cover has been blown—offer introduction and thanks. If prodded further, step lively; honesty is usually appropriate.

THE SERENDIPITOUS STUMBLE-IN

This scenario is less stealthy but more intriguing. You had no idea there was a party until the first strains of revelry piqued your attention. Under darkness and quiet of night, sound travels far and an alluring beat cocks your ear. Invariably, you are on the way home and suddenly have to decide whether to sniff out the source or continue on. Besides listening for the volume trail, look for a mass of parked cars, bodies in the window frame, or the hard-to-spot, fenced-in backyard bash. Now strategize. Do you make a move on the house perimeter and engage outdoor

---

KNOCKING

How's a gent to announce his presence? A doorbell, buzzer, or knocker? Will the door resound properly if rapped? Does the occupant own a barking dog, negating the need for a choice? A gentleman prefers knocking, except before a melodious-looking door chime or stately manor. Sample the ornate knocker. If you rap, do so firmly. More than four repetitions is excessive. As with CPR, wait five seconds before repeating the prior cadence. A gentleman may knock overhand, backhand, or with a pinky-side closed fist. Phineas favors the suave backhand strike for its smooth motion and true echo; Tesauro prefers the wrist action of a traditional overhand grip. After knocking, step back from the door, enjoy the porch daisies, and afford the host space when the door opens.

guests in conversation, or head for the front door, drafting behind others before the buzz-in expires? It's a crapshoot; likely though, the Modern Gentleman is a good candidate for a late invitation.

Upon entry, look for clues as to the event's nature. A baby shower, bon voyage, or anniversary indicates a closed group, where your presence is conspicuous and unwanted. If you spot a steady stream of traffic or "party this way" signage, this is likely a more public affair.

Note the theme. How are people dressed? Are they sipping martinis or quaffing keg beer from party cups? Stick to the high-traffic areas, as this is no time to peek into side rooms or interrupt corner tête-à-têtes. Get yourself a drink and acquaint yourself with a larger circle—start from the punch bowl area and work around the room in concentric circles. Wandering preserves your anonymity longer; if you remain in constant motion, no one can get a fix on the mystery guest.

Incidentally, a crash of either type is especially successful if a new connection is made. Bonus points if it's with the host.

COMINGS & GOINGS

Fanfare can announce a gentleman's arrival, but not every entrance will be punctuated with tickertape and paparazzi. The keys to proper coming are rooted in the assessment of conditions, ranging from hushed to raucous. Burst into the "Welcome Home" celebration with fire; slink past the boss's door at 9:35 A.M. Avoid even the slightest disgrace of under- or overstaying a welcome. Just as lingering past the host's yawns is pitiable, jumping ship prematurely is insulting to the host's group dynamic.

Here's a matching exercise to relate tactics and timing:

ENTRANCES

The sneak-in, when you'd rather be invisible or avoid the cover charge. Low profile, best executed alone or in small groups. De rigueur for gate-crashing and ideal for excessive lateness. *Pairs best with French Leave or Slip-Out.*	**STEALTH**
Pomp, grandeur, maybe a cape. Hoopla is the name of the game. Reserved for guests of honor, dress-up affairs, and Halloween. *Pairs best with Jim Brown.*	**THE PREMIERE**
Peeking in long enough to realize that you don't want to be there. You're a double scoop and they're lactose intolerant. A short visit triggers a gut-instinct abort. The club is too crowded or the party has pooped. *Pairs best with The Ditch.*	**FLY-BY**
Despite other engagements, the brief appearance, as promised. Obligatory visit with one-drink minimum and two-yawn maximum. Only there long enough for an extended hostess hug and a brief conversation with a spry stranger. *Pairs best with The Godfather or Jim Brown.*	**POP-IN**
"You didn't see me. I was never here." Hatching a conspiratorial lie in the face of trouble—rarely successful. Used for feigned office illnesses and infidelities. *Pairs best with the Slip-Out.*	**PERJURED**
Arriving arm-in-arm or with ruckus in tow. A cheerful pair or bunch incites fresh life. Unlike poker, wild pairs beat a subdued three of a kind. *Return with a Curtain Call.*	**PAIR/ GROUP**
Lying about whereabouts: "Whatd'ya mean? I was there for an hour!" *Since you were never there, no accompanying exit.*	**GHOST**
With one hand still on the doorjamb, a quick reconnoiter: "Is this the right place?" *Plot your next move based on the guest list and vibe.*	**THE LEAN-IN**

	## *EXITS*
FRENCH LEAVE	No one knows you've left until thirty minutes have passed. Best reserved for after-hours living room hangouts and among never-to-be-seen-again acquaintances. Great for anonymous opting out of 'round the clock benders and avoiding The Godfather (see below). Exit smoothly before the fun ends and group dynamic peters out.
SLIP-OUT	When a formal goodbye is undesirable, tell a few key players and forego the burdensome receiving line. A sober end to a bad night or the most dignified exit after a colossal gaffe. The group is having more fun than you: get out before your sluggish mood befouls festivities.
IN-OUTS	Revolving door of "hi" or "bye," repeated multiple times. Coming and going, with or without hand stamp; the staple of party-hopping. Usually, out to the parking lot for indiscretions or around the block on a bar circuit.
THE GOD-FATHER	An offer to stay that you can't refuse. The tractor beam of peer pressure, new arrivals, and the optimistic promise of potential merriment. "Every time I try to get out, they pull me back in." Try the French Leave.
CURTAIN CALL	"I'm back!" Unexpected encore presentation, often to retrieve forgotten items. A fallback when secondary plans falter. Use rarely, since it spoils the tidiness of a well-orchestrated goodbye. To mitigate, return bearing alms: six-pack, candy.
JIM BROWN	Retiring in your prime, with admirers wanting more. Going four-for-four, with three numbers and one kiss landed, and two assists to your credit . . . then pulling yourself from the game.
"BE RIGHT BACK" DITCH	Says it all.

TARDINESS

How long does one wait? For loose engagements, a grace period of thirty minutes is standard and given gratis. Beyond this, evaluate on a case-by-case basis. For close friends, call and leave voice mail; for acquaintances with tardy tendencies, have another drink or exercise jukebox etiquette.

For the late date or untested acquaintance, you get one phone call, like an incarcerated perp. A second call is saved for updated information or aborting the mission. A flurry of restless messages sours a fine evening's aftertaste when heard the next morning. Given cell phones, the tardy party should courteously call in their amended ETA.

REUNIONS

Family and class reunions are chances to revisit the ghost towns of your past. Whether resurrected at grandma's house or the kindergarten cafeteria, demons will not haunt a gentleman who is confident and content. At these functions, stay vulnerable but intact. A slight distance and clinical eye stave off a maelstrom of ancient issues.

FAMILY REUNIONS

Once emancipated, drop the yellowed photograph and step away from the drama. Sometimes a great distance of time exists for good reason. Perhaps your vibrant relationship with Cousin Vinnie from Rockaway has more to do with the five-state buffer than your mutual dislike of Aunt Chloe.

Make the most of it when the whole gang descends upon you to sling career advice and offer criticism of the homemade cranberry tofu sauce. Keep your ears open for dramatic one-liners or family secrets (especially if spoken in the ancestral tongue). These can be retold for years to come. Reunions, like kidney stones, are typically uncomfortable, but bearable with medication. When it's all over, consider who's flourishing and who's floundering. Next year, spend more time with the former and cross the latter off your Christmas fruit-basket list.

Family gatherings are a karmic yardstick: like measuring a growing boy's height on the wall in pencil, see how far you've come. Answering probing inquiries with an indifferent "not much" or other rote nonsense marks a stunted growth. Once matriculated from the "kids' table," speak up like Flipper, stir the pot, and ask the ever-affable Uncle Arnie about his love of the ponies and your aunt's Jordache jeans.

Bemuse those who only remember your churlish days in braces. If you are lucky enough to have living grandparents, cultivate such relations. Sip a bourbon and branch with Pop; take a Rob Roy with Nana. They are living history and should be mined for golden lore and life lessons. If you think you're a smarty-pants at thirty, triple that and imagine what Grandpa knows. As for Great Aunt Georgia—the wily one with tissues up her sleeve and a $20 bill tucked in her bosom—ask her for a dance at the next wedding.

Climb your family tree or at least carve your initials into it. Learn if any branches have been pruned or disowned in the past. Run down the family checklist: immigration and surname history; how parents and grandparents met; embarrassing adolescent anecdotes; names of men who sought Mother's hand before Dad. Leave creepy Cousin Morton snoozing in the La-Z-Boy, and repair to the back porch with Uncle Rufus. Discover why Mom's side is so neurotic—it can't be *all* genetics (you hope). Sift through topics not highlighted in the reunion getaway brochure. Find out which kin ran counter to the law, who's on first-name basis with the pharmacist, and which ne'er-do-well eloped to Vegas for the loose slots. Steer the conversation with rack-and-pinion precision and chuckle at the candor.

How to endure that Sunday/holiday time intervention? As with the company picnic, attendance may be mandatory. For the more challenging affairs, especially outdoor galas, carry the bottomless day-drink. Your wine glass is perpetually half-full from 1 to 6 P.M. When conversation yawns or devolves into an incessant medical ailment show-and-tell, spice things with a dash of hot topics ("Goodness gracious, they're closing down the Nude Emporium!"). Above all, attend occasions with a light heart and uphold the *fun* in dysfunctional.

Incest-dentally, it is not discourteous to express lingering affections for single, peripheral kinfolk. Check your local statutes, as begetting a child on your wife's sister is no longer a misdemeanor in Tennessee.

HIGH SCHOOL REUNION

Why are you going to this nostalgic spectacle of laughable one-upmanship? The dramatis personae of most high school reunions include pregnant wives of long-forgotten acquaintances, mistailored sport coats, or worse, former computer geeks who were passionate about PASCAL and now sport Audi TTs and supermodel escorts. A special trip back across the Plains isn't necessary. If within twenty miles, though, drop in for a dance to confirm your suspicions about how it all turned out. At least be nice and return the reply card with current contact information.

There are only three reasons for dragging yourself to this affair:

- **Curiosity:** What became of Miss Most Likely to Be Famous and that wacky artist who painted the lunchroom mural? Tour the crowd and classrooms, show your wife where you took the erasers for cleaning, and dash into the once-forbidden teacher's lounge for a quick flask.

- **Ego:** You want to know who made it to the top and who fell from All-County graces into oblivion. However, macho puffing is a bad reason to do anything, except maybe the boardwalk sledgehammer ring-the-bell game. Look in the mirror: self-esteem is measured from within, not against a playground chum's portfolio.

- **Debunking the Fantasy:** Despite good sense, you might be kicking around ideas that the cheerleader who snubbed you for the starting outside linebacker is ready to repent. Alas, your chances are poor. The optimal turnout for any high school reunion is usually 25 percent. Moreover, the ladies who deign to attend will either be happily married or still haunting the local bowling alley bar. Vibrant, single classmates would rather carouse the town on Saturday night than traipse the halls waxing nostalgic about Mr. Decker's metal-shop class and the pointlessness of the National Honor Society. Save your breath and rent *Grosse Pointe Blank* instead.

Exception: If you're an entrepreneur, marketing rep, or recent parolee, attend reunions for networking reasons.

A brief primer for attendees:

◆ What to wear? A jacket with a nicely ironed shirt should suffice. No jeans—this is a high school *reunion,* not actually high school.

◆ Escort? If married, remind your spouse that she agreed to stand by you "for better or for worse." For the bachelor, spare a current flame the torture or rent an expensive escort.

◆ Curtail career crowing. If you casually mention the term "six figures" within two minutes of the question, "So. . .what have you been up to?", you are an utter dolt.

COLLEGE REUNIONS

If within a 175-mile radius of such an event, it's worthwhile to make an appearance, especially if you attended a smaller school. The five-year college reunion offers an excuse to reconvene the old gang, true confidantes who shared both Western Lit and high jinks on your rickety path to adulthood. Catch up with acquaintances, exchange e-mail addresses, and develop future business contacts. Amazingly, even pickled mates and the lone stoner down the hall now have responsible positions. Often, the event is billed as "Reunion Weekend," suggesting a one-night stay on campus. Pack an overnight bag and bellow the alma mater.

College is over, so act accordingly. Skip belligerent drunkenness, breaking and entering, or sullen mood swings upon seeing an ex. A date isn't necessary, as the evening is a perpetuation of inside jokes and stories too long and furious for explanation. If a sidekick is required to fill in the dead air that used to come from campus radio, you've lost touch with too many friends.

PASSOVER

Get invited to a seder, taste the charoset, crunch matzoh, and if you arrive late, just take Elijah's seat. To Moses and the Israelites' escape from Egypt, raise a glass with wine worthy of the blessing: Hagafen or Baron Herzog of California and Yarden of Israel are kosher, yet dry and not jammy sweet. For gentiles, bring a string-tied white box piled high with kugel from a kosher bakery and make sure the wine is *mevushal* (pasteurized for handling by non-Jews).

Chapter Two

ENTERTAINING

♦ ♦ ♦ ♦ ♦ ♦ ♦

Group Dynamics 39

Hosting 44

Intimate Gatherings 49

The Active Table 51

Houseguests 54

Charcoal Briquetiquette 57

Bachelor Party 61

Best Manning 63

GROUP DYNAMICS

No need for a bullhorn or head coach's clipboard to keep a score of scallywags on task. A gentleman understands the delicate interplay between friends and acquaintances whether during playtime in the park or nights on the town. Cultivate the subtle skills of making introductions, setting a charismatic table, and coaxing the most out of groups.

PICKING THE ROSTER

A host invites according to the nature of the evening. A good roster matches temperament and charisma to environment and expression. For example, certain friends are better for a lecture and others for a Frisbee picnic. Likewise, intimate evenings are closed affairs for the inner circle; don't set out plates for casual work chums.

SIZING

Groups come in small, medium, and unwieldy sizes. The small bunch ranges from two to five, and comes with a low degree of management difficulty, as there is quick response time, easy transport, and nearly limitless possibility. Medium collectives range from six to nine, and carry a small degree of complexity regarding tables or beach spots at crowded venues, forcing tougher transportation and more involved decision-making. The unwieldy horde starts at ten, feels like twenty, moves with the speed of fifty, and makes decisions like a bureaucracy of one hundred. Its half-life is usually one event; membership falls off as soon as there's a change of place.

BRINGING IT IN BEFORE TAKING IT OUT

A group is a cohesive unit, not merely a collection of factions who happen to be in the same place. When conjoining couples and individuals for a shared event, "bring it in" by gluing the group together first. A pre-activity beverage or quick tourney of Ping-Pong in someone's basement synchronizes orbits. There's no substitute for the shared experience of a meal and sober conversation to forge common ground before "taking it out" on the town. If you don't have a home base, roll into a quiet spot prior to tossing the group into a noisy locale that hasn't room for group eye contact. Bringing it in is the huddle before a sandlot football game, when you figure out who's on your side before telling everybody to go deep.

INTRODUCTIONS

If I could remember the names of all these particles, I'd be a botanist.

—ENRICO FERMI, NOBEL PRIZE—WINNING PHYSICIST

Nameless faces equals weak dynamic. It is imperative to stress introductions early in the evening, especially with appellations like Thalia and Runn. Do not waste breath on fruitless, large-scale introductions that invariably lead to a slew of missed names. Rather, introduce guests to key players and let them make at-large acquaintances on their own. Treat each introduction as a personal connection and offer a short résumé or commonality. For example, "Maeve, may I introduce Jonah, a coworker who shares your obsession for classical Etruscan architecture."

To reinforce new familiarity, repeat each guest's name first aloud and then silently to yourself. Stick the landing on tricky ethnic names. If the name is especially syllabic, the person is likely patient with new friends and will gladly explain the phonics and derivation. Acting as liaison and bolstering name recall enriches the social atmosphere and thwarts proliferation of the impersonal moniker "dude." Be proactive and alleviate the awkwardness of someone having forgotten your name. Upon subsequent contact and until name recall is apparent, reintroduce yourself during the greeting ("Hello Ms. Zevitas. Phineas Mollod. A treat to see you again.").

Incidentally, on-the-street run-ins require less formality. Spare your escort the meaningless exchange of names with an assembly of acquaintances they will never cross again. Introductions are pointless when they would last longer than the ensuing polite and forgettable chatter.

INERTIA & FRICTION

Objects at rest tend to stay at rest and keep in motion when moving. For small groups, starting and stopping takes little more than a nimble spank. Hordes, on the other hand, take time to accelerate and, once going, rarely stop or alter course. Friction refers to the forces of motion within the group that can mar a dynamic if they are not socially lubricated. In small groups, persons of differing ilk can easily slip and twist without complaint after their ideas are considered and compromises reached ("Wait. We'll get a large pie with half anchovy and half broccoli."). In hordes, it is inevitable that not everyone's needs will be congruous with the group's mission. Thus, unlike late-night TV offers, satisfaction isn't guaranteed. With so many bodies, expect the squeaky wheels of limitations, preferences, and issues to require more grease. For decreased inertia: smoke less early-evening dope on the veranda; extinguish entertainment (turn off TV, lights, music, and air conditioning to spur a hasty departure); and exit quickly. Collect all persons and settle the tab.

THE CORE

Within every horde is a nucleus. A gentleman always allies himself with this small band committed to making the most fun, even if it requires late-night secession from the rest of the group. As the dynamic winds down, expect to jettison those flagging and pining for bed. The remaining core group will invariably catch a secondary or tertiary wind and end up with a few more highlights the others will only hear about over brunch.

THE USUAL PLAYERS

Keep an eye out for these group-dynamic archetypes:

* **The Locomotive**: Never runs out of energy or fun; keeps it going.

* **The Local Expert**: Knows the best sushi, nightclub, and picnic spot.

* **The Wanderer**: Goes missing, but always returns with a hot story.

* **The Aloof Couple**: Moody twosome who keep to themselves.

* **The Catalyst**: Buys the first round or starts the dancing.

* **The Deserter**: Cashes in the chips early; turns into a pumpkin at II P.M.

* **The Liaison**: Establishes contact with other groups and the bartender.

* **The Quiet Champ**: Seemingly vanilla persona who proves wildly insightful.

* **The Whiner**: No matter what the group does, it sucks.

TAKING THE REINS

A gentleman takes a keen interest in coaxing "nice times" into huge fun and rejuvenating floundering nights before the party poops. Don't force it; democracy should get a fair chance. When a show of hands fails to yield a plan of action, consider the greater dynamic and make an executive decision to prod the crowd. Don't be a garrulous, mic-hogging activity dictator, but when no one's guiding the bunch, take charge of the group and see to each member's good time. Leadership skills include the ability to delegate, so take a poll and deputize according to strengths: who knows the hot spots, who's the best navigator, who shakes the best martini, and who can fast-talk past any crowded door or steep cover charge.

CAPITALIZING ON THE MOOD

The gentleman strikes when the group is hot. The best time to introduce new ideas or push the envelope is after extended bouts of cheer and laughter. While the dynamic is peaking, ratchet up the fun. Suggest the daytime frolic continue into the evening, mention an after-hours club, or dare a late-night skinny-dip. On the other hand, when the mood has palled, jump-start the dynamic by acknowledging the lull before the group collapses: "Does anyone else find this band sonically dreadful?" Offer an alternative and stoke the dynamic back to crackling life.

SPLINTERING

Splintering is the sinister foe to a group dynamic. It's improbable that a group filling more than two cars will remain intact for more than two venue changes. To counter this dynamic dysfunction, keep large numbers together by finding a single place with a multiplicity of activities. Try a pub that has pool and darts or a part of town with a cluster of clubs within walking distance. In this fashion, even if the mass splinters into grouplets, they're still reachable by white courtesy phone. To prevent splintering, it might be necessary to rehuddle, which may be followed by a vote of no confidence and a hostile coup against the current group leadership. Like a half-time adjustment, reassess the group's desire and foil any mutinous behavior with a realignment of strategy ("This bowling alley isn't cutting it—let's go skeet shooting").

The friendly flake-out is a minor form of splintering, when last-minute surprises spur otherwise reliable people to disappear without warning. Should one or two crewmembers riding in a separate taxi fail to show, stick with the remaining gang and move on. Don't have a hissy fit or an episode of separation anxiety, unless stuck waiting for the cavalry alone. If this is a weekly phenomenon, reevaluate friendships.

Note: Never usurp sovereignty from someone else's group dynamic. Rather than trampling on sovereignty, a gentleman adds to the host's shine by intermixing his own crew; volunteering helpful information during dead air ("Eli mentioned another party uptown"); or playing a cameo role in the revival of a flailing host's fading dynamic (change the music, dim the lights, and make some calls).

HOSTING

Entertaining is the most revealing form of home expression, a gentleman's time to frame and impart his charms, fetishes, and qualities of life to friends and lovers. Lesser hosts allow an affair to unravel into a diluted and polluted free-for-all. Not so the modern man in his own home, who exudes full-frontal personality with structure and style.

It's HQ, you are the majordomo with supreme control over ambiance. Ideal atmosphere includes thoughtful consideration of the event, attendees, time, and season. Are the lights soft and cozy, or bright and revealing? Adjust your dimmer switches, volume knobs, and thermostats according to your joie de vivre. Is it a quiet, living-room-floor bout of gaming or a hot Saturday eve shakedown with ceiling fans on high speed? It is the host's responsibility to bestow ample comforts upon guests.

Duties do not end when the party begins. Make a point to spend time with most everyone throughout an affair. Around the room, circles should be made of newly acquainted company and not homogenized groups that arrived together. Like an experienced referee, interpose yourself on couples or familiar friends who have slumped into a clinch like tired heavyweights. Like a Lee Jeans—wearin' rustler, corral wayward, stationary sheep from couch corners. Foster new connections—say those odd names a few more times and make across-the-room introductions with either social or amorous intent ("Tamar, may I present Ishmael, lately of Yorkville. Izzy and I did time back in Sing-Sing on that trumped-up larceny charge.").

PRE- OR POST-COCKTAILS

Host a cocktail hour when you're not prepared to supply 100 percent of the fun. Provide the opening or closing ceremonies for an evening out, with or without torch lighting and dove release. Home serves as a central gathering place to wet whistles, make introductions, and divvy up the crowd into cars/taxis. This is not the time for knife-and-fork food and gratuitous rounds of shots. Simply offer one or two cocktails and await the tardy. Small bites or a cheese plate are enough, as full crudités may encourage torpor around the sofa.

Pre-cocktail hours typically settle around the kitchen and rarely find visitors sitting. Put on upbeat music and remind the group of the activities ahead—this is not the destination. Don't let easy lingering foil the itinerary. Keep one eye on the clock and the other on the ice bucket; when glasses are filling beyond your intentions, shoo the party onward.

For end-of-the-night gatherings, shoes are kicked off and cocktails are simplified. Blender-free concoctions, lighter drinks, liqueurs, or beer come into play as the group winds down. Chips and salsa may be consumed or delivery orders phoned in. Rules are relaxed at this hour as smoking patrons huddle on the balcony and the record collection is rummaged through for classics. The morning remnants of a successful post-party gathering are a teetering stack of unsheathed CDs, a batch of spent glassware, and a full recycling bin.

HAVING PEOPLE OVER

The semiweekly variety usually involves last-minute decisions to watch movies, play games, or converse in repose. A well-choreographed version finds the host merely providing the venue as comfortable guests direct their own entertainment. At this informal affair, delegate tasks and allow guests to work the stereo, mix the lemonade, or otherwise drive the entertainment, making the party self-sufficient. One person brings the hummus and poker chips, another stops for beer, and all you have to do is vacuum and dust the coffee table.

SOIRÉE

A soirée is a party for twenty or less, with a selective guest list. It's an after-nine, planned affair, more formal than having people over. With or without written invitations, goers dress per a theme—martini attire for the swank, tiki for summer rum parties, or pyjamas for a winter lingerie affair. After the bossa nova, booze, and boiled shrimp, stage a parlor game. Time need not be completely structured, but a commemorative toast to a guest of honor or announcement of exciting news fuels the frolic. Ask musicians to bring guitars, poets to share verse, and contortionists to climb into the icebox. Before widespread cosmopolitan illiteracy, soirées meant a memorable evening around the piano and a good story. Revive this salon environment and guests will remember the night for more than munchie-slaking pizza rolls.

BACCHANAL

If the squad cars aren't on their way, don't consider the night a flop. The party should have a clever thrust, capturing the naughtiness of Halloween and the frivolity of New Year's Eve. Find a theme among the calendar's alternative holidays: Arbor Day, an equinox, or a lunar eclipse. String lights, hang streamers, add food coloring to the liquor, make signs, or rent a fog machine. Decorations are an essential expression of festivity, not a twenty-minutes-prior, tacked-up afterthought. If you want a full house, print a flyer or send an e-mail with directions. Lastly, name the affair—why call it a party when you could host a St. Patrick's Day Shivaree or Groundhog Day Après-Ski? Once a decade, host a toga party.

Since each guest isn't hand-selected, provide a motleyed experience, including electronica for dancing, corners for window carousing, and lounge areas for lovers and illicit activities. Buy twice as many cups and bags of ice as you think you'll need and tap the keg in a noncarpeted, low-traffic corner, like the porch or guest shower. Buy large, 1.75-liter bottles of liquor; if you expect a mob, ask guests to bring a favorite poison to keep the bar flowing. This may be a loose affair, but don't forget your chores: patrol the bathrooms and kitchen for empties, keep the toilet neat, and make sure indoor house pets haven't been liberated.

Deputize close friends to work the door, spin tunes, mind the trash, attend to the bar, and greet guests. You are the floater, the ringmaster, so wear something unmistakable. Too often, one never meets the host at a blowout. Introduce yourself to choice strangers and find the sixth degree of separation that sourced their invitation.

Nice touch: For outdoor bashes, an ice-block booze delivery system is a chilly novelty for encouraging even the timid to do shots. Buy a body-

---

PETIQUETTE

Good hosting involves the proper training of household pets. A guest should not have to guard his designer luggage or family jewels from an overzealous Labrador. If you lack the time to clean or the resources to hire a chambermaid, avoid fur-shedding animals that foist shaggy clumps onto a hapless guest's threads after only a brief sit on the living-room sofa. Rabbit-cage linings and ferret mulch provide an olfactory assault akin to an overstocked mall petshop. Keep such creatures at least one floor away from the common space.

If you can't handle the trials of a newborn puppy or milk-feed a baby goat, try a hearty ficus or cactus, which only require air and an occasional, accidental misting. Be smart: if you cannot provide proper love and environs, don't shove a Siberian husky into your 400-square-foot studio. Cat owners must invest the extra bucks for scoopable litter that minimizes pet odors.

Incidentally, small mammals like guinea pigs, hamsters, and rabbits aren't the best investments. Like the new car that depreciates 50 percent upon leaving the lot, the novelty of rodentia fades quickly. After the honeymoon, you are left with a pea-brained, pellet-producing varmint.

sized block from an ice dealer listed in the yellow pages. Use hot water and a chisel to carve a Y-shaped channel; two tributaries (one delivering alcohol and the other a mixer) feed from the top into a well-excavated central waterway. Finish by chipping out a chin rest at the bottom. Elevate the top end of the ice block to facilitate speedy flow. Invite guests to lay an open mouth at one end as the tender pours a clear spirit down one channel, a juice chaser down the other, meeting at the maw.

INTIMATE GATHERINGS

An intimate gathering offers dinner as dénouement, a lavish affair for a few hand-selected couples who appreciate tempered tableside affections, long glances, and the sumptuousness of a well-adorned plate. Choice of garb reflects the mood. Do not allow the artichoke and arugula *insalata* to be better dressed than your guests. To accompany this more elevated evening, gentlemen and their escorts don eveningwear.

Think sensuous: candles trump fluorescent lighting, flowers over potpourri, sultry jazz over radio pop. Swap the extra hours of hanging decorations for added attention to a well-suited menu, epicurean presentation, and proper libations. Languid pacing is key: print a scripted menu, detailing each course, perhaps listing the evening's wine lineup as well. Lighter or sparkling whites jibe with appetizers, making way for full-bodied whites with the fish course, hearty reds with the roast, and port or sherry with dessert. The entire evening is a gentle rise as all five senses escalate from the toasty nose of Champagne to the silky feel of homemade mousse in the mouth. You are conducting a tactile symphony in which biorhythms are synchronized in a dance of shared secrets and open affections across the table's four corners. Red-wine whispers are perfume upon the nape of the evening.

Intimate gatherings are limited to six attendees, tapped with these considerations in mind: cultivated taste, conversational dexterity, and passion quotient. A smaller group facilitates more deliberate eye contact, subtler undertones, and a greater premium on individual needs (vegetarians, discriminating Virgos). As the evening unwinds, guests are under your subtle control, the table replete with hand-prepared delights, pretty glasses, linen napkins, chilled salad forks, and warmed dinner plates. Conversation is steeped in all things positive, personal, and pleasurable; daily triflings, worldly woes, and what you did at work that day should be left for family dinner on Sunday. Create a blissful state of escapism by choosing fare that departs from the palate's regular repertoire.

Select user-friendly, sensual foods that do not require a messy shell-cracker or a bib. Shopping should take you to the butcher, fishmonger, or roadside produce stand for ripe, seasonal delicacies. Seafood fillets over a vegetable ragout or polenta make an excellent choice; Chicken Kiev, the booby-trapped award-dinner favorite, does not. Incorporate

---

GLASSWARE

Tuxedoed guests deserve cocktails in stems or highballs. A martini in a plastic cup is not a drink. Steer a raucous bunch away from the crystal and don't place a sippy cup in an enchanting lady's manicured hand. Proper glasses are in everyone's budget and can be collected two or four at a time. Stock your cabinets with varied vessels. Versatile, attractive glassware doubles in service of sauces, puddings, and *mazel tovs*.

an exotic fruit or legume and be conscious of plate aesthetic—weave an asparagus cradle to hold the tenderloin. For current recipes consult the Internet, as Mom's fifty-year-old *Joy of Cooking* is likely dusty.

Other ideas: Spruce up a three-course meal with a simple puréed soup. In the summer, toss fruits in the blender, add sparkling wine, and serve chilled with a spoon. Try a mixed green salad that isn't all green and does not include iceberg lettuce. Experiment with red chard, edible flowers, watercress, dandelion, or endive. Arrange the greens on a plate, pre-dress them sparingly, and do not be shy with toppings—sprinkle with pine nuts, roasted beets, hearts of palm, citrus quarters, or goat cheese. Indulge in: chilled mineral water (no ice), plate garnish, bowls of olives, and a sorbet intermezzo with a dance break.

Nice touch: Move the table to an irregular eating spot. City dwellers might serve dinner with a view on the roof; others might eat alfresco in the yard, surrounded by torches.

THE ACTIVE TABLE

In classic tomes such as Emily Post's *Etiquette* and *Vogue's Book of Etiquette and Good Manners,* the order of seating around the table is a "rigid and unbreakable" representation of social rank. *The Modern Gentleman* offers a contemporary alternative. Instead of arranging place cards according to caste and importance, manage the personalities to mix the boisterous with the shy and catalyze curious conversation.

Hosting people for dinner is a sure way to push relationships further. Food and drink are but the excuse for gathering. Fostering new bonds and introducing new friends to the old circle is not haphazard and requires a deft hosting strategy. Instead of playing musical chairs when the dinner bell sounds, plot ahead according to gender, familiarity, and personality for an active evening around the stuffed goose.

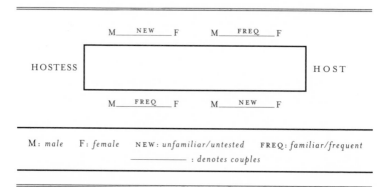

Consider the table arrangement above for a typical dinner party of ten. General rules of ratio and alternating gender are followed, with Host and Hostess at the table ends. Two couples (M **freq** F) are old friends or frequent guests, the kind that might help in the kitchen without asking. Each of these two couples sits adjacent to an unfamiliar couple (M **new** F) who've just learned where the bathroom is located. New couples include first-time dinner guests, new bedmates, or hopefully compatible strangers, and sit near the comforting ballast of a Host or Hostess. Note that the two pairs of frequent couples aren't packed tightly into an insular clique at one end of the table. Also, even if the compatible strangers *aren't* so compatible with one another, there's always help from the charismatic frequent guest seated nearby.

Next, within these parameters, mix up the seating chart according to personality.

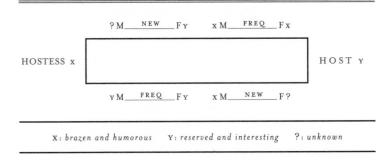

X: *brazen and humorous*   Y: *reserved and interesting*   ?: *unknown*

This is the same table, but arranged to account for charisma (*x* is a lively jokester and conversation starter; *y* is fascinating yet low-key; *?* is an untested wild card, such as a friend's new flame or a host-appointed escort). Here, the Host/Hostess and a **freq** couple flanks an unfamiliar *?*, whose zest is in question. The Host's and Hostess's own personalities balance the ends of the table. Foment crossfire, taking care that no one is left out to dry. In the table below, the *x* Hostess enlivens the unknown (M?) and the *y* couple (My **freq** Fy). The *y* Host engages unknown (F?) and feeds off the vivacious *x* couple (M*x* **freq** F*x*).

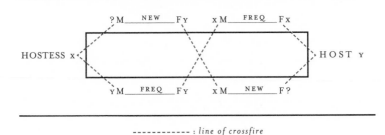

------------ : *line of crossfire*

Notice the additional lines of crossfire in the third diagram. Make sure there are opposites and like minds available across, adjacent, or diagonal. As the Host and Hostess handle the table ends, crossfire intermingles the middle of the table, lest these poor souls be caught with nothing between them but the centerpiece. Crossfire mitigates the Host's matchmaking failures, when a ? and his or her escort are noncombustive.

The Active Table looks complicated, but the principles are simple for any size table. Attention to detail extends past tablecloth and glassware to the conversational interplay of guests. If you've done it well, no one will suspect they were part of some mad gentleman scientist's social bingo experiment.

HOUSEGUESTS

When guests cross the threshold, the rules of hosting apply on a more intimate scale. Guests aren't complete strangers, so personalize the arrangements for their stay. Make room in the crisper for the vegetarian or stock up on local microbrews for the discriminating lager-head. Special snacks, cereals, and rented films always garner praise.

Polite guests often feel chary of hospitality. Anticipate needs and offer extras up front; before the first shiver, spare the timid the awkward request for an extra degree of warmth on the thermostat. Excessive coddling can be overbearing, so don't mother guests to death with comfort checks: "Are the five bed pillows fluffy enough?"; "My pet tarantula isn't bothering you, is he?" To quell feelings of imposition is to demonstrate your comfort with a guest's presence. Saying, "Make yourself at home" is passive hosting and is almost a coded warning not to touch anything.

Rather, a good host creates an inviting space where comfort is as easy to find as the bedroom light switch.

WASHROOM

Leave a small basket of nicely presented sundries in the bathroom. A bottle of aspirin, contact lens solution, hair dryer, spare toothbrush, fresh soaps, and elixirs pamper a traveler with the comforts of home. Plug in a bathroom or toilet nightlight and freshen up a guest's toilette with a cluster of aromatic herbs. The stress of living from a suitcase is quickly quelled.

GUEST QUARTERS

Stock the guest room with an abundance of towels, pillows, blankets, and linens. Mind the helplessly chilled or perpetually warm; keep an extra fan in the summertime. In any season, only a skimping host issues one meager, paper-thin, phyllo-dough coverlet. A down comforter is rarely amiss, and an afghan, space heater, or electric blanket is welcome for wintry visits. An alarm clock will probably spare wake-up-call duty and stave off flight-missing worries. Or, inquire within. Would they like reveille at 0500 hours or an undisturbed sleep-in? If the latter, pad lightly around the common space. After nine hours of REM, however, conduct business as usual; grind coffee with impunity, split cordwood in the yard, and rouse that slugabed.

An in-room telephone provides guests additional privacy for those late-night tuck-in calls to a sweetheart back home. Offer long-distance service; conscientious guests will use their calling card or dial judiciously. Guests who routinely run up the bill can be directed to the pay phone at the corner filling station.

MAKESHIFT ACCOMMODATIONS

Spruce up makeshift guest rooms with plants, photographs, and books. Barring known allergies, a colorful nosegay livens any quarters. No matter how pretty the walls, though, true guest comfort is all about the bed. Blankets on the floor are a last resort when there's no room at the inn. For guest comfort, purchase any of the following: sleeping bag, collapsible cot, inflatable mattress, or convertible futon. When a lover finally moves in, the extra mattress you'll acquire is usually the beginning of guest accommodations. Special guests or married couples passing through a bachelor pad warrant the gentlemanly offer of his bed for the night (with full conjugal privileges).

CRASH PAD

For impromptu visits, sometimes the best choice is the sofa. Remove the back cushions, wrap the seats in a fitted sheet, and dress the couch up like a four-poster. Even for the leftover party intoxicate, these are first-rate arrangements on short notice. There's usually little need or time to furnish all the trappings—your gifts of shelter and a shower are adequate.

EXTENDED GUESTS

Faster than a sublet, more powerful than a stopover, these four-night-minimum stays warrant a leap and splurge. Enjoy luxuriating yourself and the guest by upgrading to the butcher's choicest cuts, sniffing out imported cheeses, dialing up four-star meals, jump-starting the kitchen mixer, or dusting off a decorative platter for a festive antipasto.

Aid your guest's navigation about the house and town: leave the local weekly bedside to help guide their cultural itinerary. Type up instructions for deciphering your home's more curious peccadilloes: the entertainment center's army of remotes, pesky doors, loose fixtures, broken stairs, tricky switches, flesh-hungry dogs, or claw-clinging cats. To avoid lonely foraging for a drinking glass, conduct a kitchen-cabinet tour. Also alert guests to the location of the nearest convenience stores and shops.

Part of your responsibility is the guest's entertainment. Arrange some daytime outings and nighttime activities for the group to enjoy, but permit guests plenty of free time. Unlike Wayne Newton at the Golden Nugget, your guests shouldn't be booked solid for the week. The most familiar bachelor guests might afford an escort for dinner or evening affairs, the goal not necessarily being matchmaking, but the avoidance of the dreaded third-wheel syndrome. A compatible friend balances conversation and provides a dance or contract-bridge partner.

Incidentally, guest-proof for large groups, children, and first-time guests by stashing away sensitive documents and extra-special breakables. Take a quick look in the guest bathroom and remove provocative prescription drugs and embarrassing ointments.

CHARCOAL BRIQUETIQUETTE

[frankfurter] [patty] [hibachi]

Every gentleman is fully conversant in the ceremonial Olympic lighting of the charcoal grill, from its light-it-yourself briquette ancestors to today's push-button propane styles. BBQ means blue skies, piles of potato salad, and carefree, shoeless demeanors. Fingers come first.

Isn't it time to branch out past the dynamic duo of hamburgers and hot dogs? Exhibit creativity short of epicurean haughtiness by flaming on such easy trimmings as vegetable kabobs, fish fillets, corn on the cob, and turkey burgers. Italian apple sausages and bratwurst are always welcome, as are, for the meat-averse, good-quality veggie burgers. For a seasoned waft, sprinkle mesquite chips into the grill. Hot dogs are a beloved staple (especially with noncanned sauerkraut), but even if related to Frank Purdue, no chicken franks.

BBQ tools should be sturdy. Look for the all-in-one flipper (a combo razored spatula/bottle opener) for easy grilling and hosting. Before tending the dogs, a gentleman masters the delicate art of the tongs and long-handled fork. On the road, defer to the host and never assume the spatula. If you come upon an open grill, quell any emergencies, move

PICNICKING

Picnics range from brown-bag lunches under a shady tree to gourmet treats spread on table linens set with candelabra and silverware. For most outdoor affairs, pack easy fare (finger foods, prepared salads), a checkered blanket, and seasonal fruits. Go beyond the everyday sandwich and foiled bag of chips; bring stemware, a bottle of vino, votive candles, diminutive salt and pepper shakers, linen napkins, and a portable music box for dancing. To aid digestion, take in the scenery with an arm-in-arm stroll. If you're wont to picnic frequently, stow a blanket in the car and invest in a large, double-handled basket. Don't limit picnics to daytime hours or the warmest climes. Enjoy moonlit noshes and sweatered outings, especially poetic on the beach. Set a well-dressed table under the stars or in the sand for a candlelit interlude.

cooked sausage to the edges, and flip darkening patties . . . then slowly slink away. But don't tarry—otherwise, you'll get wedged behind the grill, barked at by hungry throngs like a short-order cook. For a lazy merry-maker who wants to appear helpful, arrive at the grill right around "cheese time" and assist in top-shelf bun toasting or mustard squirting.

Relish intimate tête-à-têtes around the grill, as the warm coals and air redolent of charred meat fosters camaraderie. Note quickly which side is upwind and shift accordingly. Like the soothing patter of rain, there's something about the sizzling of meats that brings out humor and confidences.

Final thoughts for the casual outdoor affair:

* If hosting a BBQ, deputize a trusted acquaintance for grilling duties to allow freer socializing with guests. Mix a batch of homemade lemonade or booze punch for all-day sipping.

* Eschew the no-frills-brand, black lung charcoal reminiscent of ante-diluvian carbon and kerosene. Also, no frozen, prepattied 50 percent befatted chuck, rivaling Gaines Burgers (with cheese). Spend the extra few dollars or visit the butcher.

* Don't panic over a "burgercide" (unfinished patty falling through the grill slots). If tongs can't orchestrate a rescue, look up, genuflect, and close the grill cover to hide your incompetence, allowing the sacrificed meat to become indecipherable ash.

* Bring booze to an occupied grill man sweating over hot coals. At night, strategically placed citronella candles fend off tsetse swarms.

- Horseshoes are the perfect accompaniment to summer-evening conversations and canned beer. Although, a gentleman never offers up that tired adage: close only counts in. . . .

- Grill on the go with a portable hibachi. Adventurous travelers might experiment with under-the-car-hood omelettes or grilled fish—make sure you've changed the oil recently and use plenty of aluminum foil.

- Leave the coals safely in the grill until given clearance by the fire marshall; grey coals still have hidden sparks.

DAY AT THE BEACH

At beach gambols and clambakes, sand pervades everything, limiting your entertainment options to the most primitive electronics. Poseidon's polyphony of meditative wave and crash is far more melodic than anything on the airwaves. If you have a boom box that functions in the sand, reggae, salsa, and surfer tunes suit the mood, but be sure you don't pollute the next blanket with loud music. Quiet play-by-play on a transistor radio is perfect for the baseball enthusiast. Also, museful guitar strumming is an ideal low-tech fit for sing-alongs and sea chanties.

Bring a GFO (gentleman's flying object); box, Hargrove, or tetrahedral kites are the most playful. For the casual kiter, beware the 300 percent markup on styles sold in lazy beach-community shops. Don't be the old pest who fails to share the spool; a gentleman plays well with others. As for boomerangs, find a vast open space, mostly devoid of people or property. Try Western Australia.

Nice touch: Leave the beach better than you found it. Tote one small piece of foreign trash from your immediate sandy area.

BACHELOR PARTY

[reels]

[MPAA rating]

[blue movie]

More hype than substance, the bachelor party has long since lost its Roman-orgy mystique. A long night out for most, police involvement isn't requisite; nonetheless, the event should be the ultimate final gesture for the bridegroom. Invite the groom's closest campadres, the male future in-laws, and a few seasoned married gentlemen—not for chaperoning, but for insightful rounding.

Many bachelors now prefer to spend their final fling over a moderately sane long weekend of skiing, golfing, or gambling with close friends. Pack your rec gear, humidor, and top-shelf spirits—whatever the climate dictates. For atmospheric elegance, quietly pack two issues of low-grade pornography for the coffee table. On these last hurrahs, spend less time on shots and more around the bonfire, steeling the groom to the responsibilities of marriage. Invoke ceremony to celebrate the rite of passage, such as by burning the bridegroom's black book in effigy.

On the other hand, when the crowd cries for blood and the bachelor himself wishes a grand finale, a corrupt and sinful outing is on the mark. The best man must shadow the groom to ensure a seamless, trouble-free evening of debauchery. Evaluate the core group to determine the groom's agenda. The troika of vice (alcohol, sex, and gambling) may seem trite, but it's a solid foundation for a decadent evening. As with a game-winning home run, make sure to touch 'em all.

♦ **Entertainment:** Favorite convivial restaurant; cocktail lounges/bars; live music; establishments with dress-code requirements; lively acquaintances for the guest list; only the fondest, softest farm animals.

♦ **Sport:** Billiards/parlor games; golf outing; biking or other active venture; ballgame; boating/fishing; late-night air hockey; playing in traffic.

♦ **Gambling:** Casino; never-ending poker game with chips and cigars as entrée; inexpensive, all-you-can-eat sushi.

♦ **Fleshy Vice:** Gentleman's club; hired help; Mardi Gras gala; PG-13 video rental (new release for a special evening).

In any case, shoot for abundance of camaraderie, cheer, mockery, humor, and excess. Start your engines with a revving round of toasts and conversation, building the dynamic before taking it out on the town. Compel the bachelor to wear something distinctive—nothing too outlandish, merely a spirited cravat or smoking jacket. Arise the next afternoon feeling satisfied, woozy, and slightly offended.

Some prefer the cityscape tour. Leave the cameras and guidebooks at home. To accommodate the entire group, arrange a central mode of transportation to cement the dynamic and prevent group splintering. Several town cars can be useful; however, the ideal arrangement is a limousine or party bus—perhaps a converted yellow school bus with long benches and a large cooler in the back.

Should professional help be desired, plan ahead. Peruse the back pages of a free weekly for services; phone several listings to compare rates, activities, and policies. Do not offer your credit card digits until informed of the itinerary, level of involvement, and the inclusion of props. Hard-earned dollars should purchase at least some novelty and shock. The higher the tips, the better the service.

Final note: Though bachelor parties are mostly harmless, sleazy fun, appearances of impropriety may prompt a next-day interrogation. Keep mum. If the bridal party remains insistent after a censored recap, unresolved trust issues remain—nothing a few years of marriage or a private investigator won't iron out.

BEST MANNING

As weddings differ in formality and micromanagement, the head groomsman is faced with either a thimbleful or a heaping armful of duties. In general, the best man is the driving force behind the bachelor party, as well as the point man for boutonnière and formalwear snags. Moreover, he's the ceremony's centerfielder, mingling among guests, lending an ear to quell service personnel flare-ups. The best man dutifully handles the groom's wallet for gratuities and checks in with the bartender to keep the ice and the bridegroom well supplied.

If the groom is the quarterback, the best man is the headset-wearing backup, calling in the plays from the sideline. More than a ring-bearer, the best man captains the other groomsman. On the day itself, the best man keeps the groom loose, like a rubdown before a prizefight. The nonchalant toss of a ball after the morning haircut calms nerves. Share a final hit on the flask before boutonnières are pinned on, and take a moment alone with the groom to bid farewell to his bachelorhood.

PREWEDDING

An attentive best man is a minority shareholder in the marriage. He has stock in the relationship and seeks to cultivate his own rapport with the bride. Early on, the best man is a confidant and sounding board for a groom overwhelmed with logistics. Late-night phone calls assuage concerns of love, lost innocence, and the transition to wedded stability. A best man doesn't wait for the cry of help the week before, but regularly takes the groom's pulse to preserve a cool head. The best man is a warm soak when caterers and cat fighting have driven a groom to cold feet.

THE TOAST

Toast preparation starts two months before the ceremony. It's surprising how many funnies are recalled when you're not pressured on the eve of the knot tying. Jot down character traits, anecdotes, and remembrances. Childhood pals can dredge up ancient playtime relics, the raw materials for a singular speech. Suitable for the flower girls and in-laws, a clever toast still has imbedded code to make insiders chuckle. If anyone can recycle your toast by merely changing the name in the opening, you have disgraced the bubbly and the groom.

Classic etiquette sanctions four libations for a proper toast: Champagne, wine, whiskey, or beer. If you are quaffing a screwdriver or inexplicably sipping a white-wine spritzer, upgrade before proceeding.

Surround the speech's body with a sharp opening and winsome conclusion. A potent lead-off seizes attention—relate a classic joke, apocryphal pronouncement, or captivating quotation. If especially creative, try beginning with a gimmick such as a top ten list or uproarious roasting, followed by warm words. No matter your toasting style, final remarks should be succinct and sober best wishes for a rosy future. To spice it further, research foreign cultures and accompanying wedding traditions, winding up the toast with something symbolic and honest. Don't forget to acknowledge the bride—the gesture won't go unnoted.

Unless possessed of stentorian voice, regale briefly and effectively. Instead of fumbling about lack of preparation or public speaking experience, grasp the moment. Shower guests with stories, sans allusions to explicit instances of substance abuse or anything that happened last night. Despite a fiendish, boyish charm, show maturity. Meaningful instances of friendship and a few minutes of heartfelt gravity make for great copy and a fine set-up for a raucous finish. Leave the crowd guffawing and wanting more. Shirk vice and rambling collegiate mischief tales that cause nonalums to roll eyes and giggle politely with tedium. Trite recollections make for limp toasts and reflexive gagging ("I knew right away they were meant to be"). Do better.

Incidentally, once the guests are rapt, don't forget to introduce yourself before proceeding with the toast.

ROASTING

A roast is an exquisite form of comedic address in which love and reverence are cloaked in seemingly mean-spirited and wry hilarity. Only those experienced with public speaking or possessing an impeccable sense of timing should attempt this style. Careful where you tread; when in doubt, tell a funny story instead. Bush-league roasting is worse than the sappiest schmaltz from the annals of Hallmark. Despite their vituperative pop, roasts end with warm sentiment and a bearlike hug that smoothes the sting and confirms affection.

CAVEATS

Despite the humorous or crowd-pleasing value, certain topics are rightfully taboo. Dodge the hisses by refusing to spin tales about the groom's prior lovers, brushes with the law, hoary secrets, the couple's rocky relationship history, divorce, deaths in the family, genitalia, and, most importantly, anything disparaging (even in jest) about the bride or her parents.

Chapter Three

WOOING

◆ ◆ ◆ ◆ ◆ ◆ ◆

Flirtation **68**

Dates 72

The Open Triangle **81**

Do-It-Yourself 84

Long-Distance Runaround **85**

Exes & Ohs 88

The Crack-Up **90**

FLIRTATION

Flirtation is a distinct act of charisma, a give and take less like chess and more akin to backgammon. Indeed, skill is involved, but the thrill of chance is always at play. Gentlemen recognize the differences between deeds of charm, manners of flirtation, and tactics of seduction.

Flirtation kicks in like a thermostat when mood and attraction are right. If you fumble for the perfect retort or regularly curse inaction ("I shoulda said something to that cute Amish girl in the black hat at the checkout line"), recall the first rule of standardized tests: trust first instincts and don't allow fear to occlude your social awareness. It is overkill to flirt everywhere with everyone, yet celebrate a heightened groove of self-assurance or a great hair day. At such times, flirting will find you.

The best techniques can't be listed because they are employed impromptu as a natural extension of demeanor and charm. Solid eye contact, the occasional wink, and first-name recall are always welcome ("Looking lovely, Carolyn"). In the freshly squeezed realm of genuine flirtation, uninvited bad techniques are sickly sweet canned orange drink. Shelve these lesser tactics:

♦ **The Jeweler:** A sudden reach for a lady's necklace too near the bustline.

♦ **The Excessive Endearer:** Sugary overdose of presumptuous pet names like "baby," "sweetie," "darling," and that boardwalk prize-wheel favorite "hon."

♦ **The Restaurant Voyeur:** Writing a suggestive note to a server, then leaving only 14 percent; asking the bartender when she "gets off."

- **The Cunning Linguist**: Overpunning with sexual terms; see above.

- **The Surprise Toucher**: The "Guess Who?" hands over the eyes game or the unsolicited, two-handed neck massage (perfected by former Senator Bob Packwood).

- **The Persistent Hello/Goodbye Hugger**: Clinging with extra-expressive squeezes, pats, and circular back rubbing.

- **The Sarcastic Flirt-Beggar**: "Wait. . .you're leaving, and you haven't said goodbye?"

SEDUCTION VS. FLIRTATION

Flirtation is the exchange of peripheral sexual energy for mutual glee and confidence boosting. Seduction is flirtation with a specific thrust to further action. Thus, seduction is only successful when consummated, whereas the gaiety of flirtation is itself the reward.

Flirtation is light and fleeting, even if continuous. Ideally, it is spontaneous, without thought to long-term effect. It need not be reciprocated, though hopefully it will be returned with at least a smirk or smile. The most intense flirtation involves dancing close to the line—as close as

PICK-ME-UP

Cognac ◆ Dubonnet blanc ◆ Dash of anisette ◆ One egg white ◆ Lemon twist another implicitly allows. With seduction, you are luring the intended to cross the line and anticipating the ideal moment to cross it yourself.

DOUBLE STANDARD

If a woman flirts, respond in kind and check the vibe before presuming ulterior motives. Men are expected to flirt, but when women are playful, lesser picaroons with pulsing ids assume the mating ritual has begun. This type of behavior causes ladies to reserve their winsome chitchat;

DANCING

The well-expressed dancing gentleman is a magnet that draws in like-minded spirits. Even if little is exchanged on the floor besides strong moves, gimlet eyes, and deep sighs, consider an intimate dance a clothed intercourse that's as breathless as the naked variety. Still, dancing is not an unmitigated tit-smash insinuating foreplay. A well-disciplined monogamous man relishes the metaphor of dance as a medium to channel sexuality without the vow-crushing infringements of exchanged digits and kisses.

In the nightclub, don't fear a circle, where the empty space is an exhibitionist's chance for inspired monologues. Hop atop a speaker when feeling brazen. Slug more water than gin and dress for twirling. Lead confidently, no one likes a limp wrist. Never mind your witty tongue, speak in the primal words of hips, dips, breath, and writhe. When the room is synchronized in a deejay's vortex of bass and shake, let out a scream and wave your arms.

Incidentally, know when to bow out. A single splendid whirl is not reason to affix yourself to a partner like a ballroom barnacle. Say thank you and step into the washroom for a splash break, then take another's hand or resume solo action. A reprise with an early-night partner is like comin' home.

women are entitled to flirt harmlessly without being asked for their phone numbers and Hotmail addresses.

FLIRTING AND MONOGAMY

The married or involved gent can share a gleaming smile and innocuous flirt without temptation. Still, biologically speaking, flirtation demonstrates health and virility as a mate. Ensure you aren't falsely flashing your feathers, leading someone to believe that you are available. Double-check the temperature before misplaced lust unwisely invites someone for a dip into your venerable gene pool. Make it a motiveless venture. Good flirtation affirms vitality, but does not leave you holding a motel key.

RELATIONSHIP FLIRTATION

Don't reserve all enticements for alluring strangers. Renew your passions at home lest they expire. Billing and cooing are essential to relationship nurturing, whether through passing whispers or tantalizing glances across the breakfast table.

ILL-TIMED FLIRTING

Don't be a sugary sycophant, trumpeting loaded compliments indiscriminately. One does not turn on the charm at a funeral or woo the bride at her own wedding; similarly, flirtation is ineffectual when the recipient is harried with other tasks. Flirting with a married woman can be a tasteful affirmation of her attractiveness. However, over-amorousness is unseemly in the presence of a spouse.

Incidentally, when someone stands between you and a simple goal, charisma can grease the wheels. An extra smile at the deli counter might get you a bigger piece.

DATES

Dating is an audition. You are both reading lines cold, looking for the spark of chemistry that leads to a continuing role. Put aside the posturing and the scoring pad; dates are meant to be fun encounters on the town. No more preparation is necessary than the personal-growth homework you've already put into making yourself attractive and interesting. Isn't that how you got the date anyway?

Thoughts for the dating gentleman:

◆ Squelch indecision. During the logistics stage, present a menu of firm, lively options. It doesn't have to be dinner or an after-dusk date. How about a brunch picnic, play, or planetarium visit?

◆ Dress appropriately: neither Sunday best nor funkiest eclectic. Smart shoes are an imperative.

◆ Be interested, not just interesting. Humor is essential, but the date is not a slapstick sketch or an *Airplane!* outtake.

◆ Praise a date's features without invading personal space. A well-placed comment about earrings is welcome and evinces a keen eye. Overpersonal compliments cause the willies ("I love that mole on your right calf").

◆ A run of first dates in the same place is unimaginative. Multitask your romantic calendar by exploring the many metropolitan curiosities. At worst, a string of bad dates leads to a pocketful of restaurant reviews.

- Too many wooing bells and whistles create a false impression. Select venues within your fiscal element. Overspending is betting $500 bottles of wine against your blandness. Overdoting with chivalry is less expensive but just as gaudy.

- When the topic swings to sex or drugs, follow the leader. Less is more, and scant hints of a tawdry résumé are better than locker-room roll calls of your vast experience.

- During gorilla August, carry a handkerchief or napkin to pat your brow and neck before first contact, so as not to appear a complete drip.

  Thoughts for the dating lout:

- Show up late, slouch in your seat, don't offer to share a morsel of monkfish, and steamroll your date with extrovertedness.

- Be the Smothering Solicitor: "Are you comfortable? Do you want another drink? Do you need anything else? Are you having fun? Do you wanna go somewhere else?" To make her smile vanish, comment to her dismay, "Do you feel all right? You look tired."

- Mistreat the service staff, giving your date a preview of what she can expect on a future Sunday morning.

- Select a venue so loud that pantomime and mouth-cupped yelling are the only methods of communication. *Exception:* a vibrant tapas joint enriches, as does the third carafe of sangria.

BODY LANGUAGE

Collate character clues before the first course. Note her entrance. Were you hugged? How does she hold her glass? Is she leaning into the conversation or searchlighting the room as if waiting for her "real" date?

A date is neither pedigree check nor portfolio review. No need to expose all desires and profiles like one of Picasso's Dora Maar portraits. Heat the pot and then prime the stew with the best ingredients and raciest conversation. Shared professions are a bridge, but bungee jump into deeper interests like SCUBA, outlandish dreams, and the arts. It's a great date when conversation hums long after the Guinness foam has caked in your empty pint glass.

You may mash each other's toes or knock knees. Don't be afraid of awkward moments or brief silences, but shoulder the responsibility to

---

ST. VALENTINE'S DAY

A dubious holiday, famous for the Chicago massacre and unfulfilled, chalky candy hearts. Can't remember the last time you bestowed flowers? Don't start now. And no eleventh-hour runs to CVS for a heart-shaped box and no-frills tray of Russell Stover chocolates (the only brand that says, "Not only don't I love you, I don't particularly care for you in any lasting manner"). Surprise her instead with a whisk to a favorite bistro for a quiet, tactile evening. The holiday should be recognized on the fourteenth, but not always celebrated then. Despite the lack of crayon-adorned desk pouches, send your friends and associates cartoonish Valentine cards like you did in elementary school.

Nice touch: Make a wine-primed beloved swoon by slipping a gift on the sly to the waiter for later presentation on the dessert plate.

moderate and stimulate. Call a time-out and offer your date the same, to recollect your confidence, leave a table hot, and consider a tempo change.

A great date leaves a mystery that won't be solved until the second episode, like a fine cliffhanger. What was that coy smirk at the end of the night? When did she live in England? Who shot J. R.?

DRINKING

A woman drove me to drink and I didn't even have the decency to thank her.

—W. C. FIELDS

Cocktail management is a practical extension of personality. Do not arrive with a head start. If you are early or your date is late, order one drink to pass the time. Should plans disintegrate, kill the pain of rejection with rueful abandon.

Pace yourself. Not all rambunctious dates are Olympic tosspots. It is bad manners to drink ahead and lap a slow-sipping companion who's lumbering around the oval like a sputtering Indy car. Avoid a deplorable evening that finds you rummied up on Captain Morgan as your date shrugs with a Chardonnay. For ungoverned elbow-benders, beach booze in pitchers and bottles of wine mask consumption rates, permitting drinking at natural speeds without reproach.

Unexplained teetotaling causes as much alarm as a besotted date who calls for whiskey by the bottle like an extra in a spaghetti western. The latter may be seeking a codependent, not a lover.

THE CLOSE

A first kiss shouldn't be first affection. A vibrant date warrants a stroke of the hair or a nibble on the fingers. Before the evening ends and the ride home begins, take a reading on the love meter to determine a date's conclusion. You should know by now if the future holds a kiss, a nightcap, or a handshake before the awkward confines of the apartment-building vestibule.

Nice touch: Be a rule-breaking mogul and whisk a first date to Venice on twenty-four-hour notice.

A FEW DATES LATER

Certain barriers have dropped, so take advantage of the openness and probe deeper. Reach across the table with an offered hand without even breaking eye contact. Enjoy same-side seating or corner-booth canoodling. Close proximity affords entrée sharing and furtive nestling.

Learn from Hitchcock's *Rope*: sometimes the ideal arrangement is in the span of two rooms. Declare the home-field advantage and rearrange the furniture for comfort. For rented black-and-white classics, schedule intermissions to take air on the balcony, fluff pillows, and steal a smooch.

Incidentally, an aquarium is a winsome venue. For advanced wooers, immerse yourself in this oceanic theme date as if it were a Jacques Cousteau bathysphere and break for sushi or a bowl of clam chowder.

DISPLAYS OF AFFECTION

Open mouths are fine for Resuscitation Annie, but one should avoid gratuitous displays in public. However, regular pecks are mutual publication of an affectionate relationship. When the mood is undeniable, hold up a menu or shield your affections behind a phone booth.

In mixed company, hold hands. Single-fingered swinging or interlaced fingers forge an unassuming bond. Offer friction in moderation, as the continuous caress numbs the receiver to the unpredictable pleasures of casual touch. For the arm-in-arm escort, offer neither a limp spaghetti forearm nor a dominant elbow—it's a lady's supple arm, not a pigskin that mustn't be fumbled.

SO, YOUR FIRST DATE IS GOING IN THE TANK

Scenario: As dinner progresses, you realize your date is not nearly as attractive as she seemed last Saturday, nor as witty as her e-mails; and frankly, the anecdote about formative years spent in a Jovian cult was not amusing. Chemistry is noncombustive and chat is disenchanting. To avoid this quagmire, schedule a preliminary cocktail summit before committing to the blind potluck of dinner. Enter the first full date with a backlog of rapport to drive communication and prevent uneasiness.

Bad dates vary in degree from innocuous to intolerable. If you find yourself starring in the classic first-date debacle, use the graded list below to help gauge hopelessness. For ease of discussion, these examples presume you are the innocent victim of incompatibility. (Though, any poor-date

---

IN CASE OF EMERGENCY, BREAK GLASS

The Ditch is an ungentlemanly, sly departure. Deploy this maneuver once per lifetime in the wake of a truly offensive act: strung-out condition, blatant disregard of your presence, or other social pathology. When no one's looking, pay the bill and dive into a getaway taxi like a mobbed teen idol. Retreat to a distant gin mill and spend reflective moments over a solitary drink. Direct remaining adrenalin into another encounter—indeed, you have a cliffhanger as an opening line: "You'll never guess what I just did. . . ."

scenario can find you in the seat of culpability—off your game, clumsy, underattractive—with a squirming mate itching to flee.)

• **C:** *A Flat Affair.* After too many long pauses, intermittent sparks fail to keep the pilot light lit. Frequent interruptions and fruitless conversation of missed innuendo: the brows never fully unfurrow. Both parties have previewed peccadilloes and committed a few mood-neutralizing conversational gaffes (off-color jokes, nail biting, excessive use of pet phrase). In short. . .can't get on track.

• **D:** *A Chilly Affair.* All of the above AND striking polarity, a minefield of schisms (Marlboro Man vs. fitness instructor, Mac vs. PC), morose temperament, or poor table manners. Hot chemistry has iced over into a job interview. In short. . .opposites aren't attracting.

• **F:** *A Calamity.* All of the above AND an outstanding annoying habit such as a hyena's shrill laugh, irksome germophobia, unstable emotional makeup, or revealed tragic flaw. Feels like a peer counseling session. There's been plenty of sharing, but too much, too soon. In short. . .too many issues, more repugnant with every forkful.

LOVE COCKTAIL

• **Sloe gin** • **One egg white** • **2 dashes lemon juice** • **Fresh raspberries** •

Incidentally, a bad date can become a good date once both parties acknowledge the dynamic. In the best cases, a next-day follow-up directly addressing a Grade C or light D bad date can foster a shared laugh and desire for a do-over or merely furnish kind closure.

PERSEVERANCE

See a poor date through to a speedy finish: decline dessert, skip the next round, and politely call it an early night. Better yet, treat the date as an anthropological survey. Revel in hearing another's life story, even if it lacks plot and intrigue. Conversing candidly with strangers develops skills as a social animal. When all else stalls, be brazen and introduce off-the-wall queries ("You mentioned you're in PETA. What's your stance on furry handcuffs?"). A little pluckiness enlivens a dormant date. One good cocktail comment, unthinking caress, or off-hand invitation for a nightcap can inspire mirth.

Don't be tempted to end the affair with a concocted excuse—the conversational equivalent of a bad toupee. Feigned medical emergencies and phantom cell phone calls are laughable. Should the situation plummet to an abysmal nadir, steal away to the restroom to consider options. Think at the sink or, for additional privacy, take solace in the gentleman's lounge with head in hands.

Two options when considering a salvage operation:

1. **Restart:** A change of ambiance livens a sagging mood. When flickering connections are still promising, chalk up discomfort to the uninspired music, long wait, or low blood sugar. A simple "Can we start over someplace else," and an open-air stroll might remind both why you wanted a date in the first place.

2. **Candor**: Be assertive and break the sullen vibe with a mid-date huddle: "This isn't quite working out as we expected." Lay out the cards and shuffle the deck, or fold. A lean-in might resurrect stalled affections. The edgy lady appreciates tactful, honest interjection to silent dolefulness. Well-played candor is a pickax upon the icy block of flailing dates.

THE WEEKEND GETAWAY

The early rounds of dating have progressed swimmingly. You've logged plenty of evenings and afternoons, but few (if any) overnighters or stretches of uninterrupted playtime. It's time to up the ante with a weekend getaway. This is a three-day crash course in cohabitation that previews relationship potential. By the ride home, you'll both have a keener sense of compatibility and toothpaste brands. The long drive up to the inn fosters deeper exploration without time constraints or the usual date insecurities. The beach or mountain getaway is ideal for filling in the blanks of personal history and outing odd music tastes on the rental-car tape deck. Pack sundries for romance and mood: candles, bubbles, toys, Duraflame logs, stimulants. They may not make it out of the duffel bag, but one should prepare for budding coupling. A cozy weekend getaway acknowledges mutual desires and acceptance of the invitation usually implies sex. Though, examining uncovered idiosyncrasies so closely might cool attraction and cause one party to reconsider. Despite passions bubbling over in the bedroom, tread lightly and respect the remaining boundaries of personal space, especially with closed bathroom doors.

THE OPEN TRIANGLE

*I think it's quite possible for a man to take care of more than one woman—
on condition that the parties concerned realize fully what they're in for . . . .
A friend of mine thinks that a man should take care of as many women as he
can keep happy. But then there are economic problems, no?*

—HENRY MILLER, *MY LIFE AND TIMES*

Courtship isn't always a prelude to nuptials, and healthy relationships
can exist without monogamy. The open triangle is for mature bachelor
gentlemen. Managing one romance is hard enough; balancing two
entails the deft touch of a surgeon and the intuitive communication of
a mixed-doubles pair.

Rarely, a gentleman finds himself immersed in a successful network
of affairs where thirsts are sated from a host of cups. Multiball play typically occurs when a man emerges from a dry spell. A wintry homebody
routine of gym workouts and cozy reading-chair sessions renews vigor
and wends into springtime outings. Suddenly, the black book swells with
phone numbers, and multiple dates are scheduled. Fast forward a few
weeks to when two semifinalists have surged ahead in the polls. Before
choosing between budding romances, consider the open triangle. Not
a pair of overlapping loves, these are two distinct and valued relationships occurring simultaneously. Enjoy a zesty Italian class on Monday
and a cerebral physics course on Tuesday. As long as the science text gets
highlighted in yellow as often as oral skills are practiced in the language
lab, there's nothing lost in this ambidextrous experience. Perhaps one
bond evolves as the other fizzles, for now the focus is on fun, discovery, and freedom.

Ideal scenario: MG is wooing lovers X and Y. X is also seeing gent A as Y sees gent B. All parties are physically intimate and nonexclusive. Outside of each twosome, none of the lovers are acquainted.

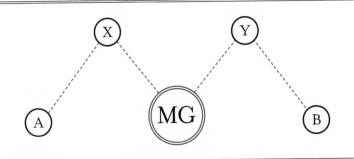

So you've begun something interesting with two and both are in similar periods of experimentation and self-indulgence. Once sexual relations are consummated, it's time for unambiguous disclosure ("I'm really enjoying this, and I'm seeing someone else"). Open consent from both lovers is mandatory. Discussion might cover condom use and other logistics, but do not dwell on intimate details ("She's into leather and Mallomars"). This conversation is an excellent early gauge of expectations and equality. Is someone more emotionally invested?

Relationships of similar intensity should depart in style and content. For instance, MG and X hit the galleries and dance floor together, while MG and Y go for coffeehouses and rock climbing. X and Y are not competing for affection and are unencumbered by talk of other amorous relations. X isn't shortchanged because MG's foibles are A's abundant strengths. Likewise, as long as what Y brings to the table is different from X, MG needn't fret over whom to like best.

Nice touch: Once all lights are green, treat yourself to the open triangle treat of double booking. Love in the A.M., love in the P.M.

The open triangle is symbiotic . . . if one relationship breaks down, the whole system fails. In a broken triangle, MG begins to lean heavily upon Y for what he used to get from X. Y cannot sustain the strain of inequality, and MG is left undersatisfied. Entropy will inevitably set in and make this affair short-lived—more than six months is stupendous.

No mere serial flings for logging notches on the bedpost, these relationships are grounded and bordering on serious. Triangles demand more than the sustenance of casual sex, dinners, and routine telephone check-ins. They work best with lovers who are mature, sane, and a little bit wild. At the crossroads? Not quite ready for the supreme soulmate? Explore multiplicity and see how two flames in the same city at the same time yield such wildly varying results in heart and bed. If all memorable couplings are plotted in the open triangle, re-examine your fear of commitment.

Tips for the triangulating varietist:

* Affections are personalized, not cheap form letters of love. Never repeat romantic notions: no identical gifts, no shared pet names.

* No unannounced visits. Ample notice facilitates an easy shift of gears. Courtesy of forewarning raises anticipation, not suspicions.

* Do not ask prying questions into affairs and schedules. Maintain confidence that your particular gift is unique and desirable, despite a lover's overnighter with someone else. Respect privacy and you will garner the same treatment.

♦ No need to tempt the fragile balance with in-your-face reminders of the triangle arrangement. For propriety's sake, look out for loose barrettes and stray undies.

DO-IT-YOURSELF

As table-manners expert Marjabelle Young Stewart's credo states: stroke the meat, don't saw it. The authors will not provide a guiding hand regarding the "solitary rhumba," "han solo," "white knuckler," or "backstroke roulette." We assume a gentleman has honed this skill through years of trial and little error. We will not chair a panel concerning the alleged myopic effects from "hand-to-gland combat" or "driving the skin bus." Rather, the following concerns the ins and outs of "fisting one's mister" during a grounded relationship, when sexual relations and intimacy are touchstones.

Certain instances require an immediate "hand shandy." No matter how stupendous a sex life, the occasional, undeniable fantasy ought to be slaked. Giving in to your personal carnality infrequently keeps it a stolen pleasure. This rare practice will not hamstring award-winning romps or tarnish your moral fibre.

"Giving Yul Brynner a high five" is a sexual supplement and a mild affirmation of autonomy that's as right as rain. No main squeeze, however wonderful, can oblige all needs, all the time. When in love, "hitchhiking under the bigtop" appears somehow fresh. So "meet your right hand man" and "pan for white gold," because cheating with yourself is not cheating.

SHARING

Play show-and-tell with an open and sexually mature lover. Nevertheless, for the overly prudish, be discreet during pillow talk:

Q. Honey, do you still. . .you know?

A. Well, dear. In the past I "pumped gas at the self-service island"
on occasion, as any man would. And anyone who admits otherwise is lying. Now, I have everything I want, you little so-and-so.
The only time I "keep down the census" is when you're away at
your parents' or attending a Junior League tea. Otherwise, I simply have no need to "qualify in the testicular time trial." Really.

LONG-DISTANCE RUNAROUND

The transcontinental affair has become more spicy since e-mail and
videophones replaced protracted post and telegraph. Mutual attraction
struck at last week's actuarial convention in Reno. What to do? Consider
the following points before you embark.

BROAD ATTRACTION

Seafaring yeomen may revel in casual flings with many a girl of port, but
the energy to maintain a land-lubbing long-distance romance requires
mutual, multitiered passion. Creativity must compensate for geographical
constraints that consign mates to second-hand contact. The majority of
interaction will be cerebral and full of fanciful yearning, so make certain
neurons are fluttering as strongly as your loins are aching.

FORESEEABLE FUTURE

Once ensconced, establish the possiblity of a conjoined future in the same area code. Ask the foundation questions: Is one party seeking a career or venue change? Are intangibles such as professional licenses, property ownership, or family proximity a factor? Glean answers early on with frank issue exchange, especially as intimacy grows lush like plush moss on a rotten log.

FREQUENT ATTENTION

Distance must be offset with frequent correspondence. In this fashion, uncover naughty thoughts and preferences for everything from the cinema to bondage strategies. In lieu of face time, unexpected flowers, gushing letters, and weekend jaunts are the tools of woo. Telephoning is important, yet daily marathons are expensive and tedious, resulting in fatigue and earlobe sweat. For habitual gabbers, a cell phone is standard and perfect for the sleepy, late-night tuck-in. Tired of the reciprocal visit routine every three to four weeks? Instead of the usual home-and-away schedule, plan a rendezvous on neutral ground in an equidistant city.

INHERENT FREEDOM

Establish the parameters early: Is it exclusive or are both parties permitted to see other people? Given the failure rate, don't foreclose an active roving eye in ascetic observance of an untested, distant love. Monogamy can be maintained through dedication and subliminal audiotape seminars without precluding harmless "catch and release" dalliances on the town. A constant interrogation of whereabouts or missed calls is smothering. For jealous types, pop a quaalude or trade in a *distancée* for a neighbor.

REPEAT OFFENDERS

A failed long-distance relationship or two is a poignant lesson in anticipation. Distanced relations should be fortuitous, unplanned acts, not fallback solutions for intimacy fears or twice-bitten souls. A serial of affairs from afar signals more than a nomadic lifestyle: namely, a fiery strain of independence or an unwillingness to tackle complex, local relationships. It's easy to participate when interaction and meaningful pillow talk are rarities. Be certain that proximate relationships are still within you.

CAVEATS

Inequality of effort and affection is fatal. When desire and bond aren't piston-firing in synchrony, end the affair. The relationship is inherently flawed, as each party observes libidinal discipline without tasting the daily fruits of hand-holding and nocturnal waltzing. During visits, intimacy is focused but limited. Departure dates and luggage in the corner loom over time together. Long evenings on the porch swing are far different than the hustle-bustle of time-conscious nights on the town. Discern whether rapture is fueled by love or the artificial excitement of intermittent trysts. Permanent transplants may unearth the rascal of incompatability. Before moving vans are rented, scrutinize your pairing.

ESTABLISHED RELATIONS

Sometimes engaged couples are temporily separated, perhaps by an out-of-state job assignment. With the perspective of space and candid conversation, see an established lover from a new perch. Between longings, take the opportunity to ponder what aspects of your relationship need fine-tuning. Upon reunion, plot any course corrections discussed via hotel phone.

Incidentally, don't worry, all those plane tickets aren't a complete waste. You'll tally enough frequent flier miles for an island trip, where you can wallow in self-pity after the relationship crumbles.

EXES & OHS

While deep emotional ties with every ex suggest lingering issues, a gentleman invariably remains in contact with a few old flames. Postrelationship interaction is a sign of maturity, and maintenance should be cultivated, if cautiously. Admit to yourself that the underlying motivation for remaining friends is continued attraction. Don't delude yourself and romanticize a rocky past; all the hang-ups are still there. Never forget why the relationship ended, even as you rekindle by candlelight.

Some postscripts resolve into deep, platonic affections; others gel into light friendships or infrequent e-mail curiosities. At most, be able to write an outline of her current life, but leave any extended essay questions blank. Don't be presumptuous: requests for cocktails can be rain checked and phone calls left dormant for a spell.

Incidentally, throaty telephone calls after 10 P.M. are booty calls, not innocent chitchat. Avoid calling an ex while drunk or horny (especially drunk *and* horny).

THE INVOLVED EX

Don't be a barnacle on the side of a spoken-for lady and make her answer to a jealous husband. Call her at the office or on her cell phone, or stick to e-mail. Repeat calls without leaving a message indicate misguided pining.

Even worse, the hovering vulture, the loathsome creature who lunges at the first sign of heartache before staging the canned "concerned" lean-in ("Oh really, trouble at home?"). Successful, long-awaited sequels are rare and fleeting, as needs change over time. Don't carry an Olympic torch for a long-past ex. Keep those old crushes pint-sized, especially when it was your fault the relationship soured.

EX SEX

In a perfect world, two people break up graciously, respect differences, and soon after sleep together for no reason other than pleasure. On Earth, sex with exes is fraught with renewed jealousies, clingy bad habits, and unwise reprises. Peek behind casual sex with an ex. Often there is an inequality, as one party longs for reconciliation. Eventually, one screws while the other makes love, setting up a dramatic take-two of the crackup when someone inevitably cries, "I can't do this anymore!" As a gentleman matures, easy sex with exes is weighed against the selfish exploitation of vulnerabilities.

WHEN YOU'RE ATTACHED

If your phone voice decidedly dips when your current squeeze comes within earshot during a call to an ex, beware a possible breach. Lines of flirtation blur when you've already danced on the other side. To avoid trust issues, disclose your status with an ex to a present love.

Incidentally, it is unnecessary to disclose an innocent run-in on the street, especially during trying times when mention will only exacerbate troubles at home.

THE CRACK-UP

First Suspicion of Crack, 8. 0:
With absolute ease. . .both agree to differ on liking football. . .or completely
modern chairs. . .and both agree not to talk much more about these subjects.
Fissure, 23. 0:
He has long wondered, now he is sure. He would rather not be present
when she is with her best female friend.
Crevasse, 64. 0:
When you start in private practising things you are going to say to her,
just as you did when you were falling in love with her.
Now with a heavy difference.

—STEPHEN POTTER, *ANTI-WOO GAMBITS FOR NON-LOVERS**

A break-up is defined as the end point of a sexual relationship that has lasted for any period over a fortnight, or the termination of a physically intimate, nonconjugal relation of at least one calendar month. The brush-off of a brief interaction with an extra base-hit requires no stratagem and is the only exception to the "never by telephone rule."

The denouement is rarely clean and swift; most relationships end

---

* Stephen Potter, *Anti-Woo Gambits for Non-Lovers.* New York: McGraw-Hill Companies, 1965. Excerpt reproduced with permission of the McGraw-Hill Companies.

with bitterness and regret, and in some cases, a distinct promise never to speak again. Outside of Act-of-God break-ups, most are doomed by a gross inequality of desire and motive.

Sometimes it's not easy to let go. The gentleman does his best to remain whole when crushed by circumstance. Temper the pall of a broken heart or the call to revenge. Evade Medea's fate: after hearing her lover Jason had fallen for King Creon's daughter, she killed Jason's lover and two sons, then fled to Athens for more high adventure.

Even if you aren't grinning like Bruce Jenner on a Wheaties box, avoid the common pitfalls following a fallout. How many of the following Despondent Decathlon events did you gold-medal in during a previous break-up?

The 100m Denial: First hints of doom are ignored and precious time for real communication is squandered.

The Furious Discus Throw: Initial aftermath of restrained anger, characterized by seething and a few temperamental outbursts.

THE FIZZLE

You've bribed the planning board and gotten all the permits, but no construction has actually begun. A few dates and telephone exchanges suggest a promising beginning. Still, loose plans fall through, poor timing intrudes, and interest slumps, dormant. The fizzle is a flame of interest allowed to smolder out without the bellows of continued contact. Is there a spark to salvage? Will a candid e-mail revive a static connection? Either invigorate relations with a second chance ("We keep missing one another, and if I don't see you soon, I'm going to forget why I like you"), or shelve it for a later reprise. All it takes is one serendipitous encounter to rekindle the chemistry: "Care to try this again?"

The Shot Put of Fury: Late-night phone calls that begin with drunken colloquy and end with. . .more drunken colloquy.

The 400m Lobby: Cherry-picking accentuation of your remaining positive traits; pleading to friends for diplomatic intervention.

The Long Jump of Lamentation: Guess who's been standing on her stoop the entire evening with a bottle of Old Grand Dad in one hand and a shaky cigarette in the other?

The Mutual Javelin Throw: The true war of negativity, when patience and niceties burst and torrents ensue.

The 110m Emotional Hurdle: The pit of despair in which crying and pleading haven't patched things up; idle threats of "I can't live without you" are bandied about.

The Heights of the Pole Vault: The false hope in the eye of the crack-up hurricane, when nurturing sentiments of "I miss you" and "I care about you" are misconstrued as signs of reconciliation.

The High Jump to the Bar: The trite, week-long swims in whiskey at the local pub, with head in hand.

The 1500m Plead: "I was wrong and you were right to leave me. I'll change, I'll do anything. I'll even stop seeing Ellie on the side."

WEEP NO MORE

◆ ◆ ◆ ◆ ◆ **Brandy** ◆ **Dubonnet** ◆ **$^1/_3$ lime** ◆ **Dash maraschino** ◆ ◆ ◆ ◆ ◆

FOUR TYPES OF CRACK-UPS

Mutual: When budding romance backtracks into indifference: a relationship's growth, connectedness, and practicality have reached a natural stopping point. Nothing has really gone awry, but sexual chemistry and date frequency have sharply abated. Long-range scanners indicate potential obstacles and little future along the current course. Rather than forcing an unfeasible togetherness, both parties agree to part ways. Following an amicable split, the opportunity remains to cultivate warm acquaintanceship. The least destructive breakup, the Mutual augurs the best chance of romantic revisitation.

Symptoms of mutual breakup:

◆ After a night together, one fails to call, the other doesn't care.

◆ Four or five days of unknown whereabouts go unquestioned.

◆ Both parties have left items at the other's apartment, but are unconcerned (his Bulova watch can sit a spell; so can her pearls).

◆ Neither references the other (or the relationship) in mixed company.

Inequality: The corrosion of balanced affection, when one party earns a poor return on his or her emotional investment; compassion and kindness are monopolized; thoughtful notions and gifts are unheeded; one side is forthcoming, the other withholding, in communication and in bed. The relationship is consumed by unilateral whims, and the teeter-totter of affection is leaving one person in the air. The same person who picks up the check is also left holding the bag.

By the time inequality reaches the crack-up stage, ample opportunities to right the balance have been overlooked. Unlike a Mutual split, the Inequality breakup has an insidious undercurrent, since no single episode caused the rift. It's a slow cancer, steadily eroding a relationship until the crevasse is wide. One person is left to question their attractiveness, second-guess their efforts, and rethink an open heart. Ironically, the more they gave, the less they received.

A rebuffed gentleman needs time to recover from a war in which no shots were fired. After replaying relationship game film, highlight bad decisions and poor execution. Rebound relationships are improbable during introspective healing.

A selfish gentleman whose decreased affections started the corrosion must reevaluate his relationship manners. Instead of orchestrating a courageous fix or definitive exit, the sheepish lad allowed the neglected relationship to curdle. Next time, go for the clean cut instead of a protracted withdrawal.

Act of God: The Fates intervene: a better job is offered in a faraway city, a saucy new soul mate inexplicably falls like manna from heaven, the lottery hits, or a false pregnancy reveals hidden cracks. There is little red tape for this crack-up; one priority trumps another. Acts of God can be a permanent splits or mere sabbaticals. Parting shots range from polite handshakes to tender swan songs of lovemaking.

Bitter: Transgressions and fiery passions explode: keys dragging across simonized surfaces; hate mail slid under the door; photos shredded; e-mails to coworkers concerning sexual inadequacy; and rabbits boiling on the Amana range. Straddled between acts of war, countless caustic telephone calls, hang-ups, and a sailor's cesspool of rarely heard pejoratives are spat in the name of vengeance. In this drama, the victim thirsts for the wrongdoer's matched suffering. As blood boils over like in a Greek tragedy, the gentleman does not succumb to the black bile of retribution. Constrain jilted emotions to short retorts, as bitter maledictions gradually subside.

In the Bitter breakup, the gentleman typically assumes one of two classic roles:

Protagonist: Living well is the gentleman's best revenge. Instead of firing salvos that stall healing, listen to the blues, dust off your collar, and reenter the scene. Schedule a singular evening of buddy-sponsored debauchery to pave over old hurt. During the postmortem, lean upon your inner circle for support, but beware an easy rebound to the very shoulder you cried upon most. Flip many (or infinite) calendar pages before entertaining thoughts of recontact with your ex.

Antagonist: A gentleman deserves his former love's malice when despicable lies are uncovered, abhorrent truths are revealed, dastardly deeds are detected, and the rapier of abuse has fatally slashed the relationship to tatters. The most respectable way to behave in the aftermath is to bear witness to the victim's pain, express remorse, and deal compassionately on their terms. Reflect upon your ruinous ways and lay off the serious dating scene until you've served penance.

FINAL DOS AND DON'TS

- Never break up by telephone, e-mail, hired third-party agent, or grapevine.

- If a breakup of live-in lovers forces one party to move out, the gentleman still offers his burly shoulders. In the case of a Bitter break-up, victims may slyly reserve all the U-Hauls in the state on moving day.

● Do not follow an entertaining evening and sexual romp with, "We need to talk." Either forgo the encounter or postpone the decision.

● Don't incinerate old photos, letters, or gifts until your rational mind deems it a sober decision.

● Before sending jilted love letters or mawkish 3 A.M. e-mails during a forlorn state, sleep on it. Dream that your words are being read by the entire Internet nation. Then, tear up the envelope or file the message in your Drafts folder for a future, head-shaking chuckle.

PART TWO

The
INNER
GENTLEMAN

Chapter Four

GENTLEMANLY KNOWLEDGE

◆ ◆ ◆ ◆ ◆ ◆ ◆

Literature **99**

Classical Music 108

Jazz 113

Fitness 117

Yoga 119

Flora 122

Soothsaying 124

Profanity & Vulgarity 126

Man Cycle 127

Fonzarelli Moves & Legerdemain 129

LITERATURE

Reading is a personal pleasure, a splash into authors, genres, and eras. Skip the CliffsNotes cram for tomorrow's *Wuthering Heights* discussion and write your own curriculum. Sample contemporary writers not taught in school, pick up nonfiction neglected by the History Channel, and crack those neglected classics.

If you're adrift between Auster and Zola, take a look at our All-Season Reading List below. Skim newspapers or free weeklies for book reviews or ask like-minded friends for recommendations. Return to a few pet authors for a familiar voice. Be a few books behind; your reading inbox should be piled medium-high with waiting volumes. But don't be afraid to occasionally cut the line for an urgent must-read that fits a current mood. During winter sabbatical, pick up a tome; on the rocks from a failed relationship, get lost in a therapeutic epic.

Keep a mental list of others' literary track records. After a string of hits, a reliable source shouldn't be dropped for promoting one dud. Though, if an acquaintance's first selection is a dull wordfest or a shiny airport paperback, decline like a coy schoolgirl ("Thank you for offering, but I just broke off a long engagement with Tolstoy, and I'm involved with another novel right now").

Don't be the persistent book pusher. The cry-wolf refrain of "You gotta read this" wears thin; not everyone cares to read every book on your nightstand. Maintain quality control: a gentleman's recommendation batting average should be 1.000, with only limited at-bats.

A book club is an effortless way to find good reads and meet an eclectic mix of fellow readers. Before diving in, find out how each month's selections are chosen: is it a democratic process, the host's choice, or some shady, local zoning board–like scheme? Book clubs are fun and should boast more wine than cheese: equal parts book discussion and carousing. Skipping a month for an overactive social life is acceptable.

Rather than frequenting megastores with trendy upstairs cafés, linger in independent bookshops that favor overstuffed shelves and a lazy cat asnooze in the biographies. Hunt down vintage hardbacks on the Web for half price and wonder over an ancient dedication or long-forgotten bookmark.

Allow the creamy goodness of a sublime read to soak in. Appreciate the gentle mind as it tosses around characters and memorable plot twists for days after a book has been shelved. The characters and themes in a gentleman's book du jour should peek into conversations. Talking about the book preserves its effect. Similarly, the shared experience of a book in common forges an immediate bond and breathless respect. The more books you read, the greater chance of forging connections (and myopia).

Carve out time. Turn lengthy train commutes into quiet book time; turn off the phone for extended stints or burn the lamp until 3 A.M. for late-night page-turning sessions. Underline favorite passages, circle unknown words, or jot crib notes in the margin; your scribbles will demark hot chapters and chart personal growth.

It's acceptable to string out a read over time, savoring every bite like a marbleized Kobe steak. Tougher tomes are like frozen lasagna and take

O H   H E N R Y !

♦ ♦ ♦ ♦ ♦ ♦ ♦ **Bénédictine** ♦ **Whiskey** ♦ **Ginger ale** ♦ ♦ ♦ ♦ ♦ ♦ ♦

a hundred pages or so to thaw. Keep at it, but don't be afraid to pull your bookmark out of a discount-bin snoozer or dull referral.

Mimic the best heavyweights: after a long, fifteen-round intellectual challenge, schedule a glass-jawed softie for your next read to maintain stamina; perhaps a light novella or fun mystery. You're on your own if you move from *Infinite Jest* to *Gravity's Rainbow*.

Are you a serial reader who tackles several books simultaneously or a dedicated one-book-at-a-timer? Serial readers are an odd bunch: should they be applauded for their thirst or treated for attention deficit disorder? Some books require undivided attention and must be your main squeeze. Other times, your coffee table can be a five-subject note-book, piled with studies. As for the nostalgic re-re-rereader, who con-sistently turns to the same volume, they just can't let go.

A bookshelf, like a music collection, is a mirror, revealing interests and personal history. Short of the Dewey Decimal System, organize it to eliminate extraneous piles. View the spines and ruminate over a treas-ured volume. When did you read it? Who was your lover?

BOOKMARKS

A bookmark holds your place while life continues outside the hardback. Bookmarks hawked at bookshop counters should be avoided like a thatch of poison sumac. Haphazard scraps of paper are better than laminated strips of cutesy bookworms spouting inane exclamations like "Look Where I Left Off!" Instead, use a heartifact or unorthodox bookmark to revisit a fond moment. Slip in a train pass from a recent excursion or a blue-movie ticket stub from a red-letter viewing.

Incidentally, some first editions are priceless and call for display, but books are not curios left out for intellectual machismo ("How *did* that Dostoevsky end up on the coffee table?").

Enjoy poetry on your own terms. A volume of verse doesn't expire and needn't be read cover to cover; it makes an excellent bedside joy or quiet valise stowaway. Like sampling regional cuisine, picking up local poetry provides a lasting memento of your travels.

Nice touch: Take fifteen minutes a night to read aloud a rousing bed-time tale to a pillowmate. Might we suggest poetry, Dr. Seuss, or vibrant classics such as *1001 Arabian Nights* or *The Lord of the Rings* trilogy?

THE MODERN GENTLEMAN'S ALL-SEASON READING LIST
Below is a wide-ranging fiction survey for a gentleman venturing beyond the best-seller list.

- **Donald Antrim**: A dark, satirical fellow whose books always twist sharply in the end, like a leg fracture. For a memorable treat, try *Elect Mr. Robinson for a Better World* or *The Verificationist.*

- **Paul Auster**: Thoughtful tale-spinner. Pick up the *New York Trilogy* or the circus tale, *Mr. Vertigo.*

- **David Bowman**: Exciting, expansive narrator. For Emily Dickinson fans, try *Let the Dog Drive.*

- **T. C. Boyle**: Solid author of quirky short stories (*Descent of Man*) and humorous modern fiction (*East Is East*).

- **Mikhail Bulgakov:** A Russian virtuoso. *The Master and Margarita* is an amazing journey through deception, selfishness, and love. Where else can you find a six-foot tomcat, Jesus Christ, and Satan in one novel?

- **Michael Chabon:** Great storyteller with sharp wit. Begin with *Mysteries of Pittsburgh* or *The Amazing Adventures of Kavalier & Clay*.

- **Robert Coover:** A dark, satirical writer; bring your headlamp. Begin with *Pricksongs & Descants*. For kink and fetish: *Spanking the Maid*.

- **Pete Dexter:** Pore through the powerful and touching *Paris Trout*.

- **Stephen Dobyns:** A philosophical writer who weaves tales through the strange byways of New York City. Sample *Cold Dog Soup* and *The Wrestler's Cruel Study*.

- **Tom Drury:** Simple prose about fictional Grouse County. Intelligent, probing, and full of dry wit. First novel: *The End of Vandalism*.

- **Frederick Exley:** *A Fan's Notes* begins a humorous, engrossing trilogy. *Last Notes from Home* is poignant and sidesplitting.

- **Kinky Friedman:** Pure joy. Marry any woman who elicits this same feeling. Begin with *Elvis, Jesus & Coca-Cola* and keep flipping.

- **William Gaddis:** The writer's writer, with a singular style of telling a story through dialogue. Begin with *Carpenter's Gothic* or *JR*.

- **Mark Helprin:** *Winter's Tale* is an incomparable modern epic set in nineteenth-century New York. Come join Peter Lake and his flying milk horse. You'll never look at snow and ice the same way again.

- **Mark Leyner:** Master of modern, satirical rants and twisted popular culture. First, try *Tooth Imprints on a Corn Dog* or *Et Tu, Babe.*

- **Carson McCullers:** Her *Heart Is a Lonely Hunter* is a singular depiction of quiet desperation and pure loneliness. Read "Ballad of the Sad Café" to better understand the human condition.

- **Henry Miller:** One of the most dynamic men of his century, whose comments on writing, conversation, love, and women are invaluable. The *Rosy Crucifixion* trilogy is among his finest journeys.

- **Magnus Mills:** Who knew he used to drive an autobus in England? Try the laconic, brooding, and droll *The Restraint of Beasts.*

- **Christopher Moore:** Fun summer fiction with a smart edge. *Island of the Sequined Love Nun* is perfect poolside.

- **Haruki Murakami:** Popular Japanese author whose panoramic stories of love and introspection are a distinct pleasure. *The Wind-Up Bird Chronicle* is his unforgettable masterpiece.

- **Flannery O'Connor:** The Southern bell-ringer, a spinner of rugged tales of betrayal and indelicate endings. Pick up *The Collected Stories* and relish "A Good Man Is Hard to Find" and "Greenleaf."

- **Cynthia Ozick**: A modern writer with a flair for big-hearted humor and religious deprecation. Try *The Puttermesser Papers* to discover what happens when a stubborn mud golem discovers New York.

- **Dorothy Parker**: Poignant stories. Who could forget "Mr. Durant"?

- **Charles Portis**: The great, overlooked American writer. *Norwood* and *The Dog of the South* are stellar; *Masters of Atlantis* is wry and humorous.

- **John Cowper Powys**: A star of the early twentieth century. His booming lectures on literature were so stunning, people were wont to faint and swoon. Try *Wolf Solent* first for a memorable tour through life's contradictions and the quirkiness of desire.

- **Thomas Pynchon**: Murky modern novelist. Tread carefully and labor for your illumination. Begin with *The Crying of Lot 49*, proceed to *V*, then (and only then) to his rewarding tome, *Gravity's Rainbow*.

- **The Raymonds**: Raymond Carver for his short story narratives, such as *Cathedral*. Raymond Chandler, whose complex Philip Marlowe offers the private dick's perspective of seamy old Los Angeles; begin with *The Big Sleep*, move on to the singular *Long Goodbye*.

- **Tom Robbins**: An erudite writer whose hilariously spun tales offer a unique slant on spirituality. *Skinny Legs and All* is a romping favorite.

- **Jim Thompson**: The premier crime fiction/*roman noir* author. Try *The Getaway* or *The Grifters* first.

♦ **John Kennedy Toole**: *A Confederacy of Dunces*. Perhaps the most humorous book ever written.

Mix up your playlist with a few classics: Joseph Conrad, *The Secret Agent*; Jack London, *The Sea-Wolf*; Malcolm Lowry, *Under the Volcano*; F. Scott Fitzgerald, *Flappers and Philosophers*; James M. Cain, *The Postman Always Rings Twice*; Ernest Hemingway, *The Sun Also Rises*; *The Letters of Vincent Van Gogh*; Kurt Vonnegut, *Cat's Cradle*; W. Somerset Maugham, *The Razor's Edge*; D. H. Lawrence, *Lady Chatterley's Lover*; James Hilton, *Lost Horizon*; Frank Norris, *McTeague*; and revisit Poe before *and* after Halloween.

THEMATIC READING

Sometimes a blustery winter calls for a large classic to curl around, and summertime, a baseball novel. When airline prices skyrocket, perhaps a foreign novel may have to suffice until year-end bonuses are handed out. Below are some of the finer atmospheric novels.

THEME	*ENTICING TITLES*
BASEBALL	Philip Roth, *The Great American Novel* David James Duncan, *The Brothers K*
DOWN IN DIXIE	Mark Childress, *Crazy in Alabama* William Baldwin, *The Hard to Catch Mercy* John Dufresne, *Louisiana Power & Light*
NEW YORK CITY	Stephen Dobyns, *Cold Dog Soup* Daniel Evan Weiss, *Honk If You Love Aphrodite*

DRUGS	T. C. Boyle, *Budding Prospects* Thomas De Quincey, *Confessions of an English Opium Eater* Hunter S. Thompson, *Fear and Loathing in Las Vegas*
DREAMS	Jonathan Coe, *The House of Sleep* Haruki Murakami, *Hard–Boiled Wonderland and the End of the World*
INSPIRATIONAL	Paulo Coelho, *The Alchemist* *The Lais of Marie De France* *Bhagavad-Gita*
TRUTH	Umberto Eco, *The Name of the Rose* Iain Pears, *An Instance of the Fingerpost*
AMBITIOUS & REWARDING	Fyodor Dostoevsky, *The Brothers Karamazov* John Barth, *The Sot-Weed Factor* Herman Melville, *Moby Dick*
HISTORICAL	Louis De Bernières, *Corelli's Mandolin* Sheri Holman, *The Dress Lodger*
ROMANTIC ODDITIES	A. S. Byatt, *Possession* Nani Power, *Crawling at Night* A. L. Kennedy, *Original Bliss*
CANADA	Howard Norman, *The Bird Artist* Wayne Johnston, *The Divine Ryans*
FOREIGN RAPTURE	Nina Fitzpatrick, *The Loves of Faustyna* Jeanette Winterson, *The Passion* Milan Kundera, *The Unbearable Lightness of Being*
ODD SHORT STORIES	Steven Milhauser, *The Knife Thrower and Other Stories* Will Self, *Tough, Tough Toys for Tough, Tough Boys* Tobias Wolff, *The Night in Question*

CLASSICAL MUSIC

The Greeks believed that Apollo and the other gods created music to help explain the universe's harried order. Later, chants and hymnals were scripted to pass the time in church while the collection plate went 'round. Before Chuck Berry, Handel and Bach wrote music that has stayed on the charts for the last 250 years.

If your knowledge of classical music is limited to humming sullied melodies from the "The Blue Danube," it's time to expand the musical catalogue. For the non-Juilliard set, approach symphonic music like fine Scotch or bourbon—sip, stop, and appreciate, and don't expect proficiency or virtuosity upon the first gulp. Once the aromas are deciphered, the complexities and wonders become accessible. Single out the individual wind instruments and horns. Recognize building chromatic tensions, releases, and resolutions. With even a smattering of musical theory under your belt, classical music is a mind-altering diversion.

If approached by an aficionado, voice admiration, but don't fake aptitude. Should cocktail party chatter turn to such things, it wouldn't be untoward to mention that Richard Strauss (pronounced RIH' ärt) was the nephew of Johann Strauss, and considered much more radiant and modernist. Moreover, should someone bring up Beethoven, you might proffer that, with the exception of his *Symphony No. 6 "Pastoral,"* his odd symphonies are generally regarded as better than his even ones. Before leaving such a talking circle, end on a high note and state with alacrity that Chopin's ballades, of which there are four, are much deeper than his showy mazurkas and waltzes.

Better than hissing tape decks, attending the symphony or a piano recital is an effective way to determine likes and dislikes. Stem adventurousness and skip modernist or minimalist compositions. Start instead with the crowd-pleasing, older canonical works like Mussorgsky's *Pictures at an Exhibition* or Rachmaninoff's *Second Piano Concerto.*

Dress for symphony hall and soak in the tuxedoed professionals on stage. Don't be the stumblebum who blows into the auditorium thirty

---

OPERA

Your first and lasting experience with opera was probably Bugs Bunny's "What's Opera, Doc?", the seven-minute paean to and summary of Wagner's sixteen hour *Ring Cycle.* (Wagner, rest his anti-Semitic soul, aspired to the best: a fluid convergence of stage, chorus, orchestra, dance, visual backgrounds, and theatric set changes. He wrote directions like: "a river runs through the stage" and "the entire set should be destroyed by flame.") With its booming arias, is opera the pinnacle of civilization? To some. For a harsh critique of this view by someone in the know, see Tolstoy's vilification of the entire form in *What Is Art?*

One should never be forced to go to the opera. Minor appreciation brews throughout the gentleman's mid-twenties, as maturity sets in like crow's feet. When attending casual opera-in-the-park venues, don't forget picnic baskets and delicious edibles; during park concerts, wine glasses are better than opera glasses. In some venues, it is common to bring fine foods and vino to nosh on during longer-than-usual intermissions—inquire before packing. At the opera house, a tuxedo is never out of place, with opera tickets secured in cummerbund (ruffle up). This is an expensive date, so choose partners wisely. If you are dubious about your ability to endure *Aida,* refer to your local psychiatrist for a sedating prescription of Xanax before Act One, to be washed down with a mighty swig of house Chardonnay.

seconds before the opening note, only to be ushered outside to wait. If late, remain quiet and ask to be seated in the back row until the first intermission. Most importantly, leave upper respiratory infections, sputum production, and smoker's hacks at home, as well as crinkly wrapped candies and activated cell phones.

Not unlike the rock'n'roll heartthrob who humps the mic stand, the maestro is the focal point of the performance. Observe his feverish arm-pumping and dramatic swoons; and when in doubt, follow the standing rituals and bravo calls of those around you. Don't mimic the clapping clodpate by applauding between movements of a concerto or sonata—the pause is part of the piece. Wait for the conductor to put his arms down before erupting.

For the Modern Gentleman's home, we suggest some ground rules and required recordings. Be discerning and avoid compact discs that are thematic anthologies issued and sold at home décor stores or coffeehouse counters (*A Little More Night Music* or *Classical Music to Garden To*). Enthusiasts prefer analog recordings by well-known conductors instead of modern, all-digital productions by over-hyped music luminaries like Seiji Ozawa. Seek out the entire package. When in doubt, consult the Penguin guide, a tome that rates classical recordings. Isn't an old recording of Rachmaninoff playing his own music more appealing than a violin concerto played by Midori?

Below are eight must-haves that, like answers to $800 and $1,000 Jeopardy questions, will show off your musical breadth.

1. **Beethoven**: Still the best after all these years, garnering the most pages in *The New Grove Dictionary of Music and Musicians*. His *Symphony No. 5* is often considered the best ever written. Listen beyond

the first movement as the master resolves the cruelty of "fate knocking at the door" in the opening chords with the triumphant C-major fanfares of the final movement.

2. **Beethoven**: Again. Enthusiasts need a double shot. Get a complete recording of the piano concertos. If *The Emperor* doesn't bring you back to eighteenth-century foxhunting country splendor, what will?

3. **Berlioz**: *Symphonie Fantastique.* This French composer prefigured modernism and the excesses of the Romantic Movement by fifty years. This symphony is about his drug-inspired, suicidal musings of love for an Irish actress (whom he actually invited to the first performance to win her hand). Highlights include his "march to the scaffold" in punishment for his love and a Satanist Sabbath with tolling bells and damnation—all 150 years before AC/DC.

4. **Tchaikovsky**: Go beyond *Swan Lake* with the *Symphony No. 6 "Pathétique."* When first performed in Saint Petersburg and conducted by Tchaikovsky himself, it received little fanfare. Tchaikovsky died nine days later (the cause of his death remains a mystery; some suggest an accident, others, suicide by arsenic.). His only extant comment following the performance was, "Without exaggeration, I have put my whole soul into this work." One of the few symphonies to end with a slow and soft deathlike movement into gloom—the final movement's tempo direction was *adagio lamentoso*—this symphony is so existentially dark, Sartre would retreat in horror. Wait for a rainy day.

Incidentally, though Tchaikovsky's *1812 Overture* and its cannon explosions are a familiar accompaniment to Fourth of July festivities, the Russian composer wrote the piece to commemorate Napoleon's retreat from Moscow, not America's little skirmish with the Brits.

5. **Dvořák**: He wrote *Symphony No. 9 "New World Symphony"* in 1893 during a stint in New York, where he discovered American native and spiritual music. Just when you tag this a lightweight classic, listen to how the ballyhooed folk themes and dissonant ur-jazz elements seamlessly mesh into the symphonic backdrop.

6. **Mahler**: Not for the faint of heart, this fin de siécle Austrian, Jew-turned-Christian composer remains hot hot hot in musical circles since his profundity was "rediscovered" by Leonard Bernstein in the 1960s. The uninitiated shouldn't dare start with anything but *Symphony No. 1*, which is infused with enough neurosis to fuel a ten-year psychoanalysis. It also has moments of exquisite beauty and affirmation, as well as a third movement with borrowed "Frère Jacques" strains in a minor key, juxtaposed with traditional klezmer music.

7. **Holst**: *The Planets.* Probably our recommendation closest to "date" music. Best listened to outdoors on a clear summer evening or while reminiscing about the destruction of the Death Star ("Mars" was a strong influence on John Williams's *Star Wars* soundtrack). Show your vulnerable side here, then initiate first affections during the light-hearted "Venus" and "Jupiter." We shouldn't have to tell you what to do during the dreamy "Neptune" and "Uranus."

8. **Ravel**: *Daphnis et Chloé.* The height of this Impressionist's career is an orchestral piece with Eastern influences and an otherworldly chorus

without words. Learn how Chloé escapes from pirates with the aid of resourceful shepherds. Incredible music to accompany any of Phineas's Phavourites or Tesauro's Titillations.

JAZZ

[keys]

[horn]

[mouthpiece]

"Do you know what it means to miss New Orleans?" Louis Armstrong mused. Whether Miles on a lolling Sunday morning or a hip quartet chomping bass in a low-ceilinged club, it's jazz and it makes your foot twitch. Jazz signatures don't play by the usual rules of meter or tone, so listen closely and appreciate the harmony.

Jazz's allure spikes when seen live and late into the night. Break up the usual and breeze into a small jazz club. Downed martinis and cordials aside, intoxication comes with the foot-tapping beat. Sample the host of genres, from down-home brass bands to Brazilian bossa nova. For newcomers, get to know the greats and work your way modern. Choice liner notes and documentaries like *The History of Jazz* and *A Great Day in Harlem* will enlighten.

Below is a shortlist of singular recordings often overlooked. Peek into the world of post-swing jazz; get beyond rote compilation discs and "Best Of" selections. As the oozy Quato said to Schwartzenegger in *Total Recall,* "Open. . .your. . .mind."

1. **Charlie Parker:** *Talkin' Bird.* No list is complete without at least one selection from Parker. The Bird is every alto saxophonist's (and dealer's) hero, the virtuoso force behind the bebop movement. No one could tame the alto so well, especially when blowing in the high register. Bird was so influential that a New York jazz club was named after him during his lifetime (Birdland). *Talkin' Bird* culls gems of Parker performances with a host of jazz giants. Bend an ear to "Lester Leaps In" and the soaring solos of Parker, his mentor Lester Young, and Roy Eldridge on trumpet.

2. **Medeski, Martin, and Wood:** *Last Chance to Dance Trance (Perhaps).* This trio of keyboards, percussion, and bass brings more to the stage than meandering jams. Each melody highlights individual talents with expert exploration and taut solos. Listen to "Bubblehouse": hear the organ mix with the funky hip-hop flourishes and jazzy melodies, and wait for the impending tempo change that piques attention. MMW is an acquired taste, but this album is highly accessible to both casual jazz fans and urban hipster know-it-alls.

3. **Charles Mingus:** *Mingus Mingus Mingus Mingus Mingus.* Listen to a stand-up bass press the band into intensity on "II B.S," or sit slyly in the foreground as horns belt sexy heartache and minor keys in "I X Love." This barrel-chested bassist/composer played with all the big names and had an indomitable, fiery spirit. He took his impeccable musical acumen and short temper to excess in the studio, storming out of sessions if bandmates flubbed a single note. Distrustful of whites, he was married four times, thrice to white women. Mingus said that his music was "angry, yet it's real, because

it knows it's angry." His headstrong behavior was legendary, and in his heyday, he busted more naysaying onlookers than Sean Penn.

4. **Marc Ribot:** *Marc Ribot y Los Cubanos Postizos* and *¡Muy Divertido!*. Swirling guitar meshes with congas, percussion, and organ. Pulsing with Afro-Cuban grooves and Latin rhythms, Ribot's arrangements sound like a sprawling urban fiesta. "Obsesión" evokes bluesy Cuban grooves with heavy guitar picking and tuba. A true romp live.

5. **Grant Green:** *Idle Moments.* A delicious accompaniment to an intimate porch-side gathering on a quiet summer evening. Play twice with plenty of water and muted solace following a night of overmedication. The album's core is tenor sax, vibraphone, and Green's smooth guitar. His licks beg morning introspection and salvation and, at times, sound like a melodic horn. Notice the pluckiness of "Nomad" and the flowing guitar solos of "Jean de Fleur."

6. **Duke Ellington with Coleman Hawkins:** *Duke Ellington Meets Coleman Hawkins.* The master composer/classy gentleman meets the stately saxophonist. Already a vaunted bandleader for thirty years, Ellington opens an arena for Hawkins to shine, in tandem with Lawrence Brown on trombone. Besides their superb taste in fine hats, this album memorializes a juicy collaboration. After hearing the infectious melody, scatting, and piano-anchored solos of "Limbo Jazz," you'll be humming it the rest of the day.

7. **Miles Davis:** *Steamin' with the Miles Davis Quintet.* Miles was a luminary who helped define cool in dress and tonality. His notes didn't leap

off the clef like Louis Armstrong's, but were introspective and bare-beautiful. His quintet was considered the Hot Five of the 1950s, and its output left an indelible mark on jazz. With a young John Coltrane in tow, Miles melded the new bebop movement with classic twelve-bar blues. This masterpiece has the craftsmanship of a hand-tailored silk shirt, featuring precision interplay of of tenor sax and trumpet. Perfect for a late dinner party. Bask in the sexual tension of "Diane" as it resolves in the final measures; "Well, You Needn't" is infectious.

8. **Wes Montgomery**: *The Incredible Jazz Guitar of Wes Montgomery.* Recorded in 1960, this album is frequently mimicked, yet remains fresh. Spin this disc for a quick escape from three-chord rock'n'roll. Montgomery is a guitar enthusiast's favorite, influenced by jazz guitar pioneer Charlie Christian. A self-taught master from Indianapolis, Montgomery's style features a thumb-picking method of vibrato variations. His first recording, *Wes Montgomery Trio,* is a subtler amalgam of guitar, drums, and organ, culminating in the classic "Escaroh." Later recordings for Verve are considered overcommercialized.

9. **Django Reinhardt**: *The Indispensable Django Reinhardt (1949–1950).* This pioneer is often considered the finest jazz guitarist. A revered European icon, Django was born a Belgian Gypsy and developed his style in Parisian *bals-musettes,* or smoky, underground cafés. Embracing his Gypsy roots, Django could neither read nor write music, but had a boundless, innate talent. While sleeping in a caravan, he accidentally knocked over a candle and suffered serious injuries to his left hand. Undeterred, Django patented a two-fingered playing style. He had multiple influences and was comfortable rearranging

various genres to the jazz idiom. Listen to his interpretations of classical music (Tchaikovsky's *Pathétique*), American roots music, or standards of the 1930s to 1940s ("St. Louis Blues"). Check out the amazing exchanges between Django and erstwhile bandmate, violinist Stéphane Grappelli.

10. **João Gilberto:** *Getz/Gilberto*. Affectionately called O Rei da Bossa (The King of Bossa), Gilberto introduced bossa nova to the U.S. Every music collector should have "Girl from Ipanema" at the ready, sung by the inspiration herself, Astrud Gilberto. Like a lilac-scented grasp of the loins, this sensual music is a soft, steamy night downtown. If you can't clear the bases with this seminal record playing in the bedroom, repeat triple-A before returning to the majors.

FITNESS

[grip]
[plate]

After a night of debauchery, isn't a bike ride around the velodrome or a football toss in the park more beneficial than the #19 Chow Fun MSG special? Life is a continuing cycle of rebirth and destruction, pruning and renewal. Toss a disc, walk a dog, eat a fruit salad, and get in the game. A desk-jockey double chin or inflationary waist size are avoidable even after thirty. Trimness requires disciplined time management. Lunchtime gym jaunts or evening workouts are enough to stay fit, but whatever the routine, exercise at least thrice weekly. Whether you hit the racquetball court for vanity, vitality, or competitive fervor, the exertion will strengthen and defog. Confidence is the foundation of sexual aptitude, and a gentleman should feel uninhibited without a shirt. A good body is contagious—as your muscle tone increases, watch compatriots dust off their dumbbells.

Despite their own drooping potbellies, most men expect a lady to be trim. Before pinching your lover's inch, develop your own varied routine of aerobics and strength training. Nonlinear fitness is more fun: think prison-cell pull-ups off the top bunk. Besides the usual treadmill and Nautilus circuit, hone your breaststroke, toss the medicine ball, or hit the heavy bag like Apollo Creed. Water and snow skiing, rock climbing, mountain biking, and spelunking build tone without the claustrophobic ennui of gymnasia. For the perpetually lazy, go with a gym buddy to keep a regular schedule. Eventually, missed workouts will cause guilty uneasiness and a jonesing for the addictive endorphin high.

Incidentally, the home poses too many distractions for a proper workout. Buying personal workout equipment will only make some future eBay high-bidder happy when your stationary bike goes for $20. Why not get out and meet like-minded people at the health club?

Points to consider as you sweat to the oldies:

- Whilst waiting to use an occupied machine, don't hover like a vulture. When an individual appears finished, politely ask, "Can I work in?" Also, know how to spot (or when to call for one) and interject a few coaxing phrases to spur that last bench-press rep.

- Fitness requires no record keeping. Plot your progress in a spiral notebook only if protein shakes are an hourly treat and Jack LaLanne is your uncle.

◆ A witless fool clangs dumbbells after each repetition.

◆ No "one up, one down" sweatpant-leg stylings, except if certified in international semaphore. Unless late for wrestling practice, no shorts over sweatpants.

◆ For tasteful peeking of others, take advantage of the wall mirror's magic properties of incidence and reflection.

YOGA

Yo-ga, yo-ga, yo-ga. . .not just for vegans and longhaired galoots, yoga means "union." The idea is to use the known (your body) to smash worldly illusions and discover the unknown (your inner spirit), all while elongating space in your body.

Books abound on relaxation, diet, and simplifying your life. Instead of straining your eyes, try a yoga class and achieve balance, flexibility, and poise in unfamiliar poses. Benefits spill over: more flexibility, space within, and inner peace. And, like Mom said, you'll stop slouching.

There are several types of yoga, each with a different focus. The most common is *hatha* yoga, a mix of breathing and stretching poses that combine strength and meditation. *Iyengar* yoga, named after a famous yogi, is a more intense *hatha* practice that uses props and deeper poses. *Ashtanga* and *vinyasa* yoga use a fluid series of poses to achieve meditative benefits through intense movement; they are recommended for intermediate students seeking variety and aerobic elements. Finally, *kundalini* stresses advanced breathing techniques and postures that channel sexual and creative energies upward. The aftereffects of *kundalini* are powerful and liberating.

It's not the first day of junior high, so don't be nervous. Instructors are patient and understanding. For those intimidated by the formal studio setting, many health clubs and gyms offer classes in which to dip your oblique. Once you find a comfortable class, be a repeat back extender.

Before your first forward bend, follow these steps:

• The instructor will invariably ask if there are any first-timers. Identify yourself and benefit from shepherding like an unenlightened lamb.

• A small nosh an hour before helps, but save big meals for after class.

• Arrive dressed for easy movement (T-shirt and sweatpants/tights). Wear gym shorts over biking tights or spandex, as poses are far-reaching and may offer an unwanted eyeful to a neighbor.

• Find the props: rubber sticky mat, blanket, belt, and blocks. Most gyms provide everything you need, though some studios levy a small mat-rental fee. New mats are slick and beg a hot water washing with powdered detergent to increase the grip.

• Take off your shoes and socks. Don't be the Squeamish Sally who keeps his tube socks on in class for fear of getting cold toesies. You'll need bare feet to feel grounded and balance the poses properly.

• Classes typically begin with meditation. Should you run late, enter the room quietly or wait outside until the active part of class begins.

◆ Bringing an activated mobile phone to class will result in muddled karma for a lifetime.

Yoga is not all headstands, back bends, and ankles behind the ear. It is a fusion of finding your breath and calming the mind through standing poses, extensions, and twists. Follow the instructor (or a neighbor if unsure of a posture), breathe only through your nose, and lose yourself in the hour-and-a-half of bountiful solace. Except for in beginner classes, don't disrupt the flow with jabbering questions. Many *asanas,* or poses, will be called out by their Sanskrit terms; listen for the explanation. Learn the names, with or without flash cards. The invocation of archetypes and animals is part of the practice: *virabhadrasana* (warrior), *bhujangasana* (cobra). Class ends with *savasana,* corpse pose. Practice is more than meditative chanting: note the pooling sweat and fatigued muscles. Minor soreness in your back, hips, and hamstrings is normal.

Forget the urban environment and leave your type-A personality outside; yoga is not a competition to see who can bend the farthest, balance the longest, or commune the deepest the with the cosmos. Leave fears in the gym locker room and attempt every pose with an inner smile. After a time, you'll marvel at the mind's clarity and the body's magnificence. There is an unexpected bonus: yoga classes have a 5-to-1 female/male ratio of illuminated, well-rounded souls who see fitness as more than fifteen minutes on a treadmill with headphones.

FLORA

A gentleman stops to smell the *Rosa borboniana*. A thorny crush on Gregor Mendel's snap peas is not a gentlemanly prerequisite, but the core curriculum mandates basic floral proficiency. Ever been to an arboretum? Can you whistle the dominant theme in Louis Armstrong's "Azalea"? A cultured man's recognition of a dozen plants on sight, Latin names excluded, adds to the joy of selecting a winning nosegay.

* Visit a botanical garden yearly. It is a glorious scientific and visual feast, not to mention an ideal early date or "me time" venue.

* Frequently (at least weekly), brighten up a white-walled apartment or bare kitchen table with a modest arrangement.

BOUTONNIÈRE

The boutonnière blossomed in the late nineteenth century and has all but disappeared from men's fashion. Yet, a lonely sport coat lapel seems unpollenated. A simple blossom from the backyard garden is far better than an elaborate topiary, and a modest triple bloom is less formal than a single flower. Try a small ivy berry or a pinned silver vial of flowers to complement an evening jacket. For added panache, wear the local flower when traveling: Virginia Beach, dogwood; Scottsdale, a saguaro cactus flower (prickly danger while hugging); Tennessee, a small TV satellite dish.

Nice touch: After hours, encourage a lover to play "he loves me, he loves me not." Count the petals beforehand to ensure the desired outcome.

♦ Banquet affairs feature flowers and centerpieces. Take the blossoms to go and bestow pick-me-up forget-me-nots upon down-and-out souls on your stroll through the cityscape.

   Flowers are best bought from nurseries, florists, or groceries, not filling stations and bus-station kiosks. Stow a tasteful glass vase in the kitchen to accommodate floral surprises. Before displaying, trim any wilting foliage and snip the stems diagonally, at varying lengths. Change the water to avoid the noisome vapors of biomass decay.

PASS THE PISTILS

Flowers are a gift that needn't be reciprocated—every lady enjoys the receipt of flowers. Select beyond the usual mundane, first-date fare. With the panoply of choices, bland purchases belie creative verve. Tulips, daisies, birds of paradise, or hydrangea strike a more redolent presentation. The surprise single flower, even a vacant-lot dandelion, plucked on a whim, is never misguided. Despite the fine gesture, seventy-five-cent à la carte carnations and baby's breath (which is a weed) should not be exchanged with even a pestiferous foe.

TULIP

♦ ♦ ♦ **Calvados** ♦ **Dry vermouth** ♦ **Apricot brandy** ♦ **Lemon juice** ♦ ♦ ♦

SOOTHSAYING

[the all-knowing   magic 8-ball]

What She Said Would Happen	1958	World War III breaks out.
	1967	Cure for cancer found.
	1995	Rush Limbaugh forced to go on welfare; Whitney Houston marries Mike Tyson; Peter Jennings is the first journalist in space.
What Actually Happened	1997	Psychic Jeanne Dixon dies.

A gentleman needs the occasional snake-oil rubdown. Keep your eyes peeled for unexpected theophany or more subtle visions of grandeur. Like I-95's lonely stretches of kitschy South-of-the-Border billboards, life is littered with karmic signposts, some (Nostradamus) more reliable than others (Dionne Warwick). When it feels like fourth and long, Notre Dame's "Touchdown Jesus" or an upright horseshoe will align your lucky stars.

MAGIC 8-BALL

If you're at loggerheads and have forgotten what comes after "eeny meeny miney," consult an old sage, that ultimate plastic Solomon—the Magic 8-Ball. The magic orb is more decisive than Indian leg wrestling and rock-paper-scissors for settling group disputes. Use it next to the night-stand, not in the office war room, as light inquiries are best.

Good: "Should we call in sick and play in bed all day?"

Bad: "Should the firm report these profits to the IRS?"

Somewhere between fortune cookies and audiences with Edgar Cayce Institute mediums, the 8-Ball awaits your vibe. Shake it awake to summon the voodoo within. While "Outlook Not So Good" hints at "No," "Ask Again Later" and other ball uncertainties require more devout persistence. Thus, if encumbered with "Cannot Predict Now," bring in the hot hand. No need to wait the maternal twenty minutes before taking another dip into the occult. Don't let a doubting dilly muck up the works and question the ball's authority. If bubbles or cracks are impeding cube legibility, resort to more basic problem-solving solutions, like a show of hands or a logical discussion.

OUIJA

Do you really think you can obtain authentic, high-grade enlightenment from a Milton Bradley board game?

FORTUNE COOKIES

Only killjoys deem these nuggets of wisdom mass-produced triflings. Rather, they are personal telegrams from the Fates. In a tale of two cookies, Tesauro follows five steps: (1) silently pose an issue before the cookie; (2) crack in half; (3) chew one hemisphere while unfolding the Confucian advice; (4) nibble upon the remnants; and (5) digest its meaning.

Nice touch: For a bit of that finding-a-crumpled-ten-spot-in-the-dryer sensation, stow a shrewd fortune in a jacket pocket for later discovery.

PROFANITY & VULGARITY

*I believe in having a good heart, a chirpy penis, a lively intelligence,
and the courage to say "shit" in front of a lady.*

—D. H. LAWRENCE, *LADY CHATTERLEY'S LOVER*

A well-rounded gentleman possesses a mature vocabulary, from sublime to inappropriate. Use profanity judiciously; four-letter words are not the only clever way to raise eyebrows. There's a high degree of cliché among cursers. Mix-and-match the filthy classics to create a string of fresh phrases that highlight your keen wit and local tongue. Proper timing and emphasis separate the nimble jawsmith from the colloquial fool.

In addition to the four-letter favorites, a seasoned gentleman peppers exasperation with a more colorful lexicon. For the occasional quirky insult, pick up a thesaurus or volume of Shakespeare for potent Elizabethan abuse. A finely crafted jibe or cultured pejorative can be shared beyond a whisper. Following "You're an ass@#$%," quip, "Your dendritic branches are thin and wispy, like the sunburned reeds of the Red River Valley." To convey profanity over a distance, build a database of vulgar gestures. Unfurl the Finger in both its clenched East Coast grip and the languid West Coast, up-yours flip.

Be cavalier in your manner or dress, but not in your deviation from the Queen's English. Profanity is generally inappropriate for job interviews or first contacts and in court. Keep it for friends, foes, and excited utterances. Tread lightly when first meeting a lady, professional colleague, or parent. Used poorly, profanity is a steamroll of useless acrimony. The quickest route to a bureaucratic clusterfuck is the raging-lunatic motif—swear at the clerk between you and a passport renewal or student loan deferment and you'll be denied. Act differently. Don't lean over the counter, elbows akimbo, and demand. Hold it in and get results. Reserve your speed-bag flurry of vituperative slurry for irksome telemarketers.

Vulgar behavior such as groin thrusts is the lowest common denominator. Behind the polished veneer and stiff ascot, a man's basic settings are rooted in the hunt and the hot blood of libido. The balanced gentleman knows when to peel back layers of correctness. The sharpest vulgarities are unexpected slips revealing fundamental traits: anger, lust, hunger, and fear. Examples include lewd tongue-and-mouth gestures, the ol' in-and-out index-finger poke, beating fists, and flashed nudity. Don't be a prude; those who can handle sophistication, but not its antithesis, are missing the grotesque beauty of vulgarity.

MAN CYCLE

Few men are ignorant of a woman's hormonal tides when she's "on her moon." What about the man? Men are moody, too, and often their sine-wave gyrations are tied less to the pituitary gland and more to local teams' playoff woes or a toothpaste error on the tie. Indeed, like thirty days on the NASDAQ, a month in the gentleman's life is plotted with peaks and valleys.

CRESTING

When the cards are lucky, up the ante and push the pot. Hot biorhythms are functions of serendipity and positivity: traffic lights are green, favorite songs litter the radio, a whole week of good-hair days unfolds, and bank errors are in your favor. When you're on, impossible billiards combos drop and romantic approval ratings hit all-time highs. Looked-up words are spotted in a single flip of the dictionary, and front-row parking spots divinely materialize. This esteem spike is not license for rash expenditures at the track, rather a chance to energize your whole life. Invigorate flagging friendships, write letters under the influence of joy, ask for a raise, or tackle that garage cleanup with an indelible spirit. With fresh legs, make huge strides. Nevertheless, like a nitrous turbo charge in a souped-up hot rod, these unbridled blasts are not sustainable. So don't waste them on the couch.

SLUMPING

It's a narrow fjord between fortune and infelicity. Yesterday, conversation was packed with profound, poetic truth. Today, your marble-filled mouth is bumbling, cranial fog preventing even a hint of wit. As the cycle turns, expect bouts of moodiness and binges of unhealthy behavior.

ME TIME

A man owes himself more than stolen moments of solace. Weekly whiles alone are essential. When inner trouble is burbling, alight to a solitary meal for midday introspection or clear a night's social calendar and take yourself out. "Me time" is therapeutic and efficient. Wash the car, hit the gym, open the diary, and purloin "me time" without turning into a scruffy, antisocial troglodyte. Remember: not every Saturday evening must be a raucous group affair. Don't fear a phone that doesn't ring with invitations. Little bespeaks the meek like a man who can't muster the self-love for an unaccompanied weekend movie or sandwich in the park.

Polished shoes and fenders are scuff-prone, red wine gravitates to white shirts, and romantic kismet falls like an overcooked soufflé. Lesser men thrive when the dice are friendly, but gentlemen are adroit in stormy weather, too. Don't panic—like Biblical scourges of locusts, droughts of glee are unlikely to persist. Usually, a lover's note in the lunchbox or peppy call from Mommy will help mitigate the doldrums. Beware an advancing devil-may-care attitude, which can snowball from a few bad breaks into a reckless bender of stubborn melancholia.

Final note: "I'm PMS-ing" will never describe those times of the month when a man is bloated with blues and misfortune. Yet, like the modern lady, a gentleman faces some days with impenetrable bliss and others with a mild heaviness. Maximize the sprints, shorten the stalls, and preserve an overall baseline of optimism. A gentleman who evenly negotiates travails and triumphs will spend more time making small course corrections and less time recovering from colossal swings of fate.

FONZARELLI MOVES & LEGERDEMAIN

Aaaayy. All decent people revere the vaunted powers of the Fonz, be it his yin-yang sartorial selections or inherent intimidation factor. His finest moments began with just a snap, and his supremacy was unchallenged.

While ordinary buckos will never master telepathic prowess over diner jukeboxes, a sharp eye and a deft hand can transform the mundane into magic. Graceful mannerisms and dexterous control over objects make up one's sangfroid, an effortless imperturbability that is the hallmark of any gentleman's cool. Cultivate a wide natural habitat and remain poised, even in unfamiliar surroundings.

The success of Fonzarelli moves is less about what's done coolly and more about what's not performed awkwardly. Learn to drive in reverse, throw a tight spiral, and carry two full martinis without sloshing. Lesser men are boorish; make it look easy. For the advanced, add a sum of numbers (division is more impressive), scratch your name in an Etch A Sketch, or slide down a brass banister and stick the dismount. On the other hand, an unflagging bag of tricks is like wearing too much make-up. Behavioral hocus-pocus is no cover-up for hebetude.

Other Fonz tactics:

- After others have failed, be the one to open an irksome jar. Open bottled beer with a lighter, spoon, or convex object.

- Practice long-distance, no-look wastebasket shooting. Likewise, demonstrate eye-mouth coordination by tossing grapes blithely into the air and catching them in your chops.

- Execute a one-handed parallel park into a tight space with three precision anglings of the wheel.

TAIL SPIN

Gin ◆ Sweet vermouth ◆ Green Chartreuse ◆ Dash bitters ◆ Lemon twist ◆ Olive

- Give just the right corrective bump to a skipping CD.

- Engage in spontaneous tossing of fragile objects (glasses, melons) with such an expert touch as to shift blame to the catcher if dropped.

- At the tollbooth, employ a passenger-side or sunroof coin flip into the basket, or pay the collector for a caravanning car or a fetching stranger behind you.

- Drain behind-the-back pool shots and hone your bank shots. If you truly feel the love, call your backgammon roll.

Chapter Five

APPEARANCE & STYLE

. . . .

Fashion 133

Business Attire 136

Accessories 138

Seasonal Toggery 140

Neckwear 142

Pyjamas 146

Eyewear 148

Men Without Hats 150

Umbrella Policy 152

Tattoos 153

Hygiene & Habits 154

FASHION

[shoelaces]

[sole]

[tassel]

Clothing is the gentleman's external reflection of mood and mode. The costume of dress—tempered with timing, texture, and color—is a keen measure of confidence and personality. Poor dress befouls a man's hygiene or panache and inappropriate dress betrays a man's lack of social harmony. Save leather pants for the nightclub, light-blue oxfords for the office, and ecru gabardine for the croquet pitch. Expression and experimentation are wonderful, yet mild adherence to tradition and seasonal conventions never tarnish a first impression.

A gentleman selects from a wide array of styles and seldom purchases fad apparel. If the far half of the closet is cluttered with once-worn garb, it's time to update. Building a wardrobe is akin to amassing a music collection. Pick up the goes-with-all-occasions basics (black dress slacks, sharp white shirt, dark blazer, smart pullover) and diversify from classics to funk. Strip the store-window mannequin; preassembled outfits are fun on occasion, but beware mass fashions likely to be copied by packs of mall rats. New pieces that complement old clothes won't leave you with sartorial pariahs that go with nothing else. For example, the orange-checked jumpsuit is ideal for Halloween and New Year's Eve, but the dark silk shirt dresses up for work or down with jeans.

Before you explore advanced techniques and boutiques, Phineas recommends finding a niche for personality and budget by browsing finer department stores, honing an eye for style. After you build a fashion foundation, Tesauro ballyhoos stepping outside the pinstriped lines into vintage shops. Shopping jaunts for uptown staples and downtown one-of-a-kinds outfit the gentleman for both work and play.

CARE

Spend one dollar to dry-clean your best shirts and they will last longer. Touch-ups at home with spray starch prevent last-minute wrinkles on the town—pressing makes for impressing. Moreover, if you don't know the cold-water care of delicates, call Mom or stick to permanent press. Use wooden or plastic hangers at home; wire leaves telltale marks on the shoulder line of heavier garb. Layering and perspiration-free outings permit a second wear. After a barhop bacchanal, air out smoky clothes before returning them to the closet.

Incidentally, plain undershirts aren't fashion, rather a protective layer between naked skin and fine clothing. At dress-up affairs, don't casualize a smart open shirt with an exposed white tee that peeks above the top button.

VINTAGE CLOTHING

Vintage clothing is like an old home. Often, there's evidence of a former tenant: a resewn button, the handiwork of an expert tailor, or an inked monogram courtesy of Sir-Marks-A-Lot.

Salvation Army stores are meccas for thrifty basics such as black pants, work shirts, or the rare treat of a terrific tie or shoes that fit. Another spot for nifty thrift, Army/Navy stores are best browsed for pea coats, boots, and gear for start-up militias. The choicest vintage shops resemble top-dollar designer boutiques chock full of mindfully chosen gems and well-aged denim; hands down, the place for purchasing economical and unique accessories. Introduce yourself to the shop-minding boulevardier and ask him or her to point out unusual acquisitions.

For the advanced gent, supplement beyond standard retail fare for an original look. In particular, vintage formal wear is both timeless (ascots and cuffed trousers) and novel (smoking jackets and ruffled tuxedo shirts). Antique studs, cuff links, crossties, and pinstriped pants are best found here. Occasionally, treat yourself to a few boutique binges and nix the hard-line penny-pinching, lest overindulgence in the discount bin brand you an outdated, sloppy fop.

FOOTWEAR

Invest in quality. Shoes last countless years with periodic maintenance and repair (resoles, reheels). Mild care is sensible and cheaper than buying a new pair. Shoehorns ease slip-in and prevent premature erosion of a shoe's backstay and lining. Caught on the go? Use the end of a belt as a substitute. Rotate your footwear, so as to evenly wear soles over time. For days of deluge, footwear needs protection. Wear rubbers or spats, or nominate dress shoes in disrepair for rainy commutes. Shoe trees, mandatory for fine footwear, preserve shape and eliminate odor.

Reserve sneakers for sporting activities and relegate comfy boat shoes to Saturdays on the poop deck or chores in the garage. On the shoe rack: sturdy black leathers, brown bucks, shiny oxblood wingtips, and throwaways to handle muddy tasks. Branch out into monk straps, split toes, slip-ons with pricey tassels, and jazzy two-tones. Be footwear-frivolous and keep two pairs of nightclub-only treads and winter or cowboy boots.

The three-dollar shine conditions leather, redarkens outsoles, and is a simple pleasure that feels like a decadent luxury. Shoeshines are for gentlemen what weekly manicures are to ladies.

BUSINESS ATTIRE

Dressing for the office isn't all bad. Two rules: neither the Saturday night funk nor the Sunday afternoon frump. Still, well-coordinated play clothes double as desk and datewear when paired with fine fabrics, smart accessories, and shined shoes.

DRESS SHIRTS

Diversify your holdings, as even mediocre clothiers stock nonwhite shirts in a host of stripes and patterns. Don the spectrum, closeting several shades of blue, ecru, and other earth tones with smart designs. Expand your hues: variants of lemon, lime, and lilac to brighten warmer months. Unlike the monsignor, vary your collar styles—the button-down collar is the least formal, and the surest way to downplay an otherwise dressy outfit. Both point and spread collars accentuate broad shoulders and allow ties room to flaunt their patterns and dimples. Tab collars provide a closer fit and confidently showcase a gentleman's tie. Wait until you've been complimented on your dress before venturing into contrasting collars or rounded French styles requiring a collar pin. Short sleeves with a tie demonstrates kinship with door-to-door vacuum salesmen.

Incidentally, once you've accrued a few pairs of classic studs and cuff links, slip French-cuffed attire into workday ensembles.

SUITS

Select a versatile medley of all-season suits for office and after hours. Every business professional's closet includes the old IBM-mandated classic, corporate blue suit and several dark-gray or black styles. Beyond color, match button style and subtle piping with body type and appearance.

Chestnut or olive suits agree with darker features; three-button or four-button models allow for more expression and are perfect for taller gents. Buttoning only the bottom button of the dressier double-breasted suit elongates lines and favors the shorter man. Buttoning the middle or waist button balances the height of a tall man and accentuates build. Piping and texture break up the banal and offer clues to tie and shirt selection. Always hang suits after use to breathe and unwrinkle; if done faithfully, pressing and dry cleaning are but a rare occurrence. Pressing a suit without dry cleaning is verboten.

Always marrying the same shirt and tie sells your closet short. Maximize permutations and look for new groupings that turn a small bounty of professional threads into a well-stocked walk-in closet.

BUSINESS OVERCOATS

The traditional raincoat (tan or olive green) never goes out of style. Unless you are an Inspector Gadget fan, don't actually tie the belt around your waist. Instead, loop it around back, clasp together, and allow it to hang harmlessly. When the arctic cold front hits, wear a calf-length black or navy wool overcoat and a stylish muffler.

TUXEDO

♦ ♦ Gin ♦ Sherry ♦ Dash sweet vermouth ♦ Dash bitters ♦ Lemon twist ♦ ♦

ACCESSORIES

Don't wear trinkets, shirt-pins, finger-rings,
or anything that is solely ornamental. . . . Don't be a "swell" or a "dude,"
or whatever the fop of the period may be called.

—CENSOR, *DON'T*, 1880

Highlight your extremities with a dash of élan. The dresser top is a handy residence for Pop's old tie tacks and other vintage trimmings. Transform an ordinary Dixie-cup, vanilla-scoop sport coat into a sundae suit by sprinkling on some sterling or gold garnishes. The investment in an array of silk handkerchiefs and sturdy studs will upgrade a wardrobe for years to come. A quality pair of cuff links, for example, should set you back; substandard accessories stick out like baseball caps with a tuxedo and demean a handsome ensemble.

TIMEPIECES

Rugged leather bands are for everyday, handsome metal bands for evening wear. Digital watches are for triathletes on the go; magazine subscription thank-you models, for the junk drawer. If so inclined, carry a pocket watch to keep forearm unencumbered by weight or tan lines. Tucked away, a pocket watch protects against pedestrian inquiries of the hour; it also leaves the gent at liberty to ask a spry lady for her time.

Incidentally, don't have a fine watch repaired by an establishment that also features a barber pole, cobbler corner, or key-copying booth. Trust a jeweler instead.

BRACES

Buttoned on the inside, not clipped on the waistband, braces are the gentleman's choice, ideal for the Scotch-sipping esquire crowd and for looking sharp after the jacket comes off. Busy suspenders worn with a T-shirt are *Mork & Mindy* revivalist, but tasteful patterns lighten a stuffy suit. Braces are comfortable, promoting coolness in the summer and roominess for the corpulent. They provide clean vertical lines without the cinch of a waist belt and permit pleats to fall naturally. Suspenders keep pant length constant; no more hourly lifting to hoist dragging cuffs.

Incidentally, belts should extend past the buckle but not snake and loop down to the crotch. Rather than driving nails into a closet or bending wire hangers, invest in an anchor-shaped belt rack that hangs on the rod.

POCKET SQUARES

A white-cotton handkerchief elevates style and costs next to nothing. Finish dressing—don't neglect a bare breast pocket, or worse, stuff in a hard pack of smokes. This is not a bow tie—cummerbund set; the best pocket squares complement but don't match exactly. Contrast texture and tone: muted linen squares with flashy ties, patterned silky handkerchiefs with solid-colored ties. Master the four folds: (1) the conservative square-ended or Presidential fold; (2) the classic one-point triangle fold; (3) the elegant multipointed Cagney fold; and (4) the dandier puffed or Cooper fold, typically worn with colored silk and handlebar moustaches. If you can master a paper airplane, the pocket square is within reach. Visit a men's shop or the Web for a fold-by-fold tutorial.

BILLFOLDS

A wallet should fit comfortably in a front, back, or breast pocket without upsetting the smoothness of clothing. Except for full-serve Texaco station attendants and gentlemen's club regulars, it is unnecessary to carry a bulging sheaf of bills. Purge the inner folds of old business cards, pay stubs, receipts, and long-lost nudie shots.

A billfold's style is as serious as a gentleman's everyday belt. Brown or black leather is a timeless selection, in regulation size, or the longer, Southern, checkbook length. Velcro models are reserved for sporting activities or for the hopelessly wealthy. If your wallet is old, faded, and cracking, retire it. For a more subdued look, seek a money clip in sterling silver or gold. This is no place to clench a weak wad; fold in at least as much as the clip is worth.

Nice touch: Stash a few stamps behind your ATM card for last-minute mailbox drops. When traveling, remove ancillary wallet materials and stick with what's utilitarian on the road. Do you really need that "buy ten, get one free" hole-punched deli hoagie card in El Segundo?

SEASONAL TOGGERY

So you don't have to wade through ski pants to reach tennis shorts, have a shelf devoted to a rotating stock of seasonal items.

FALL & WINTER

◆ **Mufflers:** The long piano-key scarf is inappropriate unless you are commonly addressed as Maestro or are a middle-school substitute music teacher. Inexpensive wool-blend models are fine for daily use, but a fine cashmere scarf accomodates workplace or evening jaunts. For transitional weather, loop a scarf about the neck even without a coat. Hit up a knitting grandmother for a custom model.

- **Earmuffs & Hats:** In modern times, new styles have emerged—ear-flapped hats and headband-like wrap-arounds. Purchase one if it suits your tenor, though quadraphonic headphone styles are best left to air-port traffic men on the tarmac. Woolen or fleece caps, with or without pompom, are essential for snow play, bald pates, and high wind chills. With a long overcoat and a tattered volume of Dostoevsky under your arm, you'll survive January with a Kremlin-issue Persian lamb astrakhan.

- **Gloves:** A gentleman owns a pair of dark leather gloves for dress and a sturdy synthetic pair for everyday freezes. No gauche Isotoners, regardless of what Dan Marino says. Unless named Enzo or driving a vintage convertible, no knuckle-vented driving gloves, either.

- **Sweaters:** Own a few oversized wool sweaters for splitting wood at the cabin or huddling on the beach in November. The remaining selections should be double-checked by a woman's eye before purchase. The sweater vest is a precarious article—great for the golf course or under the reading lamp, not for a night out with the rugby squad.

- **Turtlenecks:** Rich, dark tones in combed cotton and cashmere are versatile under open-collared shirts, tucked into jeans, or worn with trousers. Stick with the mock turtleneck until autumn leaves are raked and bagged at the curb. Watch the length, as giraffe-neck fold-overs give the impression of a whiplash recoveree.

SPRING & SUMMER

◆ **Flip-Flops & Sandals**: Flip-flops are best in the sand or for a quick dash to the mailbox. Sandals are a comfortable necessity on balmy afternoons. Brown, open-toed sandals range from casual to sporty; black and closed-toe models are typically dressier. Reserve socks with sandals for nonmetropolitan lifestyles.

◆ **Shirtsleeves**: There is no reason why summer clothes should be less fashionable. To keep cool, wear lightweight linens and breathable textures. Beyond the polo shirt, button-downs are a comfortable alternative; leave open with a solid shirt underneath or try alone with a few buttons undone. Tuck in with a belt or leave untucked with a straw hat.

◆ **Shorts**: Like the miniskirt, shorts length varies within a decade. Opt for measures between thigh-high micros and calf-covering clam diggers; anything wandering well north of the knee is suspect. Long Bermuda shorts are ideal for croquet, badminton, and walking about. No cut-off denim, though former dress pants with holes from dance-floor knee slides are converted with scissors and a roll of the cuff.

NECKWEAR

Along with boxer shorts, neckwear is one of the most telling articles of clothing. A colorful litter parallels weather and mood. Brighter ties emerge in the sunshine, sedate hues mirror the nimbus clouds. A handful of conservative dot or striped ties should fill out your (nonmotorized) cedar tie rack. Most ties match white and blue shirts, but not all stripes or patterns. When shopping, pull a few styles from the fine-shirts department for comparison to prevent a glut of strictly primary colors.

Around a swinging rack, one distinctive silk gem leers from behind discount clutter, causing a great stir in your charge card. A great tie, like a vintage car, snatches the eye and calls for attention, sometimes in a

---

═ ASCOTS ═

For those who disapprove of tight collars or full-time jobs, the ascot is a sound alternative. Four out of five *flâneurs* recommend it over the conservative cravat. If bow ties are interesting, ascots are downright curious. They are not for the everyday, but for loosely sophisticated affairs when a *soupçon* of swank and *Playboy* is not inappropriate. The ascot zests up pyjamas, fancies a cocktail hour, and elegantly denotes a frisky host. A black or white ascot is quite versatile as social lingerie, either for public gaming or intimate affairs. It remains fast to the neck with a modified four-in-hand knot or a tie tack.

Incidentally, Fred Jones, the blond *bon homme* from *Scooby Doo,* is at least a semigentleman. He wears a distinctive red piece of neckwear, singly knotted, with pointed ends over his white sweater. Hanna Barbera classifies this as an "ascot." In reality, it is merely a "cravat." In his 1978 classic, *Dressing Right,* Charles Hix clearly states, "The true ascot, sometimes seen at formal daytime weddings, has wide, usually squared ends that are worn, after the neck has been looped twice, folded diagonally one over the other and held in place by a jeweled or plain stickpin." A cravat, like a scarf, is wrapped around the neck and looped once in a single knot without a tack. Ergo, Fred is wearing a cravat, not an ascot. No squared ends + no stickpin + a single knot + a silly sweater = cravat.

whisper, other times a shout. Develop this radar. If a tie doesn't move you, don't buy it. If you can't recall the last "nice tie" compliment, ask a well-dressed sales clerk to assist among the silk.

If your ties routinely develop ripples or if the underside bar tack unravels, buy better-crafted knits or ease up when unknotting. At the end of the workday, too many unknowing gents wantonly strip their tie from a shirt, trawling it around the neck band, stretching and twisting the silk back and forth like an older brother's Indian burn. Turn up your shirt collar and untie by retracing the steps of knotting gently. Then, drape the fatigued tie back on the rack.

TIES THAT (DON'T) BIND

In the world of quick assessments, ties are a Geiger counter of character (see chart). No limp ties, except if you are allergic to silk or compliments.

BOW TIES

Long feared for its imagined intricacy, the bow tie is a special accessory. Ranging from professorial to formal to funky, it is the hand-tied bench-mark of gentlemanly virtue. Visit a vintage or men's shop and engage in this rite of passage. Never divulge to a rogue the bow tie's true ease of knot—let's keep it between us gentleman, shall we?

BOLO

◆ ◆ ◆ ◆ ◆ **Rum** ◆ **Lemon or lime juice** ◆ **Orange juice** ◆ **Sugar** ◆ ◆ ◆ ◆ ◆

FIRST IMPRESSION	*PERMANENT CHARACTERIZATION*
Small dots and diamonds, bland color, or uninteresting collegiate stripes; button-down collar	Conservative. If the Constitution permitted, third time's a charm— Reagan '88.
Computer-generated entropy design with no discernible dimple.	Likely a shut-in; plays with pogs.
Thin, older model; drab paisley; seemingly leftover from the prop department on *Hunter*. Tie tip never reaches the navel.	Lazy, dispirited. Barring that company memo, sweatpants would be a casual day option.
Nonholiday-time Loony Tunes design or other novelty.	Take one step back—lunched on a Happy Meal today.
Really tight knot the size of a pinhead.	Pinhead.
Obscenely ugly, abstract, essentially low-grade Pollock puke. Crooked, hasty, four-in-hand knot; tie drapes down over 501 button-fly jeans.	Deficiency of taste: enjoyed *Cats*, thinks Kenny G is "soulful."
Smart design, sturdy swatch of silk, instantly (but casually) eye-catching, secondary colors, well-dimpled, properly arched Windsor knot.	The Modern Gentleman, of course.

Unlike a straight tie, which isn't undone until undress, a bow tie is fidgeted with and reknotted throughout the day. Take a moment of "me time" to deliberately undo and retie when caught in a slow elevator. The undone bow is a subtle beacon; onlookers know it's a manual, not a pre-fab clip-on. Indeed, a bow tie is quite phallic. With deft manipulation, it stands soft yet turgid, puffing with stiffness or leaning askance.

You already have the clothes to go with a butterfly, or bat-winged, bow tie: it goes with almost any collar, except the tab collar, and it's not just for tuxedos or stuffy sport coats with elbow patches. Fabulous with suspenders, a bow tie doesn't require a jacket. It goes with any suit; in fact, it nearly turns a double-breasted suit into formal wear. Still, a knotted bow tied around a lackluster, ill-fitting suit looks frumpy and thrice accentuates a nerdy lack of style.

Knot a bow tie only so tightly that it may be undone by a lover's gentle tug. As Frank Sinatra hinted, attempt a keen bow no more than three times. After that, leave it. . .it's jazz.

PYJAMAS

After hours, evening wear is discarded. When revelry returns home, slip into something more comfortable. Amongst appropriately intimate company and especially when alone, slide into a pair of pyjamas. Additionally, a men's size small makes a clever hint and splendid gift for a playful love or platonic female.

Diversify your collection. In the warmer climes, collarless light-weight cotton is preferred. Try on simple patterns and prints, as opposed to shorties and pairs with childish choo-choo themes. Essentially, don't be too casual; pyjamas shouldn't seem incongruent with a snifter. For the kinds of nightcaps that are poured rather than worn, keep a sleek set for chic repose. As the nights grow long and frosty, swap for flannel and lounge by the fire. The more mature should seek out faux cuffs and buttons as opposed to snaps. A third pyjama pair should be kept as a spare or reserved for guests.

Pyjama tips:

• Flashy polyester can double as urban club wear. Once, spend the night at a lover's metropolitan pad and ride the subway home in pyjamas.

• Try an intimate hosting experience where pyjamas are required attire.

• For extra credit, find out what really goes in the breast pyjama pocket: a sawbuck for wagers and dispatched errands; mobile phone; snuff; contraception; paraphernalia?

Really nice touch: Spin pajamas in the dryer for a toasty transition from a shower or to ease a lover out of bed on a glacial morning.

ROBE DE CHAMBRE

An antecedent of the dressing gown, the robe is an undervalued article of gentleman's clothing, not merely hotel pilferage. Don't let Tabernacle choirboys, Majesties, Supreme Court justices, and Jedi Knights monopolize the garment's virtue. Ranging from dragon-print kimonos to shiny satins worn by ringside welterweights, robes are more than a bolt of terrycloth worn after a soak. There are bathrobes, usually in thirsty cotton weaves, meant strictly for post-bath comfort and cover. In the stickier months, sporty designs are casual, light, and short as a green-belt's judo *gi*. In the wintertime, don a calf-sweeping model. If dashing across snow to a gurgling hot tub, employ something hooded.

Robes for lounging and wearing over pyjamas are more elaborate. Often with contrasting silk or velvet trim, the bathrobe evolves into a smoking jacket when made with cuffs and a shawl collar and tied with a black sash. Chic patterns, sumptuous textures, and a tad of shoulder pad make for in-home formal wear that begs an ascot and velvet slip-ons.

SLIPPERS

A toe ring and well-groomed bare feet aren't uncomely, but decent fluted sleepwear deserves better than tube socks or holey stockings. Finish with comfy slippers, but no pink floppy ears or anything purchased at the hospice gift shop.

EYEWEAR

[frame]

[arm]

[lens]

It is polite for a gentleman to have 20/20 vision, but it is not rude to require prescription oculars. Until Lasik surgery is scheduled, myopic gentlemen should sport sensible and stylish frames. Accentuate cheekbones and dark lashes without resembling Mr. Magoo or Waldo. Glasses are worn front and center, so spare no extras: purchase the featherweight, scratch-resistant frames for a sleek fit. Thick lenses may be necessary, but not Coke bottles. Even wear-with-a-hangover-and-allergies spectacles should suit a business meeting or happy-hour date. For the retro set, eclectic frames are encouraged, though skip the "Goodbye Yellow Brick Road" models. No matter what, edgy frames must fit your face and charisma, lest your glasses be cooler than you.

CONTACTS

Purchase a large supply of disposables for ease of care and comfort. Avoid cumbersome and outmoded cleaning systems that require Pyrex beakers, Bunsen burners, and multiple disinfecting solutions. Colored contacts rival hair plugs as cheap forgeries; no one is born with purple eyes. Mischievously patterned lenses are acceptable for holiday amusement, costumes, or nights of deviance, especially All Hallow's Eve.

FRINGE-WEAR

A monocle, on a chain or floating solo, is a fine Austrian accoutrement; Colonel Mustard, diamond appraisers, and Baker Street antagonists shouldn't have all the fun. Balanced upon the bridge of the nose, the armless pince-nez (excellent with a vintage bow tie) was hot with Woolworth's counter-backers and nineteenth-century accountants. Lorgnettes help you get an eye on faraway arias at the opera. An eye patch is a niche accessory with its own ecstasy, though only those named Von, Erich, or Von Erich may regularly employ one for nonmedical reasons.

SUNGLASSES

State Trooper mirrors and folding Ferrari ovals are meant for lesser specimens. Jet-black, rearview mirror–sized granny brow-blockers are meant for trachoma sufferers. Backups stashed in the glove box to fight

UV rays are better than borrowed giveaways from a Yankees game. For the clumsy and absentminded, make early rounds to discount street vendors for sunglasses you can afford to sit on or forget in the backseat.

The triathletic gentleman might own sport shades. However, Jim McMahon wrap-arounds and anything endorsed by Olympic volleyball players should not leave the court or Club Med gift shop, and may never accompany a business suit. Remember, goggles are for the slopes, racquetball, chem lab, Motocross, and Lakers starting centers.

MEN WITHOUT HATS

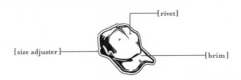

[rivet]

[size adjuster]   [brim]

After perusing the pyjama shop and fine-footwear department, nestle an uncovered head into a hat and discover the gentleman's answer to a lady's shoe fetish. Little sparks attention at an affair like a gentleman in a fine hat, dressed appropriately and well-fitted from brim to toe. A hat doesn't create gallantry, but a gent's aura and crackle is noticeably enhanced with the right tilt of a lid. When traveling, nothing restores the fancy to trains and airplanes like a man in a slim hat. However, there is a fine line between looking foolish and looking enviably dapper in a hat. If you are in the latter 10 percent, hats off. For the remaining crop of gentlemen, there are sombreros in Tijuana and hard hats for safety.

THE PARTS

Brim, band, crown, and crease: the brim shades sun, and the band holds a feather; the crown covers the head, and the crease is how the fabric or fiber is indented or protruded (center or pinch, for instance). Measurements are taken in inches, then converted to size equivalents from XS to XXL. Take a measuring tape about the widest part of your head, just above the ears and eyebrows, and wedge a pinky fingertip under the tape to account for movement. Hairstyles vary over the life of a hat, so account for a recent perm or buzz cut when determining size.

STYLES

For yachting and election night, try an Italian straw boater. For slipping into a zoot suit or anticipating a night of jazz, try a felt fedora or homburg. Chauffeurs like tweed driving caps, and Bond villains enjoy classic derbies and bowlers in wool or fur. The silk/satin, collapsible black topper is a must for the opera. Let a milliner show you around.

Matching hat style with the occasion involves seasonal considerations as well. Winter calls for beaver and lamb furs, pigskin suede, wool, and blends. Summer hats keep a head cool with weaves of straw, corn, and coconut. Poplin hats repel April showers. Nearly indestructible synthetics like Mylar take a drenching and pack without a hatbox.

Incidentally, leave the sunglasses at home when donning a hat. Not only does a hat shade the eyes, the full circumference of shadow guards against sun glare and misjudged infield pop-ups.

HAT CARE

If a proper hatbox (slightly larger than the hat) is unavailable, hang your lid on a hook or rest the hat on its crown. Always store the hat with its brim upturned, then snap it back into place when ready to wear. Unlike its shoddy cousins, a well-made hat retains its shape after years of wear.

Do not wear nonweatherized hats in heavy precipitation. Plastic rain protectors are available, a sort of hat galosh, which guard against the elements. Regular brushing with a soft bristle maintains luster. For the best chapeaus, invest in a hat jack, which preserves shape like a shoe tree.

HATIQUETTE

Famous doffers P(hineas) T. Barnum, Abe Lincoln, and Frosty the Snowman knew that style comes with responsibility. Hat manners include: (1) removal when a lady enters an elevator, when sitting indoors, or during a funeral procession; and (2) lifting after performing an act of courtesy, when passing in close quarters, or in offering up one's seat.

UMBRELLA POLICY

Umbrellas are like lighters: everyone owns one, but no one has ever actually purchased one. Carry one, but don't be the partly-sunny-day pessimist when there is less than 30 percent chance of showers.

There are two types: those routinely left in taxis and finer *parapluies* meant to be cherished. The gentleman totes a black umbrella. Forget unfurling hackneyed Impressionist motifs or anything licensed by Disney. Ordinary push-button styles are fine for commuting and routine errands. A "disposable" $3 street-vendor model is ideal for rainy barhops where the chance of precipitation and a lost umbrella are both 100 percent. Stash one in the office for an unexpected early-evening cloudburst; though, leave it at home for a mere misty mizzle and any snowstorm. Snazzier stick or malacca-handle models are for formal outings and fine duds.

Use your umbrella primarily for rain protection. Only the anal-retentive poke a pointy ferrule at discarded cigars on the pavement. An archcriminal's stick also doubles as an automatic weapon or quick getaway whirligig, à la Penguin. Do not drag your umbrella on a sidewalk or hardwood floor, nor furl a brolly in the house. The gentleman shouldn't emulate Nurse Sarah Gamp, of Dickens's *The Life and Adventures of Martin Chuzzlewit,* and carry an unwieldy, untidy umbrella, especially in mixed company.

Incidentally, prohibitions against premature affection are suspended in the rain. Drape an arm over her shoulder while sharing a pocketsize 'brella. Even in monsoons, however, early "ass-patting" is still out.

TATTOOS

Perhaps a night with the boys in Nuevo Loredo or a wrong turn off Bourbon Street left its indelible mark. The gentleman's code includes the decorated crowd. Who wouldn't say that a gent with a three-piece suit and a forearm skull and crossbones is at least interesting?

One cannot be too patient in measuring instant gratification against permanent liabilities before getting a tattoo. Before you get marked, pinpoint your motivation: Is it for a partner? Rebellion? For "entrance" into a particular subculture, like a fraternity or Kiwanis Club? Will this passion last to the wood anniversary five years from now? Lest you experience pallor in the parlor, don't vacillate on yes, no, or where.

A second-glance discovery is more furtively exciting than a center-stage neck display. To engage in blatant exhibitionism for the sake of shock or entertainment value is not an example of unflappable confidence. Similarly, ill-conceived and unimaginative art demonstrates a lack of depth. Avoid the terribly banal: trendy Asian characters, the latticed bicep ring, lovers' names (see Johnny Depp's left arm), and any styles found on mischievous NBA rebounders.

Before getting inked, seek out a recommendation from a satisfied customer and visit the parlor to peruse designs. Even if you have a sketch in mind, note the artist's work and tidiness. During an ink session, pain settles into a bearable backdrop. A prelude Pabst might take the edge off (though reputable parlors won't mark an intoxicated patron), and Tylenol eases the dull prickly pain without affecting blood clotting. Afterwards, follow the care instructions and appreciate the permanence . . . until a second mortgage comes through for laser removal.

HYGIENE & HABITS

[shaving soap] [brush] [cup]

Like that biannual visit to the dentist, perform a crown-to-sole inspection of your appearance. Once the thirties have sprung, contemplate modern issues in hygiene and habits concerning exfoliation, cavities, regularity, and squamous cell carcinoma. A gentleman's outward presentation starts with management at the bathroom sink.

HAIR

Take a cue from a handsome tomcat who keeps himself well licked: hair in obvious places should be stylish and unrumpled, be it closely cropped or loosely shorn. Whether clean-shaven, moustached, or Van Dyked, each do should be as well kept as an aging tycoon's trophy wife. This is not an employee handbook: your coiffure can venture into a ponytail or even depart completely via electric shears. Use some imagination, but be wary of chain-store salons run by beauty-school dropouts.

Long hair will make thee look dreadfully to thine enemies, and manly to thy friends:
it is, in peace, an ornament; in war, a strong helmet; it. . .
deadens the leaden thump of a bullet: in winter, it is a warm nightcap;
in summer, a cooling fan of feathers.

—THOMAS DEKKER, *THE GULLS HORNBOOK*, 1609

SECONDARY FUR

Trim neck hair biweekly with clippers or a disposable razor. Wandering unibrows must be plucked until the follicles wear out (shaving actually encourages growth). Like prescription antidepressants, tweezers will be in your medicine cabinet for a long time, so purchase a precise instrument, not a bargain model. A copse of chest hair should be hacked back monthly to a manageable length, especially around the aureole and navel region. Similarly, snip underarm overgrowth as it begins to peek out the sides.

TERTIARY DOWN

Don't ignore it, especially during the warmer seasons and most active periods of libidinous exchange. Much like a lady's flowerbed, a gentleman's boscage should be pruned monthly. A light trim around the edges will usually do, but one is free to express any latent creativity in manner and pattern. Whether you prefer the natural or sculpted look, one shouldn't play on a completely bare surface or rub in foamy mousses around the lower latitudes.

EXTREMITIES

Are your soles and palms unsightly, cracked bricks in need of a pumice stone or callus remover? It's no small feat during harsh winters and sweaty sandal season. Weekly clipping, filing, and general care of toes and fingers is sufficient for most men. For those whose career or social habits require meticulous presentation, treat yourself to regular manicures. Powder up with talc in the summer to ease humid cling; look for it at department stores or haberdasheries, not on the drug-store shelf next to medicated foot sprays. As for ears, cotton swabs were designed for make-up removal, not daily drilling of the delicate auditory canal.

CLYSTERING

Ah, the internal cleanse. Similar to clearing gutters at signs of the first robin, spa enemas are a great adjunct to spring-cleaning. There's nothing awkward about a gentleman in a comfortable room, covered in a sheet, experiencing the healthful effects of a high colonic. After a brief enemetiquette tutorial on the ins and outs, you are left in a private chamber upon a special table with control of water pressure and temperature. Like a hygienist probing your tartar-flecked teeth, the attendant should be trusted to regard your dignity in this vulnerable moment. A home enema is a milder, less intrusive Roto-Rooter for detoxifying after bouts of drink, junk food, and other pollutants.

MOISTURIZER

Crow's feet, age spots, and sagging features are successfully postponed for a few more birthdays with studious, postrinse application of moisturizers. Wrinkles might be dignified on a salt-and-peppered gentleman, but saddlebags under the eyes and elephant skin around the joints look more neglectful than distinguished. Get into the habit of taking care of your skin beyond perfunctory aloe applications after sunburn. Yearly, gift yourself a day of beauty that a lady would envy. A body wrap, cleansing facial, and deep massage are more restorative than a cigarette after sex. No matter how much lumber you cut, keep hands soft for practicing basic sensual massage techniques on a ready lover.

COLOGNE

Often, the natural scent of a well-groomed man is enticing enough. If inclined, walk into a light misting, so as not to overpower an elevator with Aqua Velva. If one is wont to spray, go beyond the latest fad. Bottled bouquets are not absolute—what smells good in a fashion magazine insert may not complement your natural chemistry. Take a lover to the cologne counter and rank the tester sticks. For the finalists, alternate arms and have her nuzzle your wrists as each scent blends with natural aroma. Choose two: light and spicy to splash with active wear, and a darker, more elegant toilette for well-heeled evenings out.

ORAL FIXATIONS

Gum is a once-in-a-while treat that makes an appearance when the gentleman is sour-mouthed and out and about. No exploding gum "Chewels," juicy "Freshen Up" squares, or gum tape. Likewise, no Big League Chew unless you are DH'ing in a Saturday stickball game. Chiclets are for senior citizens and Pop Rocks are dangerous killers. Don't be caught eating Chuckles. It's not funny.

Black licorice is an acquired taste akin to anisette. Go natural and savor the herbal flavor with a seasoned, mature tongue. Swizzle the occasional red Twizzler, especially as a straw to slurp up an ice cream soda.

Lollipops, those most elegant of the juvenile oral fixations, come in many types, from the wafer-thin Movado museum model to the boardwalk kiosk all-day sucker. Never turn down a lolly, especially a pop sent in the drive-thru vacuum tube with your bank balance from a doting teller. While not recommended for in-line skating, push-ups, or go-carting, root beer Dum Dums are blessings for birthday parties and intimate gatherings, and a respite from holiday candy-cane season.

COTTON CANDY

Hearken back to Sundays at the state fair. Even if your prized sow, Petunia, didn't win best shank, there was always cotton candy. Unless trailing a favorite niece, mind the following tenets:

- Cotton candy has two recognized hues: white and pink, not Smurfette blue or Grape Ape mauve.

- Like the Benihana shrimp special, the good stuff is produced booth-side. Get it from the spinner, collected on a white, conical stick.

- Cotton candy is not attic insulation—steer clear of the prepackaged, plastic-wrapped swag that is injected with enough preservatives to cure the meat of an eight-point buck.

The volatile mixture of too much fantasy and not enough play leads to bad pick-up lines and nervous habits. Shy away from the person who always sucks mints or hands out Certs like religious leaflets on the subway (listen for the telltale Altoid shake). Beware these Freudian tics, indicating stunted oral-stage development or a miserable month on the dating calendar: persistent ice cruncher, pen-cap mangler, pencil biter, label peeler, nervous belt aligner, Styrofoam-cup teaser, nail nibbler, swizzle-stick mutilator, cocktail-napkin baler, earring twirler, macho triceps massager, or maniacal ball shifter/pocket-pool player.

Incidentally, take heed of orthodontia. Straight white teeth are the gentleman's best accessories. Floss, gurgle, and brush so you don't piss away years of braces, headgear, and pink retainers.

BRONZING

Compliments of Apollo, sunshine is a gift to melanin fiends and photosynthetic flora. For your own freckled hide, purchase lotion at SPF levels higher than middle-school grades and select products according to quality and waterproof durability first, pleasing coconut scent second. Dark tanning oils with near-zero protection are for vain ozone disbelievers and rump roasts cooked to well done. During sun cream application, don't neglect forgotten corners of the forehead, collarbone, feet,

LOLLIPOP

◆ ◆ ◆ **Green Chartreuse** ◆ **Cointreau** ◆ **Kirsch** ◆ **Dash maraschino** ◆ ◆ ◆

and earlobes. Left to the elements, the neck will wither into an unsightly, corrugated "rooster neck" before age forty.

The George Hamilton, perpetual, all-weather, all-season, steel-belted-radial tan is overkill. If you want a little color in your wheyfaced cheeks during barren winter months, rent *Love at First Bite* or work out with the heat turned up. If a wintertime business boondoggle calls to warmer climes, soak in the rays like a hungry hippo lazing at the wading pond.

Tanning salons, or "sun centers," are discouraged. If you require extra Vitamin D, drink milk; if you favor UV lighting, step into a rave or a stoner's closet. One exception is the thirty-minute winter session the day before a wedding to look hearty and hale for the cameras. Sunless tanning creams produce an irradiated orange glow that's only acceptable should Syracuse make the Final Four.

> *"The sun, with all those planets revolving around it an dependent on it, can still ripen a bunch of grapes as if it had nothing else in the universe to do."*
>
> —GALILEO GALILEI

Chapter Six

DOMESTICITY

. . . .

Domestic Guidelines **162**

The Kitchen 163

Cooking **165**

Breaking Bread 166

The Gentleman's Bedroom **169**

Heartifacts 171

Toiletiquette **176**

Spitting, Hiccoughing & Other Expulsions 179

DOMESTIC GUIDELINES

Domestically speaking, a gentleman can major in one of three areas: the kitchen, the bedroom, and the garage. Mastery of the first two will land you romance and active Saturday nights. Being a handyman will more likely book your Saturday afternoons among twisted coaxial cables and busted fan belts. A splendid candlelight dinner or rollick in the sack is better recompense for a missed shift of house chores than rearranging the tool shed.

A gentleman's living quarters bespeak a well-landscaped personality. A poor inner habitat, with wilting plants and chintz-yarned tissue boxes, evinces a myopic decorator. A soulless home lacks framed photographs and a dictionary for looking up tough crossword clues. The archetypical bachelor, with only an old can of Schaefer, a half-empty bottle of relish,

THE STRONGBOX

So, you've accrued the requisite credits and think you're ready to matriculate? Are you actually prepared to relocate your valuable documents from an under-the-bed shoebox to something more substantial? Enter the strongbox, that fireproof alloyed container built to shelter one's dearest effects. Small, chic, and portable, the strongbox securely houses the family's cherished costume zirconia jewelry without the bother of a behind-the-painting wall safe. To qualify for a strongbox, the gentleman must be a policyholder insured for more than his auto, or he must have executed a will. Once you've met these basic requirements, toss in passports, love letters, sensitive media, paraphernalia, and anything you want to flee the house with during a twister.

and an onion in the crisper, has fallen out of vogue. A modicum of food in the fridge, art on the walls, and flourishing flora affirm vitality.

Outfit your space properly. If you must ask a kindly neighbor for a Phillips-head screwdriver or if you are using a butter knife in place of a flathead, invest in a small toolbox or designate a kitchen drawer. Candles, in holders, are vital mood setters and furnish soft, fragrant ambiance. A candy dish fills out the living room, but skip the bowls of starlight mints, caramel squares, or butterscotches—save these bundles of sunshine for your grandmother's high-rise apartment.

THE KITCHEN

Be your own health inspector. Dish sponges shouldn't be emissaries of germs consigned to double duty: nominate one for the sink, another for counter tasks. Stow a fire extinguisher for flambé gone awry and marital flare-ups. Go Southern: pick up the versatile iron skillet and learn to cure and care for it. Those with perfect parade lines of copper cookware should be culinarily proficient, able to pronounce *demi-glace* and whip up spinach *crespelle* in a jiff. If you cannot produce even a bachelor-fridge 4-A.M. scramble for a booze-flushed bedfellow, you are hopeless. However, city dwellers are forgiven when the quick flick of a StarTAC delivers bountiful goodies to the door at any hour.

A stocked refrigerator exudes balance, good health, and self-sufficiency. Like Bronson's *Mr. Majestyk,* fight for your watermelon and other produce. If you find that you have vastly more boxed or canned food than fresh vegetables, place a classified ad for a roommate with a toque and rolling pin. Rotate the perishable stock and reserve eye-level storage for daily comestibles. You shouldn't have to move the capers to get to the orange juice. Keep a jar of unsweetened applesauce chilling in the back of the icebox for near-death hangover experiences in which the colossal pain makes you realize, rather sullenly, that last night's revelry inflicted irreversible biotic damage.

Incidentally, do not horde take-out condiments. Moreover, electric can openers are for the meek, who shall not inherit the hearth.

MILK

Whole milk is for coffee and babies, not for mass consumption. For those with crystal-wearing Woodstock moms, try soy or vanilla rice milk. Two percent milk, like an unregistered Democrat, demonstrates a distinct fear of commitment. If you are torn between the fatty, womblike goodness of whole milk and the blue-tinted, waterlogged taste of skim, consider 1

TV DINNER DOSSIER

There's nothing like the splendid odor of freshly defrosted steak with pearl onions and a befoiled dessert cobbler; but don't trust the Gorton's Fisherman— who knows what lies under that long yellow slicker? These days, technology has rendered the aluminum, Army-mess, sectional tray obsolete. . .TV dinners are now microwavable. Blasphemy! Whatever skills were required to time the foil removal from creamed corn have been lost on today's hyperlazy consumers. Turkey dinners with giblet gravy and Salisbury anything are among the safest choices in the frozen-food case. Nostalgia aside, never be caught with more than one selection in the freezer. As far as Lean Cuisine goes, if nutrition and caloric intake are at issue, wheel on over to the produce section.

percent. Those few saved grams of fat may be traded in at the end of the month for an extra helping of foie gras or a Double Whopper with cheese.

COOKING

How is it that some men can replace spark plugs, decipher schematics, and fiddle with circuit breakers, but can't follow a recipe? If you've spent more time with *The Joy of Sex* than its tamer cousin, *The Joy of Cooking*, you might be intimidated by the prospect of folding an egg white or grappling with a double boiler. Collect thematic cookbooks for inspiration and watch a few cooking shows to pick up new moves. If you didn't learn how to roll meatballs from Grandma, allocate funds for gourmet carry-out and the props for hosted candlelight dinners.

DISHWASHING

The anal-retentive sock drawer is arranged by color and rayon content, yet the dishwasher remains an open forum of expression. No worries, you can safely desegregate knives and spoons to commingle in the utensil compartment. On occasion, even a glass from the top shelf can elope with a wayward mug to the lower dish level. Still, there are some rules to observe. Silver plates, wooden spoons, and sex toys are not top-shelf dishwasher safe; wash these delicates by hand (in a liberal household, the last can be aired in the drying rack). And take it from Tesauro, never substitute sink-top liquid dish soap for dishwasher detergent lest you have a foam party on the floor worse than any syndicated "zany" 1970s family sitcom.

Cooking entails more than broiled meat doused with prefab marinades. It's okay to cheat and buy bakery cheesecake, but create the entrée yourself. Log some range hours and develop a few signature dishes that can be whipped to perfection without recipe cards ("Oh yes, Marvin's famous Stove Top–stuffing tuna casserole is to die for"). With enough butter, cream, and eggs, even amateurs can speciously impress; the real goal is to achieve tasteful weak-kneed decadence without the Alfredo death factor. Instead of drowning veggies in oil at the sauté station or deep-frying fish, feed your friends from the grill. When dining out, steal ideas for winning plate combo and quirky garnishes.

Incidentally, a dessert fruit salad is transformed by a splash of brandy or Triple Sec. Turn heavy cream and a splash of liqueur into a Class I fetish.

BREAKING BREAD

[steam]

[toasted rye]

[lever]

We will not linger on the basic table manners Mom reinforced by raps upon your knuckles with a spoon or spork. Instead, brush up with our bibliography and remember when setting the table that the fork goes to the left, the knife is turned to cut the plate from the right, and the spoon rests adjacent. A wet spoon is not welcome in the sugar bowl, nor a butter-flecked knife in the jam. Ask someone to pass the pepperoncini rather than running the wine-stem gauntlet or beer-bottle slalom by reaching an outstretched arm across the table.

A few meal and manner enhancers:

BREAKFAST

It is not impolite to show appreciation for a fine bowl of Cocoa Puffs by raising it to your lips in sugary brown communion. Use the four-finger bowl hold with thumb-clasped spoon, instead of the double-handed, shivering-soup sip. At home, a used knife may return to the warped butter log—loose toasticles are signs of comfort. Whilst breakfasting, shun the meticulous waffle-square filler who drizzles equal syrup doses in each chamber. As an out-of-town guest, partake in available foodstuffs; only finicky ingrates disparage non—New York City bagels, non-Vermont maple syrup, or cheddar made outside of Wisconsin. Any meal *can* be taken in pyjamas, but only breakfast *should* be taken in pyjamas.

LUNCH

Sandwiches are instantly enlivened with a diagonal cut, a toothpick, and a green olive. Weather permitting, take a lunch in outdoor solace. For an occasional pick-me-up, treat yourself to a lime rickey or other old-fashioned fountain drink. Lastly, workday fast food promotes daytime productivity akin to a socialist state; if your recent lunch history can be plotted with McDonald's promotional game pieces, go healthier or consider a cabinet post in the Mayor McCheese administration.

SUPPER

At ease. Protocol is relaxed at home, but not jettisoned; import a touch of white-tablecloth demeanor even with a TV remote in hand. Keep a linen napkin in your lap and pair a wine with your Spaghetti-Os. This isn't the mess tent, so prewarm the plate and garnish with any handy leftover greens, fruits, or toss of crackers. Surreptitious pea-flicking wakes up tablemates, but knife licking is still out. Before digging in, set the table. Intimate meals find sauces in small bowls with spoons; but for casual feedings, bring out the Hellmann's and the Wishbone dressing to mingle tableside with salt and pepper. Preserve some supping sanctity and try not to let the phone interrupt, although a lone diner can take a call and reheat morsels afterward.

QUAFFS

Supplement orange and cranberry usuals with juicer-made concoctions. A bubbling, organic creation gurgles with life for twice-a-week health kicks, rocky Saturday mornings, and post-workout restoration.

To date, lemonade is still made from just water, sugar, lemon juice, and grated lemon peel (sprig of mint optional). As for tea, no self-respecting Southerner sips instant iced tea, except a Snapple on the go. Ideally, home brew a batch and chill it over ice. Further, Quik's artificial chocolaty goodness should not be discounted, especially when a heaping tablespoon of powder is dunked into milk and eaten like a muddy cookie.

Invest in a decent kettle, tea ball, and fresh lemons. Steep in the enjoyment of imported loose teas by the pound, not the bag. For bean types, percolate or Mr. Coffee your own workaday morning java. With a

AFTER-SUPPER COCKTAIL

◆ ◆ ◆ ◆ ◆ ◆ ◆ **Apricot brandy** ◆ **Curaçao** ◆ **Lemon juice** ◆ ◆ ◆ ◆ ◆ ◆ ◆

robust Sunday brunch or muffin-time coffee moment, employ a coarse grind and dark roast in the high-octane French press.

Incidentally, a gentleman skips instant coffee except when holed up in a country cabin or on an ice-fishing junket. Still, drink Sanka twice a year. You'll know when.

THE GENTLEMAN'S BEDROOM

A cavelike retreat of dim and dingy repose is no place to greet a bright day. Avoid the monastic childhood milieu by investing in down pillows and a handsome duvet instead of a zoo of stuffed animals (no worries, a favorite teddy can rest nearby with impunity).

Your bed is a sacred place that projects strength, style, and intimacy. Odysseus and Penelope had the most historically significant bed, featuring an olive tree as one of its posts. For those residing outside Ithaca, a lush bedside plant should suffice. A framed mattress and box-spring set is standard; the minimalist's futon rests on the floor, as long as it's not the bleak centerpiece of an ultramodern blank-walled mise-en-scéne. A

YOU (HAVEN'T) MADE YOUR BED

Phineas finds daily bed making time-consuming, unhealthful, and reminiscent of some conservative, call-your-dad-"sir" household. Meanwhile, Tesauro knows how to bolster pillows, fold a fitted sheet, and delight in the nap-tempting allure of straightened bedclothes. Both find the mitered military tuck and constricting hotel cocoon rather unacceptable.

wrought-iron or basic, nonsqueaking bed set with a headboard does nicely for the bachelor, poster beds for the monogamous.

Certain accoutrements reside near the gentleman's bed. Within arm's reach: fire, water, candles, and the makings of mild bedside activities and orated poetry. A house vibrator soaking in blue Barbicide on the nightstand is too colorful; massage oils, condoms, and other instruments of vice are housed discreetly within an adjacent drawer or box. For transition, check remote-control angles to ensure the stereo can be operated horizontally from the bed. For the nightstand library, Gideon's Bible may be filled with miraculous bedtime stories, but aren't *Grimm's Fairy Tales* or Dr. Seuss's *The Lorax* more enlightening selections?

What about the rest of the room? Artwork, personal photos, and black-and-white prints show you're not a week-to-week lessee. Garnish corners, empty spaces, and windowsills with cacti, pottery, or heartifact curiosities. Mood lighting is a must: be eclectic but subtle. Save dreamy lava lamps and glaring neon signage for cookie-cutter cocktail lounges. A full-length mirror reflects the fashionable gentleman; though, for optimal feng shui, hang the mirror elsewhere lest spirits within disturb your sleep. Recycle any rusting Chock Full o' Nuts coffee cans and procure a vintage candy dish for loose change and miscellany.

Localize clothing clutter to one armchair near to the closet. Mimic four-star inns and keep a steady supply of after-tubbing towels plush enough to soak up Noah's deluge.

The room should look lived in but not camped in. Leftover snacks and empty glassware call for a kitchen bus tub. Motivational plaques urging perseverance received from misguided family members rest comfortably in closeted mildew, next to Cub Scout merit badges. Likewise:

- No telltale lotions near the bed unless you have a serious skin condition, like leprosy.

- Aside from an absinthe-drunken whim, no Gypsy-beaded doorways to your "den of love."

- Do not "accidentally" leave financial statements or stock reports on your bureau. Secure confidential and sensitive materials out of plain view.

- No collegiate sporting equipment (baseball spikes, lacrosse gloves) displayed in the corner to dupe unsuspecting visitors about your former athletic prowess.

- The gentleman's room shall contain no "furniture" that could be used to ship Vitamin D milk or start a retaining wall. No more than one "expensive looking" particleboard bookshelf or weaved end table shoddy enough to be splintered by a white-belt's karate chop.

HEARTIFACTS

Everyone from the noble landowner to the train-hopping hobo carries a few near and dear mementos in their bindle. Even hit man Léon from *The Professional* escaped under a hail of gunfire and tear gas with a prized ficus under his arm. What's a gentleman to do with this collection of ephemera, T-ball trophies, and romantic miscellany? If any keepsakes have made the cut of a multiapartment shuffle or vigorous spring-cleaning, perhaps they are worthy of classification in the gentleman's archive. How does a gentleman determine the real value of long-held odds and ends? Put your mementos up against the following criteria, and then plot them on the graph opposite to see if they end up in the display case or recycling bin.

MEANINGFULNESS

Is the object directly related to the event or is it a secondary prop? Milestone objects that signify growth and development merit consideration—letters from first flames, diplomas, and keys to your first house.

Tone of Experience: Tokens may harken back to simple events with strong reverberations: for example, the room-service bill from a long-ago weekend getaway.

UNIQUENESS

Sometimes nonmeaningful objects are worth saving for their originality. For instance, a friend behind the Iron Curtain sent a bottle of Georgian vodka. Drink the booze, keep the label.

Collective Association: Particular objects quantify aggregate events. An engagement ring doesn't symbolize the night of proposal, but the entire courtship; a fraternity sweater, the entire fuzzy four years.

FAMILIARITY

Regardless of meaning or uniqueness, certain items latch onto you unnoticed, from dorm to apartment to the home junk drawer.

Obligation: Some ornamentals are devoid of meaning and actual retail value, yet still garner a corner in the utility closet behind the ironing board. These knickknacks are usually leftover Chanukah gifts, wedding presents, or hand-me-down family gimcracks kept out of politeness.

THE VALUE VECTORS

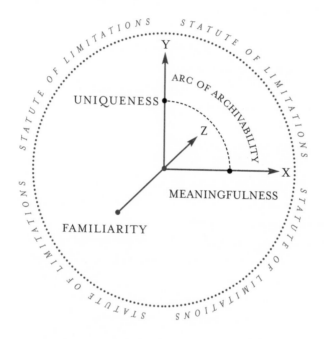

Heartifacts must be plotted on three axes before they
are allotted shelf space in the den.

X-axis . . . How meaningful? • Y-axis . . . How unique?
Z-axis . . . How familiar?

ARC OF ARCHIVABILITY

The Arc of Archivability sets a threshold of worthiness to justify retaining mementos. To avoid the bin, an object must surpass it on at least one of the three axes. For a passing grade:

- An object must be at least as *meaningful* as. . .a good first date or a farewell token from an ex-coworker.

- An object must be at least as *unique* as. . .a commemorative cup.

- An object must be at least as *familiar* as. . .something you use monthly.

STATUTE OF LIMITATIONS

The Statute of Limitations is a function of decreased value over time. It surrounds the entire graph because even the most meaningful, unique, or familiar keepsakes ultimately fall prey to decades of growth and change. Your first-place summer-camp equestrian ribbon had importance, but it faded with dust mites and adolescent neglect. Though, objects of the highest meaning or uniqueness transcend this Statute: antique family heirlooms, ancient love letters, and the Magna Carta.

To illustrate:

- A sibling mails a touching poem written on a napkin. The uniqueness of a napkin is nil, and the item is not yet familiar, but the meaningfulness is high and clearly surpasses the Arc of Archivability.

- One manual can opener has shepherded you since your twenties. During a decluttering clean, you consider tossing it. Upon deep reflection, it returns to the drawer for another ten-year stint of opening canned yellow cling peaches in heavy syrup. The meaningfulness is questionable and there is nothing unique, yet the item passes the Arc on merits of familiarity.

- Your ex-roommate scoops up a bagful of infield dirt from Fenway Park and ships it to you on a whim. If you dislike baseball, the meaning is low, but the uniqueness makes this gift worthy of a discount urn.

- Cleaning off your desk, you come across an old store-bought holiday card from an adjacent cubicle-mate. Keep it? The item is unoriginal, lacks profound meaning, and isn't a familiar fixture. Toss it.

- Rummaging through the attic, you stumble upon a junior prom commemorative Champagne glass from which you once sipped Champale with Mindi. Years ago, the flute was especially meaningful and the screen-printed glass once seemed unique. Now, Mindi's married and so are you. Pour a beer in the glass, take a last swig, and toss in the fireplace. . .the Statute of Limitations has declared this item expired.

POSTSCRIPT

Life is a collection of memorable events—don't get bogged down with the trinkets and other folderol. If curios are required for recall, perhaps the memory isn't as poignant as the commemorative cup suggests. Clean house, don't let your home become a mortuary for cobwebbed collegiate pin-ups, yellowed documents, and romantic notions of yesteryear.

TOILETIQUETTE

Let's alight to the washroom. Do not disrupt the dignity of sparkling porcelain by behaving like an ogre in the bathroom. If character is what you do when no one is looking, Toiletiquette is a free personal-growth seminar. We provide a lavatorial primer from hand-towels and soaps to nomenclature and solace, both for home and on the road.

MAINTENANCE

Neaten the restroom. Purchase only quality toilet tissue and don't store bare spares on the windowsill. Replace empty rolls during regular usage and still have time on the commode for daydreaming, humming, or reading. Moreover, blue toilet bowl inserts are unthinkable, unless you're operating an airplane lavatory. If the tub is ringed and clogged with filth and fallen hair, it has been too long since your last languid soak.

Incidentally, like Schneider on *One Day at a Time*, be conversant in flush-mechanism repair and light uncloggings. Know when to plunge, jiggle the chain, manipulate the ball cock, or walk away and call the plumber.

═══ FOUR FLUSH ═══

✦ ✦ ✦ ✦ **Rum** ✦ **Swedish punsch (or spiced rum)** ✦ **Sweet vermouth** ✦ ✦ ✦ ✦
✦ ✦ ✦ ✦ ✦ ✦ ✦ ✦ **Dash grenadine (or simple syrup)** ✦ ✦ ✦ ✦ ✦ ✦ ✦ ✦

HAND TOWELS & SOAPS

Bathroom towels come in two varieties: functional and ornamental. Workhorse cotton models are to be used; ornamental towels, often found well hung on a brass rack, with frilly lace or holiday patterns, are for admiring, not manhandling like a dishrag. However, at times, the only hand towels available are worth more than your monogrammed gingham broadcloth shirt. Faced with this emergency, delicately pat your hands dry on the backside to preserve the neatly folded façade.

Similar rules apply to dainty European leaves, papers, and soaps carved like angels or flowers. Despite your faith, don't befoul a decorative toilet-top nativity scene. If no other cleansers abound, give the angel's wing a light swipe for minimum melt.

DECIBELS

Little has been written on water-closet etiquette, leaving the gentleman to cope with such unnerving beasts as the off-the-living-room head or the dreaded everyone-can-hear-what-you're-doing-in-there half-bath. For rare times when decreased volume is desired, rim aim is vital. Further dilute decibels with wads of tissue or sit down to mum a tinkle's tintinnabulation. With more serious matters, make sure the fan is whirring, otherwise trickle the faucet for wet white noise when outsiders are in close proximity.

SOLACE

When a break in the action is desired, the bathroom is neutral ground; a sanctuary and solitary retreat to gather wits or collect loose marbles. Take a little "me time." Calm the mind, have a good long look in the mirror, and return refreshed, if not cleaner.

Nice touch: Infrequently enjoy the freedom of al fresco toiletiquette, especially when taken hands-free in the countryside.

NAMING IT

A gentleman's broad vocabulary makes it unnecessary to invoke vulgar language when announcing a trip to the men's room. Must it be announced at all? A simple "Won't you excuse me " is rarely rude. Words such as "potty" and "little wrangler's room" are no better than "crapper" or "throne," and certainly no one cares that you "have to urinate" or "do number two." When asking for directions, stick to innocuous phrases: "Gentleman's room, please" or "Where may I wash my hands?"

THE HOT SEAT

Elimination at the inopportune moment is execrable. Scenario: you have stopped at a lover's house to meet the parents and have refreshments before dinner. Suddenly, you feel a tremor. What is the proper course of action? For pressing engagements, go; this is not fourth grade anymore. Yet, if there is wiggle room, a grave decision awaits you, much like Kennedy, Khrushchev, and the Cuban Missile Crisis. Provided your business can be resolved expeditiously, quicker than an ATM "Fast Cash" withdrawal, proceed. The clock is ticking, however. If you sense an unpleasant, difficult half-hour logjam, grit and tighten up (like Archie Bell & the Drells).

In accordance with matched consideration, do not sit down unabashedly on a new lover's toilet until you have experienced this person in a congruent state of informality. Breaches of privacy force your partner to cross bridges of intimacy prematurely. Tinkle manners are generally more relaxed; the bathroom door starts out tightly latched but progresses to slightly cracked then utterly ajar as relations familiarize over time.

Incidentally, a word on the medicine chest. Avoid burrowing about the pharmacopoeia of another. Curious cats who can't resist a peer into an unlocked vault of vulnerabilities should at least avert eyes from prescription medication. Preserve privacy and enjoy the mystery—what's wrong with a little psychopathology these days?

SPITTING, HICCOUGHING & OTHER EXPULSIONS

Spitting is sometimes necessary, perhaps for watermelon seeds or the jettison of medical nuisances. Nonetheless, this act need not be accompanied by a nasal-cleansing hack that echoes about the Alps, unnerving poor Heidi and countless mountain goats.

Do not try to squelch a sneeze and emit a short, girlish squeak. Emissions happen; forget your guilty religious upbringing. Use a napkin or closed fist to temper such utterances. If coughs continue, simply leave the room; if tickles persist, go in for a lung biopsy.

HICCOUGHS

Be vigilant and don't make the record books. Charles Osbourne began hiccoughing in 1922, continuing to hiccough every 1½ seconds, and didn't stop until February 1990, dying a year later. Hold your breath, have a drink of water, and cure hiccoughs quickly. For yogis and the mentally limber, practice mind-over-body control to end spasms. Otherwise, head for the bench away from the action. Those unlucky souls with cartoonish, crescendoing reports should expect good-natured ribbing and name-calling.

Incidentally, for humor's sake, collect a few hiccough-curing old wives' tales—tongue pulling, sugar swallowing, lemon biting, tummy rubbing, or brown bag hyperventilating—as desperate people will agree to do anything when afflicted. If at the cinema, suggest the hiccougher overstuff his mouth with buttery popcorn until breathing is labored and then insert one Milk Dud for good measure. While this procedure may prove ineffective, it is delicious.

GASEOUS EMISSIONS

Flatulence should generally be ignored. Don't accentuate the effect with "whoops" or wild exclamations, unless humor of the moment dictates. Always attempt to blame any odor on a hapless pet, nearby restaurant dumpster, or faceless skunk. Note that it is acceptable for auto passengers to dispel spirits by efficiently rolling down the window and just as quickly rolling it back up. Lastly, never adjust body posture more than ten degrees in mixed company to accommodate dispersion.

VOMITUS

Most of your technique was likely perfected in college, along with a well-honed Spidey-sense auguring its onset. For an adult, expelling is a rare event. As a guest, have the decency not to unload on white carpets, fluffy bath mats, or sleeping pets. To prevent supreme embarrassment during formal events, maintain a full belly, as there is nothing as hapless as a lush spewing in a tuxedo. In public, exorcise amidst shrubbery or in the shadows between two parked cars. When a fuzzy morning at the office takes a turn, use the hallway slop sink/mop closet for ultimate privacy.

PART THREE

The
POTENT
GENTLEMAN

Chapter Seven

VENERABLE
VICES:

ALCOHOL, TOBACCO
& FIREWORKS

◆ ◆ ◆ ◆ ◆ ◆ ◆

Spirits 183
Beyond & Tonic 190
Concocting 193
The Solitary Drink 198
Oenophilia 199
Bubbly 206
Saké 208
Working with a Hangover 210
The Ethic of Alcohol 211
Tobacco 214
Drugs 218
Leaves of Grass 219
Gaming 222
Golf 224
Card Playing 228
The Ponies 231

SPIRITS

The true inability to drive safely or complete a sentence is impolite, but the appreciation of liquors off the usual depth chart is rather gentlemanly. Most college graduates matriculated with a major in malted barley studies and a minor in Russian appreciation. There is no reason to stop slurping vodka or knocking back beers, but the blooming palate and keen mind mandate an occasional tour through the higher spirits. Broaden your horizons and liver oxidation. Know the proper time for an afternoon Lillet, between-the-acts Armagnac, dessert Porto, or late-evening Madeira.

Below is a short list of underexplored, remarkable favorites and the easiest ways to indulge in them. For home-bar enthusiasts, these spirits are ideal shelf stock and will keep your decanters brimming. Put your flask to task, guided by the noted portability factors, from zero to five stars. Percentages refer to alcohol by volume (A.B.V.).

CHARTREUSE (YELLOW OR GREEN)

Unlike the Colonel's 11, Chartreuse is distilled by Carthusian monks with 130 herbs and spices. In 1605, François Hannibal d'Estrées bequeathed to the Carthusian elders an ancient manuscript entitled "The Elixir of Long Life." Brother Maubec undertook the task of deciphering the complexities, but died before finishing. On his deathbed, he disclosed all secrets to Brother Antoine, who finished the translation in 1737. During the French Revolution in 1789, the monks fled the monastery with the manuscript and the secret formula. Napoleon's henchmen, the Secret Remedies Commission, captured the document but rejected the recipe as too complex. Besides Waterloo, this was Napoleon's silliest mistake. Only three monks from this silent order know the secret formula.

Green Chartreuse is a modern ancestor of the original formula and gets its distinctive color from chlorophyll. At 55%, the beguiling green elixir is minty, spicy, and intensely aromatic. In 1838, yellow Chartreuse was produced. At 40%, its color is derived from saffron. This milder Chartreuse is sweeter, lighter, honeyed, and more viscous. Vieillissement Exceptionnellement Prolongé (V.E.P.) is an extra-aged version of green or yellow Chartreuse and is the most mesmerizing liquor these authors know. Drink it with nothing but rocks.

For the uninitiated, sample either yellow or green Chartreuse over ice with tonic or soda, perhaps a dose of cranberry. Next, move to the Alaska: yellow, gin, dry vermouth, and bitters, with a touch of soda and a cherry. The Bijou is a cool-weather classic: green, gin, sweet vermouth, bitters, and a cherry (and some juice), with a twist.

Flask factor ★, *not a moveable spirit.*

LILLET (BLANC OR ROUGE)

This flavorful French aperitif wine is from Potensac, southeast of Bordeaux. Like a jaunt with a learner's permit, Lillet privileges are revoked after dusk. Only 17%, Lillet is an excellent afternoon refresher served on the rocks, splashed with soda and squeezed with lime. Lillet blanc is light and honeyed, with hints of orange, made from Sauvignon Blanc and Sémillon grapes. Lillet rouge is fuller-bodied and sharper, with a grapey fruitiness. Blended from Merlot and Cabernet Sauvignon grapes, it's agreeable over ice with an orange slice or twist.

Flask factor 0, *needs chill.*

PASTIS

Overcome your childlike distaste for black jellybeans and try pastis, the licorice and aniseed-based Marseilles thirst-quencher. Heavy absinthe use in nineteenth-century Paris was rumored to cause absinthism (insanity) and Impressionism. When the fun burst, *la fée verte* (the green fairy) was banned in the Western world. Ricard and Pernod are its modern, law-abiding grandchildren. At over 40%, pastis is for sunny afternoons outdoors. Drink pastis with cold water and some sugar, or with fresh orange juice, soda, and a dash of grenadine. A drop of pastis adds an herbaceous twinge to fruity vodka or gin highballs.

Flask factor ★, *served neat it's too potent.*

SINGLE-MALT SCOTCH

Go beyond Dad's Chivas. Single-malt Scotch is so named because it's the product of a single distillery. Malted barley used for single-malt Scotch is double distilled and not blended or vatted with other whisky. (Blended whiskys are typically the product of several single-malts from different distilleries assembled into a smoother, lighter blend.) The Highland peaks supply much of the water, the coveted lifeblood of Scotch that wends over granite, peat moss, and heather. Melted snow never tasted so good, especially with haggis. There are four notable Scotch-producing regions, each with its own distinctive style of single malt: Lowland (light in color and flavor), Islay (heavy peat, full-bodied), Highland (balanced, most popular), and Campbeltown (also full-bodied).

All Scotches are made from sprouted barley dried in kilns fired by peat and coal, which infuses the whisky with smoky characteristics. Color comes from wood aging. Most casks are retired bourbon barrels; others are leftover from sherry and Madeira houses.

A few stylish examples: Lagavulin 16 (Islay—grassy, dry, smoky, complex; sherry wood gives extra fruit); Highland Park 12 (Highlands—malty, heathery, understated smokiness; exceptionally smooth); Auchentoshan 10 (Lowland—light and zesty, with lemongrass and vanilla); Springbank 15 (Campbeltown—salty, dry, malt-rich, and complex).

Single-malt demands to be drunk neat or with a diluting splash of water, but a few cubes are fine. For Scotch and soda, stick to blends.

Incidentally, a spelling lesson: whisky without the "ey" demarks Scotch and Canadian varieties. Whiskey with the "ey" is used by Irish and American distilleries (Maker's Mark Whisky is a notable exception).

Flask factor ★ ★ , ★ ★ ★ *if you bring a second flask for branch water.*

ITALIANI

The Romans conquered the world with might and appetite. Tuaca is a 500-year-old spirit based on cask-aged brandy. At 35%, it's a delicious compromise between potent whiskeys and sweet liqueurs. With tons of vanilla, spice, and butterscotch, it's like a kid's Halloween goodie bag. Try it neat, with an espresso, or in lieu of a favored brown liquor.

Grappa is Italy's rags-to-riches *eau de vie*—it starts as humble grape skins left for dead, and is then resurrected in hand-blown bottles. Most lump it with tequila and kerosene for palatability, but the best examples (anything over $20 from Jacopo Poli) are delicate, aromatic *digestivi*.

Flask factor ★ ★ ★ ★ ★ *for Tuaca—there's something about the taste of vanilla and pewter;* ★ *for grappa.*

ARMAGNAC

Cognac's tawdry older sister from southwest France. This full-flavored brandy dates back to fifteenth-century Pays d'Gascogne (Gascony). Many of its producers are still rural artisans, not behemoth corporations, so lesser known means better value. Made from a blend of distilled grapes, Armagnac is continuously stilled and aged in black oak, a method that yields a more rustic character than does the pot-still process responsible for Cognac's smooth richness. Armagnac is more intense, with jagged flavors of chocolate, wood, and fruit. Since caramel isn't added, Armagnac is paler than Cognac. Look for quality and age demarcations: V.S. (very special), V.S.O.P. (very special old pale), X.O. (extra old, over six years). Drink Armagnac in a snifter, but don't bury your nose in the glass, lest you get a wasabi-like nasal singe. Enjoy it at home with a cigar.

Flask factor ★ ★ , *pricey and meant for glass, not metal.*

CALVADOS

It was too cold to grow grapes in Normandy, so ingenious northern Frenchmen cultivated apple groves instead. Not just a land of applesauce, Pays d'Auge is the home of Calvados, a prized apple brandy. Quality is denoted according to oak aging. On the label, "Réserve" indicates three years, "Vieille Réserve" or "V.S.O.P." is four years, and "Hors d'Age" is six years or more in wood. Younger Calvados exudes more appley fruit forwardness; the aged versions are imparted with the oaken characteristics of vanilla and spice. The bouquet is intoxicating, the mouth feel is soft, and the finish is warming. Fans of cider open to winter exploration should drop their Schnapps and pull up a nose.

At 40%, Calvados is a sipping spirit. Réserves belong neat or on the rocks. With younger bottles, try the inimitable Calvados Cocktail: Calvados, Cointreau, orange juice, dash bitters, a squeeze of lemon juice, and a splash of soda, stirred on the rocks.

Flask factor ★ ★ ★ ★ ★ , *the height of wintry flasking.*

PORTO

When dessert is nothing but the glass in front of you, sip port. Ruby, tawny, and white ports are aged in oak casks and blended for balance. Ruby is bottled fresh and fruity; the name is derived from its color. Tawny is so named for its color, too, as years in wood turn port a golden brown. Made from white grapes, white port is a rarer style and perfect as a chilled aperitif. Vintage port is the best of its kind. Declared vintages occur only a few times per decade; rather than a blend of different years, a vintage port is made up of grapes from one harvest. Aged in the bottle, not in wood, vintage ports require simple decanting skills to separate wine from sediment. L.B.V. (Late Bottled Vintage) is a wine that was left in its cask for most of a decade, and then bottled for immediate consumption.

For port, no special cordial glasses are necessary; use smaller wine glasses. Poured properly, a bottle yields over ten servings. Port's balanced sweetness and acidity pairs well with pungent cheeses like Stilton.

Nice touch: Pouring, a port punctilio: port is passed to the left. In the formal setting, the host fills the glass to his right, fills his own, and then passes the bottle clockwise.

Flask factor ★ ★ ★ *(nonvintage), port-able sophistication.*

SHERRY

A fortified wine, sherry isn't just for cooking or for Grandma's liquor cabinet. True sherry only comes from Jerez, a small city in Andalucía, Spain. A sherry's quality remains constant year after year due to the Solera System, which requires mixing new wines with older vintages. It's said that new wine gives the old some freshness as old wine teaches the new its character.

The following several varieties of sherry can be drunk before or after dinner: fino (light and very dry; serve chilled), amontillado (darker and nuttier), Manzanilla (pungent, yet delicate), oloroso (sweeter and potent), and cream sherry (sweetest—look for high-quality dark cream, not artificially sweetened light cream). Judging quality versus price, sherry is considered by some to be the greatest value in all of wine. Still, plenty of plonk exists, so seek assistance at the package store.

Flask factor ★ ★ ★ ★, *try amontillado on Edgar Allan Poe's birthday.*

MADEIRA

Port gets all the press, but Madeira is what the founding fathers drank when they signed the Constitution. In the 1600s, ships from the East Indies stopped at Madeira, a small island southwest of Portugal. Ships were loaded with wine that would often spoil due to heat exposure and the turbulence of long voyages. Madeira, though, improved with abuse. Today, *estufas,* or large, outdoor hot rooms, mimic those squalid conditions. Four distinct types of Madeira are produced: Sercial (light, pale, and nutty); Verdelho (medium dry and smoky), Bual (medium sweet and raisiny), and the nearly indestructible Malmsey (full bodied, dark, and rich), which can last a century. Poured like port, drier Madeiras make excellent aperitifs. Older Madeiras are a graceful end to a sensual meal. "Rainwater" denotes a lightly fruity Madeira best served with a slight chill as an aperitif. The name is derived from a legend that casks left out in the rain for shipment to Savannah, Georgia, absorbed water through the wood, which yielded a pleasing, if diluted wine.

Flask factor ★ ★ ★ ★, *ten-year-old Bual, especially.*

Incidentally, other sipping wines to serve as dessert include Banyuls, Marsala, Sauternes, Trockenbeerenauslese, and Hungarian Tokay.

BEYOND & TONIC

[the whimsical   drink umbrella]

Bellying up to the bar is a call to imagination. Spicy conversations and saucy companions warrant something more titillating than fill-in-the-blank and tonic. A bartender's toys are the gentleman's booze jukebox. Mix it up. An interesting order makes a barkeep reach beyond the insipid speed rail of cliché cocktails and house-brand liquors. Exploration is a function of availability, season, and mood. While there's nothing wrong with the ol' familiar, don't let a highball of habit leave you in a single-minded rut.

Wetting one's whistle should be celebrated for the experience, not merely the effects. Ever had Chartreuse? What goes with rum besides cola? Read a vintage cocktail book, study some labels, and sate bottle curiosities with frequent doses of experimentation. There are countless original drinks that employ Triple Sec, fresh juices, apricot brandy, and grenadine. Write down a few recipes and buy bottles for mixing yourself; it is difficult to remember drink recipes without having made them first-hand. Start modestly. Adopt a pet liquor for the month and use the bottle for home concocting. The mad mixologist is overkill, but trying a few martini substitutes expands one's liquid horizons.

AVAILABILITY

With some successful home-bar experiments under the belt, a gentleman's barroom adventure begins with a survey of shelves and scene. Choices are first narrowed by what bottles are displayed. Unlike trips to the shoe department, there is no checking in the back for exotic stock. Survey the collection for areas of focus (like a bevy of small-batch bourbons), ethnic themes (a cluster of tequilas), and signs of a bar's good taste (a printed menu of spirits or specialty drinks).

If you see the proper ingredients, politely ask the bartender to make your drink. After pouring the thousandth vodka and tonic that night, a bartender will happily oblige. However, this is no time to play "Stump the Bartender" with quizzical drinks. A Pousse-Café, for example, has six ingredients, and the intricate layering is ordinarily too much to ask of a busy barkeep. Most joints are unfortunately not equipped with egg whites or rose water. In short, don't assume high aptitude or deep stocks and know the recipe before requesting an obscure drink. Don't just order a Sazerac and shrug when the bar is jammed six deep with low-brows screaming for Lowenbräu. Be prepared to recite the ingredients to the barkeep and request the proper garnish. He or she will be happy to learn a new drink for the repertoire. Tip extra for cooperation and offer a sip.

ODE TO THE MANHATTAN

Crave its bourbon-brunette hues, subtle vermouth-enhanced viscosity, and the lustful cherry treasure buried deep in the conic crux of the glass. Note how the bartender prepares the drink: is it shaken until beads of cold sweat fall from the tumbler, or is the ice barely introduced to the booze? When properly mixed with extra bitters and quality Italian vermouth (Carpano, the hard-to-find favorite), a tantalizing slick of Manhattan rapture and fading bubbles flows to the lips. Bypass house labels in favor of premium bourbon, and you'll soon share an experienced martini drinker's penchant for brand loyalty and intermittent experimentation.

Incidentally, adventurousness aside, certain venues are so loud and crowded that bartenders don't have the time to fulfill strange requests. When ordering for five or more people, keep it simple or get a table.

SEASON

Cure cocktail indecision by looking to the weather. In the warmer months, thirst-quenching concoctions are de rigueur. For July quaffs, employ summer fruits and the blender, but lighten the hand. Heavy consumption and lengthy bouts of sunshine require a moderate pace. Don't wallop a crowd with a potent first serving when a steady poolside buzz is in order.

Whereas convertibles and gulpable pitchers full of margaritas match nicely, slow-sipping fixatives ward off the snowy side of a calendar. Tall, fruity frozen drinks don't belong in a gent's December glass unless he's on holiday in the tropics. In cooler climes, tip the bottle steeper; long nights and low mercury beg warming, mighty spirits in more delicate glassware. Contemplative cordials (Marsala) and heady liqueurs (Bénédictine) in snifters are a gentleman's antifreeze. Think clear (rum, gin) in the summer and brown (bourbon, brandy) in the winter.

MIDNIGHT SPECIALS

This is the time of night when just knowing a quirky drink name is enough to sate a drunken inclination for a something-something: a cocktail of interest to break the rhythm, a capper. Show your diversity and imagination. Shout for a Harvey Wallbanger, pine for a Stinger, refresh with a Campari and soda. Recognize when it's time for the unwise shot. After midnight ("I shouldn't be having a drink, let alone tequila"), salt placement is commensurate with levels of intimacy.

MOOD

A constellation of present company, sonic environment, time of day, budget, and location, mood is the final factor in drink selection. When the boss is buying a round of pints, for instance, skip the top-shelf single malt. High-impact cardiovascular dance halls might find a clear spirit in your hand, while sultry cafés beg something darker and undiluted. Mood can cast a carefree veto upon an otherwise logical choice; the frivolous mind musters a Monday happy-hour Mojito while coworkers slug draught beer. One's attire also influences the selection process: brandy befits tweed slacks, while tattered dungarees deserve a frosty mug.

CONCOCTING

Just as drinking rookies seek out the anodynic properties of vodka (liquor so versatile it goes splendidly with tonic, juice, and most flavors of Gatorade), home-bar pretenders eschew the shaker for tepid prefab mixes that require little more than ice. The booze-crafty gent takes charge of fixing, mixing, and pouring and makes deft use of distillates in imaginative concoctions. Once you've reached martini curiosity, master a few vintage favorites and hone a feel for what goes together.

Guests appreciate a homemade Scotch and soda, but why not bestow a novel drink? Hand off living-room hosting to an able first mate so you can wrestle in the kitchen with tools that sound like Batman villains: the muddler, the jigger, and the strainer. No matter how cold the frosty shaker, grip with vim and hold on like a wing walker. You've arrived as a home concoctionist when a tumbler full of drinks requires service of the reamer, lemon spout, citrus stripper, or bar spoon.

SETTING UP THE HOME BAR

The home bar evolves from an above-the-fridge cabinet to a specially appointed furnishing or buddy-built bar with matching stools. An outlay of $150 to $200 will open your home bar for business. Start with your favorites from our list of essentials: reputable bourbon, top-shelf gin, upscale vodka, sipping Scotch, generic Triple Sec, mixing tequila and gold rum, apricot brandy, and one sexy cordial (Grand Marnier, Armagnac, or Calvados). Upgrade and deepen the collection as bottles empty, tastes evolve, and investment accounts fatten.

Besides the staples, stock some festive accessories: themed cocktail napkins; picks, straws, and stir sticks; jarred garnishes (olives, cherries, onions); and wacky drink umbrellas. Antique and thrift store decanters beautifully display your premium liquors.

CLUB SODA

King of the "big three" mixers, club soda is new-car fresh and crisp as a laundered collar, an easy cocktail topper and dimmer switch for adjusting potency. Classic recipes routinely urge a leaden pour short on mixers: assuage the sting with a touch of club. Short out of the tumbler? A jazz of soda at the top of a Collins glass keeps the garnish from languishing unseen below the rim. Stumped for mixing ideas? Fine liquors over ice with club soda are a simple, rare-miss creation. Soda regulates mood and mode. Depending on crowd impairment and lateness of evening, adjust high-octane drinks with a splash of soda, added after shaking to preserve effervescence. A hot, lingering afternoon begs refreshing, bubbly quaffs. Hesitant imbibers need a lighter hand; the first drink of a long night should allow the palate to soften. Lastly, club soda with lime is an acceptable lunchtime alternative to iced tea and makes a presentable hand-filler for the teetotaler.

Incidentally, half-empty cube trays will not keep pace with a summertime gathering over blender drinks. The forward-thinking host picks up a spare bag of ice before guests arrive.

MIXERS & MISCELLANY

Fresh juices, especially citrus, compensate for any recipe imbalances by smoothing out a distillate's rough edges. Sweeten the bracing pucker of sours with a splash of orange juice or tip the jar of maraschino cherries into a drink that needs some color. While tonic water tempers stiffness, too much quinine is an Amazonian clear-cutting of taste. Despite fitness proclivities, diet cola and energy drinks are not proper mixers. Ginger ale makes a fine companion to bourbon or rye. For expert play, shake a cocktail to a frothy finish by adding an egg white.

SEASONAL VARIATIONS

When shade is a commodity or activity is furious, a tray full of Manhattans is the wrong cure. Instead, look to the fruit bowl for tonier ideas and colorful medleys. Muddling is the best method of rescuing the last two strawberries and other fruit refugees trapped in the crisper. Don't limit yourself: blueberries, mangoes, peaches, and kiwis form the perfect

SUMMER MUDDLING RECIPE (serves 4)

◆ ◆ ◆ ◆ ◆ **4 shots premium vodka or rum** ◆ **2 shots Triple Sec** ◆ ◆ ◆ ◆ ◆
◆ ◆ ◆ ◆ ◆ ◆ **Dash crème de cassis** ◆ **Seasonal fruits** ◆ ◆ ◆ ◆ ◆ ◆

base to gin or rum muddling expeditions. Seasonal drinks are guaranteed crowd pleasers, as most bars don't use fresh fruit. Freshly plucked mint ignites late afternoon revelry every time, whether in Mojitos, Juleps, French 75s, or Harry's Cocktails.

Nice touch: Enliven any home-bar experience with a snappy soda siphon for a lovely accent of fizz pizzazz.

INTUITIVE MIXING

Often, time is short or the crowd undiscerning—a drink is desired lickety-split. There is no time for formal recipes, outlandish flambés, and origamic garnishes. Like a good cook, the booze maestro isn't beholden to the measuring jigger and occasionally dabbles in tasty improvisation. Opt for a few versatile liquors, such as rum or vodka, add some mixers, and fill the tumbler. Even without the Mr. Boston's guide, turn a friend's odd fridge full of pineapple chunks, guava nectar, lime wedges, bottle of pop, and pint of Jim Beam into a spontaneous, original punch. A touch of dry vermouth rounds out a gin drink, while Cointreau and lemon juice mix with almost anything. A hit of fruit juice or ginger ale adds tang. But beware: a heavy-handed pour of crème de menthe (white

═══ WINTER MUDDLING RECIPE (serves 4) ═══

4 shots gin or bourbon ✦ 4 dashes bitters ✦ Touch of dry and sweet vermouths
1 large shot Grand Marnier ✦ Seasonal fruits ✦ A few drops of chocolate
✦ ✦ ✦ Magic Shell will solidify on the surface as dark floating droplets. ✦ ✦ ✦

or green) smacks of blue mouthwash. When reloading, don't be afraid to give the used glasses a scant rinse, reuse the cocktail spears, and, if pressed, allow a twist to make an encore. Experimentation aside, don't overdo; mishmashes and Long Island Iced Tea clones are toxic.

MARY AND THE MUDDLER

An oft-ignored bar tool, the muddler is best known for squashing orange slices with sugar and bitters to form the base of an Old Fashioned. At home, a simple mortar and pestle or small spice pummeler will suffice.

Muddling is for the supreme concoctionist, someone who delights in the blending of light liquors and colorful fruits. Where ordinary quaffs merely rush across the tongue and pass by the teeth, muddled cocktails carry the nectar and pulp of fruits, compelling a deliberate pause in the mouth. Crushed fruit offsets the fire of the alcohol with supple body and a chewy-textured mash.

=====   **BLOODY MARY** (serves 1, in a 24-ounce mason jar)   =====

3 or more shots vodka ✦ **Fill glass halfway with tomato juice** ✦ $2/3$ tsp. spicy yellow mustard, stir vigorously ✦ **Several healthy splashes Worcestershire sauce** ✦ **Large lemon and lime wedges wrung and dropped in glass** ✦ **Repeated splashes Tabasco to taste** ✦ **Healthy sprinkling celery salt (the vital ingredient)** ✦ **Light dusting black pepper** ✦ **Stir and sniff to gauge strength and amount of ice or juice needed for dilution** ✦ **Top with tomato juice and more ice, if necessary** ✦ **Stir with a firm and fresh celery stalk; leave in glass** ✦ **Final splash of dry sherry, if available.**

Muddling requires two tumblers, "A" and "B." In tumbler A, muddle the fruit: soft seasonal choices such as ripe pear, watermelon, peach, or thawed frozen berries. Prepare the alcohol in tumbler B. Shake, then strain B into the fruit-filled A, marinating the fruit in the chilled booze. Strain tumbler A into your guests' frosty martini glasses, filling halfway. With your bar spoon, distribute the remaining pulpy mash evenly into the half-filled vessels. Top with a bubbly mixer and garnish with a colorful parasol or swizzle stick. Short of kitchen supplies? Enlist a Tibetan singing bowl and the back of a flashlight as muddling apparati.

THE SOLITARY DRINK

I like bars just after they open for the evening.
When the air inside is still cool and clean and everything is shining
and the barkeep is giving himself that last look in the mirror
to see if his tie is straight and his hair is smooth.
I like the neat bottles on the bar back and the
lovely shining glasses and the anticipation. I like to watch the man mix
the first one of the evening and put it down on a crisp mat and
put the little folded napkin beside it. I like to taste it slowly.
The first quiet drink of the evening in a quiet bar—that's wonderful.

—RAYMOND CHANDLER, *THE LONG GOODBYE*

Frequent consumption of cocktails with only the company of Jack, Jim, or Johnnie is problematic. Nonetheless, the occasional solitary drink, or three, in the taproom in the late afternoon is a solid, gentlemanly prelude to a bustling evening. Where else can one check out the afternoon baseball scores and Tour de France times, or inhale the atmosphere of screwdriver-swilling pensioners amidst the ether of generic cigarettes?

Steer clear of trendy brewpubs or restaurant lounges: the ideal afternoon is spent among struggling actors and service staffers, with just the right touch of atmospheric grunge. If you hear strains of idling Allman Brothers songs or potluck R&B, step right in. After a lazy half day of work, recline and order a bottled beer or a sipping bourbon. Contemplate and dust off the Pernod like so many expats. The bar is probably empty, save a few other gentlemen. Pocket the flirtation and steal some "me time."

This is a great time to pen a letter or prepare your upcoming best man speech. Stretch out with a hobby magazine or tabloid. Recline unabashedly, savor the surrounding sights: the peeling liquor labels, a leather-jacketed woman chalking her pool cue, and later, the restroom-stall prose. Treat this thirsty sojourn as your little secret, like that late-night soft-core adult feature you ordered on the last business trip.

OENOPHILIA

To drink wine is to sip of the land and its time. For the youngest wines, like Beaujolais Nouveau, pouring a glass means quaffing juice that's a mere few weeks old. In the oldest bottles, wine is a time capsule that offers vintage mouthfuls of long-past decades. It is astonishingly poetic that one can read the Declaration of Independence while drinking liquid crafted in the same year.

LABELS

Deduce the juice from the label. In the supermarket aisle, where bag-in-box jug wines crowd out premium bottles, it is the oenophile's onus to distinguish the nonpareil from the dreck. Like sexy covers in the record shop, labels are the first eye-catcher. A revealing one tells where and when the wine was made, the types of grapes used, the alcohol percentage, the officially designated quality (Appellation Contrôlée, Vino da Tavola), and even the level of dryness or sweetness (Brut, Demi-Sec, Late Harvest). Take time to examine the bottle, even if after emptying it.

RETAIL

Trips to the vinous retailer bolster confidence the next time a waiter drops the wine list in your lap. Without the pressure of picking a bottle before the nightly specials are recited, stroll around four continents, in five aisles or less. Are the wines arranged by region, varietal, or price? Engage the professionals and look for shelf tags that offer tasting notes or ratings. Brush up on wine vocabulary and be specific—light or full bodied, fruit or oak driven, soft or crisp? "I'm baking a ham for my anniversary," offers far more clues than, "I dunno, something good and red." This is not an auction (yet) and if budget's a concern, say up front how much you're willing to spend. Give the pros a chance to point out the best values.

> *Don't say too much about the wine being "sound" or "pleasant":*
> *people will think you have simply been mugging up a wine-merchant's catalogue.*
> *It is a little better to talk in broken sentences and say, "It has. . .don't you think?"*
>
> *Or, "It's a little bit cornery," or something equally random like, "Too many*
> *tramlines." I use this last phrase because it passes the test of the boldly meaningless.*

—STEPHEN POTTER, *ONE-UPMANSHIP*

CHOOSING

Red or white, no wine is better with a region's cuisine than its own wine. Outside of food, season and mood dictate selections. In the cool climes, bold, rich reds warm the belly. Dip into big Rhône styles from France and Australia for a deep taste of Syrah/Shiraz, Grenache, and Mourvèdre. Barolo, Barbaresco, and Amarone are Italy's answers to a blustery night. California offers young, ripe wines like Zinfandel for connoisseurs who can't wait ten years for a bottle to mellow. Lighter reds pair well with poultry and hearty salads: Gamay, Pinot Noir, and Dolcetto. Bordeaux and Burgundy deliver old-world complexity and character when the professor's in town for a steak dinner, and Spain's lush Rioja begs for nights of tapas and tango. For value, uncork up-and-comers from Chile, Argentina, and South Africa. Languedoc-Roussillon and the Pacific Northwest earn impressive marks without inflated prices.

For whites, appetites are best whetted with crisp, mineraly Loire Valley Sancerre, New Zealand Sauvignon Blanc, and dry sparkling wines. Spicy foods and hot conversations love aromatic, spicy whites: Gewürztraminer and Pinot Gris from Alsace, Viognier from the Rhône, and Albariño from Spain. The "ABC" rule of "anything but Chardonnay" is good advice when you want to avoid mismatching creamy, full-bodied whites with casual porch sipping and a delicate ceviche. For grilled swordfish, white Burgundies from France are a finesse-oriented class of Chardonnays; for buttery notes, head to California and Australia.

A note on off-dry wines and the misconstrued rosé: little in the world of wine is as pleasant on a mid-July afternoon as a glass of Tavel. Dry rosés offer gorgeous hues ranging from salmon to cinnamon, and refreshing fruit. The low alcohol and clean finish of a Lirac, Australian White Grenache, or rosé from Provence pleases the palate without weighing down the senses. Off-dry whites are lovely alternatives to tart wines with bracing acidity. Wander through bottles of Vouvray, German halbtrocken, and Argentinian Torrontes for a grapey, honeyed fix.

Incidentally, wine isn't all France and Napa Valley. When in Long Island's South Fork or the Finger Lakes, visit a local winery and try New York's *vitis vinifera.* Taste what Jefferson loved about Virginia. Don't miss a riverside detour out of St. Louis into Missouri wine country, where indigenous American grapes and curious hybrids are hidden gems.

OPINING

Feigned wine smarts are transparent. In the store, demonstrate knowledge and interest by asking questions ("How about something Chilean?") or referencing a recent article ("What's the difference between Syrah and Petite Sirah?"). In the dining room, avoid being the talky bombast. Friends appreciate a quick résumé of a wine region, but avoid puffing, "Willamette Valley? Tut tut, who drinks wine from Oregon?" If uneducated, treat wine like museum art and use your creative

B.Y.O.

For special occasions, it's a delight to pack a bottle you've been maturing in the cellar. For tiny trattorias without a liquor license, toting a smooth Brunello di Montalcino is encouraged. Call ahead and inquire as to the corkage fee. Gladly fork over a ten to fifteen dollar tariff for the right to import your own gem, but never show up with a substandard bottle or one that's already on the list. This option is for expressing taste, not whittling down the tab. Offer the server a glass from a hard-to-resist vintage and often the fee is waived.

senses. Comment on radiant hues, aromas, or how the wine feels on the tongue. While an untrained nose might not discern a Pouilly-Fumé from a Pinot Gris at ten paces, a humble enthusiast can still spot richness of color and taste, and voice an opinion.

RESTAURANT

After untimed practice rounds in retail, give the restaurant ritual a run. Encourage a round of aperitifs so you can flip through an expansive, leather-bound catalogue. Whatever the occasion, wines should be as well dressed as the company. Apportion the wine budget like an extra guest: for a couple enjoying a $100 meal, ante up at least a U.S. Grant for the bottle; pizza outings call for a $12 carafe of the house red if the company decides against pitchers of beer. A bottle equals five glasses, although as many as seven smaller servings can be divided when necessary.

Incidentally, modest pours, especially for the first glass of a bottle, allow the wine to breathe and open up. Appreciate how a wine's aroma and character develop over the course of a bottle.

Scratch-n-Sniff. The steward announces the bottle to confirm your selection—check the year against the vintage you ordered. No need to be a thermometer-wielding fusspot, but if reds are too warm or whites numbingly cold, ask the server for another bottle. Examining the cork is your chance to inspect storage conditions. Give a squeeze. A moist cork halfsoaked with wine is better than a dry, brittle plug, although neither are telltale signs of health or damage. Ordinarily, there is no need to smell the cork, but historic and otherwise interesting bottles might warrant a sniff.

The short pour that follows is the real test. Swirl to volatilize the esters and release the bouquet, and then smell the wine. Most times, a deep sniff is enough to detect a fault. If still unsure, take a sip. This is not the scorer's table with tableside spit buckets; the initial pour determines the wine's potability, not likeability. A gesture or kind word signals acceptance ("Yes, it's lovely"). Rounds of table wine don't necessitate a glassware change, but insist on fresh stems for remarkable bottles.

Sending It Back. A delicate deed, sending back a dud is by no means taboo. Approximately three in a hundred bottles are faulty, but the majority go undetected. Look for clues: a raised, moldy cork or leaky

---

EXPLORING VINO D'ITALIA

With a string of amazing vintages since 1995, the fruits of Enotria are garnering more attention than Cicciolina, the porn star twice-elected to Italian parliament. For squid-ink-risotto rookies, here's your vino crib sheet.

In Piemonte, venerable Nebbiolo grapes give rise to Barolo's age-worthy machismo and Barbaresco's sexy succulence. Barbera has bounteous earth tones, hints of currant, and bright acidity, and Dolcetto's grapey softness is the pinnacle of gourmet-pizza wine. Molto-affordable Arneis is an underrated aromatic Chardonnay alternative. In Veneto, a trio of grapes makes the fruity Valpolicella and the seductive Amarone. In Toscana, famous for its Chianti, plentiful Sangiovese grapes are also vinified into the elegant Brunello di Montalcino and a host of pricey super-Tuscans (usually boutique-style blends that offend locals but please the auction crowd: look for names ending in *aia* like Ornellaia, Sassicaia). After dinner, dip your biscotti into a sherrylike Vin Santo. Italy's boot heel, Puglia, boasts Zinfandel's forefather, Primitivo. In Sardegna, Vermentino is perfect for picnics and Pinot Grigio fans, while Sicilia reemerges with Nero d'Avola and Marsala that delights more than veal cutlets.

capsule indicates heat damage. White (tartaric) crystals, sediment, and harmless crumbs of cork are not faults, but beware strong scents of Madeira or sherry in unfortified wines, which point toward noxious oxidation. Musty, wet-newspaper vapors indicate undrinkable corked wine. When suspicions arise, summon the steward and offer the glass. "What do you think?" is more polite than an acerbic rejection.

Incidentally, if the sommelier recommends a bottle based on your stated preferences, sip early before a poorly matched wine becomes an albatross on your table.

EQUIPMENT

The impassioned wino enjoys the accoutrements of enthusiasm. Nevertheless, don't gussy up a limp wine collection with state-of-the-art lever pulls and hydraulic cork extractors. A decent opener with a rim fulcrum and knife will do. Bottle coasters and neck rings protect table linens, and stem charms help guests track waylaid glasses. An ice bucket is a must for the avid Champagne drinker, and a decanter serves both aesthetic and utilitarian purposes.

Glassware is most important. What a travesty to see a fabulous bottle poured into a substandard vessel, with no room for the wine to breathe! Glasses without stems and large bowls do not fully express a wine's characteristics. Skeptics may scream, but the otherwise-mercurial winemakers of the planet agree. . .make it crystal and make it Riedel. This Austrian family has been blowing glass for generations and has designed stemware for nearly every varietal. Their Champagne flute is shaped to preserve the bubbles, while the red Burgundy glass offers a bowl big enough for a small child to bathe in.

BUBBLY

Swirl the sparkling wine in a thin, tulip-shaped flute and appraise the star-bright color—does it register in green hues or bronze tints? Stick your nose into the glass and inhale the full aroma. Take a generous sip, swish it around, and feel the prickly tingle. Note the clean acid, fresh fruit, and soft, foamy mousse. Admire the hint of chalk and balanced aftertaste. These are the distinctive sensations of Champagne.

Champagne is a region in France; thus, sparkling wines from elsewhere must be called by another name. In Spain, it's Cava; in Italy, Franciacorta, Prosecco, or Spumante; Germany makes Sekt; other countries simply call their bubblies "sparkling wine." All Champagne is made according to a traditional process in which still wine, aided by the addition of sugar and yeast, undergoes a secondary fermentation in the actual bottle. The *prise de mousse* (capturing the sparkle) ensues as yeast activity causes carbon dioxide bubbles to form in the bottle. How do you get the sediment out without losing carbonation? Over the next eight weeks, spent yeast cells are collected in the bottle neck through a laborious process called *reumage,* or riddling, wherein the bottle is slowly inverted by hand. Later, the neck is dipped in ice-cold brine, where the sediment is frozen and disgorged out of the bottle, propelled by trapped carbon dioxide (*dégorgement*). Finally, the winemaker tops up with the *dosage,* a solution of still wine and sugar that determines sweetness and compensates for spilled wine lost in the *dégorgement.* The bottle is recorked and, voila, there is sparkle. To find a bottle made in the same style as Champagne, look for *méthode champenoise* on the label.

Given the cool climate, Champagne producers are forced to blend wines from different years to create palatable nonvintage Champagnes.

Two or three times a decade, however, an exceptionally ripe vintage is declared good enough to stand on its own. Stellar years to look for: 1982, 1985, 1989, and 1990. *Prestige Cuvée* designates longer aging and a house's top bottling: Louis Roederer Cristal, Pol Roger Cuvée Sir Winston Churchill, and Taittinger Comtes de Champagne. Though Moët et Chandon Dom Perignon may be the best known of this class, indulge in these wines for more than their designer names. Baptize yourself in Krug Clos du Mesnil, Billecart-Salmon, Jacquesson, and Salon.

Champagne labels, by law, are quite descriptive:

Blanc de blancs: "White from white," meaning that only Chardonnay grapes were used. Lighter, more floral; best for beginners. Vintage versions have great toasty richness.

Blanc de noirs: "White from black," indicating that only black grapes were used. In Champagne, this means a *cuvée* (blend) of Pinot Noir and Pinot Meunier, although outside of France other grapes are used. Fuller bodied, with more fruit and spice.

Rosé: Either red wine is added or color is extracted from red grape skins. Don't serve to the uninitiated, who might mistake the pink stuff for the house schwag at the Hotel California. At best, rosés are rarer wines with beautiful hues and charming summer-fruit qualities.

Extra brut/brut sauvage: Bone-dry.

Brut: Dry, 1% liqueur (*dosage*) added.

Extra dry: Slightly sweeter than brut.

Extra sec: Dry to medium-dry, 1 to 3% liqueur.

Demi-sec: Medium-sweet, 3 to 5% liqueur.

Doux: Dessert sweet, 8 to 15% liqueur.

Master your opening technique lest you lose precious wine (or an eye) in a Grand Prix gush of fizz. Despite the climactic pop of a fresh bottle, it is correct to ease the cork out gently. A deft touch leaves the bubbles unagitated and sounds of a lover's sigh. Pour slowly: a steady trickle thwarts clumsy overflow. Tough corks may warrant Champagne tweezers, but advanced users should experiment with the Champagne sabre, a ceremonial blade used for beheading bottles.

Champagne that's less than a pair of movie tickets is nonexistent. Fortunately, there's inexpensive sparking wine. Delicious Prosecco and Cava are priced for liberal pouring that requires no more reason to celebrate than a gathering of two over figs and proscuitto. South Africa is getting into bubbly production, and New Zealand has a suitable climate for great sparklers. Australia's sparkling Shiraz has fruity, oaky appeal.

• Don't destroy a delicate *cuvée* with spurts of OJ. Use everyday sparkling wines (something under $12) for mimosas and yacht christenings.

• Stay the fizz: a bottle topper preserves pressure for several more days.

• As an aperitif, bubbles lighten moods and crisp acid whets the appetite. Caviar, oysters, and a hotel key: bubbly at the raw bar is decadence.

SAKÉ

The deep pink softness of *toro* (tuna belly), the rich teriyaki tang of *unagi* (freshwater eel), and the strong, creamy seduction of *uni* (sea urchin). The sensual ambrosia of sushi demands equipotent accompaniment. Don't miss the libation of choice for samurai and the Japanese court: saké.

Brewed like beer, but served like wine, saké is incredibly pure; it rarely contains more than rice, water, yeast, and *koji-kin* (an enzyme). Since the body is spared the impurities that lead to hangovers, an indulgent saké high leads to virtually nil ill effects; you'll know good saké the next morning. Allergic to wine? Saké is a sulfite-free alternative.

Premium saké is served room temperature or with a slight chill, despite what your California roll-chomping friend says. Since excessive heat kills delicate flavors, only the lowest grades of saké are heated. *Hannya-to* (hot wisdom water) has its place, but the automatic machines dispensing overpriced hot saké have restaurant owners laughing to the bank.

Saké is not wine—the sensory qualities are different. A wine with little aroma would be considered substandard and perfect for a meatball hero; however, some sakés fascinate with style and palate impact alone. Besides fragrance, look for a burst in the mouth (quiet to explosive), sweetness or dryness, acidity (soft to puckering), complexity, earthiness (delicate to dank), and the tail (quickly vanishing to pervasive).

Helpful bottles and menus list Saké Meter Values (S.M.V.), a scale of sweetness to dryness from -10 (sweetest) to +10 (driest). ±0 is neutral. For example, *Nigori*-style sakés are sweet and lush, with a S.M.V. of -4 or lower. Roughly filtered and chewy in the mouth, they are the perfect juxtaposition to a mouthful of fleshy sashimi and fiery wasabi.

As with beer, freshness ensures the contents are most expressive. Bottling dates of six months or younger are best; avoid anything over a year old. Most imported sakés use Japanese dating, whereupon year one is the first year of an imperial reign: *Heisei* 13 was bottled in 2001, *Heisei* 14 in 2002, and so on. Domestic brands like Geikkeikan (CA) and SakéOne (OR) offer fresh saké at a good value.

In Japan, it is customary to never pour for yourself. Lift your *ochoko* (small cup), hold it with one hand, and support it with the other. The *masu* is a square cedar box used for traditional saké drinking, and may sometimes contain floating flower petals as though the wind had blown cherry blossoms into the drink. For the sake of saké, appreciate the pure simplicity of an ancient delicacy.

WORKING WITH A HANGOVER

Push for an active social schedule but maintain integrity to your employer by arriving daily in a saleable condition. To be sure, an incredible evening should never be cut short for the sake of prudence, but to give yourself a shot, set a sensible curfew of about 1 to 2 A.M. on school nights. This witching hour allows for adequate fun, five-plus hours of sleep, and a rock-solid gregarious reputation.

Carousing with unimpeded cohorts, career slugabeds, and agendaless *flâneurs* is fraught with danger. Invariably, actors and freelancers boogie deep into the night, staging the inevitable poesy-filled, guitar-playing be-in. This is quitting time for you; otherwise, five beers, two tokes, and three hours later, when dawn is spawning, you will still be there, confused.

Quit dribbling the snooze button. If more than two sick days per year are logged in the name of party overdose, get on the UNOS liver transplant list or drink more water before bed. If necessary, glide into work an hour late with a medical excuse (upset stomach) instead of missing the entire day with a falsified doctor's note.

The key recovery period is the precious, fuzzy hour of morning ablutions. Hydrate, pain-relieve, and swallow some B-12 before a restorative shower. Don't forget to shave, as the stubbly face/baggy eye combo is the telltale mark of an overindulgent sot. During the commute, quell queasiness with a large caffeinated beverage and something croissantlike.

At work, acquaint yourself intimately with the water cooler and keep a low profile. As residual rottenness evaporates, caffeine also aids the passage to lunch. For the advanced, pack a snuff. Ride this energy boost from 10 A.M. until 2 P.M. Place important calls, write urgent letters, and draft more substantial documents just before lunch, while the life force is still rising. Despite the ache to build a pillow-lined fort under your desk, don't squander this artificial spike. Undoubtedly, the late afternoon outbox will be barren from 3:30 P.M. until closing; the hangover itself likely receded before lunch like a soul lightening, but will reemerge like a fever sore. Do your best to endure excruciating yawns and involuntary chair slouching. Have a nice day.

Incidentally, twenty-something earners coasting in disposable jobs are exempt. Unless used as a precursor to a dream career, these McJobs are defined by extended lunches, long-distance personal calls, and furtive Friday afternoon slip-outs.

THE ETHIC OF ALCOHOL

Don't get the idea I'm a boozer. Setting out deliberately to get drunk is pathological. I like to drink just enough to change the temperature in the brain room. I'll turn to less mainstream substances if I want to rearrange the furniture.

—TOM ROBBINS, *FIERCE INVALIDS HOME FROM HOT CLIMATES*

Drinking usually evolves from a curiosity to a cultivated appreciation. Early on, beer is a shining amulet, the quaff of mystical older brothers and those with a fake I.D. For a teenager, drinking turns card games, movie rentals, or hangouts in the woods into joyous rebellion. Into the early twenties, alcohol appreciation widens, hedonistic possibilities surface, and the body becomes steeled to handle the sludge of libidinous urges. Then, one day in your mid-to-late twenties, you will wake up with a hangover, not the ordinary Sunday wooziness on the sofa, but a round-

---

CUTTING BACK TOCCATA & FUGUE (IN D MINOR)

The pipe organ pounds with stirring diminished sevenths as amnesia ensues from downed fifths. A soundtrack staple for scores of B-movie villains named Igor or Renfield, Bach's composition has a secondary meaning for a man with vices. In psychology, the fugue is a state of deep forgetfulness in which large periods of time and life completely vanish. Lapses of memory aren't always spontaneous, as anyone who's awakened from a Wild Turkey binge can attest. The term "on the wagon" is bandied about with rampant frivolity in this age of light promises and even lighter, tastier Promise margarine. Wagoneers, despite the rhetoric, are akin to teenage break-ups—inevitably they're back for one more round. Soon after the valiant declaration, booze enthusiasts return to the mahogany bar to ponder the tartness of a Salty Dog.

Like the fashionable refrain of "I want a divorce," declaring oneself "on the water cart" should denote a permanent dry-out; it is not a sabbatical or Lenten break from alcohol, but a tattoo of abstinence. Therefore, the capricious teetotaler with a bloated liver should instead proclaim a "cutback," merely a cruise control of moderation, a corporate restructuring—no Sunday bends, lip-cringing shots, or excessive excessiveness for at least a month.

house, a blow to your constitution and formerly elastic liver. With head in hand, you ponder the reasons why a mild soak resulted in such a spirit-trampling quagmire. As you gobble painkillers like Pez, it hits you—"I ain't what I used to be."

Following this sober revelation, denial inevitably follows. Feelings of invincibility mute calls for tolerance from your aging body. At some dehydrated point, your body will have a summit meeting, wherein the agenda will be graver than arms control and global warming. The end result is a deal negotiated between two old sharks. Your mind will bargain away the omnipotent hold of peer pressure and senseless excess in exchange for pragmatism, discipline, wellness, and a future first-round draft pick. The fine print states that you will occasionally refuse a drink.

In the aftermath, you'll acknowledge that getting snookered is no longer a prerequisite for amorous charm or vibrancy. Low-key nights warrant moderation and an early clock-out; one-star yawners might be skipped altogether. Eventually, you'll eschew nonproductive patterns of drinking in favor of enlightened pursuits. Fruitless drink-offs that don't end with a bang aren't worth the ensuing suffering. Put the funnel away or ditch your campadres before the fun erodes into a sloppy couch crash.

The foregoing is not a self-important essay on temperance. Alcohol is a delicious side dish and winning social lubricant for those of sound mind and body. There are singular nights (sometimes, many in a row) where ferocious incaution is the evening's keynote. Don't damper intimate conversation or amazing nights of barhopping jazz to catch up on paperwork or overdue winks.

Still, evolution is inescapable. Grow up or defend your lifestyle to those with 401Ks and healthy relationships. Recall the flower of youth, when running on slippery pool decks before hurtling into a cannonball seemed a biological imperative; later in life, wait an extra ten seconds before launching into a graceful swan dive. These boyhood lessons translate into all social behaviors, especially drinking. Be a refined tippler, the part-time, lovable degenerate. Impetuousness ripens into spontaneity, impatience into timely verve, unbridled energy into charisma and élan. Mastering alcohol means picking times to roar, not becoming the nightly wet rag or fun vacuum. Instead of floundering into slurred oblivion, revel in a sustained buzz of balance and loose chat. Aspire to be "the man that can hold his liquor" as opposed to that "old, pathetic drunk." Get in touch with your chakras and vitality; the venerable vices are not an intrusive competition, but a limbering stretch of control. The ethic of alcohol is about acknowledging personal limits, even as you intentionally step past them.

So? Who's in a hurry?

—Robert Benchley, when told that drinking and smoking are "slow poison"

TOBACCO

Smoking is a most divisive vice, cleaving Southern states from the Union and restaurants into demarcated dining zones. The cash crop of yesteryear, tobacco has a contemporary stigma that requires a gentleman to consider more fashionable sins. Nonetheless, for those who disregard well-known warnings, puff without addiction and do not sully an otherwise wholesome, yet naughty, lifestyle. Compare the raspy one-packer who fires up in bed to the weekend ring-blower who shares a couple of rollies with pub mates. Do not fear the onset of vice when enjoying a celebratory cigar, pensive pipe, or college football—game chaw.

Since the decline of the first *Playboy* empire, most homes have non-smoking policies and are not equipped with room-to-room ashtrays. Whether the host digs nicotine or not, acceptable receptacles do not include drinking glasses, houseplants, sinks, or the house toilet.

Tobacco has many delivery methods; choose wisely for each scenario. Whipping out Capri 100s at a campfire will raise eyebrows. Likewise, having a dip or chew at the opera is crass, even if spitting during intermission into the lobby's brass cuspidor.

Nice touch: Bummed a smoke from a kind soul in a bar? Later, buy your own pack, reapproach, and offer a return gesture. Get caught short-cigged too often? Quit panhandling for menthols, you mooch.

Miss Scarlet and the Penguin haven't cornered the market. Stretch your sophistication and employ the cigarette holder while in a dark lounge, bubble bath, smoking jacket, or incognito. For the infrequent smoker, tote a handful of smokes in a vintage cigarette case. As with the flask, do not put cheap fags in a silver case. To thwart an assassin's bullet, position said case in your breast pocket.

NOTE TO THE SMOKER

Pleasure smokers can regularly go two weeks without a cigarette. Persistent ash tappers, on the other hand, look foolish huffing after one flight of stairs. Where's the pleasure in shivering outside an office building in 25° December because you have been banished, like a leper, from the lobby?

SNUFF

Heralded as one of the safest forms of tobacco in ye olde England, snuff was routinely toted by the Union blue during Sherman's march to the sea. Infused with flavors such as anise and mint, snuff is tobacco ground finely as espresso and sold in a box or tin. To use, simply take a tiny pinch and sniff lightly; a pleasant aroma and mild nicotine rush immediately stimulates. Caveat: oversnuffing leads to persistent nasal drip and mistaken identity as a Fauvist-era, tights-wearing dandy.

FIVE-SECOND CIGAR PRIMER

Choosing. The wrapper leaf is the most important feature to notice when selecting a cigar. An oily, uncracked appearance means it was correctly humidified. In general, dark wrappers indicate sweeter, richer smokes than lighter ones. Length and ring gauge (diameter) determine burn time and flavor: long cigars burn slower and cooler and the extra length diffuses heat for a cooler smoke. Block out some time for longer cigars; you'll need at least forty minutes to enjoy a seven-inch Churchill.

Clipping. Debate over clipping methods continues, but the Guillotine cut is easier to execute than the Punch, the V, or the Pierce, and exposes sufficient surface for even draw and full flavor. No matter the technique, take care not to cut off too much.

Lighting & Smoking. Hold the flame about half an inch away and warm the cigar until it begins to darken evenly. Always use a butane lighter or wooden match for lighting; cardboard matches and Zippo-style lighters dispense fumes that destroy aroma and flavor. Next, place the cigar in your mouth and draw the flame into the foot. Don't hold the tip over the fire like a prong of roasting marshmallows; rather, pull on the cigar evenly and rotate it until you get a bright-red cherry covering the end. Don't rush the lighting ritual—take at least half a minute. Never bang the ash off a long cigar; roll it off, lest you ruin the even burn of a well-wrapped stick. A long ash also makes for a more mellow smoke, especially when the cigar is short. You should be able to smoke a Churchill in about four ashes and a Robusto in two. When finished, set the cigar aside to extinguish rather than snubbing it out like a mob informant.

PIPES

Don't let Holmes have all the fun. Piping is not just for trim on pyjamas. The leisure puff near a fireplace or during *flânerie* is good for the soul, albeit poor for the cheek and gums. To make a lasting impression on grandchildren, take up a pipe for its accompanying nostalgic aroma. Whether the S-shaped calabash, horn-shaped sax pipe, or Frosty-favored corncob, pick your implement. The epicure graduates from sweetened, flavored American-style tobacco to the natural English cake varieties. Seasoning new pipes with a coat of honey and water protects the bowl against burning. For a smooth smoke, light the top layer of tobacco, tamp it down, and light again. Replace filters often and slide a pipe cleaner down the stem to dry the moisture after a heavy session. Visit a tobacconist to remedy an overworked pipe that has soured.

PALL MALL

✦ ✦ ✦ ✦ ✦ ✦ ✦ **Gin** ✦ **Sweet vermouth** ✦ **Dry vermouth** ✦ ✦ ✦ ✦ ✦ ✦ ✦

✦ ✦ ✦ ✦ ✦ ✦ **Dollop white crème de menthe** ✦ **Dash bitters** ✦ ✦ ✦ ✦ ✦ ✦

Nice touch: For a change of pace and a wicked high, go to a Middle Eastern hookah joint for tea and tobacco with an eccentric group or date.

DRUGS

It is not necessary to sample every dish in the narcotic buffet, but a developed palate for flavors and doses evinces an experienced maturity. Like colicky nephews, substances are best tolerated in small amounts.

Don't venture alone or be the surreptitious pill popper; like the lifter maxing out with four plates at the gym, use a spotter. Sharing ensures buddied judgment on proper place or activity. Certain substances are delightful accoutrements to creativity, sensuality, and spiritual exploration—although, they will not "create" creativity. Sometimes drugs are instant stamina extenders for an especial night of dancing and debauchery.

Caveat emptor: as when stumbling on a suspiciously cheap used car, beware the seedy lemon. For reliable and safe service, purchase discreetly from a local bartender, rave kid, or well-greased bellhop.

Treat your body well and abuse lightly. Most drugs have a fallout effect during the next day(s), so research hard candy before its parlay. Lest they lose the forbidden wonder of an infrequent treat, drugs should maintain their supplemental status and never become necessities. Lastly, with your prestigious bachelor's degree in hand, it is now immature to grow a coke nail or routinely gurgle a postwork bong hit.

THE GYROSCOPE OF SANITY

When the mind is young and pliable, shaking things about never feels messy. Once you've stabilized your adult mind with consciousness and order, toxicity may be quite hazardous. Introduce a psychotropic parasite into a calm, complex mind and the bizarre skew of reality quickly dispels the romantic myth of drugs. Forming sentences is impossible, sleep is fought for and lost, and old friends awaken to your apologetic messages explaining last night's split of wits. It's now time to wave the candy-popping irresponsibility of your twenties goodbye and awaken to the more organic highs of jazz, sushi, and vino. Remember this the next time a bad trip leaves you wrecked on a sandbar of lost time. Isn't it more polite to keep your shit together? Be fortunate and learn this lesson at the cost of a few hundred bucks of booze bought for strangers or sacrificial objects lost to the cityscape, instead of real inconveniences, like divorce or a ride downtown in a metro cruiser.

LEAVES OF GRASS

Marijuana: besides Jolt Cola, the mildest recreational drug sold in the marketplace. Without consulting Jimi, Janis, or Jeff Spicoli, is your familiarity with pot a fleeting pastime or a recurring pipe dream? Whether you track prices per gram in *High Times* like tech stocks or scorn second-hand smoke at reggae concerts, at least keep the blunt in perspective. Is the occasional hit under the stars really a pathology? Abstainers shouldn't spurn tokers on camping trips any more than partakers should stroll around glassy-eyed, looking to score a sack.

Further expand your artistic experience with proper use of botanicals. Used right, reefer madness brushes away the clouds of confusion after a break-up or bout with traffic. Abused, it's a procrastination pill that makes progress futile. Visit a museum or gallery, write Beatnik poetry, or sip Orangina outdoors. Late-night pyjama dancing is elevated to heightened libidinous levels under the influence of jazz or blue(grass).

Marijuana can be a sexual mentor and a sublime electrician, bringing the lights of Broadway to women who have spent years in frigid darkness.

—NATALIE ANGIER, *WOMAN*

Marijuana should not be part of a man's daily utility, although it may creep into your hiking pack, weekend tote, or play-clothes pockets. Great for a spring cookout or a backyard weeding, Mary Jane should be piped in with admission at any planetarium. Pot is a poor cure for whooping cough, better than an ice pack for headaches, and perfect for movie-going, gaming, mini-golf, or bowling (but not archery).

Enlist a fruit, vegetable, or other crafty device for a primitive smoke, but remember to replace the screens borrowed from your parents' bathroom faucets. Offer to roll a joint if you've got nimble digits or skills certified by Snoop Dogg. Be resourceful. When necessary, utilize the ever-ready paperclip or wire hanger for clearing obstructions.

When might a gentleman produce this vice in mixed company? Take inventory of the mood and crowd. Might a light delight a group enraptured with talk of the arts, spirituality, music, or sex? Listen to an evening's subtext, and if so inclined, toss out hints ("Fancy that, Congress is considering hemp as a cash crop"). An offer to smoke in mixed company is a litmus test of inhibitions. Do guests rebuff with a stern legal citation or recoil with a skittish, virginal "no"? Or do they grab the green, clean the carb, blow a tube, and cash the stash faster than you can say "Cheech and Chong"? Reactions to ganja are a social filter: a polite, comfortable "no thanks" reveals as much as a hungry grin for seconds.

For sure, if there's a guitar strumming, fire it up. Find a side room and bond with an inner circle, or take a solitary smoke discreetly outside. As with kindergarten brownies (hash or birthday variety), bring enough for the class to share, but leave the quarter-pound baggie at home. Only carry as much as needed, preferably in a handsome pouch or case. As for that film canister, sure, the cops will think it's 200-speed.

Nice touch: Instead of After Eight dinner mints, leave a 2 A.M. dime bag and implement on an arriving guest's pillow.

Some dope tips:

+ It is ungentlemanly to scorch a fine pipe, cigar, or other implement with haphazard fire manners. Master the thumb-to-thumb handoff when the roach clip is in disrepair.

+ Exterminate. No roaches or other cheeba remnants in the car ashtray, excepting the cross-country road trip, moving van, or Winnebago.

+ Be a sufficient bowl packer. Watch stems, exploding seeds, and shake. A final gentle thumb push prevents a needless burning-bowl ceremony.

+ Don't pull a horse choke of smoke with complementary plume of waste. Learn what and where the carburetor is.

+ Next time you clean the house, hit the car wash, or want to punctuate a moment of solace, offer yourself the peace pipe.

+ Observe no-smoking zones: first dates, wood-chipping, holiday family dinners, and carpooling to the day-care center.

GAMING

In lieu of dueling at ten paces, feats of leisure are superlatively social and bring out laughter, drama, and drink. Your repertoire should include a host of games that don't require Windows XP. Don't be a stick in the mud who eschews board games—the box clearly states "ages 8 and up." Stock your closet shelf with a few classic favorites for rainy days and lazy afternoons (Monopoly, Life, Parcheesi, Master Minds).

Do not dishearten lesser adversaries with an oppressive tour de force that quashes others' zest for the game. Just as mixed doubles is a lot more enjoyable without your 100-MPH serve, so is a game of Scrabble without your quick recall of two-letter, vowel-only words from *The Official Scrabble Players Dictionary* (ae: earns you two points and three growls).

Incidentally, Clue fantasies don't end with puberty. Phineas still wants Miss Scarlet with the Candlestick in the Conservatory. Tesauro secretly craves being tied to the Library ladder with the Rope and flogged with tales of Chaucer by the mysterious Mrs. Peacock.

BONES

Dominoes, or bones, is a classic social game, not just for the park and prison yard anymore. Perfect poolside, dominoes catalyzes bonds as you laze in the sun holding tiles in your hand. Purchase a double-six set and glean the nuances from experienced players, as well as the proper method of holding tiles (four or more in each hand, vertically, like Steinway ivories). Listen for the lingo and note the proper time to slam pieces emphatically on a bar table, upstaging an opponent in winsome spite.

PUBLIC GAMING

What could be more disarming than a trio of grown-up eight-year-olds shouting "Yahtzee!" in a swanky lounge? Any game not requiring elaborate set-up can be ported to a pub or late-night diner. Risk and Stratego are a tad too cumbersome for travel; instead, tote Battleship, Connect Four, bones, backgammon, and anything with a Pop-o-Matic.

BACKGAMMON

Pastis, side bets, cocked dice, the Lover's Leap, and figs on the deck. Backgammon is excellent for the cat and mouse of flirtation, the rules are simple, and the thrill of chance scintillates. Measure your Man Cycle against the game's capricious dice. Play confidently and doublets will follow. Don't whine; the wily gent can squeeze a hot play from a role of 2 and 1. Backgammon exposes a player's persona: the attacker (hits no matter what); the runner (can't wait to flee); the trapper (won't let you out); the stalker (ready to pounce); and the miracle maker (leaves one piece behind to spoil a sure victory). Count using colors and points, rather than tapping out each pip like a sinking ship's SOS. The doubling cube allows you to wager for cash and cocktails, or play for your place or mine.

MAH-JONGG COCKTAIL

◆ ◆ ◆ ◆ **Gin** ◆ **Dollop Cointreau** ◆ **Dollop light rum** ◆ **Lemon twist** ◆ ◆ ◆ ◆

GOLF

Shelves are filled with paeans about golf's magical places and 2,000-word fish stories about near-quitting experiences cured miraculously by a tree-and-hazard-defying wedge-in for eagle. Golf is inherently frustrating. Indeed, if the game were easy, no one would spend hard-earned lucre on the newest oversized drivers. Unlike tennis, where mediocrity is attainable, golf is mercurial. Even old pros question their ability and enjoyment from time to time.

Except for retirees and idle law-school students, golf is an occasional treat. Without knowing the intricacies of club selection or Bermuda grass, a novice duffer still appreciates the history and beauty of golf by bringing the right ethic and stance to the tee box. Before unsheathing your three-wood, take in the scene, listen for honeyed thwacks, and cherish the sunshine as it warms gloved hands in plush surroundings.

As long as the atmosphere of play remains positive, a great foursome includes players of differing skill levels. Shooting over 100 won't ruin a

---

CROQUET

The best use for grass since hula skirts: this game is played on virtually any lawn larger than a badminton court. Topographical quirks or water hazards are minor frets providing just the terrain for sending balls unfettered into the greensward hinterland. Croquet is the perfect outdoor social accompaniment and obliges all skill levels. With proper planning, a sporting afternoon of mallets and wickets boasts women in gloves, gents in two-toned shoes, and all in hats, clutching chilly punch for all-day beak dipping.

day of golf for most sportsmen, but a tiresome, lagging presence will spoil a delightful afternoon with a bad temper and a dawdling pace. The goal of golf is a gratifying rhythm and a fervent desire to play tomorrow.

ATTIRE

Wear a plain, collared shirt, even if playing on a public course resembling a vacant sandlot. On most days, don long pants. For repeat players, a pair of water-resistant golf shoes is preferable over sneakers.

GOLF BAG

Show up to the course with your own sticks or call ahead to see if the clubhouse rents bags and irons. Pack ample tees and balls (nonwhite balls aren't kosher). A sleeve of balatas won't last three holes for a novice, so stow a handful of older balls for replacing errant shots into the drink.

For club cleaning, wet one end of a stolen white hotel bath mat and drape it over your bag—the wet end rinses, the dry end finishes. An old travel toothbrush is ideal for scrubbing irons, while matches come in handy for a smoking partner. Pack a few Band-Aids for boo boos and blisters, and a small bottle of aspirin for interminable quadruple bogies. Lastly, stow a sawbuck in the side pocket for clubhouse chews and quaffs.

Nice touch: Even if shot lines appear clean, mark your ball with a buffalo head nickel on the green to avoid hindering others' putting.

FOOD

Calories are needed to maintain a steady swing, especially on a hot afternoon with great distances between holes. Besides a water bottle, slide in a small bologna or turkey sandwich on white. A granola bar calms the blood sugar, but the beloved classic is prefab peanut-butter and orange crackers, a snack that retains a long bag life.

PLAY

Golf courses are set up as a zigzag of holes where a strident outburst on one hole may affect play on the next fairway. Unlike arena sports, quiet is required during shot making. After the group tees off, conversation flows freely among course mates, especially when a twosome splinters off to find balls on the far side of the fairway.

Pick up tips from magazines and work on a few preparations before every stroke. For example, keep a straight front arm or avoid picking up your head and your play will improve. Solid play, however, shouldn't include incessant practice swings and needless studying or delays.

IRKSOME PLAY

Rookies might occasionally ask better players for an easy pointer, but a nervous nag who pesters others for advice and swing analysis after every shot is annoying even before the first turn. If dedicated to improvement, sign up for lessons from the local pro. Likewise, accomplished golfers shouldn't puff and offer advice unless asked or correcting an obvious, recurring problem (lack of wrist cock).

HOLE IN ONE

◆ ◆ **Scotch** ◆ **Dry vermouth** ◆ **Squeeze of lemon juice** ◆ **Dash bitters** ◆ ◆

The worst offenders are those who snail the pace. If a ball veers out of bounds, don't form a posse to rescue it, especially in swampy terrain. After a quick search, take a penalty stroke or, if not scoring strictly, drop a ball on the fairway edge. Always note ball type and number (e.g., Titleist 2) to avoid the ultimate embarrassment of playing another's. Walk onto the green with only your putter, positioning your bag off the green in the direction of the next hole to ease transition after putting out.

COMMON KNOWLEDGE

Tee boxes are arranged according to gender and difficulty. For most of life, use the white tees. If ensconced in a sand trap, no practice shots are allowed; and after cursing your exit shot, rake the sand. As for gauging distance to the hole, look for the colorful markers before conducting a poll. Most courses bear markers in the form of engraved sprinklers or drainage caps, striped wooden stakes, or painted fence posts that denote yardage to the green (usually from 300 to 100 yards). Should your pitching wedge send a flying lump of grass on a rainbow trajectory, replace the divots with a light stomp to encourage regrowth; in warmer climes, pour bluish fill/grass seed into the divot (usually supplied in the golf cart). Lastly, if you must relieve yourself, use at least two trees as cover.

Most strapping lads can carry a golf bag for eighteen holes without difficulty; on sweltering days, a handcart might be best. Motorized carts are primarily moneymakers for courses and are not part of golf in the U.K. or Ireland, where the pace of play is actually faster without them. To be sure, carts expedite play on courses where the greens and next tees are separated by long, winding paths. Some clubs require the use of a cart and will post "driving rules" to protect delicate fairways. The 90-degree rule means that the cart is to be driven on the cement path, and then turned to enter the fairway at a straight line to your ball. Before walking to your ball, tote all reasonable clubs for the shot. If you think the shot's a seven, for instance, take the six and eight irons just in case.

Nice touch: Pack a deck of cards when playing at crowded courses. A hand or two of poker is more enjoyable than listless practice swings at grass blades before the first hole.

WAGERING

When money is at stake, rules and penalty strokes are strictly enforced, leaving no room for shameless "creative" scoring, friendly drops, and liberal mulligan offerings.

Incidentally, after eighteen holes (with accompanying tender shoulders and feet), a beer in the clubhouse after slipping on civilian footwear is a delight. Finally, no more than one *Caddyshack* reference per round.

CARD PLAYING

Whether gambling with a fat pot or playing penny-a-point pinochle, be a winning gentleman at the card table. There are a variety of games besides blackjack, crazy eights, and war. Have any fives? Go fish. Be nimble on the cribbage board and master at least three of the following: whist, euchre, hearts, canasta, spades, pinochle, or stud. To sock away bidding acumen for the sedentary golden years, learn contract bridge.

Cards make a splendid weeknight accompaniment for well-deserved leisure, especially when a rain-swept cityscape deters walking plans. Stow a deck in your travel bag and break monotony on trains or shaded porches. Cracking a fresh fifty-two makes great fodder for staging a small get-together. Card games are also ideal for family reunions when post-prandial *café* hasn't caffeinated the group to acceptable chitchat levels. Games involving trumps and kitties aren't just for grannies and casino-klatch belles. Most sentient beings with a G.E.D. can follow new games after a few practice hands. For those with steeper learning curves, keep *According to Hoyle* within arm's reach for further instructions—even the box-top undersides of Payday and Candyland require a quick perusal to arbitrate game-stopping rules inquiries.

STRIP POKER

Strip poker is perhaps the only game in which a gentleman may cheat; playing these cards shakes up more than just the loose-change jar. Once clever after-dinner activities have bubbled over, strip poker is the skinny-dip of parlor games. In fact, many of the same rules apply—keep those hot hands on top of the card table as you toss the jokers back in the pack. Don't worry so much about shuffling and don't fret a stacked deck or an ace in the briefs. The only flush a gentleman is concerned about is the one in the other players' cheeks. Keep the game spirited, a racy jape, and evenly distribute the disrobing so that ogling eyes aren't missile-locked on a great pair... of queens.

A spontaneous adventure requiring group consensus, strip poker is for a sexy, well-mixed four (or more)-some and not a Tuesday night with beer buddies. If partial to a bit of rummy in the raw, suggest infrequently, lest you be pegged a pervert. Match differing skill and prudence levels with sartorial handicapping. Offer the more scantily dressed a chance to don a hat, neck scarf, or extra pullover. Lastly, maintain manners and beware of unsightly raises not involving poker chips and witless jokes about one-eyed jacks.

Upon dealing poker and its progeny, be silly and brash, but don't misdeal. Shuffle three times with a smooth bridge method before distributing cards clockwise, yourself last. Boyish shuffling techniques, such as forcing the deck halves together like misfit puzzle pieces or sloppy, hand-over-hand card flipping, aren't fit for the gentleman's table. Beware the hotshot flicking of cards across smooth tables, risking misdeals or players scrambling to catch wayward aces. With money on the line, ante up without being reminded.

During play, sprinkle some lingo to liven up the game and provide broadcast-booth play-by-play ("Deuce, six, no help. Jack, king, ace, possible Broadway. And clubs for the dealer. Trio of queens is still high. Six tits, what's your bet?"). Know the poker-hand ranks cold. Asking whether a full house beats three-of-a-kind is poor bluffing technique. Keep poker variations such as high/low, Texas hold 'em, and three-card guts at the ready on dealer's-choice night. Once the action is rolling, introduce a wrinkle like jacks or better to open.

Have fun and repeat the Lotto mantra: *you gotta be in it to win it.* Fair-weather rookies are predictable and jump ship with pairs showing. Stay in a few pots with dubious hands to experience the once-in-a-lifetime thrill of pulling an inside straight. Among friends, don't allow betting with paychecks and wedding rings, though hotel keys and promises of hard labor are always acceptable. When the room is quiet and the wagering intense, fair is fair—after all, Lando Calrissian lost the Millennium Falcon to Han Solo in a card game.

THE PONIES

A brief primer is necessary for those who think that Citation is an old-model Chevy, not the 1948 Triple Crown winner. Most young professionals skip the after-work trip to the track, preferring to gamble their salaries on the stock market. The call of mud and hooves is usually only heeded for big-name races such as the Preakness Stakes or Santa Anita Derby. Look sharp and know the basic rules of pari-mutuel betting.

PREPARE

To deaden your small-time gambling losses, carry a flask and a fine cigar. If the outing is an all-day outdoor affair, cart your own packed cooler to the infield. Dress smart for steeplechases; for large, daytime gatherings of the local horsey set, stow catered foods and chilled liquor, and drive a large vehicle with accompanying tailgate.

EQUIPMENT

Bring two pens (one for the ill-prepared nagging borrower), and if you've had more than a few drinks, write down your bets before approaching the window. Buy a program for knowledge of the field. Scan the medley of stats about prior finishes, handicaps, or sire history. Read the legend or ask a grizzled, cigarillo-smoking veteran for a quick tip. Do not bet over $20 if you do not know what Lasix is.

WAGERING

If you are a rookie, don't fumble with your program and jam the betting-window line with one minute 'til post time. Despite the odds, always place at least a minimal bet on a well-named, catchy-sounding horse. Lastly, horses listed with subletters (Number 2, 2a, 2b, etc.) are grouped for betting purposes. Therefore, if you place a wager on horse "2," then you also receive 2a and 2b automatically.

Speak clearly: race number, bet amount (payouts are based on a $2 bet), horse number (not the name), and desired outcome ("Fifth race, $10 on number 4 to win"). To win, the horse must finish first; to place, the horse must finish first or second; to show, the horse must finish first, second, or third.

Always "box" exactas (both horses selected must finish first and second in exact order). Boxing is simply two bets covering all outcomes—for example, if your wager was six and seven exacta box, you would win whether the finish was 6-7 or 7-6). A win-place-show bet is three separate bets covering all outcomes, so you win whether the horse is first, second, or third. Bet a trifecta (your horses finishes first, second, and third in exact order) during a cresting Man Cycle.

DESPERATION

You never know about those photo finishes, so don't tear tickets in disgust until final results are posted. Barring something extraordinary, prompting a steward's inquiry, it is shoddy form to comb the ground for winning tickets like a metal-detecting beach geezer.

CHURCHILL DOWNS COOLER

1 jigger bourbon ✦ **1 shot brandy** ✦ **Splash Triple Sec** ✦ **Top with ginger ale**

Chapter Eight

BETWEEN
THE SHEETS

◆ ◆ ◆ ◆ ◆ ◆ ◆

Prophyletiquette **234**

XXX: Phineas's Phavourites & Tesauro's Titillations .. **237**

Kink & Fetish **244**

To the Power of [3] **246**

Gentleman's Club **249**

PROPHYLETIQUETTE

An armour against enjoyment and a spider-web against danger.
—MADAME DE SEVIGNÉ (1626—1696), ON CONDOMS

The cumbersome condom requires impeccable timing and delicate hands. How to broach the subject? Whose responsibility is it? When to don one? Before taking a hard-line *nay*, try condoms on for size and learn good manners.

Echoing the ancient Egyptians, Casanova unfurled a reusable linen model. Later, children of the '70s and '80s rode the last train from Woodstock and enjoyed the waning decades of penicillin and promiscuity. Now the game of love is played at higher stakes. Since partners aren't prescreened with a blood test and three references, it's arrogant to think that mere selectivity insulates against pesky or deadly diseases.

Modern life affords little sympathy for those who take no precautions against pregnancy. Early withdrawal might garner penalties at the credit union, but it lowers the odds of unplanned fatherhood. Barring statistical anomalies, regular condom use eliminates altogether the need for untimely car seats in your sporty coupe.

PREPARATION

After tattoos are revealed and middle names disclosed, first-time sex looms in the night air like a blimp at a bowl game. If it's your pad, no problem: condoms are stashed nearby. But what if you're on the traveling team? Is it the hostess's duty? No way. Better to impress a new lover by planning ahead than to face an eleventh-hour pickle ending with a sprint to the corner store and a no-frills sheath. On the other hand, whipping out the French tickler before appetizers is clearly crass.

A hosting gentleman offers the basic coital accoutrements for anxiety-free coupling. A cornucopia of wares from an under-the-bed valise is unnecessary, even if presented on a silver tray. Experiment early in your career with different styles before selecting a sock-drawer special.

Glean some insight from a lover's prophyletiquette. Does she keep a cabinet full of flavored condoms, organized like herbal teas? Can she manage the condom as deftly as a boardwalk ring toss? A frank discussion of rubber deepens intimacy beyond microns of latex and leads to other conversations. Some fun: "What fantasies do you have?" Some not: "How many lovers have you had?"

LUBRICANTS

Unslippery moments can be a real fly in the ointment. Preferably water based, a tube of lube restores the unctuousness of natural love. Put a little butter on your popcorn and see what a dab of lotion sets in motion.

RESPONSIBILITY

If you're intimate enough for sex, you're adult enough to oversee logistics. Whether the worry is paternity or the clap, it is polite to offer the condom option before forgoing protection. A cautious lover shouldn't feel like the bad guy; be proactive and take responsibility, particularly with new partners. Teens and inexperienced Romeos should always buckle up for safety; since the whole gig is new anyway, rubbers are little imposition.

Some gentleman insist on regular condom use, but consider going bareback under special circumstances, such as in monogamous sexual relations with a long-time lover, especially a spontaneous act in an inconvenient place. Gentlemen past their first love and twenty-fifth birthday might consider weighing the perils of unsafe sex against a lover's lust-hungry waiver. When her crazed infatuation tears at your button-fly and tosses you on the bed like a gunnysack, the mature lady is signaling for immediate action. Permission is still not to be assumed, though. If you can't get a read on your partner's state of mind or bill of health, go to the drawer. Green-light consent must be crystal clear; even if her eyes say yes, let your brain make the final call on usage. Regardless of your well-honed character judgments, this is risky behavior. It presumes enlightened degrees of maturity and honesty best reserved for trusting, sober familiars, not backroom strangers.

TIMING

Produce a condom with dignity and purpose, akin to King Arthur's knights fetching their scabbards. Don't make a stroll to the nightstand a starchless event; infuse it with levity and playfulness.

So now you've got a rubber—what next? Have the forethought to properly equip before the stroke of intercourse. When passions peak past petting, use those hands-free moments to unwrap and unravel, or ask your lover to assist. If the shot clock winds down during fumbled condom retrieval, retrace a few amorous steps before leaping in. Well-managed, a condom will not totally disrupt the smooth transition from foreplay to more play.

TAKING OUT THE TRASH

Do not attempt a walk about the boudoir with a condom dangling precariously, like a wet noodle. A gentleman should tidy up his business in discreet fashion. Wrap spent articles in tissue and toss them in the trash.

Final dicta:

- Reservoir tips are good ergonomics, not boating rules.

- Lubricated is better than non, and ribbed is indeed for her pleasure. Fruit-scented varieties mask the distinctive odor of used latex. As with beef jerky, stick to name brands and watch those expiration dates.

- Prophylactics redeemed from rest-stop kiosks are like home runs made with nonyellow Whiffle Ball bats. Every score is suspect.

- Asking if she's on the pill just before climax is generally impolite.

- If it breaks, be a hero. Either deputize a backup or spare the anxiety and fake your orgasm.

- Though ineffectual against STDs, lambskin is alright, even for vegetarians.

XXX: PHINEAS'S PHAVOURITES & TESAURO'S TITILLATIONS

[A] racing car is very much like a woman . . . . You must treat it with smoothness and caution . . . . Let's take one corner, for instance. You're approaching at maximum speed, maybe 200 miles per hour, and you've got to decelerate sharply to go round. You don't wait until the last second and then stamp the brakes . . . . And as you're gearing down, you're not banging through the gears; you're taking them smoothly . . . . She doesn't want to be rushed . . . . Now you have to take the apex . . . which can be measured in inches, and this precise spot is the climax . . . . Maybe you're going to apply a little bit of power because she's coming but you haven't really

reached it yet; and that last bit of extra power does it. She's done it beautifully, and you've done it with her. . . . The fact that every car is like a woman, of course, means that you can do all the right things with her and she still may not respond.

—JACKIE STEWART (SCOTSMAN AND FORMER WORLD CHAMPION GRAND PRIX DRIVER), INTERVIEW, *PLAYBOY*, JUNE 1972

Over the course of healthy physical relationships, shared fantasy life is a natural extension of intimacy. Embrace the bedroom as a safe space for experimentation. Whatever a lover's fancy, taste without judgment, goad without pressure. In turn, a trusting partner shouldn't have a closed mind. Eroticism is a vast ecosystem of ecstasy, a symbiosis where dominants and submissives, role-play and fantasy exploration all coexist.

BLUE STREAKING

Dirty talk finds an outlet during impassioned exchange. The undercurrent is lasciviousness, the tongue ripe with rapid-fire lyric. A mature exploration, blue speak is reserved for near-equal kinksters and is best employed with a measured temperament that does not exceed a partner's tolerance. Nothing complements a stimulated id, healthy power play, or long-distance tuck-in more than choice elemental phrases.

While quality pornographic films provide a dragnet for collecting terminology, take care to not borrow text that demeans rather than coaxes. Bluestreaking is an advanced stage of intimacy that should gradually and skillfully accelerate the moment. Thus, the use of "slut," "whore," "bitch," and the "C" word should remain on the outskirts of your nonrole-playing rotation. Conjure words that connote playfulness, beauty, and primal urges.

Normalcy is not vanilla sex, but acts between consenting hedonists who agree with Ani Di Franco: "I am thirty-two flavors and then some."

Kinky résumés are usually brandished after nervous wooing has passed into playful canoodling under and over the blankets. With whetted breath, ordinary talk morphs into, "Have you ever tried . . . ." With an open floor, share some favored off-center practices and suggest some Class I and Class II fetishes. After mutual ground is reached regarding tuck-ins, tie-ups, and trapezes, keep raising the carnal bar every sigh session as navels gravitate closer and trust breeds mischievousness. If prudish hesitation chills hot chat, table it until confiding smiles widen with each night spent. Everyone has a vice—even the straight-shooting den mother down the block—so, like dubious game-show host Geoff Edwards, relish the *Treasure Hunt*.

PORNOGRAPHY

Say *oui*. Porn is meant to be an infrequent and delectable side dish, never the main course. More than a baker's half-dozen cassettes suggest a videophile, so keep your collection current, but not voluminous. Plucky and filthy selections are encouraged; borderline, foreign, scatological choices are for parolees. Store your films discreetly, like fine liqueurs, closeted for discriminate consumption. Try the very back of your video cabinet or that neglected living room drawer or chest. Unless you still live with your parents, do not stockpile materials under the mattress.

OMNIAMOROUSNESS

The consummate epicurean, a gentleman is saturated with a curiosity to sample the feast of sexuality. During formative years, the consequences of dabbling in *délire du toucher* (desire to touch or be touched) are negligible. Before engagements and thirtieth birthdays, dabbling in alternative conduct doesn't threaten masculinity and needn't taint a reputation. A summer course in Greek won't tarnish a major in Latin. The developing gentleman should not forsake a late night *faute de mieux* (serendipitous homosexuality) because of social fears. Heterosexuality should be the personal choice of someone who prefers the opposite sex. Hetero or not, sexual identity is the fusion of what feels right and what doesn't quite leaven one's loaf. Whether you dabble for experience's sake or skip this lesson altogether, do so wide-eyed and not yellow-bellied.

ROTE & FOLLY

Not all erotic dalliances entail security clearance and a rope tutorial from the dungeon supply store. In fact, most playful romps involve mind and body, not the toy chest. "Routine" is an evil word in relationships, the surest method to romantic ennui and the early three-and-a-half-year itch. Take the same road to work everyday, but the path to hot love should be a sinuous route from A to Bewitching, sometimes a speedy shortcut and other times a serpentine, scenic byway. Break up habits with the interspersion of less familiar places, props, and times.

Don't be bashful in your birthday suit. A gentleman's naughty creativity turns ordinary into erotic, especially with unexpected attentions

===== **MORNING AFTER** =====

Absinthe or Pernod ◆ **Dash of anisette** ◆ **1 egg white** ◆ **Top with club soda**

and succulent asides. Don't give lip service . . . to lip service; overdo it to delight once in a while, with ice water and Viagra in your veins. Moreover, like the deftest topographers, use entrancing digits and a lickerish tongue to thoroughly remap your lover's clean lines, surveying for elusive valleys, firmer grades, and previously untapped natural resources.

Instead of using scholarly and poetic prose to explain preferred necking and lovemaking techniques, we offer a few bonded secrets. Always keep a full quiver, even if you only need one arrow.

POSTCOITAL BEHAVIOR

After sex, is one ready for the postgame show or merely the half-time entertainment? Don't feel pressure to communicate verbally immediately after your bodies have disengaged from sticky discourse. Sincerity and candor govern verse; avoid asking the loaded, "What are you thinking?" A trip to the washroom is an opportunity to consider options (and mouthwash).

A partner's postcoital offering of water signifies hydration loss and is a glowing compliment that punctuates continued desire. Talk of clothing's whereabouts hints at adjournment. An offer of a shower from a flushed lover is a promising prelude to frolic, now or later. Though, do not request one except on a harried weekday morning when a return home is impossible.

Next-morning relations are the sweetest plum, but don't linger like a house pest. Before departure, take a rapid inventory, lest you sacrifice a bold new Zegna tie to the connubial Goddess of Casual Sex. For unplanned stay-overs scented with regret, either tiptoe out or feign sleep. Nothing can be gained from an awkward interrogation when a bedmate (or you) is caught slinking out, singularly shod. Exits of this type indicate a poor selection of lovers in the first place.

PHINEAS'S PHAVOURITES

1. Like a footballer in a World Cup match, go hands-free and use the upper body. Complement pelvic tilt through sensuous arm pinning and employ a clever header with the chin and nose.

2. Practice the long vertical lick, centralized on the chakra meridian that proceeds from pelvic cleft, past the navel, through the mammary valley, over the smooth neck area, and to the waiting lips.

3. Induce gentle hot zephyrs as you hover beside an ear, followed by deliberate circling of the outer ear with the tongue, never entering the ear canal like a misused Q-Tip. Precede with a gentle parting of silky locks, exposing the tender aural flesh.

4. Upon initial penetration and for a brief time afterward, only engage the first one-third to one-half of your member.

5. Engage in a face-to-face straddle at edge of the bed, leading to an uninterrupted maneuver into missionary position.

6. Don't just piston-mimic; vary your speeds like a veteran left-handed pitcher, occasionally bringing the action down to a light simmer.

TESAURO'S TITILLATIONS

1. Scribble couplets with your tongue or imitate motorboat sounds with pursed lips. A light and percussive, open-palmed tap upon excited anatomy augurs innovative passions to even the most familiar lover. Expressive exclamations telegraph what tickles your fancy.

2. Prolong and tease by peppering oral pleasures with manual stimulation. Use different utensils for different dishes, don't mix peas and carrots; and never explore the fundament too early in the count.

3. Tantric breath control is the multiorgasmic male's Ace of Tarts. Near climax, short breaths of fire incite release; elongated, cooling breaths focus passion without sending it outward.

4. During heightened penetrating moments, challenge your discipline and practice teasing withdrawal or stoppage. Reengage in erogenous-zone stimulation or impassioned kissing—the return to intercourse will be extraordinarily spirited.

5. Like a top gun in the cockpit, pilot your stick as deftly as a dogfighter. A turgid pitch and yaw scintillates all points with soft savagery.

6. The refractory period: don't make all performances a one-act play; enjoy a brief intermission, but save some spunk for an encore. If necessary, bring in the stunt double.

Incidentally, there are infinite finish lines besides orgasm and physical intimacies beyond intercourse. Do not neglect gentle nibbles at the hairline, the soft undersides of wrists, fingers, and those sexy toes. Pay attention to tucking the tongue under the waistband and sashaying across the panty line. For the real epicure, journey lips from the sensitive clavicle, through the forbidden armpit, and up the tasty elbow.

KINK & FETISH

[attach to bedpost]

[attach to wrist]

While PVC piping, peter pants (briefs with a leash), and subjugation masks are not necessary fixtures in the gentleman's closet, a certain proficiency with kink and fetish should be cultivated for active minds and loins. Kink is a loaded gun, better holstered for the right occasion than bandied about injudiciously. A short list of toys and tools follows for easy reference.

Class I fetishes should be shared with the less-experienced lover gradually, with whimsy and gentility. Note, however, that the obviously adept lover needs no handholding, rather, handcuffing. For Class II, let the intensity of your interaction dictate the introduction of more vigorous kink. Such implements and positions flow from the rare combination of intimacy, perversity, and trust. No rush: learn your lover's threshold and do not exploit that line. For Class III and other felonies, mutual consent and hasty clean-up are prerequisites. Each party must also bring a permission slip from their analyst before venturing into this domain.

TABOO

Favor fetish without flaunting it. Enjoy the paradoxical pleasure of wearing a cock ring beneath a tuxedo. Beyond animal acts of sex are respectable lifestyles of lingerie and the occasional can of whipping cream. The promised land of complete disclosure lies further on, where the bed is a conduit for candid expression. Certain deviances will leave

CLASS I	CLASS II	CLASS III
HIGHLY FAVORED AND FLAVORED	**ALWAYS LURKING IN THE BAG OF TRICKS**	**THREE TO FIVE, WITH GOOD BEHAVIOR**
Oils, creams, body paint	Restraints (hand or ankle cuffs—furry, leather, or pleather)	Swinging and swapping
Feathers, tantalizers, French ticklers	Sploshing on rubber sheets, Saran Wrap	Traction devices
Scarves, delicate blindfolds, rope	Role-playing (costume rental) and public sex exhibition	Public frotteuring or trenchcoat flashing with a toothless grin
Ice cubes, foodstuffs, sundae toppings	Ben-wa balls and beads, hot wax, adjustable nipple clamps	Edge play, breath control, electrotorture
Bizarre shoes and corsets (on her)	Bizarre shoes and corsets (on him)	Le Rack
Wine bottle (spin the bottle) and deck of cards (strip poker)	Blindfolds, collars, gags, and bits	Scat play
Affection for feet, wrists, knees, and armpits	Cat o' nine tails, riding crops, spanking (designate "safe" words)	Dungeon reservations: "You are confirmed for three, Mr. Tesauro"
Exotic positions requiring a manual and bachelor's degree	Vibrators, dildos, and well-scrubbed organic vegetables	Anything involving clean-up with bleach
Your Favorites Here:	Your Favorites Here:	Your Favorites Here:

even veterans feeling flushed and prudish. Worry not; a gentleman isn't required to master water sports beyond SCUBA lessons. Still, rent a French Maid outfit for a lover, get tied up in something other than traffic, don some leather, and play "Daddy" (or "Mommy").

TO THE POWER OF ^{3}

On the winding stretch of sexual exploration, pad your résumé with statistical analyses of the cube root. Threesomes create combustion or catastrophe, depending upon how the gentleman plays a full house.

Scenario: the sought-after tango occurs between a couple (A and B) and a mutual attraction (C). Troikas are not necessarily premeditated, but signs of possibility have been exchanged in prior flirtation. Participants are ideally prescreened for open-minded, healthy (or filthy) individuals who are mature enough to separate love and lust. Either A or B (ideally both) take the lead in involving C for a shared tryst. For this discussion, the gentleman assumes the role of A.

CALISTHENICS

Warm up by stretching the twosome plus one into a shared three. Since A and B are a couple, celebrate the preexisting bond first and frequently with affections, especially when C is present. A's affection for B must not be a shallow charade put on to coax C into action; if A and B's fire is feigned, the trio's flame will fizzle.

As flirtation rises, extend the affections to C, but don't upset the balance. Always begin with B, then extend the personal space to envelop C. Invite C into the space A and B share by participating in playful activities that accelerate intimacy (cooking, swimming, dancing, gaming). Give yourselves some privacy so nothing disturbs the budding dynamic.

DEEP STRETCHING

Engage the vortex with swooning conversation, enlivened with shared secrets. Talk of poetry, art, and passion raises the pulse and evokes sensual vulnerability. Allow the pot to quietly simmer. Like an old salt, raise a dampened index finger to read the prevailing winds. Vast inequalities or jealousies are toxic (A and C get along famously, as B stews alone). If the vibe wavers, scrap the fantasy and don't let an agenda disrupt a pleasant evening. Abort if sexual leanings risk serious damage to the underlying relationships. Better to save A and B's future than to jeopardize it for a chance to see what's behind Curtain Number Three.

By now, shared experiences are common—words are addressed to the group and long bouts of eye contact are traded between all players. Here is the time to get tactile. Fingers drumming on trigger points of the neck are irresistible as are offers to massage toes. You have one hand for each neck or foot, thus it is best when B and C are closely corralled. Carefully, increase the general intimacy of the trio by reintroducing some of the behaviors visited earlier only between A and B. This time, do not exclude C from a furtive kiss, open adoration, or stroke of fingers through the hair.

Note, any *trois* is invigorated by wine, candles, pillows, or a long, thin joint. Neck rubs blossom into bare back touching and quasinaked backgammon. Lose when necessary; cheating for the sake of strip poker is within acceptable limits.

Act I: Exploration. From massages, spawn wrist kissing, blue streaks, and the shedding of inhibitions. Let your tongue speak a randy mind, and a day's worth of synchronicity will answer back in the form of vital signs rising, including deeper talk of sexual fantasies, laughter with smatterings of flitty kisses, and suggestions for more intrusive activities (spin the bottle, examination of body art or racy undergarments). Mercury rises quickly.

Act II: Threshold. Before leaping over the fence of no return, consider if flirting and coquetry are as far as it should go. Staying here is safe; pressing on carries the risk of hurt feelings and shock. Secure final consent with a wide-open display of shared delights with B and C: finger licking, lip kissing, or naughty suggestions. Steamy and yummy.

Act III: The Close. You've been waved in by the third-base coach: open love is shared by all. Maintain a balance of attention in giving and receiving. If B or C lingers too long as the other two play, he or she must be immediately seduced to rejoin. A and B's beckoning hands are a confirmation to C that C's inclusion is vital. Strays are thus reinvigorated.

Act IV: Tidying Up. After cozy interaction, pause for a lively postgame wrap-up. Poeticize about the denser regions of sexuality. Gain a consensus on how delightful the experience was. In the afterglow, reaffirm relationships by revering B as your continued favorite and acknowledging C as a welcome intimate. Always kiss last the one you loved first.

SIDE EFFECTS

Trysting is not about switching from B to C, but exploring intimacy with B through the shared enjoyment of C. In the end, A, B, and C should still know whose bed they're really sleeping in. The poorest consequence is when a threesome with C reveals cracks between A and B. Here, the experience with C accentuates inequality rather than trust.

Incidentally, if B or C shows the red card ("I don't feel comfortable"), the game is over. Retreat need not be awkward if everything has been on consent.

GENTLEMAN'S CLUB

The electric womb, where a gentleman trades dollars for D-cups. At its best, a strip club is an aphrodisiac. At worst, it's an eye-catching lick-penny that sucks money and soul by way of lechery.

Enter the club with a smile and a full wallet. Gauge the posh or sleaze factor and ask up front or over a booze order what the rules and market prices are. To optimize the experience, follow these basic tenets:

1. Spend money   **2.** Dancer ≠ Hooker   **3.** Talk light

PAYMENT

Forget the origami swan or bills held like blades in a skin-diver's teeth, and simply crease lengthwise and fork it over. Money is dirty, so keep it away from a dancer's naked rose. Amounts vary, but etiquette is stead-fast. Be bountiful with singles for girls on the stage and don't ogle an adjacent table dance without contributing toward the view.

RESPECT

Give respect, or even fat cash won't make a dancer amenable. This is nei-ther a tea party nor a locker room, and comments about her body should

══════════════ **MAIDEN'S BLUSH** ══════════════

♦ ♦ ♦ ♦ **Gin** ♦ **Triple Sec** ♦ **Dash grenadine** ♦ **Dash lemon juice** ♦ ♦ ♦ ♦

split the difference. Skip the oft heard and ineffective, "Nice titties"; try, "Lovely breasts." She shouldn't have to dwell on one unpleasant experience for the rest of her shift. Dancers are not diner waitresses, so don't point or snap to get attention. This isn't the ASPCA either: professionals are there by choice, not on display awaiting foster homes. During a table dance, allow some space. Don't put the lady on edge. If you want to maximize her experience in your personal space, read the vibes before reacting. A casual touch on the back is less cavalier than a clumsy grope.

FANTASY

The best gentleman's clubs are expressions of goddess energy, often bastardized, but nevertheless places where spiritual connections are measured one dollar at a time. Dancers fancy a mix of witty chat and nudity ("Talk to me, tell me I'm beautiful"). Probing questions about outside life, tenure, motivation, and relationship status are unwelcome ("If you ask about my boyfriend, I'll ask about your wife"). Her real name is irrelevant; she is playing a role and so are you.

Want to be a prick? Go to an upscale club with a bachelor party, spread degrading vulgarity instead of cash, and pine for unreasonable extracurricular play. Want to be original? Look into her eyes and inhale the muse, not just her ass.

Chapter Nine

TROUBLE

◆ ◆ ◆ ◆ ◆ ◆ ◆

Sticky Situations & Solutions **252**
◆ How Many People Have You Slept With? 252
◆ Your Lover Finds Evidence of Old Flames 256
◆ Your Girlfriend Says, "I'm Pregnant" 257

Conversational Gaffes 258

Secrets, Lies, & Confidences **261**

Office Romance 265

Losing It **269**

The Apology 272

STICKY SITUATIONS
& SOLUTIONS

Chaos seeps in. Whether transpiring across a booth or pillow, sticky situations demand deft strategy. Extraction with poise defines character. There are no prescribed responses or panaceas; rather, tactful strategies that don't incite second-guessed oafish acts and thoughtless blurts. Below, romantic quagmires and resolutions for skirting disaster.

HOW MANY PEOPLE HAVE YOU SLEPT WITH?

Scenario: Pillow talk moves from tittle-tattle to résumé. Minor secrets have been exchanged, but the relationship has not progressed into complete openness. As romantic and sexual histories unfold, the question is posed.

MOTIVE

The inquirer already has an acceptable number in mind; the goal of this joust is to fall within a range. The number must be high enough to demonstrate proficiency, yet low enough to evince selectivity. Falling outside these parameters may impede intimacy and raise caution flags. This line of questioning is a vane, gauging the prevailing winds of trust. An evasive or hostile attitude corrodes mounting bonds.

Amorous dalliances of old have little to do with feelings of present. Yet, bedmates expect a certain amount of libidinous disclosure. Such information is ostensibly relevant to STDs, though it makes unfair fodder for stereotypes. Until the relationship is ripe for frankness, answer with gourmet delicacy. Brutal honesty about numbers may tarnish fond feelings and ultimately cheapen a budding relationship in a cloud of machismo. Why show a full house when three of a kind wins the hand?

Consider yourself a hostile witness; this information is a gentleman's privilege, so don't give it up quickly. Open with a saucy reply and impeccable eye contact: "Including you? Two . . . give or take." If pressed further, remain cagey and state with deadpan delivery: "Once I settled my tumultuous hormones, I focused my concupiscence much more judiciously." If still on the stand, refer to the charts below.

Even the unchaste gentleman knows the number, within a trio. A lost count admits an unadvisable looseness of intimate affairs. To bolster believability and soften a hard total, round down to the nearest odd integer. Numbers ending in zeros sound staged—take a page from retailers who hoodwink shoppers with alluring price tags of $19.99. Why say "twenty" when "nineteen" may coax this potential lover to reach a milestone? This answer will stand for the length of your relationship.

KNOW WHAT'S COMING

This question rarely springs out of the blue; recognize the prequels. Start computing when conversation turns to sexual pedigree—"When did you lose your virginity?" or "When was your last serious relationship?" The carnal-tally query is close on the heels. Data indicating late bloomers,

=== **THIRD DEGREE** ===

◆ ◆ ◆ ◆ ◆ ◆ **Gin** ◆ **Sweet vermouth** ◆ **Dollop Pernod** ◆ ◆ ◆ ◆ ◆ ◆ ◆

prudish upbringing, or boarding school periods of promiscuity helps narrow the target range.

KNOW WHAT'S TO FOLLOW

Be prepared to clarify and justify. Follow-up questions include: "How many times have you been in love?" or "How many were one-night stands?" If you are scrambling and rustling your notes at the podium, focus the discourse on qualifying, not quantifying, your experiences.

Incidentally, play coy. You may invoke the Fifth Amendment and refuse to incriminate yourself. This cavalier attitude is reserved for flings. Or, after fessing up, profess indifference to hearing their number.

THE DEMURE DOZEN

Once asked for your tally, opportunity arises to return fire. Schooled in evasive maneuvers concerning weight or age, the snappy modern lady might retort, "I've enjoyed a demure dozen." Further prodding is unnecessary. Must you know more?

TALLY TABLES

Based on age, Reported Earnings helps determine an appropriate response when you don't know the questioner's tally. The Philander Forecast plots a safe tally relative to the questioner's known total. These charts are gender nonspecific and are meant to quell discomfort, not create a sexist upper hand.

Incidentally, asking "how many" may expose an inequality of sexual experience. To some, a lover with more partners is disconcerting.

REPORTED EARNINGS

BIOLOGICAL AGE	REPORTED NUMBER
Teens (at this age, women will titter at whatever answer is given)	Report 100% of your earnings, but no more than your age
20–24	Report no more than 50% of your earnings
25–29	Report no more than 60% of your earnings
30–Retirement	Not more than two baker's dozen
Retirement and Beyond	Report entire earnings + 20% for poetic license

THE PHILANDER FORECAST

THEIRS	YOURS
1–5	≤ 11
6–10	≤ 17
11–15	≤ 23
16–25	≤ Two baker's dozen, with smirk
26–49	Full candor
50 +	Full candor + literary license

YOUR LOVER FINDS EVIDENCE OF OLD FLAMES

[naughtiness] [flash] [Polaroid camera]

Scenario: While rummaging for stamps, your flame finds intimate mash notes or compromising photos amidst personal effects. Summoned to your room by your full name, you're confronted with a fistful of evidence and a scornful look. Don't invoke Fourth Amendment privacy rights unless a barrage of doubts are hurled with venom over a nonissue.

Understand the threat (real or imagined) and resolve insecurities. Overstuffed scrapbooks from a near engagement might intimidate a relationship just out of the gates. Offer reassurance of your present affections. In a long-term relationship, ancient keepsakes are worth minor fussing, not major fighting.

Most serious charges are lobbed against exes still in your life, however infrequently. Also, if there is bad blood between current and old flames, expect a housecat's territoriality when it comes to your bed and heart. Prepare to defend against the office shredder or a burning bowl ceremony. Explain that love notes no longer carry any passionate weight, but are tokens of experience and closed life chapters.

PREVENTATIVE MEASURES

Sensitive items should be discreetly (but not secretly) stowed. A shoebox of notes carries a lot less significance than wall-sized photomontages and trophy cabinets of mementos. Discovery and outrage are mitigated altogether with a guided tour through times of yore.

ADVANCED DEFLECTION

Before the seething venom of jealousy is inflicted, step forward. Nonchalantly deflect a screaming line drive with disclosure; a casual exclamation defuses the powder keg: "Oh, that letter is from Rebecca, my college sweetheart. Let me show you my favorite passage."

YOUR GIRLFRIEND SAYS, "I'M PREGNANT"

Gentlemen, we'll skip the health-class lecture on how these things happen. How you handle this situation is an excellent measure of overall gentility, as it compels a genuine appraisal of the relationship and attitudes toward children. Run away from a woman now and your character is lamentable; maintain conscience and support, and your soul will double in value.

What's the man to do? Observe her body language. Do lips quiver with regret or murmur with delight? If the latter, step in and show willingness to participate. Handle the emotional issues first before discussing practical considerations. Postpone talk of cribs or clinics until after appraising her state of mind. Later, get to the logistics: her cycle, medical history, and pregnancy test results. By now, it's an appropriate time to ask what she'd like to do next. Talk about it. Discussions of pregnancy crises either unravel weak links or bolster strong bonds. Whether the results are positive or negative, both parties come out with a more complete understanding of love, sex, and commitment.

When conception is the goal, congratulations. Three absolute don'ts when pregnancy is unexpected:

1. Don't raise the paternity issue in haste. Wait for a doctor's confirmation. There is nothing to gain in striking up mistrust without certainty.

2. Don't treat the pregnancy with lesser or greater weight than she, and certainly don't act like it's her problem.

3. Don't initiate sex. Allow your partner's spirit to dictate your next encounter. Even if the pregnancy is ultimately a false positive, restraint demonstrates remarkable sensitivity.

Ideally, a late period is not the first time babies are discussed during long-term relations. Walks down the contraception aisle should prompt the explication of viewpoints on reproduction, abortion, and adoption. Early airing of these issues prevents rocky indecision and surprises.

CONVERSATIONAL GAFFES

Take that fully shined, patent-leather shoe and shove it in your mouth. Even the most adroit gentleman stumbles on occasion. Don't panic—show poise like an Olympic skater whose triple lutz ended ass-first on the ice.

Recognize the avoidable gaffes and look to the cures when calamity strikes. Whatever the remedy, don't inflate a minor boner or trivialize a flagrant oops. Whitewash foolhardiness with panache and stand tall for half gaffes. In case of serious fallout, don't play word games.

There is no magical Rescue Remedy for any particular gaffe. Deploying the proper one depends on several factors.

Severity: Forgetting a punch line might warrant a Groucho-like Slink Away or Change of Topic, while the more serious gaffe of a racial slur begs an Immediate Confession or Subsequent Redress.

CARDINAL GAFFES

OFF-COLOR JOKE	Racial, religious, cultural, political.
THE KILLJOY	Legal, medical, financial, and other morbid topics that bring the curtain down.
ARCANE REFERENCE	Inside joke, obscure quotation.
IMPRUDENT APPLE POLISHER	Uncomely sexual advances in the wrong direction (other's spouse, roommate, boss, Girl Scout).
THE CRICKET CHIRPER	After your wisecrack, silence is deafening.
SLIP OF THE LIP	Blown cover; divulgence of secrets or past misdeeds.
DRUNKEN INSULT	Unintended malice, candor, or profanity.
THE RERUN	Breaking old news and revisiting thrice-told anecdotes.
MORE THAN I NEEDED TO KNOW	Over-reporting of undesirable details.
THE MUSICAL CHAIRMAN	The music stops and you're caught shouting.
THE UNDUE ERUDITE	Spare the townsfolk your liberal arts vocabulary.
JARGON JUNKIE	Excessive use of shop-talk tech lingo and governmental acronymns: GAAT, UNICEF.
JUNKIE JARGON	Exhibiting too deep a résumé of fringe enterprises, narcotic slang, and paraphernalia.

RESCUE REMEDIES

IMMEDIATE CONFESSION	"That was a poor choice of words."
CHANGE OF TOPIC	Move on, no major damage.
RECRUITMENT	Raise a quorum to defend a position: "Tell 'em Tesauro—Bon Jovi's from Sayreville and Bruce is from Freehold."
THE TROUBADOUR	Deft save with improvisational brilliance.
FULL-COURT PRESS	Stand on convictions: "You heard me, he's a Communist."
HOT POTATO	After a fumble, pass the mic to a surer-footed emcee.
THE TURNAROUND	Follow up an Immediate Confession with complimentary candor: "Pardon my flattery, but your dress *is* quite fetching."
SLINK AWAY	Two-word aside followed by swift departure: "Tough crowd."
THE FILL IN	Footnote a historical reference or clarify obfuscated language.
THE AMBASSADOR	Dispatch a diplomat to smooth a faux pas.
SUBSEQUENT REDRESS	Apology proffered slightly after the fact: "I'm sorry for last night."
OLIVE BRANCH	Peace offering of small gesture or drink.

Personality: A lack of comedic improvisation or quick thinking limits use of the Troubador. Less poetic tongues might pass the Hot Potato or engineer a friendly Turnaround.

Venue: Handle muffs at raucous parties and lively bistros with a Recruitment or spirited Full-Court Press. Formal ceremonies justify the Ambassador or a conciliatory Olive Branch when the mouth misfires.

SECRETS, LIES & CONFIDENCES

Secrets are deviously decadent, a sort of black-market trade between friends. White lies are the President's Physical Fitness Test of impromptu lyrical dexterity; though big, fat lies are treasonous. Confidences are gifts that should never be taken for granted.

WHITE LIES

Small departures from hand-on-the-Bible testimonials, white lies evaporate with little risk of serious fallout. Lame excuses are the most common white lie, typically aimed at saving face. Keep them believable: one part fact with sixteen parts make-believe is a rude assault on intelligence. Excuses are useful for deflecting blame when full-blown lies are inappropriate—tell the boss traffic was heavy, not stalled by a fifteen-car pile-up. Offering falsities that would be awful if true—such as apocryphal family death—is ominously prophetic. Also, don't sling insincere compliments about dress and appearance because you think you have to. However, altruistic quasi-truths meant to spare feelings are acceptable ("Honey, of course you don't look fat").

LIES OF CONVENIENCE

When the truth is too long a story or the kernel of justification is buried in complexity, one might cut corners for simplicity's sake. Lies of convenience are dashes of condensed fiction in place of truth, but they can backfire. They are best used when you're innocent of any wrongdoing, yet circumstantial evidence is stacked against you. The lie you tell: "I'm late because I ran into Gordon." The truth you don't tell: "I'm late because I ran into Gordon, who was with my old flame Angela." The reason for lying: "Mere mention of her name makes you angry." Used sparingly, lies of convenience are a proactive thwart of spats and past wounds. Snags occur when a convenient lie isn't enough or the full story comes to light and forces you to reconcile two stories.

LIES THAT BOOST EGO

Rampant among the juvenile and midlife-crisis sets are tall tales of fast cars, fat bank accounts, and phantom sexual encounters. Lying for ego gratification is laughable at best, pathological at worst. Make life a pastiche of reality and fantasy, but don't pretend to be someone you're not.

HYPERBOLE

Don't get huffish over the use of exaggeration for the sake of making a point or relating a furious tale. Aside from chats with insurance adjustors and detectives, embellishment is spice to the often bland dish of fact. Only the bore forsakes the imagination of poetic license in the interest of exactitude. In the name of fancy, add a few inches to the marlin that got away or the bust line of your first love. Watch for overkill, however, and don't jeopardize an honest nature with needless super-sizing of unremarkable events.

CHERRY PICKING

Though relatively harmless, half-truths are still lies. Don't be guilty of consistently excluding those tidbits of truth that paint you unfavorably. Your relationship with the listener determines when censorship is called for. For instance, omit details of excess in front of the boss.

BIG, FAT LIES

These tumorous canards are buildups of small and mid-sized lies, a Gordian knot of untruth. Expect inevitable collapse and a flurry of shrapnel. The only way to avoid detection is to tell more lies and deceive more people. The aftermath includes disappointment, scorned trust, and torched friendships.

CONFIDING

Have at least one tight-lipped confidant to unequivocally rely upon for silence. The ideal confidant doesn't need to be sworn in before each secret—sensitive information is assumed protected. Prefacing a divulgence with "Can you keep a secret?" means you're probably telling the wrong person. Before you invite someone into your sanctum of trust, consider the intent: are you seeking to gossip, gain counsel, or unload a stewing burden? For example, share a Saturday-

THE GREAT SECRET

✦ ✦ ✦ ✦ ✦ **Gin ✦ Lillet blanc ✦ Dash bitters ✦ Orange twist** ✦ ✦ ✦ ✦ ✦

night escapade with a racquetball buddy, but whisper moral dilemmas to a close comrade.

Incidentally, sometimes telling one person is telling two. Secrets confided to a married friend invariably reach the spouse.

CONSPIRACIES

Conspiracies are collective secrets with the joint responsibility of keeping things hush-hush. Following clandestine acts, co-conspirators are subjected to on-the-spot debriefing about what they can or cannot discuss, what did or didn't happen, and with whom they may share this information. For example, bachelor-party adventures are sealed unless the groom himself lifts the veil of silence. Groups of friends should forge certain alliances of incognito to affirm the strength of their bond.

PERJURY REQUEST

Sometimes you are made accessory after the fact by being asked to corroborate a false alibi, ranging from the harmless ("Tell him I forgot my phone") to the precarious ("Tell her you saw me leave alone"). Perjury requests are a lose-lose situation. You are lying for someone else's benefit, and should the web of deceit unravel, your character will be impugned. Though perjuring is to be avoided, it is sometimes inevitable, an occupational hazard of socializing. Ideally, perjury requests call for a single fib and not a flowchart of contingency lies to cover all angles. After this one dishonest detour, the path of truthfulness is resumed.

STATUTE OF LIMITATIONS

Secrets, like soy milk, have long shelf lives. Certain secrets come to light; others lose their efficacy. A confidence that has lost its damage potential is obsolete. When a truth is finally declassified, you are free to discuss it openly, though it's prudent to withhold the particulars of what you knew and when you knew it. For instance, a friend's vacation philandering is inconsequential once a breakup is finalized.

The responsibility of a confidant does not end when the friendship spoils. Prior confidences are grandfathered even after friendly and romantic relationships sour. Former friends and lovers deserve continued respect. Befouling a confidence at the first squabble or breakup dubs you an impetuous cur.

OFFICE ROMANCE

It's a late night at the office and neckties aren't the only things being loosened. You've been huddled over a stack of reports for thirteen hours and your back has developed a slight kink. After a friendly rub, a dinner break is suggested. Glasses of wine are lifted and talk strays from work.

After seeing the same pretty face every business day, familiarity may breed ill intent. Fight this urge—office romance is an avoidable minefield of corporate incest with more booby traps and legal complications

TEMPTATION

◆ ◆ ◆ ◆ ◆ **Whiskey** ◆ **Dash Pernod** ◆ **Dash Dubonnet rouge** ◆ ◆ ◆ ◆ ◆
◆ ◆ ◆ ◆ ◆ ◆ ◆ **Dash Cointreau** ◆ **Orange twist** ◆ ◆ ◆ ◆ ◆ ◆ ◆ ◆

than bank robbery. However, due to their industry or position, certain workers are exempt from the dangers of office romance. Entry-level workers with replaceable jobs needn't fear the pink slip. In the service industry, the ethic of post-shift drinks, shared smokes, and nocturnal confessions makes romantic trysts almost inevitable. In any case, don't prey on fresh hires, and when beginning a new job, observe a thirty-day waiting period to decipher the office culture.

PROSPECTS

Steer clear of affairs with the office magpie. If inclined, associates in other departments and part-time help are prudent prospects. Lay flirtatious rap outside working hours where shoptalk casually slips into personal life. An office romance is not a one-step close—it may require several lunches and a few group outings in weekend attire.

NONDISCLOSURE

Eventually, mutual attraction leads to candid conversation: "Do we know what we're getting ourselves into? Are we up for a little cloak and dagger?" Establish the ground rules soon after consummating romance: "Perhaps we should keep this to ourselves." Make sure there is a firm understanding of the difference between discretion and absolute secrecy. Err on the side of the latter.

DISPLAYS OF AFFECTION

When engaging in under-the-table amour, monitor outward appearances. Googly eyes at the copier are as fatal as a sudden, cold-shouldered evasion that registers as highly unusual. Mind the paper trail: affectionate jots of intraoffice e-mail and hushed phone calls arouse suspicion.

Don't risk blowing your cover with surreptitious trips to the supply closet, synchronized arrivals/departures on the parking deck, and elevator rides shared alone. If romance is truly blooming, pent-up anticipation from nine to five will be well worth discharging in the P.M.

DISCRETION

Office romance is not for habitual cheaters or the otherwise indiscreet. Think twice before risking career and reputation on a thoughtless dalliance. In ordinary romances, poor behavior disrupts your home life, but not office life. In the workplace, a rogue cheats on his spouse with a subordinate and faces double jeopardy of a divorce and a career nosedive. Leave extracurricular activities to the company softball team.

TREFOILED AGAIN

Another hazard of the workplace is meddling moms and dads shaking the charity cup. There is always a troop leader lurking behind the next cubicle like the office bookie. These cookie emissaries corner you during a weak moment and threaten you with Tag-a-Longs, Thin Mints, and the abominable Do Si Dos. Read your office harassment policy and do not succumb to this type of Lemon-Drop shakedown.

To be sure, enjoy the occasional Samoa with morning coffee. But, as with quality psychotropics, always buy directly from the source and not through some patsy runner doing the Brownie's dirty work. This goes double for personalized calendars, jump-rope or lay-up sponsorships, marching-band chocolate bars, and the dubious magazine subscription whereby some eighth grader tours Paris while you endure a full year of *Popular Mechanics.*

Until an office crush proves more serious than a fling, conceal your cross-dressing fetish and other provocative leanings, lest you give the other party embarrassing ammo that would sink you if broadcast. If things unravel, you are only one e-mail away from torpedodom.

POINT OF NO RETURN

Take stock and perform a six-month review, before things become so emotionally entrenched that a bad breakup necessitates someone's resignation. Even mature adults can't work amidst snickering coworkers and lingering hostilities following an unpleasant end. If the relationship review earns an optimistic thumbs-up, consider a public declassification. Speak to your immediate superiors before open hand-holding in the break room. To avoid future litigation, some companies will request each party to sign a "Love Contract" or consensual relationship agreement.

TOP SHELF, BOTTOM DRAWER

As a young lad visiting Dad's office, you eyed seasoned supervisors pulling bottles from desks and pouring strange brown liquid. As an adolescent, you watched the tube in awe as Barney Miller and Larry Tate deftly produced the office deal-closer. Now it's your turn. Brandish booze for celebratory closings and late-night bracings with weary colleagues.

The liquor must be of excellent quality, and brown (bourbon, whiskey, or Scotch). Accompanied by at least two rocks glasses, it must be stored upright in that deep, bottom desk drawer behind the hanging files. Noncompliant desks indicate that you are too low on the totem pole for this privilege: like at the rental car counter, twenty-five years or older, please.

LOSING IT

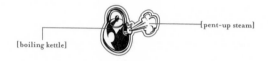

[boiling kettle] — [pent-up steam]

Don't make me angry. You wouldn't like me when I get angry.
—DR. BRUCE BANNER, *THE INCREDIBLE HULK*

Temper, temper. Even after counting ten Mississippis, taking a time-out, and sipping valerian tea, a gentleman occasionally spews his bile. When a lifetime of Anthony Robbins videos and Est seminars fails to cool the hot coals of emotional indigestion, losing it is the last resort.

The gloves come off, secrets are spilled, and the sphygmomanometer mercury spikes until the conflagration detonates into complete self-destruction. Plot your outbursts on the Bile Barometer located on page 271.

- **Cold Shoulder:** A tight-lipped and temporary uncomfortable silence; haven't had a conversation since mile-marker 57.

- **Raising Your Voice:** You can't bite your tongue any longer, so you dish out at an elevated pitch.

- **Internal Combustion:** Anger-management techniques prove ineffective; holding your breath and "going to the happy place" is not working. Shoulders are tightening—yoga class recommended.

- **Road Rage:** Knuckles white, face red, talk blue, traffic light green, and you're still stuck.

- **Flying Off the Handle:** Distinct episode of ire. This tidy tempest is typically sudden and short, a minor blemish on an otherwise pleasant day.

- **Drunken Tirade:** Now your vituperations are getting on others' nerves. Your jibes and playful breedbating have soured into an ugly stream of drunken tequila-quy.

- **Moody Fit:** Your slow-burning wick has enflamed those around you. Beyond irksome banter, this mushrooming dark spell ruins your day.

- **Rabid Billingsgate:** *You f@#%!$g so-and-so, and another thing. . .!* Eat a soft-soap sorbet for an intermezzo; your palate is feculent and foul. Crowds gather to rubberneck, take notes, and *ooh* and *aah*. Parents cover toddlers' ears and the bouncers are summoned.

- **Bitter Harangue:** Now it's personal. Ancient history is dredged up. Your rapierlike spite not only probes soft spots, but twists the blade and seasons the wound with rancor. Sacred confidences that were once affectionate are now weapons of war.

- **Nuclear Breakdown:** A Vesuvian, Krakatoan, Chernobyl-like eruption: it's all over. Book a room at Bellevue and burn your address book—no one's coming to visit.

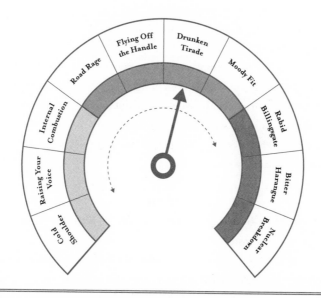

THE BILE BAROMETER

A gentleman has a long fuse. Like a well-balanced pressure cooker, let off steam in small, frequent doses and avoid the histrionic supernova that leaves a high body count in its wake. When you start to feel the Bile Barometer rise, it's time to self-monitor. After a bad day at the office, slug the heavy bag in the gym, not a fifth of Cutty Sark. Minimize ulcerous things: unpaid bills that linger, long bouts with traffic, clinging acquaintances, and a television with bad reception.

A note on getting physical: putting fists through sheetrock and sidearming dishes are unhealthy channels for anger. Violence toward people and animals is wholly unsavory, excepting the deer that hop the garden fence and munch your mums.

THE APOLOGY

When excuses expire, tempers explode, and the ash settles, practice penance and apply a mild, medium, or extra-spicy apology strategy. The Culpa Continuum efficiently divides faults, foibles, flubs, muffs, mistakes, oversights, grave miscalculations, and other blunders into a PowerPoint presentation. From the lightest transgression to the darkest betrayal, the gentleman is fittingly contrite. Oops.

MILD

The land of boo-boos, boners, and goofs. For the mildest, "I'm sorry" is not necessary—instead, sprinkle the occasional "pardon" or "excuse me." Treat forgetful foozles at face value and don't turn simple lateness or one forgotten trash day into a trust issue. Even if you have one, don't waste good excuses on trifles. Although, habitual misdemeanors accumulate on your rap sheet—every blizzard begins with just a few flakes.

MEDIUM

The arena of lapses, transgressions, and infractions. For medium-low derelictions, impromptu-yet-meaningful apologies are a start. In addition to remorseful words, furnish a modest act of good karma, such as flowers, lunch, or the more practical offer of dry-cleaning reimbursement. Close friends should shrug off these botches as long as your slate remains clean for the following week.

For medium-mediums, premeditated words or a contrite letter is called for. Lob an excuse to help explain your thoughtlessness. Further, you must furnish greater retribution, such as a homemade meal, a night on the town, or a tasteful fruit basket.

The most serious mediums also require a revisit, like an insurance adjustor, to assess the damage and confirm relationship integrity. Hopefully, the passage of time renders your fault historically curious. The phrase "I owe you one" was never more meaningful.

Often, emotional scars are less the result of severity of offense and more the consequence of untimely neglect.

EXTRA-SPICY

The pit of iniquity. One may spout profuse regret until morning, but this is merely the first peace offering of the healing process. The victim needs time and space to process the upset before renewed contact. Extra-spicy sins require third-party moderation to shuttle messages and broker a deal. This is the time to come clean and surrender. Lay yourself upon the mercy of the wronged. Excuses are despicable and represent a shallow understanding of the devastation. Apologies shouldn't focus on the reviled act, but the wake of battered emotions.

Often, you will be required to endure a difficult interrogation, with repetitive questions, uncomfortable details, and incriminating evidence. Bypass pride and answer with humble sincerity. You are lucky to be talking at all.

DEVIL'S COCKTAIL

♦ ♦ ♦ ♦ ♦ **Port** ♦ **Sweet vermouth** ♦ **2 dashes lemon juice** ♦ ♦ ♦ ♦ ♦

CULPA CONTINUUM

MILD: FORGETTABLE WITHIN MINUTES TO ONE DAY.
DEGREE OF FAULT: 0.0–2.5

0.5	Sneeze, cough, mild brushing in public, wearing a black belt with brown shoes, failing to return a friend's disposable pen.
1	Mild lateness, failing to hold the door, undercutting a fellow hailer by fifty feet to snatch a cab, filching minor office supplies.
2	White-wine spill, household chore defalcation, encrusted frying pan still in sink after five days of "soaking," forgetting to feed roommate's goldfish or sea turtle, ignoring Wet Paint sign.

MEDIUM: TIME WILL HEAL, RELATIONSHIP WILL EVOLVE.
DEGREE OF FAULT: 3.0–6.5

3	Gross lateness, blowing a mild favor, belching at a dinner party, minor fender-bender in friend's car, failing to return a telephone call for forty-eight hours, premature ejaculation, your bad mood soured an event, borrowed clothes imbroglio.
3.5	Red-wine spill, arriving home extra late and waking housemates with ruckus, failing to take dog out results in unseemly mess, being an irksome overnight guest, mild drunken slip of the tongue, failing to repay minor debt, mixing lights and darks.
4	Stood up friend without calling, large favor blown leaves friend in lurch, sharing secrets with nonrelated party, borrowing without asking, blowing off a family affair, drinking a friend's top-shelf booze and replacing it with rotgut.

5	Breaching trust, forgetting intimate's birthday or other significant date, getting visibly aroused with a lover's best friend on dance floor, extended guesting distresses host, fistless skirmish.
6	No note, major letdown, ignoring an intimate's crisis, accusing others without confronting them, major drunken spectacle, heated dish-hurling, sticking others with large bar tab.
6.5	Slip of the lip sinks friend, thoughtless racial or homosexual slur in wrong company, saying "I love you" to get sex, butting in to a breakup before the smoke has cleared.

EXTRA-SPICY: THERAPY AND SOUL-SEARCHING; RELOCATION TO NEW CITY AN OPTION.
DEGREE OF FAULT: 7.0–10.0

7	Caught in big, fat lie with fiduciary; car accident with cover-up; sharing secrets of inner circle; intentionally writing bad checks to friends.
7.5	Negligent pet care resulting in death of prized small mammal; unexplained, last-minute absenteeism at close friend's wedding.
8	Conspiratorial affairs; infidelities; getting caught with explicit, nonconsensual videotapes; breaking up after coaxing a lover to pay your credit card debt; black-eye assault.
8.5	Accidental killing of a family cat or dog, abandoning pregnant lover and other perfidy, cheating in the marital bed.
9	Stealing, fraud, abuse, and other basic unimaginables that warrant police involvement; losing your wedding band in a hooker's lair.
10	Dreadful, irreversible consequences that affect multiple parties and, indirectly, the cosmic balance; evening news–worthy betrayal. Congratulations, you just reserved that hard-to-get corner booth in Circle VII, Ring 3 of Nether Hell alongside heathens who did violence against God, Art, and Nature.

BETRAYALS OF LOVE

If felonies have affected a lover, mind your distance in the heated after-math. After betrayal, expect recoil from even the most tender caresses and hugs. Don't be cold, but offer to sleep elsewhere.

After extensive Q&A, it's time to gauge if the relationship is worth salvaging. It falls upon the offender to attempt casual recontact without pressure. Send a card or leave a telephone message when you know he or she is away. Wait until the recipient responds before proceeding further. You are on eggshell probation until further notice.

Final points:

- Reduce your sentence by turning yourself in before grapevine discovery makes your infraction public knowledge.

- Pie-in-the-sky promises won't get you off on a lesser charge. Even if you think you should say it, don't utter, "I'll never do it again" or "I'll never look at another woman."

- For medium bungles, offer (or accept) sincere apologies from good friends and keep going.

- "I was drunk" is a valid excuse for offenses 3.5 or lower; "The Devil made me do it" works for those grade 2 or lower.

Incidentally, no "to be continued . . ." Upper-medium transgressions left unsalved by an apology quickly fester into extra-spicy wounds. Clear the air before leaving town, driving away, or hanging up.

PART FOUR

The
WAYFARING
GENTLEMAN

Chapter Ten

TRAVEL

♦ ♦ ♦ ♦ ♦ ♦ ♦

Motoring 279

Asking Directions 285

Bumper Stickers 286

Jet-Setting 288

Mile-High Club 291

Sleeper Trains 293

Theorem de Valise 294

Guest Decorum 298

MOTORING

[authority vehicle] [dreaded siren]

Driving is a mobile form of hosting. Arrange passengers like dinner-table invitees. Take initiative to keep ladies and escorts together and guide the tall or large to the front. You are the pilot: if you'd like, illuminate the No Smoking sign and point out exits at the front, side, and rear of the cabin. With windows down, give a breeze check for backseat patrons (and the hair conscious), especially during freeway travel. When air conditioning or heat is involved, note passengers' body language. Are they huddled together, conserving hot breaths? Have they pressed their flushed cheeks to the glass in an effort to cool down? A little "How's the weather in here?" goes a long way.

Make transport time socially productive. Nothing separates the front and backseats like loud speakers that drown out conversation. Although, road ditties can be blasted ("Radar Love" is more crowd-pleasing than sing-along Neil Diamond hits; above the Mason-Dixon line, "The Devil Went Down to Georgia" is questionable).

In Italy, where machismo and horsepower merge on winding highways, the law of *il sorpasso* (to pass with an automobile) dictates Andretti speed and blind passing. In America, preserve riders' sanity by not stopping hearts with near misses, hair-raising banked turns, or shoulder passing. Unless trying to annoy, do not drive the way you drive alone. Running red lights, slamming on brakes, and doing donuts in snowy parking lots are reserved for easily impressed mistresses. The most overlooked aspect of a seamless ride lies in the driver's artful ability to smooth stops and starts. With a full manifest on board, consciously manage brakes to prevent rocking quease and miniwhiplash at every stoplight.

Incidentally, the Modern Gentleman always uses his signal, not necessarily to ask permission, but to indicate intent.

SPEEDING

For novices, a posted speed of 55 MPH does indeed suggest a limit. Interpret speed postings as a gauge of terrain. Typically, 70 MPH signs aren't found on winding trails. Of course, there is the law. One weighs the benefits of speed with the inconvenience of moving violations and night court. In general, reserve the lead foot for open stretches, familiar territory, and summertime trips with the top down.

No need to break into triple digits except to test new wheels at full throttle. Speeding is utilitarian for the perpetually tardy, but recklessness is reprehensible, especially in a shimmying jalopy that was manufactured during the Bush administration (the first one).

Sharpen eyes for fellow Sunday drivers flashing headlights and return the favor next time you see the sheriff poised in a shaded gully. Ease off the accelerator at intersections, bridges, on-ramps, and swaths

═ SCOFFLAW ═

◆ ◆ ◆ ◆ **Rye or bourbon** ◆ **Sweet vermouth** ◆ **Dollop lemon juice** ◆ ◆ ◆ ◆
◆ ◆ ◆ ◆ ◆ ◆ ◆ **Dollop grenadine** ◆ **Dash bitters** ◆ ◆ ◆ ◆ ◆ ◆ ◆

cut across woodsy highway medians where cruisers make U-turns. Drop to reasonable speeds when approaching the crest of a hill or a stopped vehicle. Ludicrous speed is unnecessary; enjoy the countryside.

Incidentally, play "follow the leader" and draft slyly behind a blazing sports car with its radar-detector LED lights beaconing from the dashboard. Don't fret; like Lee Majors, the 'vette will be the fall guy when smokey emerges from the median.

CLOCKED

If stopped for speeding, pull over slowly, turn off the engine, unroll the window, and place your hands on the steering wheel. Before a word is spoken, you must appear unarmed and compliant. Always address the officer with a clear, curt "Good day, officer," and nothing more. Wait and allow the deputy to explain your defalcation before volunteering any excuses. Never answer the question, "Know how fast you were going?" with an actual integer. If pressed further, state valid excuses with contriteness,

---

DULLARD ON BOARD

A gentleman does not parade cutesy back-window stuffings, windshield-obstructing rearview-mirror danglings, or side-window suction-cup signage. Eschew the stupidity of fake limbs dragging from the trunk and raccoon tails in the gas tank. Window placards announcing mothers-in-law or toddlers on board are the marquee of blockheaded drivers and guarantee curbed courtesy from other motorists. A single strand of Mardi Gras beads is permissible, but graduation tassels, cheap garters, or rotating CDs are unwelcome dashboard trinkets. Festooned fuzzy dice are encouraged for vintage hot rods.

not drama. The most effective requests for leniency are truthful (medical or family emergencies, relationship heartache) or a simple petition ("Could you kindly issue me a warning this time?"). Alas, the waterworks and flirtatious smile reside solely in the ladies' quiver.

STEERING

Besides the prescribed ten-and-two position, perfect the loose, one-handed noon grip for lazy lanes, allotting a free hand for gratuitous pointing or itinerant affections. The reinsman and steering wheel should get acquainted at a cordial arm's length. Engage the tilt steering and drape back the seat a smidge. Not too much: you should resemble neither the super-reclining Memorex Man nor the tottering granny with chin raised one inch from the windshield.

Nice touch: Master the art of knee driving, especially on carefree sunny days whilst employing the cruise control. Nudge your patella into the steering grooves for effective control and increased safety.

PASSENGER ETIQUETTE

Take control when the driver's radio and climate choices have nullified the joy of being chauffeured. Before usurping the host with a discourteous stretch across the console, preface with a statement. When engaging heat: "Mind if I throw a log on the fire?" or whilst changing a Celine Dion song: "Seeing her live really takes the thrill out of studio recordings." Never touch the dial when the motorman is singing along, unless you're older, cooler, or have a backup ride home.

Take advantage of constrained personal space to pose revealing inquiries that might be unsuitable in larger crowds or more open environments. Gather personal inventories: where from, current (romantic) affairs, or books read. En route, cultivate group dynamic. Later, "same-car" people can count on each other for cocktail retrieval, restroom trips, or escape hatches from bland conversation.

FORE & AFT

Passenger roles are based upon seat position. The shotgunner is the conversation and music moderator, with a deft hand for volume and

---

ROAD TRIPPING

Motorcarring for the sake of rolling scenery and the joy of crossing state lines is worth more than discount airfare. Peanut baggies at 35,000 feet have nothing on craggy coastlines and the salty wind smacking at your T-top along the cruise north on U.S. 1 from Los Angeles to San Francisco. At the rental car counter, always inquire about convertible upgrades, except for January visits to Fargo for the Eastern North Dakota State Curling Finals.

Don't leave home without: a pack of tissues or wet-naps, coolered drinks, crunchy snacks, beach towel for dips and spills, travel journal, night-driving stimulants, and music collection all-stars covering moods from daytime rock and operatic exuberance to mellow acoustic. Designate a rest-stop brown bag for litter to prevent thoughtless defenestration of empties.

With or without a map, solitary road trips are therapeutic and clarifying. Forget a bad breakup, decide which grad school to attend, or merely feel space beyond the city block. Stop at a scenic lookout and get high on the mountain air. Skip the broadest routes and interstates. Hop off the exit and get lost on a back-road whim. With an empty passenger seat, periodic cell phone shout-outs satisfy cravings to share. Slip out of shoes and into pyjamas, or after a dash to the sea, sit on a sandy towel in swimming trunks.

channel selection. Responsibilities include quelling conversational secession when obstructing headrests and blaring tunes threaten to cleave the
car into front and back cliques. Over the din, only the backseat middle-
man has the ability to poke forward for catching snippets of news or randy
asides among the front circle. Thus, frontseaters should nominate the
backseat hump person to act as the booming chorus to the masses.

Shotgunners should also earn their keep by helping navigate. Know
that north and south are different from up and down, watch exit signs,
and make sure the driver isn't suffering from highway hypnosis or
Moon-Pie deprivation. Take the wheel when the driver needs to shed a
sweatshirt or burrow under the seat for a CD. Keep the car straight and
compensate for bad alignment. Decline requests when traveling at excessive speeds or if the car is careening down a mountain pass with more
curves than late-night Cinemax.

HONKING

Horn blowing, on the decline, has been unduly criminalized. In some
urban areas, the "La Cucaracha" soundburst is a Class-E felony. Gone
are the halcyon days of Saturday afternoons filled with intermittent beeps
commemorating victory by the varsity football team.

Sound off in the following situations:

* The light turns green and you are immobilized behind an import luxury sedan, driven by a reptilian matron buried in her Chanel compact.
Lay it on, hopefully causing creative beauty lines.

* When lively conversation in the cabin boils over in delight, give a
medium burst to alert the heavens to such joy.

- Give a bunt to persistent lane-drifters, a soft staccato to alert cyclists.

- While respect for the elderly is a proper pillar of society, sharing your lane is another matter. Let her ring.

CARAVANNING

For traveling in tandem, red lights and stop-and-go traffic warrant passenger shuffling, water pistoling, spontaneous driver switching, selective flesh flashing, or the jettisoning of foodstuffs toward brethren autos.

Incidentally, when returning a borrowed auto, fill up the tank and reset the presets. If borrowing for longer than a week, give the car a wash.

ASKING DIRECTIONS

There is nothing ungentlemanly about getting lost. It's the method of getting found that evokes style and cunning. Except for Prince Henry, no navigator is infallible and everyone should employ a certain amount of navi-guessing. Keeping mum as you secretly question your whereabouts is acceptable if the sun position or highway signs verify that you

WHICH WAY

◆ ◆ ◆ ◆ ◆ ◆ ◆ ◆ ◆ **Brandy** ◆ **Pernod** ◆ **Anisette** ◆ ◆ ◆ ◆ ◆ ◆ ◆ ◆ ◆

are at least traveling in the right direction. If temporarily fazed, practice some "discombebopulation" and lower the radio to focus concentration. However, if frantically adrift like William Bendix in *Lifeboat,* never use the "back of my hand" analogy to hide your desperate situation. Better to sigh and gently pull over if directional hopes rest on some pipe dream of magical signage or trail of breadcrumbs on cold pavement.

Decide to ask for directions before a passenger suggests it—this nip in the bud will save your gentlemanly reputation. Passersby may be referred to for venues in the general area when you're within mere blocks. Otherwise, it is acceptable to ask a policeman or stop at a gas station to quietly peruse a map.

Steer clear of sinking, ominous auto vibes that pall the cabin after the discovery of an unplanned twenty-mile detour. Everyone dreads the realization that precious life energy was drearily squandered on a barren country road or interstate. After such a mood blow, regain bearings. Like a Saint Lawrence breaker, smash the conversational ice, lest you have a boatful of sulking, Caine-Mutinous passengers ready to pounce on a single four-way-stop hesitation. Should morale plummet, give up the keys and fall upon the mercy of clamoring backbenchers.

BUMPER STICKERS

These auto op-ed pieces incite tailgaters to honk in good humor, recognize fellow alums, or dream of later keying your fine hatchback. Bumper space is valuable: the gentleman limits himself to two items on the fender, if any. Sticker creep is not tolerated; peel away refugees that have migrated to the lower trunk. Err on the side of none; like convenience-store shoplifting, extreme prudence and moderation are the touchstones. Abstinence, dare we say, is best.

Choices are legion; taste is limited. Express affiliations, music tastes, and philosophical leanings, not corporate pap or travel logging ("This car [and 40 million others] climbed Mt. Washington"). Expired seasonal decals denoting access to exclusive beach communities are pretentious. Election-time stickers are advisable for the active voter, but like holiday lights, they should be taken down in timely fashion—after defeat in the primaries or following the joyous innaguration. A single university decal is acceptable. Multivehicle owners should affix stickers to the utility car, not the touring sedan. Before applying a sticky witticism, suppress your giggle and ask: will it be as witty a month from now? To an irascible motorcade during a ten-mile summertime backup?

Like a tattoo, the bumper sticker is personal, if less permanent. Avoid giving too much away. Be proud of proclivities for skiing or bathhouses without the rear-window advert. For the botanist who fancies hydroponics, posted cannabis leaves are probable cause for police stops in suburban enclaves.

Be a sticker stickler. Select clever over choleric, zippy over zealous. For instance, "My other car is a Ferrari" might work best on another sexy import or pasted on the muffler of a moped. "I brake for Jesus" is common, but the lesser-known "I brake for hallucinations" is more expressive. "My karma ran over your dogma" is well regarded by these gentlemen, though the baffling "I ❤ Quisp" is more singular. Then again, a clean bumper, perhaps with a small scuff from last Saturday night, is wisest.

JET-SETTING

Jetiquette should accompany you from the ticket counter, metal detector, and departure gate to your window seat. Too many travelers vent poor time-management skills on airport staff or act like helpless cattle, pestering personnel and attendants with silly bothers ("I have a boarding pass, do I need to check in again?"), endless queries ("When do we take off?"), and childish wants ("Can I have three pillows?"). Match their impudence with kindness; you're more likely to receive a smile, an extra bag of nuts, or an upgrade to business class.

A preflight ritual settles nerves. Tuck away a few familiar items every time you fly: a tattered writing tablet for tray-table haiku, a current read for escape, and a small lunchable or snack for the inevitable delay. Whisper a short affirmation while taxiing down the runway: "May the pilot's skills never waver and may my fellow passengers' karma be turbulence free."

WAITING

Don't get mired in needless delays. A wily veteran seeks out plan-B solutions by confirming departure times or rerouting flights to alternative airports (if Washington National is snowed in, try Dulles or BWI). Leave your apple-pie insecurities at home. Arriving in advance spares hassles, but arriving too far in advance counteracts the convenience of flying. When security clearance goes smoothly, make the most of unexpected terminal time instead of exhausting your snack pouch and temperament. Watch for corner arcades, the rare airport health club, and opportunities to weasel entry into VIP lounges.

DRESSING

The gentleman's wayfaring attire should be comfort based but not contrary to gallant style. Observe a relaxed return-trip protocol, but always look dashing on the outbound. Wear a pocket square or straw hat for deplaning via rollaway island steps, and always dress for the unexpected bump to first class. This is not gym class—sneakers and swishing Lycra sportswear are for traveling teens or retirees. Tank tops are prohibited, even for one-way trips to the hottest runway at Hades International.

SIPPING

If you tote your own booze on board (which is apparently against FAA regulations, but not good taste), discreetly stow a sturdy flask and a spare bottle of water, as the beverage cart isn't rolled out during take-off delays on the tarmac. A flask should be stowed in a carry-on, not on your person. The jetway is the perfect place for a last-minute package adjustment or last flask before Palookaville. Due to cabin pressure and dehydration, in-flight alcohol uptake is especially potent, exacerbating jet-lagged haggardness. Imbibe for ease of comfort but don't be a rowdy souse sauced on Scotch nips and flask sips.

PERSONAL SPACE

Mile-High Club ambitions aside, not every rowmate wants to be chatted up. Still, a polite introduction fosters agreement over dinner tray passing, gum borrowing, and future lavatory aisle scoots. Establish territory early but mind unwieldy newspapers, clicking laptops, elbow management, and snoozing lean-overs into a sovereign seat space.

LUGGAGE

Unless traveling for an extended period, packing sports equipment, or bearing holiday gifts, only chumps check one bag. Even if it must be opened and laid flat, a sturdy black garment bag or medium-sized grip-sack easily fits in the overhead compartment and can house enough belongings for a generous stay. For multiple bags and packages, take advantage of skycaps for curbside check-in. Tip adequately ($2 per person, more for leaden suitcases) or risk sending your belongings on a one-way trip to Honolulu while you wander in Boston.

THE RED-EYE

If you have trouble sleeping at a 92° angle in a foam-filled, 1978 DC-10 "buoyant" airplane seat, try popping an over-the-counter sleeping pill before take-off for uninterrupted winks. After reaching cruising altitude, commandeer an unoccupied row toward the aft. To skirt the

---

BAGGAGE CLAIM

Prepare to snake your way through the clutter of golf clubs, snow skis, and caged pets to lay claim to your effects. Get a ringside spot but avoid standing mesmerized in front of an empty carousel before the bags are spit out. Once ready, get in the paint, box out, and crash the boards; it's all about positioning and the occasional off-the-Samsonite rebound. Since you're not the only one with a black duffel bag, adorn your valise with a marker, ribbon, or travel tag. Be nice: rescue a wayward bag that has turned the corner out of someone's reach, assist a neighbor with lumbering trunks, and clear the mouth of lodged impediments to maintain flow.

stringent upright-seat-for-landing rule, mildly recline your seat and the empty others to create the illusion of compliance. For greater comfort, raise the armrests and nestle into your three-seat boudoir.

Lastly, be a courteous traveler, cognizant of others, especially on full flights during holiday travel. As the plane rolls toward the arrival gate, don't be the early claim jumper who chokes off the aisle, scrambling about the fuselage in a vain attempt to wrassle scattered baggage from three different overhead compartments. Note one exception to the courtesy rule: when the irksome lout in front reclines so far into your lap as to afford a molar-and-dandruff check, be mischievous. Aim the air conditioner nozzle accordingly and adjust to maximum blow. Results may vary from immediate seatback ascension to a post-flight stiff neck.

Nice touch: Skip the potluck roulette and request the fruit plate (which actually contains fresh fruit) when making reservations.

MILE-HIGH CLUB

This badge of travel lust is a tawdry exhibitionist feat that has little to do with romance. Saying you're in the club is likely more impressive than the act that inducted you. Membership has no privileges, newsletter, or motel discounts—at best, it is useful as locker-room fodder or for a shared laugh with your lover. Mile-High Club membership should be a natural extension of arousal from window seat to lavatory, and not a coax into action for the specific reward of earning your wings.

Notes on the rapacious pastime of some frequent fliers:

+ No schematic or intricate plan is necessary. After breathing a few randy
  come-ons, dare a lover to meet you in the aft starboard lavatory in
  three minutes. The in-flight movie provides excellent cover and built-
  in diversion, as the dimmed houselights obscure comings, goings, and
  flushed faces. For tactical advantage, wait until the aisle-blocking beverage trolley is near your row. Slip to the back while busy attendants
  and other passengers are stranded on the far side of the cart.

+ Send a scout to sweep the area for long lines, nosy flight attendants, or
  any impediments that might queer the deal. Secure the vacant restroom and await your partner's knock.

+ Upon conclusion, do a thorough mirror-check and leave the restroom
  with aplomb, clothes intact, head held high, as you slide the door lock
  from *occupado* to vacant and face the world. At this point, even if fin-
  gered by the captain and copilot, it is fait accompli. Give a wink for
  style and return to your seat. Sorry, no smoking on U.S. domestic
  flights, even in the afterglow.

+ Keep it to once per flight, please. In fact, once *ever* is sufficient.

Advanced technique: When renewing membership, up the ante. Try
the forward cabin lavatory or, when in extra-wide first-class seats, the
blanket-covered silent spoon. For the most seasoned club member,
attempt rare maneuvers in a turbulent, open-cockpit propeller plane.
Of course, a love connection made in-flight between strangers is the
most naughty and daring form of aviator intercourse.

SLEEPER TRAINS

Sleeper trains connect the gentleman to century-old luxuries across the bucolic tracks of Americana. Read some Ambrose Bierce, order a whiskey in the club car, and enjoy the caboose, as sleeper cars are typically found at the rear. There's something particularly hypnotic about gazing down the tracks as endless rail converges in the distance.

Today's sleeper trains are tops in rail travel, well worth a coach-fare upgrade. Designed by calculus-wielding space maximizers, sleepers waste no space. Pack light so luggage neither cramps the area nor blocks the air-conditioning vents. Most sleepers feature top and bottom single bunks with little extra room, though a spooning twosome can squeeze on one and toss baggage on the other. The toilet is similar to an airplane lavatory, with a fold-down sink that harkens back to days of bedside wash-basins. Travelmates not accustomed to an open bathroom-door policy might splurge for a first-class sleeper with a separate three-quarter bath.

For maximum privacy, close the door and draw the drapes to avoid peeping passersby. Conversely, leave the sliding door open to catch the corridor breeze. Bed linens are provided and there's a set of straps either for securing yourself in sleep or restraining a lover. Either way, they are best deployed during bouts of turbulence.

═══ BLUE TRAIN ═══

◆ ◆ ◆ ◆ ◆ **Gin ◆ Cointreau ◆ Lemon juice ◆ Dash blue curaçao** ◆ ◆ ◆ ◆ ◆

Nice touch: When booking a compartment, select the sunrise side and then leave the shades open and awaken to the percussion of a chugging locomotive at first light.

THEOREM DE VALISE

The classic overpacker chokes his bag with a different ensemble for every moment and mood. Conserve. Mix, match, and plan to depart and return in the same outfit and bulky coat. Tote workout attire for unexpected fitness opportunities. A voluminous wardrobe isn't at your disposal when traveling; no one will fret if black pants get a second-night reprise. Learn from prior packing mistakes. Notice what was left unworn from the last trip and pack lighter next time.

Our Theorem de Valise replaces guesswork with mathematical certainty. Dust off your abacus and see below for practical packing ratios that measure shirts, pants, and shoes against nights away.

Beyond efficiency, traveling affords the chance to pack your closet's greatest hits. Instead of taking two months worth of hot-date ensembles, tote a bagful of favorites for four days and three nights of nonstop style and mood changes. It's okay if everyone thinks you dress this way all the time. Know the mercury and itinerary ahead of time. City avenues and mountain hikes call for different clothes and shoes. For long weekends, pack daytime kicks and a snazzy pair for the evening. Shoe color, black or brown, determines pants and belts. Fill a valise with interchangeable clothes that match these shoes. Shirts and pullovers are the wild cards that stretch two pairs of slacks into four different outfits. Special shoes that go with one outfit are forgivable for extended stays when extra footwear isn't frivolous.

Five steamer trunks is overkill for a simple getaway, but stowing a little comfort is essential. Before stuffing a suitcase with practical items like toothbrushes and airline tickets, gather personal bits of home. Turn any motor inn into an inviting abode without paying $8.95 for the edited late-night feature. Stow a scented candle, a pet photograph, pyjamas, choice tunes, and a strong dose of vitamins to counter local bacteria.

Nice touch: Don't forget the fun stuff—water pistols for a picnic, handcuffs for the fetish club, flannel for a hayride, or a ski mask if short of cash.

CHECKLIST

Pack carefully before embarking for a wedding or formal gala that requires a bevy of accoutrements often left behind. Perform a thorough

---

TOILETRY KIT

Something small, black, and durable, containing at least two compartments, is adequate for all affairs. Skip the haphazard pile of beauty products strewn about the bottom of one's luggage. A toiletry kit should reflect simple preparedness without medicinal overabundance. Travel-sized products or holders ease congestion and mass. With purchase of this book, you hereby promise to destroy forthwith your old, periwinkle-blue or vomit-beige, wide-stitched, canvas-like American Tourister toiletry bag won at the church raffle ten years ago.

In addition to reloadable basics like deodorant and toothpaste, have an inventory of in-a-pinch essentials like: a diminutive bottle of aspirin and multivitamins; decongestant; extra contact lenses; bowel remedies and antacids; disposable razor; condoms; small bar of facial soap; safety pins; nail clippers; Band-Aids; and styptic pencil.

sartorial run-down before zipping the bag. A simple recitation averts a last-minute trip to a sporting-goods store for black tube socks to wear under tuxedo pants.

A garment bag oral checklist (literally meant to be spoken aloud):

❏ Shoes	❏ Socks	❏ Pants	❏ Belts	❏ Undershirts
❏ Boxers	❏ Shirts	❏ Ties	❏ Jackets	
❏ Cufflinks	❏ Handcuffs	❏ Large Medallion Necklace		

ADVANCED TROUBLESHOOTING

Don't forget the extras that are bag mainstays: business and playing cards, pens, loose change, and matchbooks from prior trips for nostalgia. To lower stress, pack a spare pair of dress socks in case of an inadvertent step into an invisible hotel bathroom puddle. Moods change between packing day and the big event. Bring various dress shirts and ties and decide at the last moment. When going to a black-tie event, be the warm-bosomed schoolmarm: stow a cheap spare bowtie and set of cufflinks in your tuxedo pocket for a forgetful chum. To prevent a mishandled-luggage catastrophe and a $500 dry-cleaning bill, store shampoo, cologne, hair gel, and other powder kegs in a sealed Ziploc bag.

THEOREM DE VALISE

Algebra finally serves a gentlemanly purpose: whether your triangle is isosceles or scalene, you are bound to find value in this easy, plug-and-pack Theorem de Valise—a mathematical construct as riveting and complex as Fermat's own. Punch in your data to calculate how many articles of clothing should be packed for the holiday.

This is not your father's quadratic equation.

$$\text{SHIRTS} = \sqrt{(\text{PANTS}^3 + \text{SHOES})} + \text{NIGHTS}/\text{DAYS}$$

Note: nights / days refers to the respective number of days and nights away.
Equivalents: shorts = 0.5 pants, sandals = 0.5 shoes,
short sleeves/pyjamas = 0.5 shirts, blazers/coats = 1.5 shirts

A WORD PROBLEM

Phineas is taking a beach weekend in the Hamptons. He is leaving Thursday after work and shall return late Sunday afternoon. He will bring a pair of dress shoes, a pair of casual shoes, and sandals. He shall also pack one pair of jeans, evening trousers, and swimming trunks. After work, he will board the 5:51 P.M. eastbound train from New York; however, a westbound train leaves Montauk at 6:10 P.M. Both are traveling at the same speed. How many shirts should Phineas pack?

Hint: the gentleman departs and returns in the same ensemble, thus his travel shirt, pants, and shoes are not packed (or counted). Also, do not forget the lounge-about T-shirt (pyjamas may be substituted) for lazy mornings. You will not receive credit for the answer if you don't show your work. Let's compute:

$$\text{SHIRTS} = \sqrt{\{(2.5)^3 + (1.5)\}} + 3/3$$

$$\text{SHIRTS} = \sqrt{(15.63) + (1.5)} + 1$$

$$\text{SHIRTS} = \sqrt{(17.13)} + 1$$

$$\text{SHIRTS} = 4.14 + 1$$

$$\text{SHIRTS} = 5.14 = 5.0$$

Incidentally, a *Flashdance*-esque torn sweatshirt is not O.I4 shirts. Stick to the nearest half integer. To avoid overpacking, always round down.

Phineas should pack two stylish shirts for Friday and Saturday nights, two casual short-sleeve shirts for the days, a blazer for dress-up or protection against an evening chill, and one polyester pyjama set.

Other formulae solve for different variables:

$$\text{SHOES} = (\text{SHIRTS} - \text{NIGHTS} / \text{DAYS})^2 - \text{PANTS}^3$$

$$\text{PANTS} = \sqrt[3]{(\text{SHIRTS} - \text{NIGHTS} / \text{DAYS})^2 - \text{SHOES}}$$

GUEST DECORUM

Be a welcome guest, not a trying inconvenience. Common sense, privacy, and humility go a long way—even long-standing college intimates deserve a tad of respect. Be nice: offer to walk the dog, wash the dishes, or make the mortgage payment. In addition to consolidating your bags and wiping excess toothpaste spittle from the mirror, learn a few other considerations.

"Make yourself at home" doesn't mean: dialing 1-900 numbers or ordering Pay-Per-View WWF specials; drinking out of the milk carton (even the buttermilk carton); belching like a rabbinical shofar blower; drawing an uninvited bath; recharging anything larger than a cell phone; annexing the living room like a conquistador (clothes strewn, sofa bed out, VCR reprogrammed, coffee table littered, multiple pizza boxes holding court); making your presence known as an early riser; bringing home an unsolicited nightcap to your aunt's house (if you have broken this guideline, do not invite your guest to breakfast); ball-playing or nakedness around the house; leaving adult magazines by the bed; exhibiting New Age or ethnic idiosyncrasies (lighting incense, curing tofu, frying curry, or hanging *soprasetta* from the rafters); hanging undergarments to dry from the shower rod (especially black bikini briefs); packing a load of laundry (except when visiting Mom); ordering take-out on the house account; littering the bedroom with a multitude of empties; smoking dope indoors (blowing smoke out the window is still considered inside); guitar strumming after 10 P.M.; using the living room as a putting green; hosting an all-night poker game.

Incidentally, if you need an extended place to stay, say so up front instead of fudging intentions with the vague, "I just need a place to crash for a few days." If your "short" visit begins to affect the host's electric bill or your guest towel sours, you have overstayed your welcome.

DON'T TOUCH

As a guest, keep out of: any medications in the bathroom; the dining room or any room designated for "hunting"; the "master study" (unless accompanied by a snifter of brandy); the humidor; expensive bottles of wine without asking; anything autographed; any piece of furniture with a historical or explanatory placard; the whiskey decanter; the family car, even with a note; hope chests; glass curios or anything in an étagère; other people's razors; any family member (in that way) including great aunts, cousins, babysitters, and farmer's daughters.

BRING A GIFT

A gentlemanly guest bestows the hosts with a small token, larger if the visit is significant. Something personal should suffice, such as a bottle of infused olive oil, novelty corn-on-the-cob holders, or an obscure Xavier Cugat vinyl LP. For others, vices are appropriate. A bottle of vino or liquor is proper if nothing more original comes to mind. However, wrap the bottle in something other than a recycled brown paper bag and don't forget the bow. Regional comestibles are winning ideas. For example, outsiders will appreciate Vermont maple syrup, New York City bagels (however, the Sunday *New York Times* is not a gift), Kansas City BBQ sauce, or local fresh flowers or plants. When in doubt, browse a museum shop or patisserie, or mail a gift ahead via the Internet.

Want to make a bigger impression? Think small, overlooked pleasures: 1,000-piece puzzles, stationery, or an array of jams, fine teas, or coffees. Indulge the host's hobbies: a twin-boxed set of playing cards for a big whist player or quirky lemon reamers for the gourmand.

Something tucked in the valise for a "meet-the-parents weekend" arrests querulous sizing up and might upgrade you from the basement couch. Gifting forges a favorable impression, earning clemency for those festooned with body art or lacking viable careers. Bestow shortly after arrival or the next morning following breakfast.

Nice touch: For longer stays, treat the host to a memorable meal (in or out) and leave a ten spot under the telephone to cover your calls.

PART FIVE

The
CEREMONIAL
GENTLEMAN

Chapter Eleven

PUBLIC
RELATIONS

◆ ◆ ◆ ◆ ◆ ◆ ◆

Correspondence 303

Answering Machines 307

E-mail 311

Gifting 315

Handy Gifting Guide 319

CORRESPONDENCE

I cherish little notes from some of my old lady friends in their eighties,
because they know how to turn a sprightly phrase in even the briefest notes
while some of my contemporaries freeze up at the sight of note paper . . . .

AMY VANDERBILT'S COMPLETE BOOK OF ETIQUETTE, 1958

If all your post arrives in windowed business envelopes, it's time to dust
off thy wax seal, clean thy nibs, and write a letter. Despite the surge in
electronic mail and cordless everything, there is nothing more intimate
than a smudged pen-and-ink shot of love.

LONGHAND

Personal correspondence is ideally in longhand, written with a favorite
pen (not the Eraser Mate 2) or clacked out on a manual typewriter with
quirky, crooked characters. The best letters are intimate, humorous, and
insightful, if slightly illegible. Pour a glass of port, light a candle, and
shrug off prime-time television. Crack epistlers suffuse a note with at
least three non sequiturs and one self-fashioned abuse of the official lexicon. Letters are forgiven occasional misspells and overstrikes. If keyed
on a computer, do not justify the margins or otherwise gussy up a note
with fancy fonts and fallacious French phrases.

PENMANSHIP

Outside of midterm-examination blue books, hen scratch should
morph into fluid cursive or cogent Courier. Befuddle the graphologist
with a ransom note but delight an interstate pen pal with crackling imagination and fine handwriting. Revel in loopy letters with soft strokes or

slanted etches with sharp, inky jerks; but be it print or script, wield a mostly legible font. For garnish, trademark a few oddities: crossed zeds, typewriter-style a's, double-scooped 8's, and flamboyant serifs.

Invest in a fine stylus that transmits a prominent line. Black or blue ink is recommended for most correspondence, but crayons and colorful hues are appropriate for birthday cards and construction-paper projects. Practice your autograph on the take-out menu while waiting for a pizza and master the perfect expression of your name in ink. A gentleman has a few signatures to work with:

+ **The Half-Second Scrawl:** For unimportant documents like package delivery receipts, put your mark by the X but omit the last few letters of a long surname.

+ **Simple Script:** For job applications and personal checks, nothing fancy, but apply unique characters that are forgery proof.

P.S. YOU ARE AN IDIOT

A P.S. is acceptable for small oversights, randy asides, or last-minute news flashes. P.P.S. dangles you over the precipice, and anything more "post" than this likens you to a fifth-grade note passer. XOXO may only be used for doting mothers, matronly kin, and long-distance tic-tac-toe games. "Sincerely" and "Very Truly Yours" are staples for business letters. For cozy communiqués, use more creative and endearing forms, ranging from "Fondly" to "Love and Other Words Between Lick and Lycanthropy in the Dictionary."

♦ **The Ornamental Hand:** For stationery, cards, and documents of consequence, apply a distinctive John Hancock.

Nice touch: Go incognito and sign innocuous office-lobby log-in books with an imperial sobriquet like Oliver Cromwell.

GREETING CARDS & SOCIAL PAPER

The most common missive is the holiday card. We prefer a slice of stringy notebook paper with actual sentiment over a store-bought greeting card scribbled with a meager "Dear __" and a signature. Artistic blank cards serve all-purpose use; a box of smaller thank-you cards and classic bond stationery are versatile. Whatever you'd use for a first-class résumé makes handsome social paper. Don't rule out craft-class scissor work or deft use of graphics software to create distinctive letterhead.

THANK YOU

Most guests inform a host or hostess they have enjoyed themselves. Few will affirm it the following week; rarer still, the guest who mails a note of gratitude. Thank you, get well, and congratulations are common sentiments commonly overlooked. Discipline yourself (and your lover at times) to deliver essential thoughts in a timely fashion.

═══════════════ **X Y Z** ═══════════════

♦ ♦ ♦ ♦ ♦ ♦ **Dark rum** ♦ **Cointreau** ♦ **Dollop lemon juice** ♦ ♦ ♦ ♦ ♦ ♦

LOVE LETTERS

A single line, posted on the way to work, expounding on the scent of her hair is as meaningful as a transcontinental "Thinking of You" post-card. Longhand woo is like a late-night, bedside peek-in by an adoring lover, usually begetting several under-the-covers rereads.

Incidentally, handwritten letters must be answered in kind. Letters lose their efficacy if left fallow and unanswered. Don't cheapen the effort with a reply via e-mail.

POSTCARDS

Send these quick, witty notions to recount recent adventures and remind addressees they are in your thoughts. Avoid "____ City at Night" or "The Babes of ___" cards, or any designs featuring smiling, nonindigenous animals. Postcards are alluring View-Master images, causing recipients to miss you and envy the exotic surroundings. Those purchased the last

---

LETTER OPENERS

Long the favored murder weapon of Ellery Queen serials, the letter opener out-classes the paperweight as an ancillary desk accessory. We prefer a stand-alone hand-me-down to an opener poorly paired with matching pens and a tape dispenser. A stiff index finger swipe is the default opener, but why ruin a good manicure mangling 24.9% A.P.R. credit card offers? For the everyday pile of utility bills, have a standard sabre, preferably lifted from the conference room or won at the company-picnic egg toss. When the mail escort delivers personal post and airmailed curios, unsheathe a top-shelf opener bequeathed by Grandpa. Savor plunging the blade into the folded nape of an envelope.

day of a trip, written on the airplane, and mailed from home are phony and nearly felonious. Plan ahead and carry postage and an address list.

Nice touch: Load the home office with generic stamps for remitting bills, but keep a stash of illustrative postage for adorning personal mail. Try to match philatelic themes to receiver or subject matter. For example, Enrico Fermi for the scientist, carnivorous plants for the vegetarian.

ANSWERING MACHINES

Since fewer and fewer machines have spinning cassette tapes, a gentleman must be proficient with the pound key. Voice mail is a digital note tacked upon someone's door. Instead of a litany of sober facts and limp requests, deliver a delicious minute worthy of a return call.

OUTGOING MESSAGE

A gent's greeting should be appropriate for business calls, friends, and parents. Thus, after age twenty-five or retirement from the rave scene, skip the licks from a techno disc recorded over a throaty "You know what to doooo. . . ." Ambient background accidentally caught on the recording is acceptable, but no need to play deejay for thirty seconds of greeting. Show personality but maintain basic formality. Confirm that callers have reached the correct line by identifying your name or number. Skip the tutorial on message formatting and beep management.

OUTGOING EXTRAS

When there's a special event, use the outgoing message for party directions, last-minute changes of plan, or personal asides (". . .leave a message. If

this is Lockie, the house key is under wicket five"). During a bout of
entertaining, redo the message to capture festive spirits.

SCREENING & CHECKING MESSAGES

Some machines still allow incoming messages to be heard live. You are
not bound to answer the telephone. Ignore a disruptive chime or pick
up upon a sprightly message. If accused of self-important call screening,
assure the caller, "I wasn't in the mood to talk—until I heard your voice."

Don't be the persistent message-checker, especially around others.
When plans aren't hinging on a timely call, don't be a contemporary
cowboy dork, quick-drawing beepers and mobile phones from hip hol-
sters at the slightest seismic vibration. Furthermore, like good e-mail,
noteworthy messages should be preserved for renewed laughs. With early-
stage romance messages, mimic a forensic voice technician and replay
them a few times to gauge intent from tone and inflection.

OPEN MIC

Leaving a message isn't mere delivery of a terse data stream. Besides
leaving record of the time and purpose, a message should be imbued
with charisma. As when singing in the shower, discard inhibitions.
However, there is a fine line between newsworthy entertainment and
querulous rambling. When regularly trailing "I guess I'm blabbing, I
should go ...," find a sandbox and bury your head. If it's not working
for you on a particular day, bow out with just the vitals: name, time,
and number.

Take up some tape. A gentleman's message can be a spoken-word
piece or running dialogue. Make a midday call to a love's home or extra-
late-night shout to a cell phone when you know your party is unreachable.

If inclined, read a passage from a nearby book or sing along with a favorite radio song. These are oral love notes.

Certain situations dictate discretion. For business calls, quiet the room, temper the tone, and be purposeful. Repeat your name and number and get to the point in twenty words or less. For new love interests, avoid umming or hawing into the receiver. Rehearse a five-second outline of what to say if the machine picks up.

VOICE-MAIL CONVERSATION

Turn telephone tag into a conversation rather than a string of "Sorry I missed you again." Be productive—why tell someone you'd like to talk to him or her when you can share ideas now? Give an update, relate a story, or work out a thought in your head. A good voice-mailer will reply with answers, not just a return number. For hot news that can't wait, call a compatriot while still in the throes of adventure, just to get it on record.

Nonetheless, don't let voice mail do your dirty work. No one is fooled by lame attempts at reconciliation or futile callbacks, usually occurring at 5:05 P.M. ("Oh, I guess you left the office already").

DO-OVER

Treat every message as live radio—no dead air. If there's a flub, keep going. However, most voice mail allows one to listen and rerecord a message. Take advantage of this eleventh-hour bailout to self-censor an underwhelming message. Collect yourself and take two. For colossal gaffes, pull the emergency brake and hit "pound" immediately. If not prompted further, hang up without a sound; a decent reply and fibbed apology of having been "cut off" is better than more cloddishness.

DOUBLE MESSAGING

Nothing sings of desperation more than a voice mail followed by another voice mail a half-hour later. This is especially true in the critical early stages of a new relationship, in which every foible is scrutinized. Double messaging is acceptable when you are timed out midsentence by the voice system or when a dramatic dispatch is better left in two acts. A follow-up call to the cell phone after striking out at the home phone is acceptable. Kindly alert the caller to your previous attempts.

HANG UPS

Don't be the persistent redialer/no-messager. Given the prevalence of caller I.D. and screening, not leaving a message carries as great an implication as leaving one. There are three types of hang-ups:

♦ **The Mid-Dial Bailout:** An incoming call or distraction interrupts.

♦ **The Message Skip:** Urgency demands a try on another line.

♦ **The Cowardly Click:** You're still on the line past the beep, and your hang up is caught on tape. Indicates fear of no return call.

Incidentally, unless you have heard their answering-machine squawk or confirmed the existence of rolling minicassettes, a gentleman needn't prate, "Are you there. . .pick up. . .are you there?"

NOTE TO SELF

Profound words sometimes spring out of your mouth, as if you've had an entire lifetime to ponder and rehearse. To preserve these pearls sans audience, leave a message of revelation, insight, or poetry in your own mailbox. Additionally, cell phones are portable microphones, ideal for capturing snippets of live action or ideas you can't write down.

E-MAIL

E-mail juxtaposes the immediacy of a telegram or telephone with the thoughtfulness of a posted letter and the casual dash of a postcard. Etiquette is a function of timing and typeset, strict form and looseness of tongue, and information and entertainment. With the opportunity to edit, fact check, and cite quotations, even short messages should sparkle.

STATIONERY & FONTS

Although the aesthetics of e-mail can never match engraved bond paper for tactile delight, there are ways to lessen e-mail's white-screen sterility. The simple employ of a low-resolution digital image makes all messages uniquely yours, but beware a mottled background in which noisy color and pattern muddy the text. Fonts are another story. Overly intricate choices end up illegible to recipients with older operating systems. Ideal font size is between 10 and 14 points; a tiny font induces blindness, towering ones resemble screaming. Adjust margins for short notes. End stops and stanzas communicate exclamations, news, and poetry better than perfect paragraphs.

Incidentally, signature lines with contact information work well in the business forum. Tacked-on quotations befitting high school yearbook captions or photocopied propaganda leaflets are irksome.

GREETINGS & CLOSINGS

Some e-mails warrant a smart greeting and witty close, others, an anonymous string of words requiring a click to the address book to identify the sender. A gentleman introduces himself, though messages under fifty words can be closed with initials or a pet name. When there's a rapid-fire exchange regarding travel plans or dinner arrangements, skip the salutation and lengthy sign-off ("Catch you at 8—Ph").

GRAMMAR & SPELLING

For first-contact e-mails, mind your grammatical manners—you never know if a potential employer's pet peeves include colloquial e-mail expressions or haphazard punctuation. This is not an excuse to be long-winded and sloppy. Don't rush off a flurry of typos and fragments; although the occasional, inadvertent "iwth" or "olve" may sneak past a hasty writer. Emoticons are fine for intermittent wordless expressions, but overuse is akin to dotting your i's with hearts. :-)

SPAM

Do not spam your friends with "special offers" or "business opportunities." Mailing such tripe to five friends may land you four acquaintances. Skip the jokes du jour and shameless chain letters, too. Sign a Spam Non-Proliferation Treaty with frequent e-mail pals and quit slinging inbox trash like so much hash. Do you really hold your friends in such low regard that you worry their good fortune will evaporate if a stale Zen message isn't passed to ten others within 24 hours?

Nice touch: Employ the Block Sender function and purge unwelcome solicitors and their spam from memory like revisionist history.

ATTACHMENTS

Attachments require deft care. Persons with free e-mail accounts can rarely open files over one megabyte. Moreover, low-speed connections make accessing these files unbearable. With attachments of singular importance or hilarity, offer a testimonial in the message that justifies the download. For unfamiliar recipients wary of viruses, explain any attachments in the message text. Offer a caveat for sensitive materials inappropriate for office computers or prying eyes. Attach first, write later; don't be an inbox nit who sends messages with phantom attachments.

DISTRIBUTION LISTS

Send special-interest messages to targeted recipients. Guard these lists and protect against poaching by employing the Bcc (blind carbon copy) function, rendering all receivers invisible to others.

E-FFECTIONS

Prequalify prospects for courtship and upgrade the love interest status of persons who meet standards of witty subtext and typed "tally-ho"s. E-mail is a tool of the cyber-savvy who communicate thoughts that aren't quite ready for the telephone, but would lose efficacy while pining away in a mailbox. Open with basic humor, luminous references, and a mild dusting of innuendo. Successive messages raise the bar of arousal, until there is a mutual flurry into intelligent hot-chat.

E-mail is a wonderful adjunct to courtship, but beware the pitfall of substituting tasty text for actual affection and body language, or worse, hiding behind e-mail's protective cloak. Some wooing must be breathed in person; too much e-mail and not enough trysting will devalue your allure. If e-mail becomes a more open forum than face-to-face dialogue, retreat from the mouse. Cagey, bleeding-heart exchanges are for tête-à-têtes over a latté. On the other hand, a confessional midday e-mail might spur important pillow conversation later.

KEEPING CURRENT

Check that box. Once a gentleman is in the game, it is impolite to let an account lie fallow as amusing messages pile up. Reply promptly, as neglecting a return post may negate a cunning joke. E-mail runs on out-box karma: whatever you send typically comes back manyfold. Prove this by going on vacation and watching your inbox dry up.

Entertaining messages should linger on the inbox leader board, allowing joyful revisits during a neap tide of nifty notes. Phone numbers and important web links can hang around as well. Secondary e-mails that don't require immediate follow-up might lurk and lobby for attention, but they shouldn't infect an otherwise orderly inbox.

E-CARDS

Phone calls, gifts, and written notes will never go out of style. E-cards are not substitutes for the real thing, but are best for minor events and appreciation. The random e-card amidst other small notions is a like-able tool of wooing when highly original and unexpected.

OUT OF THE BLUE

Thanks to sleuthing search engines, chances are high for the unexpected drop-in of old flames, homeroom chums, or past coworkers. Reply quickly, while the novelty is hot, and don't worry if the relationship returns to a dormant state after a few traded updates. It's nice to know those faraway persons are now only clicks away from renewed contact.

STEALTH ACCOUNT

When content gets too racy for the office or for shared e-mail, open an anonymous account. This secure base is below radar, perfect for sensitive files and hot-chat outside the cyber-salon. Another advantage is spam deflection: when an address is requested for website registration, use this throwaway account to route the daily influx of corporate dreck.

GIFTING

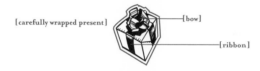

[carefully wrapped present] [bow] [ribbon]

A gentleman's gifting skills should transcend the holiday fruitcake or elk-embossed wool sweater. Do friends and family bellow, "Whoa! Where did you get this?" or force a tight, polite grin and trail, "Ohh. . .that's nice. Thanks"? The most expressive gifts do not wow with expense, but with the unmistakable stamp of "I knew you would like this." Jog creativity with a flip through catalogues or stroll through the online marketplace, but don't leave the house in search of the perfect gift until narrowing choices down to animal, vegetable, or mineral.

Gifts to best friends, a fraternal sibling, or house pets should be so individually tailored that in anyone else's stocking they would make little sense. Garner insight into tastes and listen for unconscious clues dropped as you and a future giftee pass shop windows. Thoughtful gifts are sourced from need (are they missing a small appliance?), personality (hard-to-get playoff tickets?), hobbies (anything in a bottle for the wine enthusiast?), and guilty pleasures (a day at the spa?). A good test: does the gift mean something to _you_? If you are tempted to keep it for yourself, the only thing better is bestowing it upon an intimate.

Don't be a December 24th rote wrapper. The best gifts are those you serendipitously stumble upon months before the occasion. Though it's only May and a friend's birthday isn't until October, better to snatch up that combination backscratcher/shoehorn you know she'll love than be caught scrounging for a present at the last minute. A wish list recited months before is forgotten by the time a ribbon-wrapped box is in hand; the recipient will be doubly delighted by such premeditated gifting.

Be attuned to occasions when gifting is an obligation of relationship maintenance. Such gifts of duty to the in-laws, a cubicle mate, or the doting probation officer are efficiently bought and delivered without the usual mires of cost and selectivity—like a vacation souvenir.

Incidentally, wrapping is rarely optional. The surprise is enhanced with thick paper, colorful trappings, and a small card. Even if it's your favorite Snoopy pattern, don't eye the paper for reuse.

FOR THE LOVER

Never give a gift that would make the recipient uncomfortable. Thus, diamond-studded earrings after the third date are inappropriate, while a small book of poetry or objet d'art is fun. Always be cognizant of subtle hints or casual asides. Does she repeatedly linger over something in the same shop window? Or perhaps she used a more direct approach ("Umm, I really want that catamaran").

The most memorable gifts are often uninitiated notions handed over without occasion. Do you want to be another afterthought at the dusty bottom of her overstuffed jewelry box, or the first to escort her to a ball game? Fine alternatives: frame a picture of the two of you, take your thoughts to paper (a poem or sweet letter) or canvas (can you water-color?), or hit the wood shop for a handcrafted creation.

Nice touch: Present four courses instead of a one-dish meal. A bevy of books, framed photographs, and bathtub pamperings are ne'er amiss.

GIFTING PITFALLS

A gift bespeaks your relationship with the recipient. Beware these common gifting blunders when exchanging affections:

- **The Stale Hint:** The lady offers a clue, but failing to act on it quickly proves fatal. In an whimsical mood three months ago, she may have wanted that Belgian teakettle, but now . . .

- **The Projection:** The six-tape Sean Connery James Bond set is a great gift . . . for you.

- **The Candy Dish:** "Look, honey, another toaster." The wedding gift table is sagging with Crock-Pots and food processors. Think harder.

- **The Useless Gift:** Oops . . . that fantastic imported lamp has an Albanian-issue European five-prong plug and would short out a city block if used.

- **The Obvious Overpay:** Don't show up with a velvet box when you know she's bringing a paper bag. A Tiffany necklace is an expensive, finely crafted commemoration of a two-year, not two-week, relationship.

- **The Wild Pitch**: A gift so off the mark that it raises serious talk of a trade. Expect a mound conference with the manager.

- **The QVC**: Don't pawn off shopping-channel schlock hawked by Joan Rivers as something special.

- **The Agenda Gift**: "I got you this LSAT review book, just in case you ever tire of life in the theatre." Don't push your hidden agenda through gifting.

WEDDING GIFTS

Brace yourself for the three-year, nonstop, summer-wedding binge, beginning at age twenty-six and petering at age twenty-nine. A wedding gift is a dual gift for the bride *and* groom. No golf clubs or mono-grammed bowling balls.

While writing a check or choosing from the registry is suitable for most, closer friends and family deserve singular attention. Don't give your life-long chum a seven-piece saucepan set; let others make the domestic pur-chases of bone china and candlesticks. Creativity aside, a cash gift of $125+ for struggling newlyweds is on the money. Anything less barely covers your chair-rental cost at the ceremony. If the pockets are light, pool resources among friends for a colossal bequeath of a large-screen television or first-class hotel accommodations on the honeymoon. Lastly, do not impose your avant-garde tastes upon the conservative. Margaret and Donald might not like the geometric mobile sculpture or minimalist armchair.

Belated gifts are acceptable only when tardiness is instantly forgiven by the overwhelming thoughtfulness. Thus, a paltry check mailed 11 months and 29 days after the wedding smacks of a miser's crazy scheme to earn interest on the money for an additional fiscal year.

HANDY GIFTING GUIDE

The following is a red-hot poker to stoke the fires of creativity.

PRACTICAL

Soft leather wallet; change purse; high thread-count linens; boxers/dress socks; fine white dress undershirts; oxblood dress belt; hearty house-plant; DVD player; travel clock; cordless phone; scarf, wrap, or cloak; silver brooch or lapel pin; framed print; dress watch for the sophisticate, training watch for the athlete; loose teas and accessories; cordless blender; used acoustic guitar; peppermill; digital camera; comfy wool socks; wall clock; silk boxers or lingerie; Marx Brothers video; entertainment software; hobby-oriented magazine subscription; uncommon glassware (snifters and cordials); distinctive kitchen accessory (pizza stone, bread maker, ice cream maker, tortilla press); photo album; colorful cups and saucers; CD wallets; loaded toolbox; whistling teakettle; sex toys; pocket umbrella; mix tape or CD; French coffee press or espresso machine; local restaurant guide; small electronics (Dustbuster, power drill, portable boom box); dried flower arrangement; leather satchel or briefcase; sushi bowls and chopsticks; wine or spirits reference book; unabridged dictionary; board game; slippers.

Nice touch: Identify a well-used cream or elixir on the bathroom counter. Replace this sundry with a fresh one. Tie it with a bow and slip it on the shelf as your sweetheart bathes.

CLASSIC

Fine cigars; fountain or glass pen set with inkwells; liqueurs or cordials; a flight of wines with rack; pearl earrings; desk lamp; first-edition classics;

monogrammed handkerchiefs; orchids; flask; antique corkscrew; cufflinks; shaving equipment (brush, mug, mirror); stationery and wax correspondence sealer; fragrance; bow tie; soft-covered address/phone book; puppy or kitten; napkin rings and serviettes; favored vinyl LP; antique picture frame with photo; decanter; portable bar set; manual typewriter; personalized cocktail napkins; soda siphon; vintage toiletry kit; a worn copy of a favorite children's book; specialized obsolete item (slide rule for engineer, old Singer sewing machine for clothier); shoe-shine kit; wine and cheese basket; talc; baseball mitt or football (especially for a lady); world globe; cocktail shaker set; chess, backgammon, or cribbage set; autographed picture or book with dedication; anything created by you (poem, painting, drawing, elementary-school diorama); pocket journal; flowers delivered to the office; original work of art; pyjamas.

MORE INDULGENT

Gift certificates for spa/massage/salon visit; scented bath salts and lotions; paraffin or aromatherapy lamp; feather bed; caviar; stocked exotic aquarium; imported chocolates or candies; wall sconces and decorative vases; luxurious shower head; microbrew of the month club; cashmere anything; Champagne; hard-to-get theatre or sports tickets; surprise party; express-mailed smoked meats, cheeses, exotic fruits, and dessert specialties; museum membership; paying off a credit card balance; the entire *Modern Gentleman* recommended reading list or classical/jazz recordings.

Incidentally, don't go empty-handed to a friend's home affair or to the office on Secretary's Day. Stock the pantry with small notions for unexpected exchanges or last-minute offerings for hostesses. A cupboard full of candles, teas, and tins of sweets that are wrapped and ready saves the day for the thoughtful. . .and absent-minded.

Chapter Twelve

BEYOND BACHELORHOOD

◆ ◆ ◆ ◆ ◆ ◆ ◆

The Rock 322

Proposals 323

Vows 325

The Good Husband 327

THE ROCK

Never mind the two-months' salary dictate—it was disseminated by insidious gemstone cartels like Communist dogma. For the man of means, his booming wallet buys a shiny boulder with change left over for airfare to the South African diamond pit from which it was mined. For a young couple with postgraduate degrees and staggering loan debt, wouldn't $5,000 be better spent as a down payment? No bring-home-to-Mom girl wants a husband in serious hock for a rock, anyway.

In any case, don't sell your lover's unique qualities short with a dime-a-dozen, four-prong setting. Search for designs worthy of bequeathing to grandchildren. Visit a sophisticated dealer, find something vintage, or commission a signature piece from a local artisan. You can't get a gourmet meal at the Arby's drive-thru (despite the delicious Horsy sauce), so do not expect to wow a lover with strip-mall trinkets.

Selecting a ring is the ultimate romantic surprise and a demonstration of taste and confidence. Anything over two carats is usually garish. Don't let size predominate over the gem's interest. There are more salient criteria with which to judge jewelry.

In contemporary relationships, the diamond rule is no rule at all. Society has unduly imbued the diamond with sentimentality. Respect the customs and indulge her ring-finger fantasies, but don't constrain creativity. Emeralds, rubies, sapphires, and other beguiling precious stones have bejeweled countless crowns and digits with timeless beauty.

Rediscover these gems. Phineas, nevertheless, warns against a lazy skimp who substitutes for imagination with a chintzy, champagne-colored pebble. The eclectic option is reserved for like-minded modern couples for whom tradition is merely a point of departure for their own customs.

For the four Cs (color, clarity, carat, and cut), do your homework. Browse through the Tiffany's showroom for facts and classic ideas. Don't be prejudiced on weight alone, as bright, brilliant jewels are more eye-catching than massive, dull duds. As for flaws, if a suitor has forgivable imperfections only seen under a lover's loupe, can't a B+ engagement ring commemorate A+ thoughtfulness?

Final note: For those with frozen garlic toast on their grocery list, by all means, put a day's pay toward a cubic zirconia. If even the tiniest speck is prohibitively expensive, offer another token of betrothal. Ask Grandma for an heirloom to proffer as symbolic collateral toward your commitment. Paint a picture, write a poem, or hang one of your rings about her neck. At the very least, slip a candy Ring Pop onto her finger and promise to deliver before it is licked to a nub.

PROPOSALS

You will remember the time, place, and details of this day until both of you are gumming food in the Florida sunshine. Be creative. A lover should be swept away by torrents of affection. Besides, magnificent tales of surprise and romance are more fun for her to brag about later. Do not divulge the big news to any friends or coworkers until after popping the question.

Creative presentation suggests mystery and astonishment, along with hidden accoutrements (Champagne, glasses, chocolates) for afterward.

It's too intimate for a crowded restaurant (possibly a sexy bistro) or the football stadium Jumbotron scoreboard, where a hesitant "yes" may simply be polite aversion to embarrassment. Instead, select a secluded spot that promotes unchecked emotions and passionate, bare celebration.

DECLARATION

Prepare a few cogent phrases beforehand, but skip crib notes scribbled on sweaty palms; for those in broadcasting, a teleprompter is permitted. By now, you've visualized the scene. Be assertive and engaging, and break from the working script when appropriate. If you have prepared a snazzy sonnet, recite with fervor. Kneeling is optional—those with thinning hair may want to strike a more flattering pose.

Verbal options abound. Whether it's a premeditated love monologue or courageous blurt of sincerity, there is one essential closer: "Will you marry me." The statement ends with a period; you're already attuned to the answer. Lastly, do not ruin the moment with disclaimers or a

---

ASKING PERMISSION

Before taking the lady aside for a heart-to-heart, make a pilgrimage to her papa. Don't leave Daddy with chest pains at a surprise engagement and rouse him to squash all suitors. Asking for a love's hand is less about permission and more about declaration. Certainly, an unsupportive relative may throw a spanner in the works with a flat "Over my dead body, Tesauro." Still, in-law rapport was likely cemented as the courtship deepened. When a face-to-face is impractical, a letter in longhand is a better alternative than e-mail, postcard, or balloon-o-gram. Follow up with a phone call.

follow-up "I'll get a job" or "Did you hear me?" Permit the words to sink in and remain quiet until the answer is given.

Surprise is preferred, but measure an unsuspecting mate's mood and choose a time befitting the moment. Know the calendar date and its significance (is it a full moon, Yom Kippur, or a somber anniversary of a favored relative's passing?). Once you're prepared, consider the upshot. Is there time and a place to kiss, cry, and embrace afterward? Are you running late for a flight? Make sure appointment books can be tossed aside in deference to engaged merrymaking. Plan to spend the rest of the date together and brace for awesomely tender and powerful lovemaking that affirms the proposal and delivers the relationship unto new heights.

Nice touch: Bask in the bliss. Delay public proclamation for a week and enjoy the budding secret at the tip of your tongues.

VOWS

Fill your promises with personal hopes and feelings, not cookie-cutter, book-recited vows. Do not completely neglect the classic stencil—the exchange is not an avant-garde production, performance-art piece, or tearfest. Instead, work around the traditional format, observing old

HONEYMOON

• **Calvados** • **Bénédictine** • **Dash curaçao** • **Lemon or orange juice** •

standards without slavishly conforming to convention. Honor, respect, and loyalty share the stage with spirit, pleasure, cherish, and fetish.

Write realistic vows, uncluttered with minutiae, lest broken promises be hurled against you in a domestic scuffle. For example, "I promise to fulfill each and every one of your dreams, however small," inevitably spawns a needling spouse two years later: "Honey, it's my dream that you take out the trash, clean up your whiskers, and just forget about that pipe dream you mentioned over dinner." Skip the archaic "obey," as this term needlessly and rightfully angers even nonmilitant women. Besides, an overly pliant mate is dull—isn't someone who requires cajoling and sensual favoring more interesting? This goes both ways, as a man shouldn't be an uxorious, shackled simp.

At the altar, answer with an unblinking "I do" not the corny "I will" (which suggests compliance in the indeterminate future, not necessarily

---

BRIDAL TOURNAMENT SELECTION

Just like the NCAA hoops tournament, there are automatic and at-large bids. Upstanding family members and long-time compatriots are easy picks; other groomsmen are culled from the larger lot of prospects. Consider the responsibilities these people must shoulder. Are they on another continent or can they participate in wedding preparations? Choose persons relevant to the relationship who share a smooth rapport with your fiancée. Also consider the nuclear pairings of groomsmen and bridesmaids. Ratio makes for neat photos, but it's less important than chemistry. Create a sacred inner circle that is the fount of integrity and energy for the ceremony. If you have to count upon some rented band to effuse sentiment, perhaps elopement is a better idea.

anytime soon). To seal the blessing, plant a soulful-but-tasteful kiss, namely, a slight open-mouthed smooch that appears presentable from the third row. Marriages consecrated with a prudish, cold peck are doomed from the start.

Nice touch: Surreptitious altar flasking, not for alcoholic benefit, but as a final toasting with a treasured friend. If there is a 100 percent chance that a flask can be shared with the best man during a huddled altarside, feigned-shoe-tying conference, have a nip but don't greet the bride with saloon-style whiskey breath.

THE GOOD HUSBAND

You are hard work.

—DANIEL ROOP, *LOVE POEM #39*

Divulged ATM pin numbers, commingled laundry, and a ring exchange equal marriage. Be the kind of husband who makes her friends want to find a man like you. And cultivate in-law rapport, even if you don't call them Mom and Dad (or call them).

She's still the same person, especially if cohabitation preceded the nuptials. Marriage is a confirmation, not a poker bluff to exact behavioral changes concerning fidelity, maturity, passion, or finances. The real change should have occurred after the engagement, when practical concerns and latent insecurities were aired and resolved. For instance, check-balancing acumen demonstrated responsibility and wading through sexual turbulence proved thick-or-thin commitment. Now that you're hitched, maintain the parallel paths that got you here—play, arts, goals, and attraction. Branching off into excessive solitary pursuits (vice, religion, crochet) leads to alienation and, eventually, divorce.

RENEW THE WOO

Newlyweds are pegged by their glowing demeanor and a distinct lack of seasoned scowls, but courting should not stop when the honeymoon is over. Continued courtship rituals and flirtation make you feel lionhearted and her feel alluring. Maintain the rapport you developed together as smitten singles by setting aside "alone" time, complimenting her every day, and surprising her with the kind of sex that you wanted on the third date but didn't get. Anyone with a long-playing Sade record can sustain three to five weeks of unbridled humpery, but marriage is long-term hunger. Stoke the flames, even with morning face, and the wedding day cheer will outlast most gifts from the registry.

ARGUING

The marital bed is a sanctuary. Don't drag an argument to the pillows. If you leave the house angry, sooth a blister with the salve of communication. A humbled dash of "I'm sorry" zaps cancerous, brooding silences.

JEALOUSY

You are not the only man who will recognize the goddess in your woman. Her tall, black boots and sexy clothes are not just for you. Interfering with her night on the dance floor with single friends is an insecure sign of ball-and-chain mistrust. After outings without you, sit her down for an adventure recap and not a strap-down on the polygraph.

MONOGAMY

A wedding ring is a badge of respect, if a tattoo of restraint. Don't quash longings; discipline is about boundaries, not numbness. Nightclub distractions that cloud judgement and evoke swinging days of singledom are to be brought home as kindling for the eternal fire of your marital bed. Fantasized sex with today's stranger is best expressed during tonight's lovemaking.

Run temptations through the filter of fidelity. It's about channeling, not romanticizing about what single life was really like. In marriage,

---

≡ TRY A LITTLE TENDERNESS ≡

The good husband knows expressions of love more potent than screwing, and his acuity alerts him when tenderness trumps physicality. When a couple hasn't spent enough time together, tenderness is their carnal chicken soup. Sometimes, heavy emotions (upset, making up, erectile dysfunction) call for more than high-impact P.M. tumbles. Tenderness and explicit acts are not incongruous; however, it behooves the good husband to recognize when the sport of ass-smacking cardio sex diminishes the sacred union. Ease off the lust. Sex within the context of tenderness is less goal-oriented to your orgasm and more focused on caressing, talking, or just lying naked. Such heartfelt lovemaking ends with tears of contentment.

The path to exciting, kinky sex is not always through the toy chest. Sacred sex establishes trust and opens the door to experimentation. A mature lover is amenable to diversions once the baseline of love is satisfied and revisited, as sincerely as play. An action-adventure flick leaves your pulse pounding, charged for a romp; captivating drama moves your heart to a vulnerable state of sharing, ready to divulge and grow. Kinky sex is the juicy reward of the yeoman's careful, tender stewardship.

---

you relinquish the infrequent serendipities of mind-blowing casual sex—those beachheads of pure lust, connection, and unexpurgated ecstasy that defined bachelorhood. What you're getting in return are rainy-night security and a baseline of sensuality that define your life the other 364 days of the year.

Consummation of fantasies is not the first, but the final, step of an infidel. Should you entertain extracurricular affairs, measure the risk. Will a rendezvous leave you satisfied or burdened with constraints of lies, treachery, and compensation? Are you just horny or has the home bed gone all the way cold? A spouse's dearth of sexual passion is but a symptom of more fundamental turmoil. Sex is a barometer of relationship wellness, and the closed heart of a philanderer is a poisoned apple among the fruits of monogamy.

Incidentally, a long, leering look is worth a thousand thrusts. Just knowing that you could have it is enough; reaffirm sexy esteem and cash in on the fantasy value. Avoid the heartache and karma-crunching logistics of bad decisions that set in thirty nanoseconds after climax.

AFTERWORD

◆ ◆ ◆ ◆ ◆ ◆

A gentleman is a gentleman is a gentleman. Being married, involved, single, gay, or naked doesn't dictate one's character or charm. Similarly, the venue or medium of interaction should heighten, not hamper, exchanges. Engaging and keenly naughty behavior is possible in nearly all situations. Wherever you are, make an impact—don't just take up space. Know how to speak well and when not to spoil a meaningful silence. Cultivate an energy that makes people smile and watch your stock rise.

The Modern Gentleman offers a slide rule of respect for solving the deepest conundrums of love and vice. Respect decency, life, and the dignity of men . . . their rituals and foibles. Respect women and the virtues of their grace and intuition. Respect quality over greed, meaning over appetite. Respect action and fitness, health and spirituality, learning and enrichment. Seek a diversity of experience and respect the liberating and instructive fruits of fun and frivolity. Keep your eyes open and respect the potent allure and sometimes grotesque beauty of vice and its peripheral curiosities. Rejoice, read Joyce, and "forge in the smithy of your soul" the man of your own desire.

One day soon you may stand in a crowded elevator, straighten your bow tie, and offer a spry comment that lifts the dull mood—at least for a few floors. As you tote an umbrella, wrinkled salespeople will marvel at your stiff collar and secretaries will feel the tug of your magnetic confidence. Congratulations, your daily journey is the cultured man's way.

Applying *The Modern Gentleman*'s lessons is a contagious process that evolves into effortless gestures. It begins by bringing relaxed charm to a first date, trying a new cocktail, perusing new aisles in the bookstore, or peeking into the leather store. Then, like any discipline, it will infuse other aspects of livelihood, from timely thank-you cards and delicious messages left on voice mail, to the joys of flasking when the theatre lights are low. Others will take notice and inquire about the steady inner improvements: "There's something different about you . . . have you been doing yoga? When did you start ordering Manhattans? Wait, I know. . . Grecian Formula." "No," you might reply, "just being a gentleman."

Put simply, your refurbished character is like last year's wardrobe: updated, enhanced, and pruned, with the outmoded remnants boxed and donated to charity. Remember, much of your past behavior and music collection is laughable. The idea is continual growth, not personality replacement or complete makeovers: discard imprecisions, but keep time-tested classics in your quiver. On occasion, a gentleman should take stock of past achievements and miscues.

Be proud of inspired revelry and review limitations, the mishandling of last year's love affair, or flagging friendships in need of a handwritten letter.

Best of luck to you, noble Cavalier of Life. Go forward with strength, grace, mindfulness, and an occasional glass of Chartreuse. The world will follow behind you.

—Phineas Mollod & Jason Tesauro

BIBLIOGRAPHY

Ames, Elinor. *Elinor Ames' Book of Modern Etiquette*. New York: Walter J. Black, Inc., 1935. The book Grandma lived by. Terrific for niceties of classic social affairs: gifting, correspondence; features a what-to-wear chart.

Angeloni, Umberto of Brioni. *The Boutonnière: Style in One's Lapel*. New York: Universe, 2000. School yourself in the botanical sharpness of a man's boutonnière. Great sections on proper pairing with clothes and occasion. Exquisite photography.

Aywyós. *Hints on Etiquette and the Usages of Society with a Glance at Bad Habits*, Third edition. London: Turnstile Press Ltd., 1836. Compact, bedside primer. Quick essays with terrific color illustrations. A little stuffy at times and loose with the term "vulgar."

Black, Kathleen. *Manners for Moderns*. New York: Allyn & Bacon, 1938. Very practical regarding group dynamics, proper courting, and introductions. Eye-catching 1940s caricatures and sound, accessible advice from an American perspective.

Censor. *Don't: A Manual of Mistakes and Improprieties More or Less Prevalent in Conduct and Speech*. Whitstable: Pryor Publications, 1982 (originally published circa 1880). Headmaster finger-shaking etiquette. Gleefully outdated, yet useful. Get a sense of how far "nice" society has come (or how far we've degraded it).

Diescher, Victor H. *The Book of Good Manners: A Guide to Polite Usage for All Social Functions*. New York: Social Culture Publications, 1923. The book of true gentility, not pretense. Whereas the MG touches on Prophyletiquette, Diescher touches on finger bowls.

Duffy, Patrick Gavin. *The Official Mixers Manual*. New York: Halcyon House, 1940. A mixological masterpiece. Classic and complex: more cocktails listed under absinthe and Calvados than under vodka. Infallible recipes and essays on wine and beer.

Editors of *Esquire* magazine and Ron Butler. *Esquire's Guide to Modern Etiquette*. New York: J.B. Lipincott Co., 1969. More loose in its rules than anything above. How to look the part. Slanted toward the male perspective, hitting modern topics like sporting etiquette and sex in the office.

Eichler, Lillian. *The New Book of Etiquette*. New York: Garden City Publishing Co., 1940. Wonderful prose and commentary about the self-improvement and sincerity of manners, not just table dressing.

Flusser, Alan. *Clothes and the Man*. New York: Villard Books, 1989. Worth tracking down this gem just for the fold-by-fold pocket-square and cravat-knotting tutorials.

Frost, Griffith and John Gauntner. *Saké Pure and Simple*. Berkeley, CA: Stone Bridge Press, 1999. An appetizing introduction that will make you swoon for toro, wasabi, and the banishment of hot saké.

Green, Jonathon. *The Big Book of Filth*. London: Cassell, 1999. F!*$@%# indispensable phrase book for honing the well-balanced, profane tongue.

Herbst, Sharon Tyler and Ron Herbst. *The Ultimate A-to-Z Bar Guide*. New York: Broadway Books, 1998. Keep it next to the jigger; it's okay if you spill on it. Handy reference for everyday concocting.

Hix, Charles. *Dressing Right*. New York: St. Martin's Press, 1979. Casual and fanciful splashes of clothing; dressing for "now," not necessarily for all time. Great explanation of fashion terms and collar styles.

"M."*The Sensuous Man.* New York: Lyle Stuart, Inc., 1971. Worth the purchase for "Party Sex Etiquette" and the list of ten exercises not involving dumbbells that will make you a better lover. By age seventeen, you should've already perused a stolen copy from your uncle's nightstand.

Martine, Arthur. *Martine's Hand-Book of Etiquette and Guide to True Politeness.* Bedford: Applewood Books (originally published in 1866). A man ahead of his time. A concise guide, written before the era of etiquette tomes. Relish the art of carving, taking wine at the table, and etiquette on the street.

Meade, Marianne. *Charm and Personality.* New York: The World Syndicate Publishing Co., 1938. This book gets into the charm and grace of things. The author stresses that before one can excel in social manners, one must tend to inner care and hygiene.

Mrs. Humphrey ("Madge" of "Truth"). *Manners for Men.* Whitstable: Pryor Publications, 1993 (originally published 1897). A small book with sidebars for easy reference on classical etiquette on and off the omnibus. Especially helpful refresher on the formal calm and order at dinner parties.

Post, Emily. *Etiquette (The Blue Book of Social Usage).* New York: Funk & Wagnalls Co., 1945. Classic treatise, perfect for gleaning the fundamental principles. Written in friendly language—the early, preagitated Miss Manners.

Potter, Stephen. *The Theory and Practice of Gamesmanship: Or the Art of Winning Games Without Actually Cheating.* New York: Henry Holt & Co. A humorous guide to the subtle art of gentlemanly jousting on the golf course or billiard table. Every gent should master a few psychological ploys to unnerve a pesky opponent.

Random House Hostess Library. *The Random House Book of Etiquette.* New York: Random House, Inc., 1967. Great source for practical etiquette such as gifting, tipping, and party manners. Classic cover art on an early 1970s Italian restaurant banquette—red hardback.

Reid, Lillian N. *Personality and Etiquette.* Boston: Little, Brown & Co., 1940. Finishing school textbook with manner exercises. A family book, perhaps read to young children before the "Birds and the Bees" lecture.

Sherwood, M.E.W. *The Art of Entertaining.* New York: Dodd, Mead & Co., 1892. A revisit to the classic age of "parlor games and cocktails hours around the piano. Breaks down entertaining into popular venues-in the city, on a picnic, clam bakes.

Steele, Valerie. *Fetish: Fashion, Sex, and Power.* New York: Oxford University Press, 1996. Less a how-to book than a visual dictionary, with a slight bit of history. Good for your fetish vocabulary and for corroborating your mischievous fantasies.

Stevenson, Tom. *The Millennium Champagne and Sparkling Wine Guide.* London: DK Publishing, Inc., 1998. Essential bubbly basics with history, tasting notes, and ratings.

The Savoy Cocktail Book. New York: Arno Press, 1976 (originally published 1930). A glorious reference and recipe manual for atmospheric drinks. Best illustrative art of any cocktail book. Though recently rere-leased, track down a worn copy if you can.

Vanderbilt, Amy. *Amy Vanderbilt's Complete Book of Etiquette.* Garden City: Doubleday & Co., 1958. One day you'll be stuck setting a tea tray. . . The comprehensive, authoritative text from the etiquette maven with line drawings by a young Andrew Warhol.

Walton, Stuart and Brian Glover. *The Ultimate Encyclopedia of Wine, Beer, Spirits and Liqueurs.* New York: Hermes House, 1999. Coffee table—sized behemoth providing histories, pairings, and pourings for all things alcoholic. Great for maturing booze enthusiasts who collect bottles like baseball cards.

INDEX

A

Accessories, 138-40
Affection, displays of, 75-77, 266-67
Air travel, 288-92
Alcohol, 183-214. *See also* Cocktail recipes
  on airplanes, 289
  cocktail hours, 45-46
  cutting back consumption of, 223
  dating and, 75
  drink selection, 190-93
  ethic of, 211-14
  flasks, 15-16
  glassware, 50, 205
  hangovers, 210-11
  home bars, 193-98
  saké, 208-10
  solitary drinking, 198-99
  spirits, 183-89
  wine, 199-208
  at work, 268
Anger, 269-71
Answering machines, 307-11
Apologies, 272-76
Arguing, 328
Armagnac, 186-87
Ascots, 143

B

Bachelor parties, 61-63
Backgammon, 223
Baggage. *See* Luggage
Barbecues, 57-60
Bars. *See* Alcohol
Bathrobes, 147-48
Bathroom etiquette, 176-79
Beach, day at the, 60
Bed, making the, 169
Bedroom decor, 169-71
Belts, 139
Best man, 63-66
Betting. *See* Wagering
Beverages, 168-69.
    See also Alcohol; Cocktail recipes
Billfolds, 140
Body language, 74-75
Book clubs, 99-100
Bookmarks, 101
Books, 99-107
Boutonnières, 122
Bow ties, 144, 146
Braces, 139
Break-ups, 90-96
Bronzing, 159-60
Buffets, 24
Bumper stickers, 286-87
Business attire, 136-37

C

Calvados, 187
Cameras, 17-19
Candy, 158, 159
Caravanning, 285
Cards
  e-mail, 314
  greeting, 305
  playing, 228-30

Cars, 279-85
  caravanning, 285
  decorating, 281, 286-87
  horn blowing, 284-85
  passengers in, 282-84
  road trips, 283
  speeding, 280-82
  steering, 282
  valet service, 10
Cats, 48
Catsup, 23
Champagne, 206-8
Chartreuse, 183-84
Cigarettes, 214-15
Cigars, 216-17
Classical music, 108-13
Clothing, 133-52
  accessories, 138-40
  for air travel, 289
  business attire, 136-37
  care, 134
  hats, 141, 150-52
  neckwear, 142-46
  packing, 294-98
  pyjamas, 146-48
  seasonal, 140-42
  undershirts, 134
  vintage, 134-35
Club soda, 194
Cocktail hours, 45-46
Cocktail recipes
  After-Supper Cocktail, 168
  Alaska, 184
  Bijou, 184

Bloody Mary, 197
Blue Train, 293
Bolo, 144
Calvados Cocktail, 187
Churchill Downs
    Cooler, 232
Devil's Cocktail, 273
Four Flush, 176
Great Secret, 263
Hole in One, 226
Honeymoon, 325
Lollipop, 159
Love Cocktail, 78
Mah-Jongg Cocktail,
    223
Maiden's Blush, 249
Morning After, 240
Oh Henry!, 100
Pall Mall, 217
Pick-Me-Up, 69
Scofflaw, 280
Summer Muddling,
    195
Tail Spin, 130
Temptation, 265
Third Degree, 253
Tulip, 123
Tuxedo, 137
Weep No More, 92
Which Way, 285
Winter Muddling, 196
X Y Z, 305
Coffee, 168–69
College reunions, 36
Cologne, 157
Colonics, 156
Condoms, 234–37
Confidences, 261, 263–65

Conspiracies, 264
Contacts, 149
Conversation, 5–9
    gaffes, 258–61
    small talk, 5, 20
Cooking, 164, 165–66
Correspondence, 303–7
Cotton candy, 158
Cravats, 143
Croquet, 224
Cuff links, 136
Current events, 20

D

Dancing, 70
Dating, 72–80. *See also*
    Relationships
    affection and, 75–77
    bad dates, 77–80
    body language, 74–75
    drinking and, 75
    e-mail and, 313–14
    first dates, 72, 75–76,
        77–79
    flowers and, 123
    music for, 112
    tardiness and, 32
    weekend getaways, 80
Diners, 14, 22–24
Dinner parties, 49–54
Directions, asking for,
    285–86
Dishwashing, 165
Dogs, 48
Dominoes, 222
Drinking. *See* Alcohol
Driving. *See* Cars
Drugs, 218–19. *See also*
    Marijuana

E

Earmuffs, 141
Elevators, 19–20
E-mail, 311–15
Enemas, 156
Engagement rings,
    322–23
Entrances, 28, 29, 30
Exaggeration, 262
Exercise, 117–19
Exits, 29, 31, 77, 241
Ex-lovers, 88–90, 256–57
Eyewear, 148–50

F

Family reunions, 32–34
Fashion, 133–35. *See also*
    Clothing; Footwear
Fetishes, 239, 244–46
Fingernails, 156
Fitness, 117–19
Flasks, 15–16
Flatulence, 180
Flip-flops, 142
Flirtation, 68–71
Flowers, 122–23
Flying. *See* Air travel
Footwear, 135, 142, 148
Fortune cookies, 125
Future, predicting the,
    124–25

G

Gaffes, 258–61
Gambling. *See* Wagering
Games, 222–23. *See also*
    Sports
    backgammon, 223
    card, 228–30

dominoes, 222
in public, 223
Gas, bad, 180
Gate-crashing, 27-29
Gentleman's clubs, 249-50
Gestures, vulgar, 126
Gifts, 300, 315-20
Glassware, 50, 205
Gloves, 141
Golf, 224-28
Grappa, 186
Greeting cards, 305
Grilling, 57-60
Groomsmen, 326
Group events, 39-49. *See also* Dinner parties; Parties
archetypes at, 42
core group at, 42
hosting, 44-49
introductions at, 40-41
leadership at, 43
picking roster for, 39
size of, 39
splintering, 43-44
starting and stopping, 41
Guests
being, 298-300
hosting, 54-57
Gum, 157-58

H

Hair, 155-56
Handkerchiefs, 139
Handwriting, 303-5
Hangovers, 210-11
Hats, 141, 150-52

Heartifacts, 171-75, 256-57
Hiccoughs, 179-80
High school reunions, 34-36
Horn blowing, 284-85
Horse races, 231-32
Hosting, 44-60
barbecues, 57-60
dinners, 49-54
houseguests, 54-57
parties, 45-49
Hotels, tipping at, II
Hot tubs, 26
Houseguests, 54-57
Hygiene, 154-57
Hyperbole, 262

I

Interruptions, 7
Intimate gatherings, 49-51
Introductions, 40-41
Invitations, 39
Italian wine, 204

J

Jazz, 113-17
Jealousy, 328
Jukeboxes, 12-14

K

Kitchen equipment, 163-64
Knocking, 28

L

Letter openers, 306
Letters, 303-5, 306
Licorice, 158

Lies, 261-63
Lillet, 184
Literature, 99-107
Lollipops, 158
Love letters, 306
Lovers. *See* Dating; Relationships; Sex
Lubricants, 235
Luggage, 290, 294-98

M

Madeira, 189
Magic 8-Ball, 124-25
Manhattan, 191
Manicures, 156
Mannerisms, graceful, 129-31
Marijuana, 219-21
Marriage, 323-30. *See also* Relationships; Weddings
Masturbation, 84-85
Meals, 166-68. *See also* Dinner parties
Medicine chests, 179
Mementos, 171-75, 256-57
Me time, 128
Mile-High Club, 291-92
Milk, 164-65
Mistakes, apologizing for, 272-76
Moisturizers, 157
Monogamy, 329-30
Moods, 127-29
Muddling, 197-98
Mufflers, 140-41
Music
classical, 108-13
jazz, 113-17
jukeboxes, 12-14

N

Names, remembering, 40–41
Neckwear, 142–46
Nervous habits, 158

O

Office romance, 265–68
Opera, 109
Ouija, 125
Overcoats, 137

P

Packing, 294–98
Parties. *See also* Dinner parties; Group events
    arrivals at, 28, 29, 30
    bachelor, 61–63
    crashing, 27–29
    exiting, 29, 31
    hosting, 44–49
    types of, 45–49
Passengers, 282–84
Passover, 37
Pastis, 185
Penmanship, 303–5
Perjury requests, 264
Pets, 48
Photography, 17–19
Picnics, 58
Pipes, 217
Pocket squares, 139
Poise, 129–31
Poker, 229, 230
Pornography, 239
Port, 188
Postcards, 306–7
Pot, 219–21

Pregnancy, 257–58
Profanity, 126–27
Proposals, 323–25. *See also* Engagement rings
Pubic hair, 155–56
Pyjamas, 146–48

R

Raincoats, 137
Reading, 99–107
Refrigerator, 163–64
Relationships. *See also* Dating; Sex
    betrayals and, 276
    break-ups, 90–96
    ex-lovers, 88–90
    flirting and, 71
    gifts and, 316–18
    long-distance, 85–88
    masturbation and, 84–85
    multiple, 81–84
    office romance, 265–68
Restaurants, 21–24
    bringing your own wine to, 202
    buffets, 24
    diners, 14, 22–24
    fortune cookies, 125
    tipping at, 9–10
Reunions, 32–37
Road trips, 283
Roasts, 65–66
Robes, 147–48

S

St. Valentine's Day, 74
Saké, 208–10
Sandals, 142

Scarves, 140–41
Scotch, single-malt, 185–86
Seating arrangements, 51–54
Secrets, 261, 263–65
Sex, 234–50. *See also* Relationships
    avoiding routine, 240
    blue talk, 238
    condoms, 234–37
    with exes, 88–90
    fetishes, 239, 244–46
    lubricants, 235
    masturbation, 84–85
    Mile-High Club, 291–92
    monogamy, 329–30
    partners, number of, 252–55
    pornography, 239
    postcoital behavior, 241
    pregnancy, 257–58
    techniques, 240–43
    tenderness and, 329
    threesomes, 246–48
Sexual identity, 239–40
Sherry, 188–89
Shirts, 134, 136, 142
Shoes, 135
Shorts, 142
Skin care, 157
Skinny-dipping, 24–26
Slippers, 148
Slumps, 128–29
Small talk, 5, 20. *See also* Conversation
Smoking, 214–18, 219–21
Sneezing, 179
Snuff, 216

Soothsaying, 124-25
Spam, 312
Speeding, 280-82
Spitting, 179
Sports, 20, 117-19.
    See also Golf
Stamps, 307
Steering, 282
Strip clubs, 249-50
Strip poker, 229
Strongboxes, 162
Suits, 136-37
Sun, exposure to, 159-60
Sunglasses, 149-50
Suspenders, 139
Sweaters, 141
Symphony, attending the, 108-10

T

Table manners, 166-68
Tanning, 159-60
Tardiness, 32
Tattoos, 153-54
Taxis, 11-12
Tea, 168
Teeth, 159
Telephone calls, 307-11
Temper, 269-71
Tenderness, 329
Thank-you notes, 305
Threesomes, 246-48
Ties, 142-46
Timepieces, 138
Tipping, 9-12

Toasts, 64-65
Tobacco, 214-18
Toenails, 156
Toiletry kit, 295
Travel, 279-301
    asking for directions, 285-86
    by car, 279-85
    guest behavior during, 298-300
    packing for, 294-98
    by plane, 288-92
    by train, 293-94
Triangles, 81-84
Tuaca, 186
Turtlenecks, 141
TV dinners, 164

U

Umbrellas, 152-53
Undershirts, 134

V

Valet service, 10
Video cameras, 18-19
Vintage clothing, 134-35
Voice mail, 307-11
Vomiting, 180
Vulgarity, 126-27

W

Wagering, 228, 230, 231-32
Waiting, 32, 288

Wallets, 140
Watches, 138
Weddings. *See also* Bachelor parties; Marriage
    best man and, 63-66
    choosing groomsmen for, 326
    gifts for, 318
    vows for, 325-27
Weekend getaways, 80
Whisky/whiskey, 185-86
White lies, 261
Wine, 199-208
    choosing, 201-2
    corked, 204-5
    dessert, 189
    equipment, 205
    fortified, 188-89
    Italian, 204
    labels, 200
    opinions on, 202-3
    at restaurants, 202, 203-5
    retail shops, 200
    sparkling, 206-8
Work
    celebratory booze at, 268
    charity requests at, 267
    hangovers at, 210-11
    office romance, 265-68
Workouts, 117-19

Y

Yoga, 119-21

❖ ❖ ❖ ❖ ❖ ❖

PHINEAS MOLLOD (right) received his law degree from Vanderbilt University. He lives in New York City and esquires just enough to keep his attaché out of hock and court clothes free of mothballs. JASON TESAURO (left) recently moved from Atlanta to Richmond, Virginia, with his newlywed, the Fair Elizabeth. (Faced with the quandary of nothing to write for Beyond Bachelorhood, Phineas and Jason drew straws and Tesauro had to marry first—not only for his Southern beloved, but for the inherent research value and shiny fondue pot.) He is a performance poet and the marketing director for Barboursville Vineyards.

OVERTIME

DAVID SKUY

Scholastic Canada Ltd.

Toronto New York London Auckland Sydney
Mexico City New Delhi Hong Kong Buenos Aires

Scholastic Canada Ltd.

604 King Street West, Toronto, Ontario M5V 1E1, Canada

Scholastic Inc.

557 Broadway, New York, NY 10012, USA

Scholastic Australia Pty Limited

PO Box 579, Gosford, NSW 2250, Australia

Scholastic New Zealand Limited

Private Bag 94407, Botany, Manukau 2163, New Zealand

Scholastic Children's Books

Euston House, 24 Eversholt Street, London NW1 1DB, UK

Library and Archives Canada Cataloguing in Publication

Skuy, David, 1963-

      Overtime / David Skuy.

(Game time)

ISBN 978-1-4431-0798-3

      I. Title. II. Series: Game time (Toronto, Ont.)

PS8637.K72O83 2011   jC813'.6   C2011-902070-X

6 5 4 3 2 1   Printed in Canada 116   11 12 13 14 15

TABLE OF CONTENTS

1. Rebel Rules 1
2. Trouble Overhead 6
3. Do or Die 11
4. Rain Delay. 16
5. Movie Marathon 26
6. Where's That? 34
7. Trying Times. 42
8. Defeated 51
9. All In. 59
10. Rain, Rain Go Away 67
11. Dress For Success 77
12. Heads Up 85
13. In the Red 95
14. A Long Shot 104
15. Pad Battle 110
16. Two Steps Forward... 120
17. Linemates 127
18. Bright Lights 138
19. By a Thread 144
20. Going Down 152
21. Page One. 156
22. Go Terriers 163
23. Battle Stations 169
24. High Hopes. 177
25. Northern Exposure 183
26. Reversal of Fortune 194
27. The Walking Dead. 207

To my many proofreaders over the years:
Percy, Ambrose, Unah, and Lorie; Donna,
Danny, and Charlie — and a special thanks to
my editors, Yasemin and Diane.

1

REBEL RULES

Charlie Joyce cradled the puck at the left hash marks. With the man advantage, he wanted to take his time and set it up properly. He faked a pass to the point to force the winger higher, then curled down low towards the corner. His linemates recognized the play and jumped into action; they had practised it a hundred times. Zachary Jackson, his right winger, peeled off from in front of the net and headed to the opposite corner. Charlie banked the puck off the back wall onto his stick. His other winger, Pudge Moretti, stormed the net to occupy a defender, using his powerful frame to get close to the goalie.

The Rebels' left defenceman, Spencer Bowman, a smooth-skating offensive star, was new to the team this season. He cut decisively into the high slot to force the winger to cover him. Charlie circled to the blue line. Zachary faked a pass to Spencer, then slid the puck to the right point where Nick Katsopoulos, a wizard with the puck in his own right, took it easily, raised his stick for a slapshot to freeze the centre who had come out to pressure him, and passed it across to Charlie.

Pudge pushed against the defender, exposing the bottom left corner of the net. It was a perfect screen. Charlie didn't hesitate, sending a laser-like one-timer on net.

The crowd let out a roar — another Rebels goal!

Charlie loved to score; what player doesn't? But there would be greater challenges this season than getting the seventh goal in a 6–0 game. The Tornadoes were the worst team in the league.

Nick held his glove out. "Personally, I would have blasted the puck under the crossbar, just a fraction of a centimetre off the post," he said, "but I guess a shot to the bottom corner when the goalie is completely screened is good enough for you."

"I take 'em any way I can," Charlie said.

Spencer tapped his shin pads. "Third power-play goal this period," he said. "Tornadoes might wanna think of playing by the rules."

"This is fun, dudes," Zachary said. He and Charlie punched gloves.

Pudge patted Charlie on the helmet.

"The screen made it easy," Charlie said to his left winger and best friend. "It was your goal more than mine."

Pudge laughed. "I already told the ref to give it to me. Anyone can shoot one-timers from the point. It takes real talent to stand in front of the net like a statue."

They went to the bench for a change. Scott Slatsky jumped over the boards. He was Nick's defence partner, but lately Spencer had taken his place on the power play. Scott was a stay-at-home defender, and one of the best in the league. He was also too good-natured to mind.

But this time he was shaking his head and didn't look at all happy.

"What's up?" Charlie asked him.

"It took you thirty-two seconds to score," he said. "That's not acceptable. Coach Hilton's so nice he won't say something, so I have to. We all know the Rebels won their first four games of the season because of me. So if we're going to remain undefeated, you're going to have to pass to me all the time — and I should be captain — and probably coach. I guess I'm just an all-around awesome player."

Charlie sighed. Would he ever learn not to take Scott seriously?

Nick looked taken by surprise. "I didn't know you were on the team," he said. "When did you join the Rebels?"

"Last season," Scott said.

"Weird. What position?"

"Defence. I'm with you."

Nick shrugged. "You must be really useless because I don't think you've ever touched the puck."

They skated to the blue line for the draw, while Charlie took a seat on the bench next to Pudge. Charlie grabbed a water bottle and took a long sip. The cold water burned the back of his throat. Like Zachary said, this was fun. He was playing with his buds, on maybe the strongest team in the league. Last year had been a struggle with only ten players. But winning the championship had attracted some attention. Spencer and his defence partner Philip rounded out the defence, which, with the twins, Christopher and Rob, gave them three great pairings. Nazem, Brandon and Will formed a potent new line, so now the Rebels had three forward lines capable of scoring.

Coach Hilton tapped him on the shoulder. "I liked the puck movement," he said. "Nice read to move to the point." He leaned closer. "Perhaps a touch faster getting it to Zachary," he added, before moving away.

Charlie and Pudge exchanged a glance. That was classic Hilton. No matter how perfect, he always wanted more. Of course, Charlie loved him for that. He was the best coach in the league — at least in Charlie's opinion — and a great English teacher too. Charlie had him for grade ten at Terrence Falls High School.

Matt's line had taken the ice, with Dylan on the right and Jonathon on the left. Nick whipped the puck cross ice to Scott, who one-timed it to Matt, cutting hard to open space. He took it on his backhand and slipped in between the Tornadoes' front line. Dylan came off his wing and Matt snapped a pass to him. He took it without breaking stride, and beat the Tornadoes' right defenceman to the outside. The other defenceman came over to cut him off, and Dylan flipped the puck over his stick to Matt streaking up ice. Matt took two steps and blasted the puck from the slot. The goalie did not even move.

CLANG.

"I can't believe that," Pudge said, slapping the top of the boards. "That's the third post he's hit this game."

"Let him save the goals for our next game against the Wildcats," Zachary said. "These dudes are done."

Jonathon and a Tornadoes defender battled for possession in the right corner.

Charlie couldn't agree with Zachary more. The

Rebels had played the Wildcats in the finals last year. Jake Wilkenson was their captain, and Charlie's least favourite person in the world.

"The Wildcats should've been suspended from the league," Pudge said. "Coach Schultz pulls his team off the ice — in the finals no less — and he's allowed to keep coaching? Crazy."

"He's been coaching a long time," Zachary said. "He's got friends."

"What he's got is problems," Charlie said, grinning, "because his team's gotta play the Rebels."

"Ain't that the truth!" Zachary said, and they punched gloves.

Charlie looked up in time to see Matt lift the puck over the Tornadoes' fallen goalie.

"Finally," Zachary said. "The curse has lifted."

"Change 'em up," Hilton called out.

Charlie shifted down. He could hardly wait to get back out. He felt a little bad for the Tornadoes, though. At this rate, the game would end 15–0.

"Let's not try too hard to score," Charlie said to his linemates. "This game is out of control." They both nodded. "I'll tell the others," he added.

As captain Charlie figured it was his responsibility. As cool as it was to be winning, the Rebels were not show-offs, and he did not want them to turn into that kind of team.

2

TROUBLE OVERHEAD

Slightly out of breath from dashing up the stairs, Charlie burst through the second floor doors and raced down the hall, his math textbook banging into his back with every bounce of his knapsack. He was late again, and praying Hilton had not started English class. He skidded to a halt when he saw a piece of paper taped to the door.

ALL STUDENTS TO THE CAFETERIA
FOR A SPECIAL ASSEMBLY.

"Relax, Charlie."

He spun around. Pudge was leaning against a locker.

"What's so special about this assembly?" Charlie said.

"No clue," Pudge said. "It's a major mystery."

"How come you're still here?"

Pudge raised his eyebrows. "I had a feeling you might be late."

Up ahead a door opened. A mop of sandy-blond hair popped out — Scott. He shook his head. Nick came out a second later.

"I am shocked by what I'm seeing, gentlemen," Scott

said, doing a pretty good impersonation of Principal Holmes. "An assembly is called, and all I see is vagrant young men roaming the halls looking for trouble."

"We expect more from grade tens," Nick said.

"Aren't you sort of doing the same thing?" Charlie said.

"Not at all," Scott said cheerfully. "Our math teacher mistakenly believes Nick and I were talking last class and she made us come in early to clean her chalkboards. Of course, we are completely innocent."

"I feel sorry for her," Nick said.

"Me too," Scott said. "To be all alone, without friends."

"Isn't that like you?" Nick said.

"I feel sorry for me, then," Scott said.

"If it helps, I also feel sorry for you," Nick said, and he patted Scott gently on the shoulder.

Charlie and Pudge laughed as they made their way to the cafeteria — it would not be a normal day without Nick and Scott dissing each other.

"They're probably announcing the tryouts for the Champions Cup," Charlie said. The Champions Cup was an annual high school tournament. Last year Terrence Falls had lost in the final seconds to their archrival Chelsea, and Charlie and his friends had been dreaming of revenge ever since.

Pudge held the cafeteria door open for the others. A loud voice caught Charlie's attention. It was Jake, sitting on a table talking to Liam, Roscoe and Thomas. Funny how nervous he used to get around Jake and his crew. But a lot had happened since he'd arrived last year, not knowing a single person. Their lame trash talk no longer got to him — not now that he had his own crew.

"Hey, it's little Bo Peep, with some of his lost sheep," Liam said.

"No. It's Little Miss Muffet, with his tuffet friends," Thomas said.

"No. I got it. It's the Pink Sweater Gang," Jake said, and his friends broke up.

If it had been anyone but Jake, Charlie would have laughed too. The Rebels' sweaters last year had been a bit pink. Fortunately, their sponsor had come through with new ones this season.

Pudge pushed Charlie to the left. "Zachary's over there," he said.

Zachary was waving his arm overhead. "I had to fight off about twenty angry grade twelves to save these seats," he said, as they filed in.

"Well, as you know, we're far too important to waste our time waiting for an assembly," Scott replied.

Zachary put Scott in a headlock and gave him a noogie.

"If you pull hard enough his head comes off," Nick said.

"Do you think they'll announce the Champions Cup tryouts?" Charlie said.

"We should've started practices already," Pudge said. "Last year the team was picked by this time. Why the wait?"

"It's gonna be tough without Alexi," Charlie said.

Alexi was an awesome goalie, but his family had moved in the summer and he was going to another school.

"And as much as it kills me to say it, it'll be tough

to win if Jake and his crew don't play," Pudge said.

"I've been thinking the same," Charlie said. "Is it even worth asking them?"

Pudge rolled his eyes. "It's never worth talking to them."

There was a rumour that Jake and his buddies were not going to try out for the Champions Cup junior team. That would make it easier on Charlie because he wouldn't have to deal with them — but hurt their chances of winning because they were solid players, especially Jake.

"Ladies and gentlemen," Scott announced in a deep voice. "I give you . . . The Assembly."

Principal Holmes had walked onto the stage.

"Hey, move over guys," Matt said, pushing in next to Charlie. The other students in the row grumbled at having to squish over. "What did I miss?" he asked.

"Nothing. We just got here too," Charlie said.

Principal Holmes shuffled to the mic. "Welcome to the special assembly," he began.

The students kept chatting. He cleared his throat into the mic, which only seemed to encourage more talking and to increase the volume.

"I think I should help Holmesy out," Scott said. "I'm probably the most popular student here. The kids listen to me."

"What do you have in mind?" Nick said.

"I think a day off is in order," Scott said.

"I gotta hand it to you — you might have the greatest mind in education today," Nick said.

"I really need your attention," Principal Holmes pleaded.

"Yeah, and I really need a club sandwich," Scott said, "but I ain't gettin' one."

"I really need help with my math . . ." Nick said.

Suddenly the cafeteria got quiet. William Hilton had stepped onto the stage.

"Can we have your attention, please?" Hilton said in an even tone. "We have a very serious situation facing the school that Principal Holmes needs to tell you about."

Principal Holmes cleared his throat again. "Thank you, Mr. Hilton. Unfortunately, students, I have a difficult announcement to make. Due to circumstances beyond our control, we will have no choice but to close Terrence Falls High School in November."

Charlie's jaw dropped. His mind was sent reeling. Was this for real? Closing? It made no sense!

3

DO OR DIE

Principal Holmes ran his fingers through his hair.

"There's little I can do about it," he said. "I have been in meetings with the school board and the trustee for the past week. Unfortunately, our roof has developed leaks, and there could be severe damage if substantial repairs are not carried out, especially if the snow is allowed to collect. It means we will be dividing the student body into six groups, and each group will attend one of six designated high schools."

"We don't want to go to another school," someone called out.

"I understand your disappointment," he said, "but I'm afraid my hands are tied. A letter will be going home with each student today to explain the situation to your parents. The bussing schedule and locations will be posted at the main bulletin board tomorrow . . ."

Everyone began talking at once.

"Please hold it down," Principal Holmes said. "We must simply make the best of it. We need to work together to make this an efficient transition. Now please listen closely for the activities that will have to be cancelled for timing or budgetary reasons: the jazz ensemble, jazz quartet, and senior jazz band will still participate in the Ralph Sanderson High School Jam Session on October twenty-second, but the string quartet, both junior and senior, will unfortunately not be able to go to the String It Up Jamboree Festival in December."

There was a big groan from some of the students, and one shouted, "That's not fair."

Principal Holmes turned a page in his notebook. "Please understand, this is difficult on everyone. Music classes will . . ."

"How could this happen?" Scott said.

"Why didn't they fix the roof over the summer?" Nick said.

"It'll be awful going to another school . . . and buses . . ." Charlie said. "I can't believe grade ten is ruined. What if we all end up at different schools?"

His friends stared at him. He'd said what they were thinking.

"We've gotta think of a way out of this," Charlie said fiercely.

". . . and the boys' and girls' volleyball teams are cancelled, along with the Champions Cup teams, and also . . ."

Charlie felt all the energy leave his body. No Champions Cup! No grade ten at Terrence Falls High. This was crazy.

In a daze he listened to Principal Holmes rattle off the programs and events that would have to be cancelled. Finally, Holmes ended by saying, "Unfortunately, we have to divert our entire budget to the roofing issue, and there is simply not enough money in the kitty this year to do the things we normally do. I really am sorry. Again, the lists for bussing and schools will be posted on the bulletin board in the main hallway tomorrow."

Hilton reappeared on stage. He whispered in Principal Holmes's ear.

"Okay. Certainly. You're right. We should do that now," Principal Holmes said. Hilton lowered the microphone neck and Principal Holmes leaned towards it. "Your Fundraising Committee president wants to say a few words," he said.

Charlie had never paid much attention to student politics. "When did we get a fundraising committee?" he asked Pudge.

"No idea," Pudge said. He seemed confused as well.

A girl stepped up to the microphone. "My name is Melissa Witherspoon," she began. "I was a grade eleven rep on the student council last year. We only learned of the school closing this morning, like you. We need to act fast, because if we don't, the school will close in November and all of us will have to go to other schools. For those of you in grade twelve, that means not graduating from Terrence Falls and no prom. For the rest of you, the repairs may take longer than expected, and you could lose another year."

Charlie looked around the cafeteria. Every student was sitting upright, staring up at the stage. He could tell they were as shocked as he was.

"There is a way to save our year. The school board can do temporary repairs to get us through the winter. Then they can finish the roof off in the summer over the vacation. Principal Holmes has allowed us to form an emergency committee made up of student council members from last year, with Mr. Hilton as our advisor, to spearhead the fundraising effort. We have to raise the money for the temporary repairs. The school board won't pay for that."

"How much?" a student demanded.

Melissa paused and took hold of the mic again. "It'll cost one hundred and fifty thousand dollars."

A gasp sounded from the students.

"I know it's a ton of money," she said. "But there are seven hundred fifty students at Terrence Falls. If we all pull together, along with our parents and the community we can do it. At least we have to try."

One hundred and fifty thousand dollars! Charlie remembered the Rebels' car wash fundraiser last year. They'd made five hundred dollars, and were lucky to do that.

"We don't have time to hold the regular student council elections," Melissa said. "We'll do that once we save the school. For now, we want you all to think of as many fundraising ideas as you can. Think of anything. Over the next two days you can present them to the committee. We'll pick the best and get started."

Principal Holmes shuffled to Melissa and took the mic. "Um . . . yes. Thanks. I'm hopeful the fundraising will be successful. But we must also prepare for the worst. As I said, look for the bus schedules and school assignments on the main bulletin board." He cleared his throat. "Please make your way back to your classes in an orderly fashion."

The students rose from their seats. A million

thoughts raced through Charlie's mind. "How unlucky can we get?" he said, as much to himself as his friends.

"At least we don't have to worry about losing to Chelsea in the Champions Cup this year," Scott said.

"It's still a huge rip," Charlie said.

"I wonder what schools we'll have to go to?" Zachary said.

"Hey," Nick said to Charlie. "You're late every day, and you can walk here. What are you gonna do when you have to catch a bus?"

"It means I have no choice — we're going to have to raise that money or die trying," Charlie replied.

"Nobody can live forever," Scott said. "I'm in."

"Me too," Pudge said.

"Do or die," Zachary said.

"We've been through tough times before," Charlie said. "Last year we organized the Rebels by ourselves, and won the Championship. This year we're gonna save the school."

"Rebel Power!" Nick said.

"Go Terrence Falls!" Matt said.

"I think I'd better go look for a part-time job," Scott said.

Charlie laughed, and they all joined in. He actually felt better too. It was a massive amount of money, but maybe, if they came up with some great ideas, they could pull it off.

Maybe.

4

RAIN DELAY

Charlie followed his buds towards the stairs as they made their way back to the cafeteria at lunch. He passed the second floor window and looked down wistfully at the concrete pad that was surrounded by small rocks on three sides and a hill on the other. It was their ball hockey rink — not theirs exactly, but the school's. They had started playing there at the end of grade nine, at lunch and after school, and what had started as a few mellow games had morphed into some serious five-on-five battles.

It had started to get aggressive, and Principal Holmes had threatened to ban all ball hockey, until a kid named Dalton began to ref. He drew up some rules and posted a schedule, and the problems had disappeared for the most part. Charlie looked out again. Darkening clouds were threatening rain, which was probably why no one was there. But Tuesday lunch was the grade tens' turn to play. He stopped by the window.

"Boys, just to let you know — I see an empty hockey pad at the back of the school. I know we were gonna play after school, but . . . it makes me sad to see it all alone like that," Charlie said.

"That's just plain wrong," Nick said.

"It's more than wrong," Zachary said. "It's evil."

"We need to do something about it," Pudge said.

"But there's the small matter of lunch," Scott said.

Scott's appetite would be a difficult hurdle to overcome. The kid liked to eat. "You can eat after science," Charlie said. "There's five minutes between classes."

"Besides, you need to practise because you really suck at ball hockey," Nick said. "And I mean *really*."

Scott looked at his lunch bag. "I'm sorry, old friend. Duty calls. To the pad!" he cried.

He turned and leaped down to the landing. They raced after him, taking the stairs three at a time. Charlie was at the back, laughing, and looking for a way to sneak inside and get down first, but he was too far back and Pudge was cutting him off.

"Curse you, Moretti," he said. "I shall have my revenge."

Charlie turned the corner and jumped, figuring he could take the entire flight in one leap and get past Pudge. What he did not figure on was Principal Holmes walking up the stairs, and Scott, Zachary and Nick screeching to a halt. Pudge had managed to grab onto the banister to slow himself down. Charlie was in midair and could do nothing but crash straight into Nick and Zachary, sending all three to the ground.

"Gentlemen! What is the meaning of this?" Principal Holmes said. "Are you fighting in the halls?"

"Not at all," Scott said. "We were just in a hurry to get to the library."

"Sorry guys," Charlie whispered as he helped Zachary and Nick up.

"The library is the other way," Principal Holmes said.

"We were running to the cafeteria to eat lunch, so we could get back to the library," Nick said.

Principal Holmes rubbed his chin with his left hand. "I admire your enthusiasm for your schoolwork, but we cannot have students jumping down stairs on top of each other."

"I agree," Scott said. "And we're very disappointed in ourselves. Aren't we?"

"We are," they chorused.

"Don't let me see this again," Principal Holmes said.

"You won't," Nick said. "It's my fault, though. When I get a math problem in my head, I get carried away."

"I admire your sense of responsibility," Scott said, "but as your math tutor I really should have kept you calm and focused on the numbers."

"Now that you mention it," Nick said, "you are really to blame."

"On the other hand, you did make a good point," Scott said. "You were behaving badly, and I am rather shocked."

Principal Holmes looked tired. "I think I'll continue to my staff meeting," he said flatly, and walked past them and up the stairs. When he was out of earshot, Nick put a hand on Scott's shoulder and said, "I knew there was a reason my math mark was so low."

"We better boogie, boys," Charlie said. "Our empty pad could be full of guys by now. Let's go."

They ran off, Charlie out in front. He turned the

corner towards the pad, and this time the others had to swerve to avoid him as he skidded to a halt.

"Joyce, do you have a death wish today?" Scott said.

"I have a wish to play ball hockey," Charlie said. "But look."

Ten players were lined up, ready for the drop of the ball — ten girls!

"We seem to have a problem," Pudge said.

"Dalton's reffing," Nick said. "Let's investigate."

Charlie followed uneasily. He had a bad feeling about this.

"Hey Dalton," Nick said. "What gives? Tuesday is our day."

"Correction. Tuesday is grade ten day," a girl said.

Charlie had never seen her before. She was tall, with her hair in cornrows. He certainly knew the girl opposite her, though — Julia.

"Hey, boys. We thought we'd take a turn," Julia said. "You can play the winner."

"Yeah . . . but . . . girls have never played before . . ." Scott's voice trailed off.

"So?" another girl said.

"Oh, hi, Rebecca," Scott said to her. "I didn't see you . . . there . . . behind Alexandra . . . there."

Scott was never at a loss for words except when Rebecca was around.

"You boys take a seat," Alexandra said. "We won't be too long — maybe half an hour, or so."

"Watch and learn," the tall girl said. A girl behind her laughed; she was much shorter than her friend, but looked strong and athletic.

Dalton bounced the ball a few times. "I had to

concur that it was only fair that they have the opportunity to play," he said.

Charlie tried not to laugh. Dalton had a funny way
of talking, always using big words. But he was a good
guy, even if he might be a bit geeky — and he had a
point about it being fair.

"Let's watch from the hill," he said, pulling on
Scott's arm. "At least you can eat lunch."

Charlie sat on the ground, and his friends plopped
themselves down too. The game was first to score two
goals. Julia, Rebecca and Alexandra were the best junior
girl hockey players in school, and he figured they would
win quickly.

"Julia and the girls will smoke 'em, and we'll be
playing in a couple of minutes," Charlie said. "Eat up."

"I know the fourth girl on Julia's team is Michelle,"
Charlie said to Pudge. "I remember her from the
Champions Cup. But who's the girl in net?"

"Not sure," he said. "Who's in net for Julia's team?"
he called out.

"Why?" Scott said.

"Charlie wants to know."

"I thought he was in love with Julia?" Nick said.

"Are they breaking up?" Zachary said.

Charlie could feel himself go red. They were always
kidding him about Julia. He knew it was pointless to tell
them she was just a friend; he had said that about a
thousand times already.

"I think her name is Cassie," Pudge said.

"If you knew, why didn't you just tell me?" Charlie
said.

"More fun this way," Pudge said.

He growled and pushed Pudge on the shoulder, and his friend laughed.

Dalton held the ball over his head, and Julia put her stick down for the draw against the tall girl.

"Time for the ol' razzle-dazzle," Alexandra said.

"Back to you, Becca," Julia said.

"In your dreams," the tall girl said. "It's right to you, Emily."

"Number two when you win the draw, Trisha," Emily said.

"They have plays?" Charlie said. He wondered if they were any good.

Dalton dropped the ball. Trisha knocked Julia's stick aside, stepped forward, and muscled the ball to Emily, who cradled the ball a few times, drifted to her right, and then rolled it across to her defence partner. Alexandra pressured and passed it back to Emily, and she in turn flicked it up to Trisha, and took off up the right side.

Trisha one-timed it perfectly and Emily roared down the wing with Julia in pursuit, and Michelle angling over. Charlie watched Trisha glide up the middle and then take off full speed at the net.

"I think I get Number Two," Charlie said.

Emily was a right-handed shot and she wristed the ball into the slot. Trisha kicked out her left foot to control the ball and coolly blasted it into the bottom corner, beating Cassie on the glove side.

Zachary whistled in appreciation.

"That was a bit of skill," Charlie said.

"I can't believe she meant to do that," Scott said. "Lucky bounce."

"We should probably replace you on the Rebels with her," Nick said, "just in case."

"So who is she?" Scott said.

"I thought you loved Rebecca," Nick said.

"I do, but I want to know the name of the girl who's taking my spot on the Rebels — so I can be her friend on Facebook," Scott said.

"I heard her friend call her Trisha," Charlie said.

"Okay, Joyce," Scott said. "That's the second time we've caught you cheating on Julia. Behave yourself."

"She's new," Pudge said. "She's in my science class. Her friend's name is Emily. Both of them look like they've played before."

"Even if they haven't, we should replace Scott," Nick said.

"We may as well go ahead and replace Nick too," Scott said.

Dalton dropped the ball and again Trisha won the draw. The ball came to Emily. Her defence partner ran up the left wing and she gave her a pass. Alexandra chopped at the ball and it bounced off the rocks that formed the boards and ricocheted backwards. Trisha raced over, taking it on her forehand. Julia trotted over, holding her stick out. Trisha whirled around and passed between Julia's stick and her left foot up the middle, where Emily calmly took the pass, went forward, and beat Cassie in the right corner over her blocker.

It was 2–0, and the game was over just like that.

"I guess we're up, boys. Who's ready?" Charlie said. He felt a few drops of rain. "And we better hurry. Those clouds look angry."

Zachary tossed his sandwich back in his bag. "I'll eat

this later . . . maybe. I'm ready."

"Count me in," Pudge said.

"Fine. I'll play, but only because you're lost without me," Scott said.

They wandered slowly onto the pad.

"Awesome snipe, Em," Trisha said, and she gave her friend a high-five.

Alexandra's brow wrinkled as Charlie came over. "That was just a warm-up," she said. "We're playing for real now."

Charlie felt himself go red again. "The rules are first to score two goals wins. The losing team sits . . ." he said.

"We've been waiting to play for weeks. You guys have been hogging the pad the whole time. Give us a break," she said.

"Who wants the honour of giving me their stick?" Scott said, as he joined them.

"I will," Alexandra said. "But let us play one more goal."

Scott looked confused. "I thought they got two goals already?"

"Come on, guys," Rebecca said. "That was like five seconds."

Charlie felt ridiculous, as if he had been caught doing something wrong. But the rules were the rules; and he wanted to play at least one game. "I know. It's just that . . . you can play the winner." The rain fell a bit harder.

Julia had come over. "It doesn't matter. Take it." She threw her stick on the ground and left the pad.

It did not take a genius to figure out the girls were

ticked off; and maybe Alexandra was right about the boys hogging the pad. But then again they'd never asked to play before.

"It's cool. You go again," Charlie said. "I didn't even finish my lunch. Go ahead."

"I didn't know the rules," Alexandra said. "You boys play."

She put her stick down, and Rebecca, Michelle and Cassie did the same, and all five of them walked back to the school. Charlie closed his eyes and sighed. How did a simple game of ball hockey turn into a fight? When he opened his eyes Trisha was looking at him closely.

Trisha tilted her head to the side. "You're Charlie Joyce, right?"

He felt himself blush. "Yeah. Sure. I guess." Emily laughed, and Charlie knew he was blushing even more. "I mean, I know I'm Charlie Joyce . . . rather than . . . guessing . . ."

The rain began to fall in earnest, the drops bouncing off the pavement and stirring up the dust.

Trisha leaned her chin on the butt of her stick. "It's nice to meet you, Charlie Joyce, but it looks like we'll have to postpone this game." She held her hand out to catch the raindrops. "What do we do with the sticks?"

"I'll put them away," he said, and she and Emily gave him their sticks.

"Thanks, Charlie Joyce. Come on, Em."

"See you later, Charlie Joyce," Emily said.

They jogged towards the school.

"It doesn't look as if we'll be able to fit in another game," Dalton said. "With any luck, this inclement weather won't last long and we can play after school. It has been raining something terrible this fall, hasn't it?" He took the sticks from Charlie.

"Yeah, it sure has," Charlie said mechanically. He was watching the two girls turn the corner.

Scott put a hand on his shoulder. "Joyce, I'm very impressed by the way you remembered your own name," he said. "I think Trisha was impressed also."

His buddies were grinning from ear to ear. He had to laugh at himself.

"I can spell it too," he said.

"You are one special kid," Scott said.

A crack of thunder interrupted the ribbing.

"Gents, I suggest a mad dash to the school before the tsunami hits," Nick said.

"All in favour," Scott said, "say 'Aye'."

A chorus of Ayes sounded as they started to run. Charlie kept thinking about Trisha and Emily. Those two could play. He wondered what they could do on the ice.

5

MOVIE MARATHON

Out of the corner of his eye Charlie caught sight of Zachary kicking his board into high gear. He cruised into a nose grind and stopped a etre in front of Charlie.

"Howdy, Mr. Charlie."

They exchanged a high-five. "Where's everyone else?" Charlie asked.

Zachary flicked his eyebrows and nodded over his shoulder. Charlie heard the unmistakable whirl of skateboard wheels growing louder. Pudge, Scott and Nick rounded the corner of the school and rode over.

"Zachary Jackson, you better slow down or you are going to hurt yourself," Scott said in a high-pitched voice.

"Yeah. He'll get wind burn," Nick said. He pointed to Charlie's board. "How's the Buy-A-Real-Board fund coming along?"

Charlie held his board up. It was so old and beat-up the nose was falling apart. He was saving up money by working at his mom's café.

"A few more weeks and the new board is mine," Charlie said.

"You should buy this one," Scott said. He had nicknamed his ride Black Beauty, on account of its shiny, black deck.

"The deck is too wide," Zachary said. "I'd go with a slimmer model." He held his board out.

"I'll take them both," Charlie said.

"You'll go twice as fast," Nick quipped.

"Not sure the weather's gonna cooperate," Pudge said.

"Yeah, and the rain's scared off the competition," Scott said.

Charlie had convinced the guys to play ball hockey after school. The rain had let up, but it looked bad now.

"We wanted a tougher game, but we'll take you guys on," someone called from a distance.

Charlie turned in the direction of the voice. Alexandra was laughing as she made her way towards them, with Julia and Rebecca at her side.

"Let's divide up and play before we get dumped on again," Zachary said.

"Sure, sounds good," Julia said.

An awkward silence followed. Rebecca crossed her arms, and Alexandra pulled her hair back from her face and tied it with a scrunchie into a ponytail. The boys kept their eyes on the ground or looked off into the distance.

Charlie knew they needed to clear the air. He took a deep breath.

"We were talking, some of us, about how you girls were right, about the ball hockey. I mean, that we were sort of hogging the Tuesdays — the boys, I mean . . ." Everyone was staring at him. He felt his heart pounding, and he prayed his voice wouldn't crack. "I think we should speak to Dalton about the days, and share them,

I mean the boys and girls, and maybe . . . we should . . . share the pad."

Alexandra raised her eyebrows and stuck her tongue in the side of her mouth. Rebecca looked down at the ground.

"That would be awesome," Julia said. "We don't have to play all the time — but some of the girls have been talking . . ."

"It works for me," Alexandra said.

Again, there was quiet, but it did not feel so uncomfortable to Charlie now.

"Actually, it's good that you guys are here," Julia said, finally.

"It's always good that we're here," Scott said.

They all laughed.

"It's good that you're here because we were trying to come up with ideas to present to the fundraising committee," Julia said.

"Do you really think we can raise that kind of money?" Nick said.

"I think you're forgetting my penny collection," Scott said.

Nick slapped his head. "Oh yeah! What are you up to?"

"Twelve bucks," Scott said.

"TFH is saved!" Nick proclaimed, shaking Scott's hand.

Julia eyed the two jokesters. "Maybe we should come up with one or two more ideas?"

"Car washes, bake sales and chocolates are too lame," Nick said. "I pray we don't have to do that."

"Never diss chocolate," Scott said.

"You can count on those," Pudge said, "and probably the parents will be asked to contribute. We have seven hundred fifty kids in school. If every parent puts in a hundred . . ."

Charlie suddenly felt worried. That would give them seventy-five thousand dollars, which was a huge amount — but only half way there. He felt a drop of rain — as if he were not depressed enough.

"Whatever we come up with will have to be indoors. It's been raining every day," he muttered.

"Do you have an indoor idea?" Pudge said.

He paused, hoping one would come to him — and then it did! "What about a movie, for the whole school, in the gym, and we can sell popcorn and drinks and charge admission."

He waited for Scott and Nick to make a joke.

But they didn't.

"That's a great idea," Pudge said, and the other guys seemed to agree.

"We could easily raise a few thousand," Zachary said. "People would pay ten dollars each, for sure. The whole school will show."

"We could do a double-feature — clear out the cafeteria and everyone can spread out sleeping bags," Rebecca said.

"What movie?" Zachary said.

"It's gotta be a zombie flick," Scott said. "Who doesn't love to see humans eating raw flesh?" He started chewing on his arm.

The girls groaned.

"I saw a great movie on the weekend with my folks," Pudge said. "It's an old movie, about poor people trying to raise money by winning a dance marathon. It's called *They Shoot Horses, Don't They?* It's from the sixties. It's really funny — even Scott will like it."

"Do the zombies eat the horses?" Scott said.

"Or do the horses eat the zombies?" Nick said.

"Or do the zombies ride the horses eating themselves?" Alexandra added.

Pudge flushed and lowered his eyes. Charlie knew they were only being funny. But Pudge was sensitive sometimes.

"I like the idea of an old and a new movie," Charlie said. "We should mix it up. Maybe we could watch the movies ahead of time to make sure everyone would like them."

"As long as I don't have to watch more than one zombie movie, I'm in," Rebecca said.

Pudge cheered up. "I have it on my computer. We can watch it any time."

"I didn't know there was money in dance marathons," Scott said. "Are you guys thinking what I'm thinking?"

"We're never thinking what you're thinking," Nick said. "That's what makes us normal."

"We don't dance . . . but we can skate!" Julia cut in. "We should have a skate-a-thon. We can get pledges and skate for eight hours, at ten dollars an hour, or whatever."

Zachary agreed. "I actually like that too. At least it's not chocolate."

"If you don't stop insulting chocolate . . ." Scott began.

"And both ideas might even be fun," Rebecca said, ignoring Scott.

A roll of thunder crashed overhead and the sky darkened.

"I'm not sure we're going to get our game in," Zachary said, looking up.

"It'll blow over," Scott said. "Nick, you get the sticks and nets from the shed and I'll watch and cheer you on."

Another sharp crack sounded and suddenly the rain began to pour down. In seconds they were all soaked.

"You might want to hold off on that," Scott said to Nick.

"Why don't we watch that movie?" Charlie asked Pudge.

"Sure. If you want," he said.

"Anyone into Pudge's movie?" Charlie said.

"Yes!" they all answered emphatically.

"Let's move!" Nick yelled.

The boys took off on their boards, with the girls running alongside. But the rain fell even harder and Charlie decided hurrying was pointless. He was totally drenched already. He got off his board and began to walk.

"Those were good ideas," Julia said, coming up beside him. She wiped the rain from her eyes and smiled. "We should present them to the committee. Don't you think?"

"Yeah. I guess."

"We could do it tomorrow. The committee is meeting before school."

She seemed to be suggesting that they go together, but he wasn't sure. "Do you want me to come along? I can if you want, or not. Whatever. I'm easy."

"Movie night was your idea," she said quietly.

"I guess," he said. "What time?"

"I think it starts at seven-thirty."

He gulped. Usually he wasn't even awake by then. "If my alarm clock cooperates, I'll be there," he said.

They walked along, in the rain, not saying anything for a while.

"You really are getting wet, Charlie Joyce," Julia said.

His conversation with Trisha must have made the gossip rounds. It was amazing how that worked. It was probably on Facebook already. The water was streaming down the street and they hopped up on the sidewalk.

"I'm thinking this walking thing is a bad idea," she continued.

He scrunched his mouth to one side. "I see your point."

Together they took off towards Pudge's house. Charlie was a good long-distance runner, but Julia had no trouble keeping up.

"There it is," he said, pointing to the house.

The others were waiting.

"Shark!" Scott yelled out to them. "Swim for your lives!"

Julia pretended to do the front crawl. Scott took off his shirt and threw it at them. "Use this as a raft. It's your only chance," he said.

Julia picked it up, and pretended to smell it. "I think I'd rather drown."

Pudge opened the door. He was holding a pile of towels. "Come on in, guys."

Charlie followed his friends inside. Pudge handed him a towel.

"Is this movie really any good?" Charlie asked.

Pudge pointed to the door. "You want to stay outside?"

Charlie rubbed his hair with the towel. "Where's the popcorn?" he asked.

6

WHERE'S THAT?

Charlie ignored the drizzle as he half ran, half walked his way to school. He did not want to break his promise to Julia and be late to present their ideas to the committee. Unfortunately, when he was leaving, he couldn't find his left running shoe, and then he somehow misplaced a science assignment. The result, as usual, was a mad rush.

"Hey, Charlie. What's the hurry?"

He stopped short. Julia waved at him and came over. She held a garbage bag in her hand. Peering at him, she added, "Did you just wake up, or something?"

He looked down and realized his jacket was unzipped and his shirt was half tucked in.

"I encountered a few setbacks on my way out the door," he said. "Maybe I should have stuck with the pyjamas." He hurriedly pulled his shirt out.

"I'm impressed you actually got here on time," she said. "That's got to be a record for you."

It was obviously no secret that he had issues with punctuality. He changed the subject. "What class is that for?" he said.

"It's not for class," she said. "I thought it would

help if I laid out our ideas on Bristol board. I'll show you when we get inside. I don't want it to get wet."

Charlie held the door open, and then she pulled out her work.

"When did you have time for that?" he said. "It's totally awesome." Julia was a massive brainiac, so he knew he should not be surprised. Even still, he had spent all night playing video games, and now he felt a bit guilty.

"I finished up my homework early and whipped this off," Julia said. "I figured it would help the committee. I had to make up some stuff, especially the costs. They will have to give us some money up front to rent the ice."

"Looks good to me. You'll blow them away," Charlie said. It was a total understatement. He could spend two weeks on something like that and it wouldn't look half as good.

She interrupted his thoughts by pointing at the cafeteria. "We should probably actually show them . . . ?"

"Right. Sure. In we go."

Six students were sitting at a table near the stage.

"Hey, guys," Dalton said. "Great to see you."

"How are things going?" Charlie said.

He made a sour face. "We were hoping for a more enthusiastic turnout," he said, looking around the empty room.

"It's still early," Julia said.

Dalton nodded. "Perhaps you're right; and maybe more students will present tomorrow. Anyway, did you come up with some ideas?"

"We did," Julia said. "I prepared this to make things

easier to explain." She held up the Bristol board.

"Can I see it?" Melissa said.

"I'll hold it for you," Charlie said to Julia.

"A few of us came up with two ideas," Julia began. "First we thought it would be fun to have a movie night in the caf, show a double feature — maybe a zombie flick and a classic too. We found one about a dance contest, which is sort of like raising money — anyway, it's a great movie, and we can sell popcorn and drinks and treats, and charge admission."

"I see you want to charge fifteen dollars a ticket," Melissa said. "I think that's too much. I don't think people will come. That's more than going to a real theatre."

"We could change it," Julia said.

"Five dollars for a bag of popcorn," a girl next to Melissa said. "That's bit of a rip, no?"

"It's good idea, A.J.," Dalton said to her. "Like Julia said, we can always adjust the pricing."

A.J. shrugged. "I like my idea for a pancake breakfast better," she said. "People love breakfast."

"We can do both," Dalton said.

"We will also need the school's permission. And we have to get a permit, and that's not always easy. What if things get out of hand? We'll need teachers to supervise, and they might not want to," Melissa said.

Julia's eyes narrowed and she looked over at Charlie.

"We can take care of the permit," Charlie said. He had no idea how, but he had to say something. "And we'll make sure there are lots of people around to organize things."

"Like who?" Melissa said.

"Like . . . me . . . and Julia . . . and our friends . . . and we'll ask some teachers."

"You're in grade ten, right?" A.J. said. She did not sound impressed.

Charlie nodded.

"This isn't gonna work, Mel," she said.

Julia kept at it. "As you can see here, we could raise between four and seven thousand dollars, and maybe more if . . ."

Melissa cut her off. "What's your other idea?"

Julia stopped, took a breath and answered slowly, "We also thought that we could organize a skate-a-thon, at the Ice Palace or somewhere else in town. If kids get sponsored, and I've guessed fifteen dollars an hour, or something like that, we could easily raise a few more thousand. The ice costs around a hundred and fifty an hour, and maybe we can get a deal from the rink since it's for charity, so with only a hundred kids participating you can see here that we can make . . ."

"It seems like you're being rather optimistic," A.J. interrupted. "Maybe we should shelve this one."

"I also don't think you can get that many kids to show up," Melissa said. "Look around. So far we've had three people, other than you, come up with any ideas. As usual, the student council is going to have to do all the work."

"But we have it figured out," A.J. said.

"I know, but still, it's irritating that we have to do it ourselves," Melissa said. "And as if we'll be appreciated."

"I hear ya," A.J. said.

"If I may interject," Dalton broke in gently. "This is

a unique idea. I agree that your ideas are going to be very successful. Everyone loves chocolate, and certainly the bake sale and pancake breakfast should bring in some funds. But perhaps we could let Julia and Charlie see if they can organize a movie night and a skate-a-thon, and report back to us in a week or so. Then we can judge."

A.J. looked even less impressed than before. "They're in grade ten. It's a lot of work."

"We can do it," Julia said. "We can raise some good money; and chocolates are . . ."

"Great," Charlie cut in. He could tell Julia was mad; and he could also tell Melissa and A.J. would freak if she criticized their ideas. "We just want to help out. Give us a chance. Our friends are totally stoked about the skate-a-thon, and we've already found a great movie."

Melissa took a deep breath. "I guess it's good to get the younger grades involved." She leaned forward. "Let us know by next week how things are going."

"I think we should focus on the other ideas," A.J. said. "This is a waste of energy."

"Maybe you're right, but it can't hurt," Melissa said. "Just don't expect this committee to have any time to help you guys out," she added, looking at Charlie and Julia.

"I'll be happy to lend my assistance," Dalton said. "I'm only organizing a ball hockey tournament."

"Thanks, Dalton. That would be awesome," Julia said.

Melissa shrugged and picked up a pen. "Okay. Thanks . . . what are your names again?"

"Julia Chow and Charlie Joyce," Dalton responded for them.

"Thanks, Julia . . . Charles," Melissa said. "We have another meeting in a week. You can report your progress then."

A few other kids had come in. Melissa waved them over. "You can present next," she said.

Julia stared hard at the committee members. Charlie had never seen this side of her. He pulled her gently away.

"They said we could go ahead. No sense hanging around. They seem pretty busy," he said.

Her expression remained dark. "Why did I bother wasting my time last night? I mean, do they really think chocolates will raise a hundred and fifty thousand dollars?"

"We can share a box," he said.

"I'll get my own." She took hold of his elbow. "Don't tell anyone, but I'm kind of a chocoholic."

"I gotta admit I've snarfed a few bars in my time." He paused. "But it's still a lame fundraising idea."

"Without question."

Another student was beginning to present her idea to the committee. ". . . so we thought we could print up some T-shirts with the school crest, and on the back it will say, 'I Saved My School From Drowning.' I have a list of companies that can do them for us, and here are the colours."

"I love the silver," A.J. said.

"Let me see those," Melissa said. "I'm in love with that blue."

As they left, doubts began to crowd Charlie's

thoughts. Chocolate, pancake breakfasts and T-shirts were not going to cut it. The committee had better come up with some better ideas — or grade ten at Terrence Falls High School was as good as over.

As they walked down the hall, he noticed a large crowd of students around the main bulletin board near the front doors. "Something exciting over there?" he said.

"We've got forty-five minutes to kill. Let's check it out," Julia said.

His heart sank when he saw the sign above the sheets of paper — *Student School Assignments*.

"It's the list of where we have to go . . . when TFH is closed," he said to Julia.

Her shoulders sagged. "Aren't they going to give us a chance to raise the money?"

They waited for their turn. Charlie soon found his name. "Where are you going?" he asked Julia.

"I'm at Flemington. Alex is at Chelsea and Rebecca is at Palmerston. That's totally unfair. Who decided that?"

"Do you know where Kennedy West High is?" he said. Julia shook her head.

"Well, that's where I'm going. Pudge is at Flemington with you. Scott is at Chelsea. Zachary is going to Beaverton — not sure where that is either. Matt's at Central." He looked at her in dismay. "We're all split up."

He thought of something. He looked back at the list, and quickly found Jake Wilkenson's name — and his head began to swim. Jake was going to Kennedy West too.

He turned and headed to the front doors.

"We need to petition Holmes, or at least talk to someone," Julia said. "I bet lots of kids are willing to switch to be with their friends."

"I hope everyone else likes chocolate as much as us," was all he could say.

7

TRYING TIMES

The sudden high-pitched crackling from the loudspeakers made Charlie practically jump out of his chair. He heard some grade twelves sitting behind him snicker.

"Sorry, students," Principal Holmes said, as he fiddled with the microphone. The feedback got worse. Hilton came out on stage and checked the cord. After a moment he nodded and left. Principal Holmes cleared his throat and leaned forward.

"Check, check, check. One, two, three. Check." He held up his thumb. "That's better. Sorry for the delay."

The talking continued.

Principal Holmes cleared his throat again. "I want to welcome all of you to this update assembly." He paused. "Students, please may I have your attention. Please. We need some quiet, please. Students! We have some important news to share with you about the school closure."

That got people's attention, and the cafeteria quieted down.

Charlie elbowed Pudge. "I bet he's figured out a way to keep the school open."

"There has been some water leakage reported in Mr.

Yevgeny's and Ms Charlton's classrooms," Principal Holmes continued.

"That doesn't sound encouraging," Pudge said. Charlie felt his hopes fade.

"As you know the rain has been very heavy this fall — quite remarkable, really — but then Mother Nature is a fickle lady." Principal Holmes chuckled. The students remained silent. "The engineers are very concerned about this new development, and this may force us to close the school earlier than anticipated . . ."

A murmur arose as the students reacted to this latest development.

Principal Holmes went on. "We are going to monitor the leakage situation very closely. The engineers resealed the edges of the roof, but I was told if the rain keeps up there is a strong chance that the repairs will not hold. The budget is already strained, and the engineers and I are in agreement that it does not make sense to carry out any further minor repairs if we're closing the school anyway."

"On Monday, posted on the main bulletin board, you will find a schedule for visiting your designated school. You will meet with a transition representative, and a student from that school, and you can have a tour. At the same time, students will have the chance to review their courses with a guidance counsellor. Some of you may have to change a few courses depending on availability. Please do not worry about this. We have things well organized. I understand this is a difficult and disruptive event, but by working together, we will get through it."

The absolute quiet unsettled Charlie even more

than the possibility of the school closing early. Things were getting downright weird. Now students were actually listening to Principal Holmes during an assembly!

"I will now turn the mic over to the president of the Fundraising Committee, who wanted to have a few words. Melissa?"

Melissa lowered the mic. She looked shell-shocked. "The committee wants to give you an update," she said in a soft, shaky voice. Charlie could not hear her. She went on like that until Hilton came over and whispered in her ear. She pulled the mic down lower and spoke louder. "I said, the committee has come up with some fundraising options, although maybe . . . as we just heard . . . there's no point."

Her voice cracked, and she stopped and stepped back a bit. She rubbed her eyes with her fingers. "We have organized a bake sale, a silent auction and a pancake breakfast for next week. We have also been in touch with a vendor about selling boxes of chocolate. As well, the parent committee will work with us to approach community businesses for donations. Our best hope comes from the parents, though. We will be sending out a donation package next week, asking for parents to provide donations in the amount of fifty, one hundred, or two hundred fifty dollars. We'll take more, of course." A few kids laughed.

Melissa took a deep breath. "That's all for now. We hope to have another assembly soon to let you know what else is planned." She looked to the side. "And now a junior member of the committee will make a few announcements."

Dalton came on to the stage. In a loud, clear voice

he said, "Thanks, Melissa. The Fundraising Committee has been working hard on your behalf. I am as alarmed as you about the recent news, but I am confident you share my belief that we cannot get discouraged, especially not so early in the campaign. If it turns out we cannot save the school, then wouldn't you be happier if you knew you did all you could?"

His words seemed to energize the students, and a few of them sat up straight, or began whispering to friends. The room was coming alive; Charlie felt it too. Dalton was right. The school was not closed yet, and until it was, they had to do everything they could to keep it open.

"The junior grades had a few ideas," Dalton said. "Charlie Joyce and Julia Chow are organizing a movie night at school — a double feature — and also a skate-a-thon at a local rink. That should be fun. Contact me or those two directly if you want to get involved, or sign up on the sheets that will be posted on the main bulletin board."

Scott leaned across and tugged on Charlie's sleeve. "Can I please, please, please get involved?"

"You can't," Nick said. "You'll scare the other kids away."

"I'll try to get you in," Charlie said, giving Scott a nudge with his elbow.

"Huge mistake," Nick said.

"I will be organizing a ball hockey tournament, so get your teams of five ready and let me know," Dalton continued. "The tournament will cost fifty dollars a team, and it will start next week."

There was a collective cheer.

"The teams must be co-ed," he said. "Two girls must be playing at all times."

Charlie and Pudge looked at each other. "This could get complicated," Charlie said. "How do we pick only two girls?"

Pudge did not have a chance to answer. "This is awful," Scott said. "All the girls are going to fight over me. It's unfair. I'm going to have to clone myself — but I'm willing to do it for TFH."

"You do realize the universe will explode if there is more than one of you," Nick said. "There will be too much hot air."

"We're going to have to divide everyone up," Zachary said. "I wonder which girls will play."

"There is one more thing," Dalton said. The boys turned their attention back to the stage. "Ms Cummings, our phys. ed. teacher, received notice of a co-ed hockey tournament sponsored by Bee-Bees Boutique." A huge cheer went up from the girls.

"Who are they?" Charlie said to Pudge.

"I've seen their stores around. They sell yoga clothes, I think."

"Bee-Bees sponsors a co-ed tournament in a different area every year — to promote gender equality in sport as well as health and fitness among high school students. This year the tournament is in Carling, which is not too far from here, maybe an hour. I know a lot of kids were extremely disappointed when the Champions Cup was cancelled. The Bee-Bees tournament is a couple of weeks before, and there are junior and senior divisions. There is no entry fee, and the winner in each division gets a twenty-five thousand dollar donation to the school for athletic programs."

Dalton looked out at the crowd. "Sign-up sheets will be posted for the hockey teams and the skate-a-thon. We'll be announcing the date and time for the movie night soon too." He nodded. "That's it, I guess."

Principal Holmes took the mic. "As always, please depart in an orderly fashion. Can I have the first ten rows rise and return quietly to your classes."

All the students got up and began milling around in the aisles. Principal Holmes leaned forward as if to say something, then shook his head and left the stage.

Charlie's friends crowded around.

"It occurred to me that you guys will all want me on your ball hockey team," Scott moaned. "It won't just be the girls fighting over me, but you too."

"And what about this co-ed team?" Zachary said. "Are we going to bother?"

"We can win a lot of money for the school," Charlie said.

"We're doing enough already," Nick said. "And we have to focus on the Rebels. I don't need to play co-ed hockey."

"There are plenty of other guys to play," Zachary said. "Nick's right."

Pudge grimaced. "I could give it a pass," he said.

"What about this leaking roof, then?" Charlie said. "There won't be any ball hockey or co-ed hockey if this rain keeps up."

Matt came over. "I've been thinking, boys," he said.

"What's thinking?" Scott said.

"Don't try it. You'll get hurt," Nick said.

"Remember last year when I worked for that roofing company?" he said.

Charlie sure did. Matt almost had to quit playing hockey because his father lost his job. He began working to help at home. Luckily, his dad had started his own carpentry business, which went well, and Matt had joined the Rebels.

"We did a few temporary repair jobs," Matt said. "Sometimes you can't get to a roof for a few days and you lay down plastic sheets in case of rain. It's usually not supposed to be for too long, but there's no reason it wouldn't work here. The roof is flat, so it would be easy."

"Why doesn't the school do that?" Charlie said.

"You heard Holmes," Matt said. "It's a lot of money — not in materials but in labour. He doesn't want to spend that kind of money just to keep the school open a few extra weeks, or a month."

Charlie understood him. They could do what the school would not. "Can the plastic hold up that long?"

Matt nodded. "We'd have to keep checking for holes, and fix things if it gets too windy. Sometimes the sheets get messed."

"Holmes isn't going to pay for it," Zachary said, "and there's no way he's gonna let us do it. How does this help?"

"We don't ask for permission," Charlie said bluntly. "Desperate times call for desperate measures."

"Are you sure desperate times don't call for submarine sandwiches?" Scott said.

"That's only part of it," Charlie laughed. "The most important part is taking a risk. How much would this plastic sheeting cost?"

Matt shook his head. "I'm not too sure. But the guys I worked with always said it was dirt cheap. The expensive part was the labour. It takes time and man-power to lay the sheets down right, and then secure them with sandbags. But with a big group of us, it wouldn't take long — about an hour at the most."

Pudge looked incredulous. "You're not really think-ing of . . ."

"Why not?" Charlie said intensely. "Matt knows what to do. Holmes doesn't believe we can raise the money, so he's focused on the transition to other schools. Two or three weeks is all we need to get the fundraising going, and it could make all the difference. We should try is all I'm saying."

They all looked at Charlie.

"So what do we need to do?" Pudge said.

Charlie looked at Matt. "Tell us."

"There's not much to it. Basically, we just buy the plastic sheets, the bags and the sand. I know where to get that stuff, and I can get one of the guys I worked with to order the supplies and have them delivered to the school. We need the money up front, though."

Charlie suppressed a groan. His long board fund was quickly disappearing again. Desperate times, he thought.

"We could do it Saturday morning," Charlie said. "No one will be here, and we all heard Holmes say they won't be doing any more repairs, so no one will be checking on the roof any time soon, or at least until school closes. What do you guys say?"

Charlie held his hand out. Pudge put his on top, and then one by one, Matt, Zachary and Nick did the same.

Scott hesitated. "Are you going to make me the foreman, and force me to be in charge?"

"We promise to treat you badly, and make fun of you behind your back," Nick said.

"Then I'm in," he said, slapping his hand on top.

"The Rebels are taking charge," Charlie said, and they threw their hands in the air.

"Are you guys practising the school cheer?" Alexandra said from the aisle. Julia and Rebecca were next to her, as usual.

"It doesn't sound like you'll need it," Julia said.

Charlie looked at the girls thoughtfully for a moment. Matt had said the plastic sheeting took a lot of manpower — maybe some womanpower would help!

"If you ladies can keep a secret," he said in a whisper, "Matt will explain his plan to stop the leaking."

Julia's face brightened and the three girls came closer.

"If you'll excuse me, I have to speak to Dalton for a sec," Charlie said.

"How come?" Pudge said.

He pointed to a door. "We need someone to let us in, so we can carry the supplies to the roof, and I bet a member of the Fundraising Committee can get a key."

He ran off to intercept Dalton at the back of the cafeteria.

8

DEFEATED

Charlie let his hockey bag plop to the floor as he squeezed in beside Pudge.

The usually loud dressing room was quiet. Scott and Nick dressed intently in the corner, barely talking. Charlie had to force himself to unzip his bag. It was like someone had drained the energy from his body. All day they had been talking about the other schools, and Julia had followed through by organizing a petition to protest. But he hadn't heard anything yet. Pudge always had the inside story on things. Maybe he knew how it went.

"Did you find out about the petition?" he asked Pudge.

The Terrence Falls kids looked over.

Pudge stuck a foot into his skate and reached into his bag for the other one. "Apparently, Holmes refused to accept it. He said the decisions were final because if he allowed one student to switch, everyone would want to switch and it would be . . . I think he said . . . an administrative nightmare."

"The school assignments are a nightmare," Scott said with a scowl. "Me at Chelsea? I've spent most of my life hating that place, and now I'm supposed to wear the school colours?"

"You do look good in blue and gold," Nick said.

"That's the worst part," Scott said. "I'm going to be miserable, and at the same time look absolutely fabulous."

"I heard a rumour that some kids were going to protest by dressing in black," Zachary said.

"I saw a few posters around school," Matt said. "I wondered what that was all about."

"It's a day of mourning," Pudge said.

"I'm definitely in," Scott said. He nudged Nick. "And it doesn't hurt that I look even better in black."

"Damn you and your fabulousness," Nick said.

That lightened the mood and the boys began to joke around a bit more.

"Have you made any new friends at Kennedy?" Scott asked Charlie.

"I'm still working on it," Charlie said. "It might help if I knew where it is, though."

"You'll love it there if you like buses. It's about an hour away," Pudge said.

"Finally, you and Jake can spend some quality time together," Nick said.

"So what's going on at Terrence Falls?" Spencer broke in. "I've heard they're closing the school."

Charlie filled him in.

"Anyone going to Central?" Spencer asked.

Matt raised his hand.

"Awesome, dude," he said. "Our Champions Cup team just got a whole lot better. Our coach is gonna freak when he hears you're coming."

"I never thought of that," Scott said, slapping his thigh. "Chelsea's Champions Cup junior team won last year. In fact, they've won the last six years. If I play for them—"

"They'll definitely lose," Nick jumped in.

"And I will get my revenge!" Scott yelled.

He and Nick shook hands.

"Actually, the only good thing about the school closing early is maybe we can still make a Champions Cup team after all," Pudge said. He looked around the room, and his face turned red. Slowly, most eyes in the room turned to Charlie.

Charlie was about to put on a skate. He dropped it back in his bag. "Kennedy doesn't have a team, does it?" he said.

The guys started laughing.

"Who would want to play in the most awesome high school hockey tournament of the year?" Scott sputtered, doubled up with laughter.

"He can work ahead in English," Nick said, and the roars rebounded off the walls.

Charlie could only shake his head. He reached for his skate. "It's not certain that TFH is closing early," he said.

No one heard him. They were all joking around and talking too loudly. Then Pudge tapped him on the arm.

"What time did Matt's friend arrange for delivery tomorrow morning?" Pudge said quietly.

"Six-thirty, dude," Charlie said. "But we need to get there earlier so Dalton can let us in."

"Is he going to help?" Pudge said hesitantly.

"I didn't exactly tell him what we're doing, only that we got a bunch of stuff for movie night. You know Dalton, he was happy to meet us. I felt bad about lying, and making him get up so early, but . . ."

Pudge grunted and began to tape his shin pads. Charlie could tell Pudge was worried, and so was he. Everything depended on Dalton.

"I think Charlie and Jake should join the book club at Kennedy West first, and then start up their own glee club," Scott was saying when Hilton walked in holding a clipboard, followed by Jeffrey, the assistant coach.

"Let's settle down a bit and get ready for the game," Hilton said. "Finish dressing and then we can go over the lines. I want to make a few changes."

Charlie stuffed his foot into his skate. They were getting really tight. He ignored it and began tugging on the laces. Snug skates were the least of his worries.

* * *

Scott circled the Rebels' net and Charlie curled high in the slot. Uncharacteristically, Charlie wasn't thinking of his next move; he was picturing himself on the roof tomorrow morning. They had ordered the plastic yesterday. Matt had sneaked upstairs to scope things out and take measurements. What if it didn't come on time, though? The whole thing was risky, and the later they started and the longer the work took, the higher the chances of getting caught. Just then Scott passed the puck to him. It was a bit behind, and instead of reaching with his stick, Charlie figured he could drag his left skate and deflect it.

A roar went up from the crowd. Charlie watched helplessly as the Tigers' centre stormed in on goal. The puck had clipped the heel of Charlie's skate and bounced behind him. Nick had to cover the left winger in front, so it was a semi-breakaway. Martin came out to cut down the angle, but he had not anticipated such a sudden turnover and was slightly off his line. The puck carrier hesitated, took aim and snapped a wicked wrister down low to the glove side. Martin barely had time to move.

Charlie put his stick across his shin pads and coasted to his goalie. "Totally my bad," he said, and slapped Martin's pads.

Martin dug the puck out of his net and backhanded it towards the other end. The ref gave him a dirty look, but fortunately just turned and gave chase.

"Bad pass," Scott said, joining them in front. "Sorry about that, Joyce. My goal."

"Nah," Charlie said. "I should've had it. I didn't move my stick. It was laziness."

"This game has been one continuous bad bounce," Nick said. He slapped their shin pads with his stick. "How much bad luck can we have? I think all five of their goals came off stupid turnovers."

Charlie had nothing to add. The game had been a disaster from the start. In his first shift, he had lost a faceoff in their end, and the Tigers had converted that into a goal in the second minute. A few bad passes, some sloppy defensive coverage, and now this, and the score was 5–1 for the Tigers. The Rebels had punished them 8–2 in an exhibition game!

He saw Matt's line hop the boards, and Spencer and Philip come out for the defence. "We don't deserve to play," Charlie said. "Let's change 'em up."

He drifted listlessly to the bench. It was weird how tired he felt.

"Did someone steal all my energy?" he said to Pudge, as they settled on the bench. There were only two minutes left, and he doubted they would get another shift. "It's like I'm skating in mud."

"We didn't wake up until the third period," Pudge said.

Zachary settled down beside Charlie. "I think our line got four shots on goal this game and we're at minus three. Basically, we sucked."

Charlie took a sip of water. Matt carried the puck across the Rebels' blue line. Jonathon cut into the centre of the neutral zone, wide open. Matt snapped a pass, but it was too wide and it bounced off the boards to the Tigers' defenceman, who pounded it down the ice deep into the Rebels' end.

"Have we made a pass all game?" Hilton grumbled behind them. He walked to the end of the bench.

"I know I haven't," Charlie said. He slammed the water bottle back on the ledge. It bounced off the boards and fell to the floor, rolling under the bench. He rolled his eyes as he fished for the bottle. "That was perfect. I can't even do that today."

This time he stuffed the bottle on the ledge with two hands.

"So much for the undefeated season," Pudge said.

Obviously Charlie and Pudge both knew the Rebels were going to lose a game eventually. But it hurt to know they lost because the effort was missing. "My head wasn't in this game," Charlie said. "All I could think about was the school, and the roof, and a hundred and fifty thousand dollars, and —"

Another roar from the crowd interrupted him. Martin was in a butterfly, his head down, holding his glove and blocker across his chest. A Tigers forward was leaning against the boards, his stick over his head, and his teammates were going over to congratulate him.

"Who turned the puck over this time?" he said.

"Don't ask," Zachary said, shaking his head.

"At least it wasn't me," Charlie said.

Matt's line headed off, and Brandon's jumped the boards. Charlie's line shuffled down the bench to make room. The new guys had played well. It was the Terrence Falls boys that had let the Rebels down. Charlie felt doubly bad about that. There was a minute and twenty left on the clock.

"Let's get one back, Brandon," Charlie yelled out, but his heart wasn't in it. He watched in silence with his teammates as the clock wound down.

"I've never loved the sound of a buzzer more than right now," Charlie said to Pudge.

Charlie skated to their end to console their goal-tender. He could not get off the ice soon enough. He needed to put this entire game behind him, and he promised himself this would be the last time he would let what was going on at school affect his hockey. He was captain, and his teammates deserved more.

"We let you down," he said to Martin.

They had a tradition of head butting after every game. "It was bound to happen," Martin said, and he bonked Charlie gently on the head with his facemask. "We didn't have any jump today."

"No biggie, Rebels," Charlie said. "Next game

we're going to actually play hockey. We just learned we can't just show up and expect to win. We gotta earn it."

His serious words were met with solemn nods. His teammates followed him to centre to shake hands with the victorious Tigers.

9

ALL IN

The sun had just come out, and there was still a chill in the air. Charlie and Pudge shivered as they waited for Dalton in the parking lot near the back of the school. They had arranged for the driver to drop the supplies there, so people wouldn't notice as easily from the street; and there was a side door where they could get everything inside quickly. Charlie's mind was racing for a way to convince Dalton to just open the side door and leave. There was a bigger problem, however. Dalton hadn't shown up yet.

"Dalton doesn't strike me as the late type," Charlie said. "I bet something's wrong. The supplies will be here soon, and we'll be messed."

"We still have ten minutes," Pudge said.

That didn't help, and ten minutes later his nerves were totally on edge.

"This is a disaster," Charlie moaned. "We're going to have plastic and sandbags in the parking lot for everyone to see, and no way to get in the school."

Pudge looked concerned too. "If Dalton doesn't come, we're going to have to tell the driver to take the stuff back."

"But we paid for it already," Charlie said. "Will they give us a refund? Everyone chipped in." He looked up to the sky. The only good thing he could think of was that it wasn't raining.

The sound of footsteps set his heart pounding. He turned, expecting to see his friends, or worse yet, the driver.

It was Dalton, red-faced and out of breath. "I must apologize for my tardiness," he said, gasping. "My sister has an early hockey game and we had a mini-crisis trying to find her sweater."

"No worries," Charlie said, feeling more worried every second. The truck would be here any minute, and his friends would be coming soon too. Dalton would know he was lying. "Why don't you give us the key? We'll lock up when we're done."

Dalton ducked his head slightly and squinted. "I kind of promised that I wouldn't lend the keys. Principal Holmes was quite insistent on that point. Besides, I'm always up early to read the newspaper or my magazines. Did either of you get the new *Economist*?"

Charlie and Pudge shook their heads meekly.

"Anyway, I'm happy to help carry the supplies in. He paused and added, "And where are the supplies?"

Charlie and Pudge stared at him.

Charlie wanted to yell, "They're coming," but instead he said calmly, "The truck's late. He just called to say they'll be coming in half an hour or so . . . under the circumstances I'm sure Holmes wouldn't mind if you opened the door. We won't even go in. Right, Pudge?"

"Yeah. Right."

Dalton looked at his watch. "I'd feel guilty making you do all the hard work."

Charlie was the one feeling guilty, and from the look on Pudge's face, his friend was feeling the same way. But it was too late now.

"Why don't we open the door and clear out some space in the gym storage room?" Charlie said, hoping to lure Dalton away.

"As you wish," Dalton said cheerfully. "Now where did I put those keys?" He tapped his pockets and pulled out a key chain with several keys attached. "Gotcha."

"Awesome! Dalton is the Key Man." Scott and Nick had come from behind the school. Scott slapped Dalton on the back and Nick flashed a thumbs-up.

"Um . . . yes. Just helping Charlie and Pudge with movie night — it's a fundraising initiative and . . ."

"I know what's going on, Key Man," Scott said. "Are you gonna help us? I can't wait to get up on that roof."

"The roof . . . ? Why the . . . What do you mean?"

Charlie felt sick. This was done. Dalton would be furious and they'd have to send the supplies back. And since he'd messed up, he should probably pay his friends back. But he didn't have enough money. All because Dalton was so ridiculously nice!

"Dalton, I owe you an apology," he began slowly.

"You probably owe me one too," Scott said, but his voice trailed off when he saw Charlie was serious.

"Whatever for?" Dalton said.

"This is a bit awkward," Charlie began. "The truth is we ordered roofing supplies to stop the leaking, so we could buy more time to fundraise. We needed a way to get in . . . and I didn't want to get you involved . . ."

Dalton rubbed his chin, holding his elbow with his other hand. He did not respond for a time, and then he said, "I confess I did not expect this. I can see that you wanted to protect me from getting in trouble for performing repairs on the roof without permission — I assume you do not have permission?"

Charlie and Pudge shook their heads.

"We could get suspended for this," Dalton said pointedly.

Zachary and Matt arrived on their long boards.

Zachary greeted them with a "Yo, dudes," and kicked the board to his hand.

Matt waved his phone in the air. "My bud called me. The driver will be here soon. He's running a bit late."

"At least that was true," Dalton said.

Charlie froze, uncertain if he was serious or joking.

"Hi, Dalton," Zachary said. "I didn't know you were going to help us."

"I didn't either," Dalton stated.

Zachary and Matt looked at Charlie for an explanation.

"I'm really sorry," Charlie said. "I should've trusted you. I . . . um . . . it was wrong. We ordered plastic sheets to lay on the roof to keep the rain away, and it's paid for . . . and it's coming soon."

"And the six of you are doing the work?" Dalton said.

"With Julia, Rebecca and Alexandra," Pudge said.

As if on cue, the girls came into view. Dalton spun the key chain around his finger. "I appreciate we don't know each other very well . . ." he said. He stopped spinning the keys. "Desperate times do call for desperate measures."

"I told you they don't call for subs," Nick said to Scott.

A large flatbed truck pulled into the parking lot and, with a high-pitched squeal of the breaks and a gush of air, came to a stop.

The driver hopped out of the cab. He held some papers. The girls slipped in behind Charlie and Pudge.

"How's it going?" Julia whispered to Charlie.

"So-so," he answered.

"I have an order for delivery to this address," he said, holding the paper towards Scott.

"That's right, sir," Scott said.

The driver looked around. "Where's the contractor who called it in? I didn't know this was for a school."

"We're waiting for him too," Charlie said.

The driver's face clouded. "I need a signature for the materials, and I have about ten more deliveries, and I'm already late."

Scott pushed forward. "I'm happy to sign, Mr. Driver," he said.

"I meant an adult's signature."

Scott held up his phone. "We're working for the contractor. It's part of a new school program to teach young kids construction skills. We're all very excited to get going." He beamed a smile.

The driver crossed his arms. "So this is some kind of school project?"

"Exactly," Scott said.

"Why do you need plastic sheeting and bags of sand? What are you making?"

"It's . . . like . . . a . . . the teacher has the plans," he said in a rush. Scott held up his phone again. "I just spoke to him and he's running late, so if you want to wait about another half an hour . . . or maybe an hour . . . or two."

The driver's shoulders slumped. "I don't have time for this." He peered intently into Scott's eyes. Scott smiled back. "Okay. I'll leave the stuff with you. But I need you to sign." Scott took the pen and signed with a flourish. The driver ripped a copy off and gave it to Scott.

"Where do you want me to put it?" the driver asked.

"Right here is fine," Charlie said.

"Are you sure you can leave it in the parking lot?"

"It'll be gone in five minutes, tops," Charlie said.

The driver chewed on his pen. "Fine. I've wasted too much time already. Stand back."

He ran to his truck and used a hoist to lower the plastic sheeting and the sandbags. They were on a wooden skid, bound by metal straps.

He leaned out the window. "Bring the skid back to the shop and you get fifteen bucks," he yelled, and then pulled away.

"Should I rip this up now, or wait until we're really bored," Scott said, holding up his copy of the invoice.

"Why don't you frame it for your bedroom?" Nick said. "You can put it next to your miniature glass kitten collection."

"Nick, you know it's *our* glass kitten collection," Scott said.

Nick wiped his eyes. "Is he not the best pal in the world?"

Charlie's and Dalton's eyes met. Charlie was feeling worse every second. He couldn't imagine how ugly this was for Dalton. "Hey guys, I kinda messed Dalton up," Charlie said. "I didn't tell him exactly why we are here and . . ."

"It's okay, Charlie," Dalton said, nodding slowly. "I understand your motivations, and I admire your school spirit and initiative. But, at the same time, the dangers of being caught cannot be exaggerated." He gave his keys a whirl. "We would be wise to hurry. In order to determine the availability of the gym for fundraising events I did a search of permits given to community groups. The gym is booked every Saturday starting at ten o'clock."

Dalton selected one key and held it out to Charlie. "I believe you are more fleet of foot than I. This key opens the front doors. I assume we'll be moving the supplies in through this side door, so you'll have to walk through the school." He held up another key. "You need this key to open the door leading to the south stairwell."

Charlie wanted to give Dalton a hug — obviously not a good time for that. "I'll see you guys in a sec," he said, and took off with the keys in hand. It was weird to be the only person in the school. Only a few lights were on, and it was a bit creepy. As he reached to open the side door, for some reason he felt compelled to look back. This place meant a lot to him, and he realized how much when he saw it empty like this. It filled his heart with a heavy feeling. This was the place where he had come after his dad died, when he thought he would never be happy again. Here he had made the best friends of his life; and he had expected grade ten to be an even better year.

He opened the door. Matt was snipping the straps. Scott and Nick were staggering under the weight of the sandbags and coming towards him. Charlie quickly stuffed a rock into the corner of the door to keep it open and ran over to help.

10

RAIN, RAIN GO AWAY

Charlie and Pudge struggled up the last few steps. "My arms are gonna fall out of their sockets," Charlie said. "Hold on." He rested a corner of the plastic wrapping on a stair. "How can plastic weigh so much?"

Pudge was breathing heavily and he put his end down too. "Maybe another school ain't such a bad idea," he said.

Charlie grinned. He picked up his end, and together they carried it over to the stairs that led to the roof. He'd sure learned something about school security! A lot of the doors were locked by the same key — what Dalton called a skeleton key. The same key that opened the stairwell door also opened the door to the roof.

"Are they making any progress?" Charlie said to Zachary.

"Matt actually seems to know what he's doing," Zachary said. "We've already laid down a few sheets of plastic. But the wind is kicking up and the sheets won't stay flat. I'd say it's complete mayhem and things are spiralling out of control."

"That sounds better than I'd hoped." Charlie grunted, as he heaved the roll of plastic sheeting through the door. It caught on something, and he pushed harder.

Matt came over — and he greeted them with a frown.

"Guys, I know it was heavy, but we needed to be careful not to rip it," he said.

There was a large gash on the side.

Charlie banged his thigh with his fist. "I'm beyond stupid. I bet I ripped it when I pushed it through the door."

Matt looked more closely at it. "Let's unroll it. I'm sure we can use most of it."

Scott and Nick began to cut away the ties.

"We've covered about half the area," Matt said. "We'll be done in about twenty more minutes."

"I need a sandbag!" Dalton said urgently.

"That doesn't sound good," Pudge said.

A row of plastic sheeting began tumbling across the roof. They could only watch as it gathered speed and sailed off the end into the air.

"Who was supposed to sand that strip down?" Alexandra said.

Dalton, Julia and Rebecca looked at each other guiltily. Alexandra started to laugh. "Maybe we should hold off on our plans to start a roofing company."

Charlie hung his head, his hands still on his knees. "I think we should launch a search and rescue operation — now." He stood up. "Sergeant, are you with me?"

Pudge saluted. "Ready when you are, Major."

"We'll start laying out this roll," Matt said. "Hurry up with that piece, and we should almost be done when you get back."

Charlie and Pudge practically flew down the stairs and out to the field at the back of the school. Charlie saw the plastic sheet rolling towards the fence.

"This is becoming a comedy," he said. "I'm so tired I feel like I've played three hockey games in a row."

"I wish I was only that tired," Pudge said. "I had no idea roofing was like running a marathon."

Together they charged out onto the field and wrestled the plastic sheet to the ground. The wind was getting downright unruly, and it was no easy task to fold the sheet so they could carry it. Every second that ticked by made Charlie uneasy. This had already taken too long.

Pudge grabbed one end, and Charlie the other, and they ran back to the side door.

Charlie looked at Pudge. "I guess it didn't occur to either of us to leave the door open."

Pudge pursed his lips. "Doesn't look like it."

A car pulled into the parking lot.

"*Retreat*," Charlie hissed, and they scampered around the corner. Charlie poked his head out. Four adults wearing track pants and T-shirts were walking towards the front doors. Two of them tossed a basketball back and forth.

"Aren't they a bit early?" Charlie said.

Pudge pulled out his phone. "I'll call someone to come down and let us in."

In less than a minute, Dalton opened the door.

"Good timing," Dalton said. "This piece is all we need to finish."

They made their way cautiously to the stairs while Charlie explained the situation to Dalton. He glanced at his phone. "They may have come early to practise, or the permit changed. It's almost nine o'clock. This is a very worrisome development, because someone would have had to open the door for them."

"Janitor!" Charlie and Pudge said together.

"We're totally busted," Charlie said.

"Not if we don't get caught," Pudge said.

Charlie titled his head to one side. "Sergeant, that's the kind of bold talk that will get you that promotion."

"I like the sound of General."

"That might be a bit too bold."

They began to creep upstairs. About halfway up the first flight, Charlie heard a noise. Someone was whistling — and Charlie knew that whistle.

He mouthed the word "janitor," and flung his head backwards frantically. They tiptoed as fast as they could down the stairs and out into the main hall.

"Let's go south stairwell," Pudge whispered. "It's away from the gym."

The coast was clear until they got close to the main washrooms. Up ahead they heard two men talking.

"We're sandwiched," Charlie whispered.

"The boys' washroom," Pudge hissed, pulling Charlie's arm.

They ran inside, and Charlie opened the door a crack. The voices were getting louder.

"They're coming in," he said.

Their eyes met.

"Into a stall," Dalton said.

They stuffed the plastic into one stall, and then all three boys climbed up on the toilet seat of the other.

"The door," Pudge whispered.

Charlie reached out and pushed the stall door shut, and slid the bar across to lock it. The boys held their breath.

"I could have sworn Mackie told us nine o'clock," a man with a deep voice said.

"No big deal. We can warm up. I spoke to the janitor, and he's cool with it. Besides, you could use the practice."

The man with the deep voice laughed. "It's bizarre being back here," he said. "I can't believe we graduated from this high school twenty years ago."

"I hear it's closing down."

His friend gasped. "What? Why?"

"I think the roof has to be replaced. A neighbour was telling me the school is trying to raise the money to do some temporary repairs so the kids can finish the year off. He was not too happy about having to reach into his wallet, believe me. He said most of his friends were not happy about it either. But I don't see how they can raise the money without the parents."

They washed their hands and left. Charlie opened the stall slowly. He made his way to the door and looked out.

"The coast is clear," he announced.

Pudge pulled the plastic out of the stall. "Do you think that's true? Do you think the parents don't want to help with the fundraising? If it is, we're done."

"Of course some parents aren't going to be interested," Charlie said. "Same with the students. That's always the way. But everyone will get into it." He wasn't sure he really believed that, however. It was an unpleasant thought.

They raced to the stairwell and carried the plastic to the roof.

"Over here," Matt yelled, waving at them.

"*Shh!*" Charlie said, his finger to his lips.

He and Pudge carried it over.

"We need to keep quiet," Charlie said. "The janitor is here, and some people came early for a basketball game."

Matt inspected the plastic for damage. With the help of Alexandra, Julia and Rebecca they laid it out, while Zachary, Scott and Nick placed the sandbags around it to keep it in place.

"Maybe you guys *should* start that roofing company," Charlie joked.

"Maybe we should get out of here," Alexandra said.

She definitely had a point.

"I don't think it's a good idea for all of us to leave at the same time," Charlie said. "We should leave in groups of two or three. We'll see you leave from up here, and then send the next group. Sound like a plan?"

They nodded.

"Why don't Julia, Rebecca and Alexandra go first," Charlie suggested. "Then —"

"Because we're helpless little girls who are afraid?" Alexandra said in a mock-sweet voice.

"No. I just . . . was just saying off the top of my head . . ." He hesitated. "Uh . . . maybe it makes more sense to get the tools off first. Matt, you have all your dad's tools?"

"I'm loaded." He held up a red toolbox.

"Zachary. You want to help him?"

Zachary flashed a grin and bowed. "Should we

rendezvous at The Hill for a long board session?"

"See you there," Charlie said.

Matt and Zachary left.

"Let's keep a lookout," Scott said to Nick. "And if you fall over, just do like the ninjas and float on the air and land with bended knees. After you hit the ground, hold one arm high and one low."

"Thanks for the tip," Nick said. "But I'm not quite clear on how you do it. Can you show me?"

They went over to the edge. Charlie had the feeling Alexandra had only been messing with him, as usual. But it made him feel uncomfortable. Was there some truth to what she said? Why had he chosen the girls to go down first?

"Do you guys have your ball hockey teams set up?" Julia said suddenly.

"Not really," Charlie said. "Have you guys committed to a team?"

"Not really," Julia said.

"We should organize things," Charlie said cautiously. "We need three guys and two girls on each team."

"Give me the names and I'll enter you right now," Dalton said. He pulled out his phone and began poking at the screen.

"Why do we need three boys and two girls?" Alexandra said. "Why not the other way around?"

Charlie wished he could take Scott's advice and jump off the roof. "I just assumed, I guess, that we would . . . have . . . three boys."

"Because that would be better?" Alexandra said.

A flash of inspiration came to him. "The problem is

73

there are six guys here. We'd have to have three teams, and . . ."

Alexandra shrugged. "Makes sense. It'll be fun. Right, girls?"

"Yup," Julia said.

"Pudge, what do you think we should . . . ?" Charlie's voice trailed off.

"We could keep our line together: you, me and Zachary. And Nick, Scott and Matt. That could work," Pudge said.

"Why don't Alex and Rebecca play with Nick, Scott and Matt. Michelle and I will play with you guys," Julia said. Dalton began entering the names.

"What about Trisha and Emily?" Charlie said. "They can play."

All three girls glared at him. Wrong thing to say, Joyce, he realized.

"They're out," Scott announced. "Next group."

The three girls had their arms crossed.

"Are you boys ready?" Charlie said.

Nick and Scott stood up.

"If we die trying to escape we might be late to the Hill," Scott said. He reached for the door handle. "Hey, Dalt-Man, you may as well escape with us."

Dalton looked up from his phone. "Sure. If that suits you."

"See you, Dalton," the girls chorused.

"Thanks for the help," Charlie said to him. "And thanks for letting us in."

Dalton surveyed the roof. "If it works, it will have been well worth it. I enjoyed myself. I've never been up here before. It's a nice view."

They climbed down.

Julia leaned forward on her toes. "So are you guys excited about the hockey team?"

"We had a bad game last night," Charlie said. "But we won our first four, and we have a solid squad. We picked up some new guys, especially this one defenceman named Spencer. He's awesome . . ."

"I didn't mean the Rebels," she interrupted. "I meant the Bee-Bees team — the co-ed tournament."

"Are you playing?" Charlie asked.

"Aren't you?" She sounded surprised and maybe a bit angry.

"I was thinking about it," Charlie said.

"What's there to think about?" Alexandra said. "You were going to play for the Champions Cup team."

No way could he tell them his friends didn't want to play co-ed hockey. "I'm probably gonna play. Not sure how the tryouts work . . ."

They turned to Pudge.

"I'm thinking about it," he said.

"The sign-up sheet is up already — it came out Friday," Julia said.

Rebecca had wandered over to the edge. "The boys are out. Why don't you go next, and we'll come last."

Charlie had absolutely no intention of arguing.

"Thanks for the help. This will be epic if it works," Charlie said.

The girls said goodbye, and Charlie and Pudge climbed down. They waited to hear if the janitor was around, and then made a beeline outside.

"I think my skateboard stuff is at your place," Charlie said. "I forgot it last time."

"You forget it every time," Pudge said, giving Charlie a push.

"I'm waiting for you to clean it," he joked, pushing him back.

They headed towards Pudge's house. When they were about halfway up the street, Charlie held out his hand to Pudge, and they shook.

"We pulled it off," Charlie said. "That should take care of the leaks. Now we just have to raise a hundred and fifty thousand bucks, and we're home free."

"Piece of cake," Pudge said.

"Speaking of cake . . ." Charlie rubbed his stomach. "Maybe we should stop by my mom's café."

"We have some apple pie left over from dinner last night," Pudge said.

"Then we'll go to the café after the Hill."

"The perfect plan, Major."

The sky had darkened, and after a sunny morning Charlie feared it might rain again. This had better work, he thought, or it would be a lonely school year. And an hour-long bus ride every day — with Jake.

Brutal.

11

DRESS FOR SUCCESS

Kids were heaving major sighs after school as they came down the stairs in groups of two or three and saw the rain. Charlie and his friends sighed louder than most.

"Does it have to rain on all our ball hockey days?" Charlie grumbled.

"Water polo would be a better bet," Nick said.

"We might consider building an ark," Scott said. "I hear that worked out well for Noah and his family."

Matt and Pudge came bounding down the stairs.

"Rain!" they said in unison, and their friends laughed.

"What're we gonna do?" Pudge said.

"We could head over to the café and have a snack-erino," Scott said, nudging Charlie.

"How about an air hockey tourney?" Zachary said.

Charlie had a table in his basement. "That's fine. We could all go to my place."

"Yeah. But we did that yesterday," Scott said. "And even though I'm obviously the best, Charlie always cheats and wins. Frankly, I'm sick of it."

"So we've decided to stand here and stare at each other?" Zachary said.

"That's the best idea so far," Nick said.

Charlie noticed a crowd of students at the end of the hallway around the main bulletin board. "Holmes must have put up another announcement," he said. "Might as well check it out."

"This should amuse us for eight or nine seconds," Scott said.

Alexandra spotted them. "Look at this. The great and mighty Rebels are finally going to sign up."

Julia and Rebecca were there too, and then Charlie noticed Emily and Trisha off to the side watching intently. The boys exchanged uneasy looks. Charlie and Pudge had not told the others about the conversation on the roof with the girls.

Charlie walked up to the bulletin board. The junior team had nine girls signed up and the senior team had four girls, and neither team had any boys.

"The girls are certainly enthusiastic," he said.

The girls' silence made it clear they did not find his joke particularly amusing.

"Seriously, though. We were just talking about it," he said, thumbing at his friends.

"I forgot to sign up — got busy . . . and forgot," Pudge managed.

Alexandra rolled her eyes. "They don't want to play. I told you," she said.

"We have lots of time to find guys," Julia said. "No one has to play. It's . . . whatever." She didn't look too happy, though.

Nick had a resigned look about him. Zachary was leaning against the wall, his hands in his pockets. Scott had a huge grin. He hesitated just slightly, flicked his eyebrows at his friends, then took a pen resting on the ledge of the bulletin board and signed his name for the junior team. One by one, each of them signed. Charlie went last.

"Ladies. You know you can count on the crew," Scott said. "We bleed Terrence Falls High blood. As a natural centre, and the obvious choice for captain, probably coach too —"

"What about general manager?" Nick said.

"I figured that goes without saying," Scott said, without skipping a beat.

Julia laughed. "I didn't know you were a forward."

"I didn't know you played hockey?" Nick said.

"You're hurting my confidence," Scott said.

"We have a practice this Thursday after school," Rebecca said seriously.

"Your captain–coach–general manager will be there," Scott said.

That garnered a groan.

"I'm glad you decided to play," Julia said to Charlie.

Trisha and Emily walked away.

"We need to win that money," he said, flustered.

"We definitely do," Julia said. She looked down at the floor. "Maybe we should meet to organize the skate-a-thon?"

"Yeah. We should. Definitely," Charlie said.

"Sounds like you've practically got it done," Alexandra said sarcastically.

"Thanks for the encouragement," Julia joked.

"I gotta blow this place," Alexandra said. "See you guys later."

"I'll come with you," Rebecca said.

"I should probably just do my homework," Zachary said, shooting a glance at the other guys. "I'll catch you dudes later."

"Me too," Matt said.

"I keep hearing about this strange thing called homework," Scott said to Nick. "Is that a kind of sandwich? I'm starving."

"It's more like something you do between meals," Nick said.

"Okay, we could go to the library and plan things out," Charlie said to Julia. "We can also get movie night going."

His friends were grinning from ear to ear.

"See you guys," he said, and he and Julia walked towards the staircase to the library, Charlie feeling his friends' eyes on him the whole way.

"You don't really have to play if you're too busy," she said.

"I said I'd play," he said.

"But you don't have to. I don't want you to think I'm pressuring you."

"I don't. It'll be fun — and if we win, that's a mess of money."

He hoped she didn't notice the lack of conviction in his voice. He couldn't understand exactly why, but for some reason playing with the girls made him uneasy.

Julia stopped at the first step. "I kind of had another idea too . . . sort of didn't want to talk about it in front of everyone. I was talking to Dalton earlier and he wondered if Bee-Bees would care that we want to use the prize money from the tournament for the roof. It's supposed to go for athletic programming."

"Good question. We should probably find out before the practice."

She pulled him back from the stairs. "I gave them a call already, and I'm supposed to meet someone at the mall in an hour, and I thought, well, I could use the company . . . and we could talk about the skate-a-thon and movie night at the same time." She paused. "That is, if you're not doing anything . . ."

Charlie tried his best to keep his voice casual. "Sure, I guess. I don't have anything going on, and we can figure stuff out: movie night, and the skate-a-thon . . . and whatever."

"Awesome. Thanks."

"Yeah. Sure. No problem."

They looked at each other.

"We should probably just get going then," she said.

Both slightly red in the face, they headed out of the school.

* * *

"Hey, they have the new BBs in," Julia said, pointing at the black yoga pants displayed in the store window. She laughed when she saw his expression. "You should pick up a pair."

"I assume that's your zany sense of humour," Charlie said.

"Okay. We'll start you off with a sweatshirt."

They went to the front counter.

"Is Joanne Bettencourt in?" Julia asked the girl behind the counter.

"She's in the back," she said. "I'll buzz her."

They did not have to wait long. "Are you the young lady that called me about the hockey tournament?"

"Yes, Ms Bettencourt."

She laughed. "Call me Jo-Jo, please. Everyone does. Now, you said your school might close?"

"We hope not. But the roof needs to be repaired, and if we can't raise enough money, we will all have to go to different schools in November. So we thought entering your tournament would be a good idea, because it will be fun, but also because of the prize money," Julia said.

Jo-Jo nodded vigorously the entire time.

"We were wondering if Bee-Bees Boutique would allow us to use the money for our save-the-roof fund — assuming we win, of course."

"I'll need to call head office," Jo-Jo said. "We've been doing these tournaments to promote sports and healthy living. This is a bit different. I'll get back to you. I'd like to help."

"We wouldn't ask if it wasn't so important," Julia said.

Jo-Jo laughed. "You're such a serious girl," she said. "I like you, and I like that you're taking the initiative." She pointed at Charlie. "And who's your boyfriend?"

Charlie could only imagine how deeply he was blushing. Julia did not seem that bothered.

"This is Charlie. He's helping with the fundraising, and he'll be on the team too."

Jo-Jo took a step back and looked them both over. "Wait here a second." She went to the back of the store.

Moments later, she came back holding some clothes. "Julia, you simply must have a pair of the new BBs. I got you ones with the red waistband. I thought they'd suit you."

Julia's eyes got big. "Thanks, Jo-Jo. That's so awesome of you."

Jo-Jo handed Charlie a blue sweatshirt. "We actually sell men's clothing too. We've come out with a whole new boys and men's line. Everyone thinks we only sell to girls."

"Try it," Julia said to him.

Charlie slipped it on.

"Check it out in the mirror," Jo-Jo said. "It looks great."

He had to admit it was a nice-looking sweatshirt. "Thanks. I . . . needed a new sweatshirt. Thanks."

"Making people look good is what we do," Jo-Jo said. "You two take care. I'll call you when I hear back about the tournament — and blue is a great colour on you, Charlie. We also have some awesome pants and T-shirts. Come back any time."

They walked out.

"I guess I should go this way," he said, pointing to the left. "I'm supposed to meet my mom at her café for dinner."

"So you'll ask Pudge if he wants to come with us on Thursday after school to check out ice times for the skate-a-thon?" Julia said.

"I'll talk to him tonight."

"So I'll see you later. Thanks for coming with me. It made it easier."

"You did all the talking. You didn't need me."

"I enjoyed the company," Julia said.

His embarrassment level rose. "Me too. Hopefully, they'll let us use the money for the roof."

"We have to win first."

He grinned. "That's the easy part."

She laughed. "See you, Charlie." She waved and left.

He went the other way, trying to imagine what his friends would say if they saw him in a Bee-Bees sweatshirt.

12

HEADS UP

The whistle blew as the boys filed onto the ice. The girls were kneeling at centre, crowded around Ms Cummings.

Julia had told him Cummings was a great coach. Charlie had never been coached by a woman, and he was interested in hearing what she had to say.

"Why isn't Hilton coaching?" Scott said, as they skated over.

"I bet he can't be bothered," Nick said.

"Neither can I," Scott said, "but I'm still here."

"Hurry up," Cummings called out. "You're a bit late, boys."

Charlie knelt down.

"The great ones have arrived," Alexandra said.

Next to her Trisha and Emily snickered.

"We didn't hear the Zamboni," Charlie said.

"I was just welcoming everyone to the team," Cummings continued. "I hope we all have fun and enjoy the tournament. I know we have some excellent players. Many of you played on the Champions Cup teams, right?"

Most of the players nodded.

"Let's try to be punctual for practice, please. A friend of mine was kind enough to donate some ice to help our fundraising efforts, and out of respect for that we should try not to waste any time. Now, why don't we line up at the far end and start with a few skating drills."

As if an invisible hand divided them, the girls all went to the right of the net and the boys to the left.

"We don't need to be quite so gender-sensitive," Cummings said. She began pointing at them and counting, one, two, one, two, all the way down the line. "Okay. The ones go first. Skate to the red line, back to the blue, all the way to the far end, and then back here."

She blew her whistle, and the ones took off. It was a fast group: Nick, Zachary and Matt, along with Julia, Rebecca and Emily. It was close, but Charlie thought Nick was first and —

Cummings blew her whistle.

Charlie wasn't paying attention, and most of the twos got a jump on him. He put his head down and took a few short, choppy steps, then lengthened his stride and caught up to the slower girls. Pudge and Scott were still ahead, but he didn't worry about that. Both were great players, but they were not fast skaters and he knew he'd get them on the way back. Alexandra and Trisha posed more of a challenge. They were a good four metres ahead. If he came in behind them, Alexandra would never let him live it down; and Trisha worried him too.

Charlie timed his sliding stop perfectly, tapped the back boards with his stick, and powered back to the blue line. At the top of the circle he looked up. Alexandra was two metres away, and Trisha was well past the blue line. That was impossible. She must have cheated on the turn. He put his head down and lengthened his stride. He was gaining on Alexandra, but it was over for Trisha. She was already coasting to the goal line. At the blue line he was almost even with Alexandra. He expected her to slow down — only she did the opposite and got to the goal line ahead of him.

Charlie was in shock. He couldn't remember the last time he'd lost a race. Breathing heavily and dreading what was coming, he leaned his stick across his knees and turned away from Alexandra.

There was no avoiding it, though. "You need to bend those knees a bit, Joyce. You skate like a ninety-year-old granny," Alexandra chortled.

"You should start with the cheese cutter skates," Trisha said. "They give you more balance."

Even his friends laughed. He knew he'd sound like a doofus if he got mad — even though he was. "I didn't know it was a race," he said, in between breaths.

Thankfully, the whistle blew, and the first group took off again. This time Charlie paid attention, and when it was his turn he sprang off the line like a tightly wound coil. The three of them were in a dead heat at the red line. All three hit the boards with their sticks together, and when he crossed the goal line, Charlie honestly did not know who had won. Stick resting across the tops of his shin pads again, he tried not to look too tired, but he was seriously winded. Those girls could flat out skate!

"Give it up, Joyce, before they kill you," Scott said, and his friends broke up.

They did a few different skating drills, but none of the racing variety: gliding on one foot, dropping to the knees and up, rounding the faceoff circles. Soon Charlie had worked up a good sweat. Cummings sure knew her stuff.

The whistle went.

"Bring it in," Cummings said, waving her stick over her head.

Charlie followed everyone over.

"That was great," she enthused. "Lots of energy and I see we'll have a fast team. Obviously we have to put Charlie, Trisha and Alexandra on a line together."

The kids all whistled and oooh'd and ahh'd, much to Charlie's embarrassment.

Alexandra thought it was hysterical. "I need Julia as my centre," she said, still laughing. "No old men on my line."

Cummings laughed. "It was just a joke. We'll worry about lines later. Now I want to split into defence and forwards. We'll do some one-on-ones and then two-on-twos. We only have the ice for forty minutes: they're doing some maintenance. We were lucky to get this time. The upshot is, we won't be able to scrimmage."

Most of the kids booed.

"Give me all the defencemen at this blue line and the rest of you in the left corner at the far end. We only have Cassie in net, so we'll only go one way. The forward passes to me at the blue line, and then takes a return pass in on the defenceman. Curl back to your lines after the shot. Remember, boys; there's no contact."

She blew her whistle. "Let's do this, people."

Charlie drifted slowly to the far end with the other forwards. Alexandra was already lined up.

"Behind me, Joyce," she said. "Watch how it's done."

What did she have against him, anyway?

On the whistle she snapped a pass to Cummings, took the return without breaking stride, and rocketed into the neutral zone. Michelle was on defence, and Alexandra took the puck outside. With one hand on the stick she brought it back across, stopped it halfway, and bounced back outside. Michelle stumbled slightly and that was all the fleet-footed Alexandra needed to break in alone. She glided on one foot, faked a wrist shot, and deked to the stick side. Cassie proved her worth, and got her right pad down to take away the bottom of the net. Alexandra tried to raise it, but Cassie used her blocker to knock the puck to the corner.

Charlie was still impressed by the move. He reached to the boards and snagged a puck, kicking it between his feet as he shuffled forward waiting for his turn.

"Have you played much hockey before?"

He turned around. Trisha smiled back. She had to be joking. Might as well play along.

"This is my first time," he said. "What about you?"

"My first time also," she said. "Could you explain the rules to me?"

"I'm not sure I know them. I think the game has to do with this little round thingy."

"It's called a pluck," she said.

"Not sure that's right."

"It is. I saw it on the Internet."

"Then it has to be true."

"Hey. You should be careful. Your skate lace is undone."

He looked down. They were done up. "Very funn—"

Trisha passed to Cummings and took the return pass without slowing down. The girl was crazed. She had done that just to butt in front of him.

"I guess she got you," Julia said dryly. She was behind him.

He shuffled his feet a few times and took a deep breath. He couldn't think of anything to say. At least Trisha had to go against Scott, who never got beat one-on-one, and had the deadliest poke check in the league. Trisha went directly at him, holding the puck in front of her. That was child's play for Scott, and a metre inside the red line he lunged at the puck. A right-handed shot, Trisha pulled it back with the tip of her stick, brought it even to Scott's right shoulder, and then back to his forehand side. One hand on the stick, she cut hard around him at the blue line.

The only way he could stop her was to haul her down. For a second, Charlie thought he would; and no doubt he would have in a game. But he let her go, and Trisha roared in on Cassie. Unlike Alexandra, she did not bother being fancy. She teed it up and slapped it from the slot. The puck was in the net before Cassie could react. Trisha banged her stick on the ice a few times and then held it over her head. Scott lowered his head and skated to the boards. Charlie could only imagine what Nick was saying to him now.

"You're up, Charlie," Julia said.

Cummings banged her stick on the ice. "Charlie, let's keep the drill active," she called out.

Cummings took his pass and slid it back along the blue line. Charlie curled slightly to take it on his forehand, and only then did he look up. Emily was three metres away, which caught him by surprise. That was aggressive defensive play. She carved deeply on her left leg and then pushed back on her right to gain momentum, stick forward, her left hand in the air — the classic defensive posture. Charlie felt a bit silly — as if it was so serious.

"Stuff him, Em," he heard from behind. It sounded like Trisha.

He didn't want to show Emily up, but Trisha's tone was too much. He decided to put a move on Emily, but then let her get back into the play so as not to rub her nose in it. As he crossed the red line, he figured it was time. Emily was in a good position, though. He needed to confuse her. Charlie increased his pace, faked a double move to his left, did a half-stutter and brought the puck right, then backhanded a soft chip past Emily's left leg.

She remained facing him. It was all he could do not to laugh out loud. He had her. Charlie crossed over to his left and carved around her, reaching for the puck spinning two metres behind her. He pushed off once with his outside foot.

The next second he was flat on his back. Emily had smoked him with a bodycheck.

Trisha began whooping it up. "Woo hoo! Emily The Destroyer!" she yelled, and repeated that a few times.

Most of the girls were laughing and banging their sticks on the ice.

Charlie fought to control his temper. He couldn't believe she had plowed him.

"Keep your head up, young man," Emily said.

"Those house league moves don't play with me."

"House league!" he sputtered, as he got to his knees. "There's no hitting!"

"Sorry. Forgot. I'll be nicer next time." She curled her arms into a bodybuilder pose, and the rest of the defence cracked up.

"That's enough of that, Emily," Cummings said. "There's absolutely no body contact allowed. You know that's a penalty."

Charlie stood up. Emily looked at him and winked. She was grinning from ear to ear. For an insane moment he almost gave her a two-handed shove. But she was a girl, and he obviously couldn't do that.

He heard a few girls still laughing. Charlie had never felt so humiliated. Trashed by a girl practically half his size. Pathetic. The next forward was coming, so Charlie peeled off to the side.

Charlie glided on one foot along the boards. He was in absolutely no hurry to get back in line. He dreaded the dissing.

"I would pay to see that again," Trisha said, as he got near. "That was awesomeness in action."

Charlie ignored her.

"Don't mess with my girl Emily," Trisha continued. "She'll take ya out."

He still did not respond.

"I'll tell her no more hitting," Trisha said. "That was *waaay* too rough."

"Do you actually ever shut up?" he snapped. The sound of her voice was too irritating to take.

Trisha's face coloured. "I'm just joking . . . no big deal," she said softly.

"Tell her to try that again — I dare her," he said.

Alexandra turned around. "Maybe this co-ed thing is a bit too much for you, Charles," she said. "And if you think Emily's tough, wait till Michelle pummels you. She's a monster."

He caught Pudge's eye. Pudge turned away and looked into the stands. Zachary was behind him, and he wouldn't look at Charlie either. They were obviously embarrassed for him.

The unfairness of the situation hurt ten times more than Emily's bodycheck. Obviously, he had not expected a hit; he was not going full out — it was like he had his eyes closed; and since Emily was a girl there was nothing he could do about it.

Alexandra passed a puck to Cummings and took off.

Charlie looked over at the door. It was five metres away. He could leave; it would be that easy. Now, even if he beat Emily a hundred times on a one-on-one, the guys would still remember the bodycheck, and the girls would never let him forget it either.

Then it hit him, full force. This would get around school. Wait until Jake heard about it. His rep was done. He would forever be the guy who got checked by a girl.

"It's your turn," Julia said.

He spun around angrily. Julia's smile faded.

"Charlie, please keep the line moving," Cummings said.

He looked around for a puck.

"Here, take mine," Julia said.

"Keep it," he said. He raced over to the net and dug a puck out instead. In one motion he whirled around and fired a wicked pass to Cummings. It was too far to her right, and it slid the length of the ice.

"Forget it," he said to Julia. "You go."

Charlie skated to the back of the line, behind Matt. His friend looked quickly at him out of the corner of his eye, but he did not say anything.

Charlie was grateful for that.

He should have trusted his gut — this hockey tournament was a big mistake.

13

IN THE RED

Squish. Squish. Squish.

Some committee members tried to hide their giggles as he walked across the cafeteria floor. His shoes were soaking wet from the rain, and lately they'd started squeaking. Scott and Nick had taken to calling him Squeakers — definitely not a nickname he wanted to catch on.

It was hard to keep a low profile, though. Apart from the Fundraising Committee members, he and Julia were the only ones here for the pancake breakfast.

"Could I get some help, please?"

A.J. sounded totally stressed. Milk, juice, tea, coffee, hot chocolate, fruit, butter and syrup were organized at one end of a table. A.J. had two electric skillets at the other end, and she was busily making the pancakes. She had decorated the table nicely, with a tablecloth and the school crest in the middle, cut out of coloured paper. Everything looked great.

Charlie looked at the clock: 8:25. No wonder A.J. was nervous. This was her idea. Where was everyone? He had agonized over coming, on the one hand wanting to support the school, and on the other preferring to hide at home after the disastrous hockey practice. He'd already undergone a bit of good-natured ribbing from his buds, which actually made him feel better. He knew they didn't think any less of him because of it. It was other kids he was worried about. At the very least, Trisha and Emily would be blabbing about it.

He felt his stomach growl. Charlie approached A.J. She looked past him.

"Hi, Mr. Hilton and Ms Cummings," she said loudly. "How about a special save-the-roof pancake breakfast to help the school's fundraising? Comes with fruit and your choice of beverage."

The teachers walked over.

"It might not be the best for my waistline, but it's for a good cause, so why not?" Hilton said.

"Count me in too," Cummings said, patting her stomach.

A.J. reached for two plates and began loading them up. Charlie stepped to the side to be polite.

"So how are the pancakes, Charlie?" Hilton said.

"I haven't had one yet," he said. "I'm . . . waiting."

"I was telling Mr. Hilton about the co-ed team," Cummings said. "It's a terrific collection of kids. I was amazed at the skill level. This really is a remarkable school for hockey."

"What's the senior team like?" Charlie said.

Cummings sighed. "There was a less than enthusiastic response from the older students. We only have a junior team."

"But Bee-Bees Boutique is giving twenty five thousand each for the junior and senior teams," Julia said. "They agreed to let us transfer the money from our athletic department to the roof fund. It's a chance to win fifty thousand dollars!"

"What's this about transferring money?" Hilton asked.

"Charlie and I went to one of their stores and spoke to the manager. She texted me last night, giving us the okay," she said.

Hilton whistled softly. "That was good initiative on your part."

"We still have to win," Charlie said.

"Here are your breakfasts," A.J. announced, handing the plates to the teachers.

Cummings laughed. "You're certainly trying to fatten us up," she said.

"I gave you each an extra pancake," she whispered.

Hilton gazed at the pile of food. "I was being such a good boy lately," he said. A.J. reached over and poured more syrup on top.

"That's enough, A.J." Hilton laughed. "Thanks."

"I was thinking that you, Alexandra and Trisha would in fact make a formidable forward line," Cummings said to Charlie.

Charlie felt his stomach turn.

"I usually play with Zachary and Pudge," Charlie said.

"We can only have two boys on the ice at any time," Cummings said. "Every defence pair has a boy and a girl, so we can't have two boys on one forward line. You'll be great together. You're all such fast skaters, and Mr. Hilton was filling me in on your hockey talents."

All he could manage was a half-hearted smile and a quiet, "Thanks."

"I think I'll need to finish this in the staff lounge. I have some work to clear up," Hilton said. "It looks great, A.J. You and the committee have done a great job."

"We could do with actually selling some pancakes," Melissa grumbled.

"It's not my fault," A.J. snapped. "Stupid rain, and the stupid kids are too lazy to wake up two minutes early."

"I didn't say it was your fault," Melissa said. "But so far we've sold eleven breakfasts, eight to committee members, one to Julia, and one each to Mr. Hilton and Ms Cummings."

"I'll try to round up some more teachers," Hilton said.

"I think I'd better run too," Cummings said. "This is lovely. Thanks. Take care, kids."

She and Hilton left.

A.J. seemed on the verge of tears. She stomped off and sat on the stairs leading up to the stage. Melissa shook her head and made her way to the other end of the table. The other committee members were off to the side talking. Charlie stared wistfully at the pancakes.

Julia tipped her head in A.J.'s direction. "Drama on the committee," she whispered.

"Were the pancakes good?" he asked.

She shook her head. "Awful," she whispered.

His stomach growled again. "Awful sounds pretty good to me," he whispered back.

She laughed. "Are we still good to go to the rink after school to ask about ice time for the skate-a-thon?"

He had forgotten about that. "I guess. Sure. What time?"

"How about right after school?"

"Cool. It shouldn't take long. I think Pudge can come too."

"Cool."

He nodded a few times. She nodded back.

The warning bell sounded. "I'm not going to be fed, am I?" Charlie said.

"It appears not."

"I'm not much of a breakfast guy, anyway. See ya after school. We can just meet in front?"

"Sure. No problem."

"Bye." He took a last longing look at the pancakes and turned to leave.

Julia reached out and touched his elbow. "Charlie, I know it's not a big deal, and it's probably dumb to even mention it, but I thought that maybe you were a little . . . embarrassed when Emily bodychecked you."

Charlie looked down at the floor. She had to bring that up? "It's no big deal — whatever. I admit I'm not stoked about it getting around, but there's about a zero percent chance of that not happening."

"People say all sorts of stuff. You can't listen to them."

"That's easy to say when they aren't saying it about you. I bet Emily was bragging about it in the dressing room."

"Not really. I saw Trisha talking to her, and Emily barely said anything after that. There were a few comments, but most of the girls were actually not that impressed. You obviously weren't expecting it." She paused. "Everyone knows you're a great player."

Her kind words took him by surprise, and he felt at a loss for what to say. "I admit I might have been a teensy-weensy bit embarrassed by getting stomped on by a girl, but I'm over it."

She screwed up her eyes. "You saying a girl can't stomp?"

He grinned. "I'm living proof they can."

She laughed. Every once in a while he noticed that Julia was kind of cute — especially when she laughed.

"Get lost before A.J. puts you to work cleaning up," Julia said.

"After school then."

"Bye."

Dalton came over just as Charlie was starting to leave. "I wanted to ask if you had made any progress on the skate-a-thon," he said, and then nodded at Melissa. "The general is demanding a report."

"We're going to the rink today to arrange the ice time," Charlie said.

"Outstanding," Dalton said.

The conversation lagged for a moment.

"I think A.J. is pretty upset," Julia said.

"It was not an impressive turnout," Dalton said.

"So much for our first fundraiser. We ended up losing money," Charlie said.

"The rain didn't help," Dalton said.

"No one coming didn't help either," Charlie said.

"The ball hockey tournament got a positive response," Dalton said. "I've got thirty-two teams entered at fifty dollars each."

Julia did a quick calculation. "That's sixteen hundred," she exclaimed. "Dalton, that's awesome."

He blushed and bowed his head. "Just doing my duty," he said.

"We better get handing out pledge sheets for the skate-a-thon," Charlie said.

"Might I suggest leaving some in the teachers' boxes in the office? They can hand them out in homeroom, and then we can have an announcement in the morning to publicize it."

"I'll design a poster and we can hang them up around school," Julia said.

"Awesome. If we can just get one hundred kids to raise one hundred dollars each . . ." Charlie said.

"It would be better if they each raised fifteen hundred dollars, and we'd be done with it," Julia joked.

"I don't actually skate," Dalton said, "but I imagine I can get some pledges from various family members."

"That would be great," Charlie said.

"I really would appreciate some help here, please," A.J. said. She was glaring at them and her eyes were a little red.

"This is a Fundraising Committee event," Dalton said to them. "I'll do it."

"No problem," Charlie said.

He began to pick up the paper plates, and soon they had put almost everything away.

"We should keep all this," Dalton said to A.J., "so we can do it again. We didn't hang many posters, and the weather being what it is probably scared people off."

"Do you really think so?" A.J. said.

"Absolutely," Dalton said. "We've been busy dealing with other matters; and sure, the rain . . ."

"That's true," A.J. said. "Who wants to get to school early in a storm."

"We only need some good weather," Dalton said reassuringly.

The bell rang.

Principal Holmes came scurrying over. "Hurry up, boys and girls. School's starting and we must get the cafeteria tables back in place."

"Would you like a quick breakfast?" A.J. offered. "Only three dollars."

"Oh no, thank you," he said. "I only eat bran cereal and fruit in the morning."

A.J.'s face fell.

"But . . . well, of course a pancake or two wouldn't hurt," he said.

A.J. piled some pancakes onto his plate, and then threw the rest in the garbage. Charlie had to fight off the urge to reach in and pull one out.

Principal Holmes looked at his watch. "I have to get back to the office for announcements. I really don't have enough time in the day. I'm running around from morning till night."

As they finished cleaning up, Charlie began to plan the skate-a-thon in his head. He figured they should hand out the pledge sheets at the front of the school in the morning and after school for a few days to make sure everyone knew about it, even the kids who were late for school and missed the announcements. A poster would be good too. He hoped they could book a good time at the Ice Palace. The hockey season had started and it might be tough. But he knew the rink manager from last season, so he was not too worried. Gus loved them. He had even given the Rebels free ice for practice last year. Charlie tightened the lid on the orange juice and put it in a box.

"Could you guys carry this to the front of the

school?" A.J. said. "My mom's probably waiting for me outside to take it home."

"Sure," they all chorused. Charlie grabbed a box and with the others hauled it out to the curb. He looked at all the kids filing past to get into the school. Would it have been too much to expect a few of them to come for breakfast?

What would they think of a skate-a-thon?

14

A LONG SHOT

A distant rumbling in the clouds threatened another downpour. The ground was still wet from the morning, but for now the rain held off. The sinking feeling in Charlie's stomach grew with each step. If they didn't get a good time, the skate-a-thon might not work at all.

"Gus will come through," Charlie said, mostly to convince himself.

"I got the names of a few more rinks if we need them," Pudge said, waving a paper in the air.

"We need the Ice Palace," Julia said. "Otherwise people can't walk to the rink."

Charlie didn't even want to go there. "Maybe we won't get the best day or we'll have to cut down on the hours. But it'll be okay — Gus loves us."

They went in and headed straight over to Gus's office. It was a legendary spot in Terrence Falls, filled with classic hockey memorabilia: signed photos of famous players, sticks from the fifties and sixties, old skates hanging from wall hooks, equipment scattered about — it was like visiting the Hockey Hall of Fame in miniature.

"It's the Rebels," Gus declared in his gravelly voice.

"But who's your lady friend?"

"This is Julia," Charlie said. The warm greeting boosted his confidence. "Hi Gus," he said. "We wanted to talk to you about some ice time."

"You guys sure are serious about defending the championship, aren't you?" Gus said.

"It's not for the Rebels . . ." Charlie said.

"A bit of shinny? I love you guys — never too much hockey. I got some time early Sunday morning."

"It's for a fundraiser," Julia interjected, "for Terrence Falls High. We're raising money to fix the roof. If we don't hit our target, the school will close and we'll all have to go to other schools."

"So we had this idea for a skate-a-thon," Charlie added. "We wanted to rent the ice for a day. We're collecting pledges and a bunch of kids will come and skate."

Gus scrunched his nose. "You need a whole day?"

"Well . . . not necessarily the entire day," Julia said. "But . . . you know . . . a chunk of time."

Gus didn't look happy. "I'd love to help you, of course. I'd do anything I could. But other than a couple of hours here and there, like that Sunday slot, we're totally booked. You know how busy this place gets after the summer. If you'd talked to me back in April or May, we could've swung it."

"We didn't know about it then," Charlie said.

Gus seemed genuinely upset. "You could try the Flemington Arena, only I doubt you'll have much luck there. I know for a fact Cliffcrest is booked. Ice time is as scarce as hens' teeth."

Charlie didn't exactly know if hens had teeth, but he guessed they didn't.

"There's Ted Beeve over at St. Briar and Central. I know the manager there. Let me give him a call."

Gus picked up the phone and dialled. After a quick conversation he hung up and shook his head. "Sorry, kids. All the rinks in town are booked."

Charlie made himself sound cheerful. He didn't want Gus to feel bad. "No problem. It was just an idea. We can do something else."

"Good luck," Gus said, "and if I can help you some other way let me know." The phone rang. "I've gotta take this," he said and waved. They waved back and left.

Outside the office Pudge pulled out his list of rinks.

"At least we won't waste any more time running around to those rinks. According to my list we have one last chance — Humberside," Pudge said.

"Which is where?" Julia said.

"About an hour away. I think it's near that Kennedy West High School you're going to. Let me call my dad and see if he can give us a lift. Otherwise, it's the bus."

"Maybe this skate-a-thon idea isn't going to work," Charlie grumbled.

"Any other suggestions?" Pudge said.

"We could win the lottery?" Charlie said.

No one laughed.

Pudge punched the numbers on his cell phone.

* * *

Pudge's dad was busy, and after two tortuous hours — the result of going the wrong way at first — the three weary friends finally trudged up the walkway and into Humberside Arena.

"Does anyone think this is even worth it?" Charlie asked for about the tenth time.

Pudge shrugged.

"How are we gonna get anyone out here?" Charlie fretted.

"We could rent a bus," Julia said.

"Let's get the ice first. Then we'll worry about that," Pudge said.

Charlie didn't see an office. "I'll ask that guy in the pro shop," he said. Charlie pushed the door open. "Excuse me?"

The guy was sharpening a pair of skates and didn't answer.

"Excuse me," Charlie said, a bit louder.

Again, nothing. The machine shut off, just as Charlie yelled, "Excuse me!"

"I'm not deaf, dude," the guy said. "What d'ya want?"

"Um . . . Is the rink manager around?"

"Look in the office." He grabbed another skate, inspected the blade with one eye and turned the sharpener back on.

"Where's the office?" Charlie asked.

There was no answer, and Charlie was not going to yell again.

"He's in the office," he told his friends. "It must be around here somewhere."

Five annoying minutes later, Charlie and Pudge ended up back in front of the pro shop.

"Is this office protected by an invisibility spray?" Charlie said.

Pudge rubbed his chin.

"Yo, boys."

Julia waved them over. She pointed up a flight of stairs.

"Are we smart enough to organize a skate-a-thon?" Charlie said, as they neared a door with a large *OFFICE* sign.

Charlie knocked and a loud voice invited them in.

"Hi, sir," Charlie began tentatively. "My friends and I . . . I'm Charlie and this is Pudge and Julia. We're from Terrence Falls, and we're running a fundraiser for our school. We need to rent ice, for a day, or maybe a bit less, for a skate-a-thon."

With furrowed brow, the manager asked, "You're from Terrence Falls? Isn't that a bit far from here? Why not use a rink in town. There's the Ice Palace or Flemington . . ."

"We couldn't get ice there," Julia said. "There were scheduling difficulties."

"They're all booked up, right? And you thought you'd come to little Humberside and get the ice, is that right?"

"We were hoping for something in the next week or so," Charlie said.

The man took a deep breath and typed something into his computer. "Okay. What do we have? A weekend is out, of course, because of the house leagues. Monday has short-track, and then Tuesdays are rented by a school group for three weeks. Wednesday and Thursday . . ." He turned back to them. "I can give you next Friday from eight till three; then we got the figure skating club. Will that work?"

That was a school day. Would Holmes ever agree to let them take a day off? Charlie was tongue-tied.

"That would be great," Julia said.

"I'll need a deposit of two hundred and fifty dollars," the manager continued. "Since you're renting such a large time slot, I can let you have it for a hundred an hour, so with tax it's . . ." He punched the numbers on a calculator. "A total of seven hundred ninety-one bucks. Your school can call me with a credit card, or send a cheque."

"It's a school fundraiser," Charlie said. "Is that the only price?"

"Can't do better. Already gave you a ten percent discount." He held his hand out. "You want it?"

Charlie looked over at Julia and Pudge.

The committee had never said they could spend close to eight hundred dollars.

Julia shook his hand. "Thanks. We'll take it."

"Send me the deposit in two days," the manager said, and he turned back to his computer.

15

PAD BATTLE

Charlie looked in dismay at the brackets for the ball hockey tournament. Thirty-two teams, and they had drawn Jake's in the first round? Sometimes he had to wonder if the dark clouds that seemed to haunt Terrence Falls lately were meant for him. As if that wasn't bad enough, Jake had recruited Trisha and Emily.

A crowd had lined the pad to watch. Jake was bouncing a ball on the blade of his stick. After several bounces he flicked it over to Trisha. She kept the ball up and knocked it to Emily, who one-timed it to Liam. He tried to knee it a few times and the ball squibbed to the side.

"Doofus," Jake scoffed. "We were gonna set a record."

Liam retrieved the ball quickly. "We needed some razzle-dazzle. Trust me."

"We needed you to keep the ball in the air," Thomas said.

Jake and Thomas laughed; and then all three boys stopped as Charlie stepped onto the pad.

"Hey Joyce. I hear you're fighting girls now?" Jake said.

"And getting hammered," Thomas said.

"Guys, come on," Emily said, but they kept up the dissing. Charlie ignored them completely and went over to his friends.

"That was a big surprise," he said to Pudge.

"They've been mouthing off for ten minutes," Pudge said with a scowl.

Zachary pointed to the goalie pads. "Suit up, shut-out king," he said.

Charlie dropped to his knees and began strapping on the pads. He loved to play goal in ball hockey.

"We promise not to shoot that hard, Joyce. I know you cry easy," Jake said. "Maybe you should quit now and go home to mommy."

Charlie felt a chill sweep down his spine.

"He was blubbering on the ice after Emily dropped him," Liam said.

"Like you were there," Charlie snapped.

"Didn't have to be there. Emily filled us in."

"I did not," Emily said.

Trisha whispered in Emily's ear, and Emily shook her head.

"Didn't he bawl his eyes out this summer at that hockey camp too?" Thomas asked Jake.

Jake rolled his eyes. "Don't remind me. It was beyond embarrassing. He was like, 'I don't wanna get in trouble. I don't wanna go home. Boo-hoo,'" he said, in a high-pitched voice.

Charlie kept his eyes on his equipment. He tightened a strap on his left leg.

"Pudge looks like he's gonna start bawling too," Thomas said. Pudge was leaning on the butt-end of his stick with both hands. "We better get him a doughnut, quick."

"Could you guys give it a rest for even five minutes? It's tiring." Julia said, her eyes blazing.

Jake smirked. "Charlie's girlfriend is angry. I'm scared."

"At least you got someone with a bit of toughness to defend you, Joyce," Liam said. "Wise move."

Charlie knew Julia was trying to help, but the more she said the worse it would get . . .

"You guys are such a cliché," Julia said. "You're jealous of Charlie because he's a better player than you'll ever be, and everyone knows it. And he's a better person, and you know that too."

They burst out laughing.

"You're right. We're so sorry. I want to apologize on behalf of my associates. Where can I go to join the Charlie Joyce Fan Club?" Jake said.

Liam pretended to be shocked. "I can't believe you're not already a member. You get a picture, and a pin, and one of those pink Rebels hockey sweaters."

Dalton came running from the school onto the pad.

"Sorry, guys. The committee had an emergency meeting that I couldn't get out of."

Charlie turned his focus back to the goalie equipment. He'd never wanted to win a ball hockey game more.

"Dalton, good ol' buddy," Jake said. "I feel the need to score. Drop the puck and get out of the way."

"Games will start with a regulation faceoff," Dalton said. "If everyone is ready, we can begin. I'd just like to take a moment to explain the rules."

The two teams gathered at their respective ends.

"The first to get two goals wins," he said. "If the ball hits a player or their stick and bounces out of bounds, the other team gets possession. I will call penalties for tripping and hooking." Dalton laughed and added, "And of course, no bodychecking or rough stuff."

Everyone else stayed silent.

"Can I have the two centres, and Emily, may I have the ball?" Dalton requested cheerfully.

Emily passed a ball to Trisha, who stickhandled a few times, and rolled it to Dalton. Her eyes met Charlie's. She seemed troubled.

Charlie's team huddled around their net. Scott and Nick jumped up from the hill where they were watching with Alex and Rebecca and joined them.

"Obviously, the easiest thing would have been for me to be on your team so I could control the ball the entire game and score at will," Scott said, "but unfortunately," and he patted Nick on the back, "Nick here is too scared to play without me. He's also scared of turning his bedroom light off at night — but maybe that was supposed to be a secret."

"I'm way better since I got my teddy," Nick said.

"Bottom line is you have to beat these guys," Scott said. "It's unbelievably beyond important. I hate them — and not in a good way. Victory. Triumph. Please. *Win*."

"No pressure, of course," Nick said. "But we do really, really, really need you to win."

"Thanks for the pep talk," Charlie said.

"It's what we do," Scott said, and they trotted back to the hill.

"Go, Jules!" Alexandra and Rebecca called out.

Julia looked totally intense. So much for a friendly game, he thought. It felt like the playoffs.

Zachary and Jake leaned in for the faceoff. Dalton blew his whistle, held the ball over their sticks, and let it drop. Zachary was a winger, and Jake a natural centre, so Charlie was not surprised when the ball darted back to Liam on the right side. Zachary stuck with Jake; and Julia pushed forward to pressure. Pudge and Michelle were both hanging back, which made sense since the pad was not very big.

Liam grinned and took a step forward. When Julia got close, he pulled the ball to his forehand, and then tried to slip it between her feet. But he didn't count on her being so quick. She dragged her left foot behind her to deflect the ball to her right, then she spun and snagged it close to the "boards." Michelle moved up, and Julia passed it back. Zachary cut into the middle and Michelle put it on his stick. He continued diagonally through their zone and cut towards their net.

Liam was out of position, and Emily came racing across. Zachary hesitated, and then snapped a shot. Charlie could barely believe it when Emily dropped to block the shot. It hit her in the shoulder. From her knees, she shovelled the ball back to her goalie, and he passed it to Jake, who had set up to her left. Those balls hurt, and Charlie had to admire Emily — she had guts, that was for sure.

Jake took the ball up the side, with Zachary watching him warily. Trisha came to centre, and Charlie readied for her to get the pass and cut up the middle. Jake kept it himself, however, and ran past her. Pudge stepped up, and Jake reared back and let it fly. Charlie caught it easily. He was grateful for Jake's selfish play. He hadn't had a chance to warm up, and it was good to get the feel for the ball.

He threw the ball to Michelle, who had run back. She rifled it to Julia on the right side. Zachary ran across again and she passed it, then ran diagonally towards him. He angled his stick and the ball went back to her. Emily and Liam had over-committed to Zachary, giving Julia a clear shot at the net. She raised her stick for a slapper.

Pudge had joined the attack and gotten behind both defenders, who were preoccupied, apparently, with Zachary. Julia shot, but it turned out to be a pass to Pudge. He redirected the puck over the outstretched left pad of the goalie.

Goal!

Charlie banged his stick on the ground and pumped his glove in the air at his bud. That was huge. How sweet would it be to smoke Jake 2–zip?

They lined up again. This time Julia took the draw. She tied up Jake's stick and tried to kick the ball back. Jake pushed her, forcing Julia to stagger back a few steps. She tripped and fell.

Jake calmly passed the puck to Liam.

"No contact, ref," Alexandra yelled. Then she added, "Real tough, Wilkenson."

Jake blew a kiss her way and laughed. Charlie saw Julia spring to her feet.

She charged and hit Jake with her shoulder right in the chest. He was caught totally by surprise — they all were — and he went down hard.

Julia glared at him. "Now you and Charlie have something in common," she said.

Jake looked up at her. "You've lost it, girl." He shook his head and slowly got to her knees. "Is she for real?" he said to Dalton.

Liam and Emily came running. Zachary was there first, though, and that made Liam stop. Pudge stood next to Julia, and Charlie took off his mask and rushed over.

Dalton blew his whistle. He looked bewildered. "Julia. That would be a penalty in real hockey; in fact, I think it's a game misconduct."

Thomas took a step towards Julia. "That was lame, Chow. You hit him because you know he won't hit you back."

"What about you?" Julia said.

Thomas rolled his eyes. "I'll say this. You're tougher than your boyfriend."

His two friends laughed.

Dalton rubbed his forehead with his hand. "Julia, I'm sorry, but I have to give you a penalty . . . and probably . . . I'm sorry, but you really can't play this game. That was an intentional hit."

Julia did not answer. She threw her stick on the ground and went to sit next to Alexandra and Rebecca.

"Joyce, I admit your girl packs a mean punch," Jake said, rubbing his chest. "I think I'm going to have a bad ouchy here." He showed his chest to Liam. "Not sure how hard I can go. This might even turn out to be a boo-boo."

"Okay, everyone," Dalton said. "We need to cool down a bit. If this game is going to get out of hand, we might have to forfeit you both. We're just trying to have fun and raise money for the school."

"We didn't do anything," Jake said. "Chow turned psycho. Give her the lecture."

"Your team will have to play one short, unfortunately," he said to Zachary. "It's still first to two goals. We need to hurry. The next game is supposed to start in ten minutes."

Charlie glanced over at Julia. She was staring straight ahead, arms crossed over her knees, talking to Alexandra and Rebecca.

"Hold on a sec, Dalton," Charlie said. "Huddle up, guys."

Zachary, Pudge and Michelle came over.

"I'm not all that stoked to play these guys, and especially not a player short, and I'm also thinking we don't need a fight over ball hockey," Charlie said.

"If you're suggesting we bail on this, I'm okay with that," Pudge said. "The less I see of those guys the better."

"We'll look like we're quitting," Michelle said. "I don't care . . . but are you sure?"

Charlie didn't know her very well. She obviously understood the situation. If they forfeited, Jake would never let him live it down. But all the same . . . He looked over at Julia. She had gotten up and was walking away with her friends.

"Wait up," he called to her.

Charlie waved at Dalton to come over. "Sorry, but, what with Jake and all that, we basically don't feel like getting into a fight. Anyway, we forfeit. Let them advance."

"I could talk to them," Dalton said. He sounded truly concerned. "I'm sure they're here to play, and are not interested in a fight either." He lowered his voice, "And to be honest, Julia was the aggressor . . ."

After Dalton's help with the roof, Charlie wasn't going to give him a hard time; and he obviously didn't know Jake very well. "Forget it. There's not enough time before the next game anyway, and it'll slow down the entire tourney. We're good with it. They can win."

"Okay, Charlie. I'm . . . um . . . tell Julia I'm sorry about having to send her off."

He really did sound upset.

Charlie tapped the ground with his stick. "Between you and me, I think she knew what she was doing. It's not your fault."

"Thanks, Charlie. I'll tell them."

Charlie dropped to his knees and began undoing his straps. Then he heard Liam say in a loud voice, "You don't have to pray to our greatness, Joyce. You can get up."

"You've hit a new low, Joyce," Jake said.

Charlie got the pads off. He stood up. "I've told you before, Jake. I'm not interested in anything you have to say. Irritate someone else."

Jake didn't say anything right away. But as Charlie left, he called out, "Tell your girlfriend she hits like a girl."

He could picture Jake's face exactly — the cocky grin, eyes closed slightly, laughing a bit. It took every bit of his self-control not to turn back around.

Then he heard, "I have to go to Kennedy with that clown."

As they left the pad, Zachary said, "That was pleasant.

Suddenly, Beaverton doesn't seem like such a bad place. I need a holiday."

"With my luck, he'll be in my classes," Charlie said.

They caught up with the girls.

"Sorry," Julia blurted. "I totally lost it."

"Jake can have that effect on people," Pudge said. Charlie and Zachary laughed.

"I shouldn't have done it, though. It just gave them more ammunition." She was upset. "What are Emily and Trisha doing hanging out with those guys? I guess I overestimated them."

"Trisha didn't look too impressed," Charlie said, and immediately got the feeling he hadn't said the right thing. "Anyway, are you . . . um . . . okay?" he said to Julia.

"I'm fine," she said. "We'll see you guys later."

The girls walked away. Scott and Nick ran up behind them.

"We had to exchange cupcake recipes with Jake and Liam," Scott said. "Is everything cool?"

Everything was definitely not cool.

16

TWO STEPS FORWARD . . .

Charlie's shoes squeaked with each step. They were still wet from the soaking they had gotten last night coming home from Pudge's. He was supposed to meet Pudge early this morning and sneak into school to check on the plastic, but he had forgotten to reset his alarm. Breakfast had been a banana and a piece of untoasted bread, followed by a mad sprint. He was also supposed to speak to the committee about getting the deposit for the ice time. They were already late and the rink manager had sent him a stern email.

He knocked twice, waited three seconds, and knocked once more. The door opened, and Pudge poked his head out.

"I knew you'd be late. I'm surprised you actually remembered the secret knock."

Charlie flicked his eyebrows and held out his hand where he had written the knocking pattern with a pen. Pudge pushed open the door.

"I came in with the janitors," Pudge whispered. "I told them I was presenting to the committee and must have got the time wrong."

"That's not a total lie," Charlie whispered back.

"You *are* presenting later."

They began their way up the stairs to the roof. At the first landing, Pudge glared and pointed at Charlie's feet. Charlie held his hands out apologetically. He knew his shoes were ridiculous. Then he got an inspiration. He took the shoes off. Pudge flashed a thumbs-up.

When they reached the door, Charlie put his shoes back on. He opened it with the key Dalton had given him, and they went outside. The sun had just begun to peek out from behind the clouds. The warmth felt good.

"I almost forgot what the sun looked like," Charlie said, holding his face up to it.

"Let's tan after. Matt told me what to do after school yesterday."

"When did he get sick?"

"Not sure. I called last night, and his mom said he was down for the count. Anyway, check the edges and see if any water is running under the plastic, or if there are any holes. We can move the sandbags or adjust the plastic around if we need to."

"I'm on it, Sergeant."

They exchanged salutes.

Charlie inspected the plastic for any signs of leakage. He felt underneath the plastic and, with great satisfaction, found the roof was dry. The plastic sheeting was doing its job.

"All good at my end," Charlie said.

"Other than some bird poop, we're good here too," Pudge said.

Charlie looked around. "They should set up a rooftop patio where we could hang out. The view is killer."

"Not sure it's in the school's best interests to have Scott and Nick up here on a regular basis."

"Wise words, Sergeant."

"Speaking of wise words, we should probably skedaddle before we're spotted."

"Sergeant, Phase I of the mission is complete," Charlie said, once they'd made it back to the main floor. "Phase II is far tougher, however. In fact, it's a suicide mission. Our objective is to convince Melissa and A.J. and the rest of the committee to front us the money for the ice deposit."

"Can't live forever," Pudge said. "Onward."

Charlie opened the door to the cafeteria. The committee members sat at the far end behind two tables pushed together, and two students were presenting to them. A few others were sitting off to the side, waiting for their turn. As they walked down the stairs, Julia rose slightly from her seat and waved. There was one spot next to her. Charlie felt his throat tighten.

"I'll go around to the other side," Pudge said.

"Hi, Julia. How's it going?" Charlie said, trying to sound relaxed.

She looked up at the clock. "Don't tell me you forgot the time."

"We had to check on the leakage situation," Charlie whispered.

"And?" she asked.

"So far so good."

"Not so good here. Melissa and A.J. are on the warpath. I've picked up that the fundraising is not going well. The parents had a meeting here last night, and apparently a bunch of them don't want to waste money on temporary repairs." She paused and smiled. "Anyway, thanks for coming."

"I said I would."

"Next is the skate-a-thon. Who's presenting for that?" Melissa asked.

"I guess we're up," Charlie said.

"I have Julia Chow and Charlie Joyce and . . . Anthony Moretti," A.J. read.

Charlie almost laughed. It was weird to hear Pudge's real name.

"So what's the status?" Melissa asked.

"We have rented the ice," Julia said. "We do need some help from the committee for the deposit, though. We'll get it back once we collect the pledges. The manager is asking for it up front. It's two hundred and fifty dollars."

A.J. had been chewing on her pen. She tossed it to the table and said, "We are trying to raise money, not give it away."

"It's just a deposit," Charlie jumped in. "In a week, we'll have it."

"Maybe," A.J. said.

Melissa was shaking her head. "Every group is asking for money to buy this or that. You guys need to get with the program. We get money, not give it. No wonder this is turning out to be a disaster. People think it's a fundraiser for everyone else . . ."

"How is the skate-a-thon looking?" Dalton interrupted.

"We have about twenty commitments," Julia said, "and I think we can easily triple that once word gets out."

"How much did the ice cost?" Dalton asked. "The Ice Palace is expensive."

"We didn't exactly get the Ice Palace," Charlie said. "It turned out to be booked. We were able to get cheap ice at Humberside Arena."

"Humberside?" A.J. barked. "Never heard of it."

"It's not that far," Charlie said. "We took a bus and it didn't take too long . . . an hour or so . . ." His voiced trailed off.

"We could use a school bus for everyone," Dalton said. "That would make things easier."

"I don't want to waste a bus on this," A.J. said.

"It would be helpful. Humberside is quite a distance," Dalton said.

Charlie loved the idea of a school bus. "How much would a bus cost?" he said.

"The local bus company is contributing free bus trips for the fundraising. But we only get ten, so we have to be careful when we use them," Dalton said.

"We might need two buses," Julia said tentatively.

"This is becoming too much," A.J. said.

"How about we take care of the deposit," Charlie said. "Then could it work?"

Melissa and A.J. exchanged a glance. A.J. shrugged. "I don't love this idea, but if they take responsibility for the cost of the ice, then okay."

"That means you cover the deposit and the full cost of the ice," Melissa said. "If you lose money, we're not responsible."

"We won't lose money," Charlie responded. "I mean, the entire cost is about eight hundred dollars, and if each kid raises only fifty dollars we'll be fine."

"And if you only get ten kids raising ten dollars each, you won't be," A.J. said.

"I think it's a good compromise," Dalton said.

The other members nodded.

"Then we can have the buses?" Charlie said.

"Yes," A.J. said sharply.

"When is the skate-a-thon scheduled?" Melissa said.

"This Friday," Julia said. "Charlie spoke to the vice-principal and she said the participants could have the day off school. We just need parent/guardian permission forms."

"Okay. Arrange with Dalton about the buses," Melissa said.

"We can talk after," Dalton said to them.

"Thank you," Julia said.

A.J. was scanning a list of names. "I think we have the bake sale report next. Are you guys here?"

A few kids stood up.

"I guess we should go," Charlie said to Julia and Pudge.

They left the cafeteria.

"That A.J. is no skate-a-thon lover," Charlie said, when they were outside. "What luck to get those buses, though. I didn't think we had a prayer."

"The buses?" Julia snapped. "What about the money? We need two hundred fifty by tonight or we lose the ice, and then we're on the hook if we don't get enough pledges."

"I can cover the deposit," Charlie said. "I was saving money for a new long board. The roofing supplies took a chunk, but I still have about one hundred and fifty. If you guys can cover the rest . . . ?"

"We'll go halves," Pudge said. "I have money from working at my dad's restaurant."

Julia sighed. "I have some money too," she said. "Alex, Rebecca and I ran a day camp this summer for some neighbourhood kids. We'll go thirds."

"Then it's a deal," Charlie said. "Humberside skate-a-thon, or bust."

"I like the first option," Pudge said.

Charlie laughed, but without enthusiasm. If this was a bust, not only would they look dumb, but it might cost them a lot of money — and it would be goodbye long board. But there probably wasn't anything to worry about, he thought. They had twenty kids already, and a day off school was sure to be a draw. He'd personally already raised seventy-five dollars in pledges, and Pudge told him he was up to a hundred. That was almost the entire deposit already. He was worrying about nothing.

But a nagging feeling kept the butterflies in his stomach going. The fundraising seemed like a mouse running on a wheel — lots of activity, but it wasn't going anywhere.

17

LINEMATES

Charlie bent over and stickhandled rapidly for a few metres, and then from the blue line launched a floating wrist shot at the net, caught easily by Cassie. Charlie looked fretfully at the dressing room door. It remained unopened. Where were they?

Cummings blew her whistle from centre, and Charlie joined the group of girls who had surrounded her; and it did not take the girls long to make it clear they were definitely not impressed with his friends' tardiness.

"Is your crew busy fundraising?" Alexandra asked.

He knew sarcasm when he heard it.

"I'm sure they're doing something wonderful for the school," she continued.

Julia's eyes narrowed.

"I think they got held up . . . or something," Charlie offered.

"They should come on time, don't you think?" Alexandra pressed.

"We may as well get started," Charlie said to Cummings. "They don't need to do the skating drills."

"Of course not," Alexandra said. "But we girls need all the skating practice we can get."

"I didn't mean that," Charlie said.

Cummings interrupted. "I'm not particularly impressed by some of the players' apparent lack of commitment, but it makes sense to run through some warm-up drills. Then I want a scrimmage. I might be able to organize an exhibition game on Saturday against Flemington and it would be nice for linemates to play with each other first."

Charlie's heart did a flip-flop. The Rebels had a practice.

"Do you know what time the game is?" he blurted.

"Their coach said he had ice at nine in the morning." She paused. "Is that a problem?"

"Kind of," he said. "I can't do it — and neither can Pudge, Zachary, Matt, Scott or Nick. We have a practice."

Cummings pursed her lips and seemed about to ask another question, when she raised her whistle and let out a short blast. "Let's line it up on the goal line," she said.

As they skated over, Alexandra asked, "Can't you guys miss one practice?"

Julia and Rebecca glided over, with Emily and Trisha trailing behind.

"We . . . um . . . uh . . ." He had a feeling they were not going to be happy with the answer. "We lost our last game, so . . . Hilton won't be happy." The truth was the boys would never miss a practice to play co-ed hockey. They weren't that stoked to be playing in the first place.

The girls stared at him for a few moments and skated off.

* * *

By the time the boys got there, the skating drills were done and they'd spent a few minutes doing two-on-ones with Cassie in net. Cummings blew her whistle and called them to the bench.

"I told you this ice time was given to us by a friend of mine. The team he coaches agreed to let us practise. I am disappointed that you do not respect their sacrifice enough to get here on time," Cummings said quietly.

The guys lowered their gaze to the ice.

Cummings turned to address the rest of the players. "It also doesn't sound as if we can get it together for an exhibition game."

Pudge shot Charlie a questioning look. Charlie shook his head.

"In the meantime, I want to announce the lines, so you can at least get some practice time together," she continued. "Remember we need three girls on the ice at all times." She held up a whiteboard.

LW	C		RW
Alexandra	Charlie		Trisha
Julia	Zachary		Rebecca
Sandra	Matt		Li
	Michelle	Nick	
	Scott	Sophie	
	Pudge	Emily	
	Cassie		

A smile spread across her face. "We're not at a funeral, people. Don't take things too seriously. This is fun — it's hockey. Let's put the negatives behind us, and come together to win this tournament. With the talent on this team we can do it — and win a lot of money for the school."

Her attempt to lighten the mood fell flat. Charlie tried to help out. "Let's do this, Terrence Falls," he said, slapping the ice with his stick.

All that was missing were the crickets chirping.

Emily broke the silence. "Coach Cummings, why is Trisha on the wing?" she said. "She's a centre."

"We'll try things this way, and then make adjustments if need be," Cummings said.

Emily scowled. "I don't think it's right that the boys get to be centre, as if none of the girls can play. Trisha's the best player on the team, and you put her on right wing. It's not fair."

Trisha looked straight at Cummings. "I've always been centre," she said. "I've never played wing in my life."

"I can play the wing," Charlie said. "It's all the same to me."

The girls were not satisfied.

"Julia is a centre too," Alexandra said, "and Zachary is a winger, so . . ." She shook her head, and leaned on the butt end of her stick.

Zachary tried a joke. "I'm just happy to be allowed to play after being late."

The girls were in no mood to laugh.

"You've seen Trisha play," Emily said. "She scored fifty-two goals last year in Bantam. We need her at centre."

"We need Julia at centre," Alexandra said firmly.

"I'm okay at the wing," Julia said. "It's . . . fine."

Charlie didn't believe her. He was pretty sure she

was not happy either. Then he noticed how Trisha, Emily and Li were standing together on their coach's left, and the rest of the girls were grouped on the other side. He knew those three hung out together. It occurred to him there was more going on here than who played centre.

The smile had long since disappeared from Cumming's face. "I think some of you have forgotten a simple rule in hockey. The coach decides the lineup. I welcome you to approach me after practice to discuss anything, including your positions, but remember I make the decisions. Second, my decision to put the boys at centre is based on the reality that Charlie, Zachary and Matt are bigger and stronger physically. It's not about skill level. I think the other teams will put a boy at centre, and we can't get pushed around there. Trisha and Julia are terrific players, and I expect a lot from them."

She pointed her stick to one end. "Cassie, you set up down there. The other team has to hit the post to score. Charlie and Zachary's lines will start. We'll rotate the lines, with Zachary coming off first. We'll do the same for the defence. Nick and Michelle and Pudge and Emily will start. Let's move it. We've wasted enough time already." She gave her whistle a blast and skated off.

Charlie was impressed. He figured Cummings for a softie because she was always so nice to the students. But she had delivered that in no-nonsense language, and she was right.

Charlie lined up at centre with Zachary. "That wasn't the most relaxing moment," he said.

Zachary laughed. "Next time I make a joke remind me that I'm not funny."

Matt joined them. "Which one of us is big and strong again?"

"It ain't Charlie," Zachary said. "We know Emily can take him." He had that lopsided grin of his firmly in place.

"Who said you're not funny?" Charlie deadpanned, and all three of them had a good chuckle.

"You guys just take this so seriously." Alexandra's eyes were blazing. "Everything's a joke to you, including this team. And obviously the Rebels think it's a joke to play with girls."

Charlie finally ran out of patience with her. "We're here to win the tournament for the school, no different than you. There was no dissing."

"Right. I must have totally misunderstood," Alexandra said.

"Give it a rest, Ms Drama Queen," Trisha said, from her left. "I'm finding it hard to concentrate."

"I'm not sure I asked for your opinion, Superstar," Alexandra shot back.

"That's Ms Superstar to you."

Alexandra opened her mouth to say something but was cut off.

"Alex. We should focus on the hockey," said Rebecca, who was lining up next to her.

Matt wisely skated to the bench. Zachary leaned over for the faceoff and Charlie followed suit. No chance he was getting between Alexandra and Trisha. Pretty funny, he thought, since, as their centre, that's exactly where he was.

"You just can't stop yourself from laughing, can you, Joyce?" Alexandra said.

He could not let that go. "I'm in my happy place — so maybe you could give me a break."

"Charlie is right. You definitely need to hit your Happy button," Trisha said. "You're bringing everybody down."

Cummings came over with a puck, Julia by her side. Alexandra shook her head and pressed down on her stick. Julia lined up next to Trisha.

"Get ready, boys," Cummings said.

Out of the corner of his eye he noticed Trisha had put her stick across Julia's. Julia pulled hers away, but as soon as she put it back down, Trisha did it again. And again.

"Set up, Charlie," Cummings said.

He had been distracted by the stick drama.

Cummings blew her whistle and straightened up. "Can you two girls line up properly, please," she said to Julia and Trisha.

Trisha grinned and put her stick to her side. Julia scowled and held her stick at her waist.

Cummings held the puck over the centres' sticks and let it drop. Zachary was a winger, but he had quick reflexes and Charlie wasn't going to take anything for granted. With a reverse grip, he timed his sweep well, and sent the puck spinning back to Scott. Zachary sidestepped him and pressured the puck. Scott hesitated, and then slid it across to Sophie. She took a few steps across the blue line to her right and banged it off the boards, where Trisha and Julia gave chase.

Trisha got her stick on the puck first and knocked it

forward, but Julia established body position and cut her off. Trisha could do nothing but watch the puck roll to Michelle. Charlie veered towards the puck and saw Trisha give Julia a shove with both hands.

Michelle saw Charlie coming, and she passed quickly to Zachary at the bottom of the centre ice circle. He took it on his backhand and headed up the ice. Alexandra cut him off, but not before he had gained the red line and fired it in deep. Scott was on it first, and he was able to whack it up the boards to Alexandra. Charlie hustled to support her; and was surprised when she passed him the puck.

She might hate him, but it seemed that would not interfere with her play, which made him feel better.

Trisha broke across the neutral zone wide open. Julia was sitting on the ice near the boards. He dished the puck, and Trisha took it without breaking stride. He set off, without much hope of catching her. Nick and Michelle backed up warily. Three metres from the blue line Trisha bounced outside to her left, puck on her backhand, with Nick content to let her run herself into the boards. By this time Charlie had crossed the blue line. Trisha had her head down and she was bombing down the wall; and then without slowing she spun almost backwards and whipped her stick around her right hip on her forehand.

The pass was timed perfectly, and Charlie was in alone. Nick and Michelle had been caught napping. Cassie came out to challenge him, and he was about to try a low shot to her glove side when he caught a glimpse of a green sweater flying past and heading to the right post. That decided things. He cut to his left on his forehand, drawing Cassie with him, and then slid a hard pass back to the right. Alexandra calmly deflected the puck into the open net.

Charlie and Alexandra looked at each other.

"Nice pass," she said hesitantly, and skated to centre.

He felt a glove tap the back of his helmet. "Slick pass, dude," Trisha said to him. "Even she couldn't miss that."

For some reason, it bothered him to hear her diss Alexandra. But Trisha's pass to him had been sweet, and he had to give her props for that.

"Your pass was slick too," he said. "I didn't expect it."

"Keep two hands on the stick and go to the net," she said. "You'll score lots of goals that way with me." She tapped his shin pads with her stick and skated back.

That bothered him too. Like he needed to be told how to play?

"Keep up, Jules," Trisha said. "That was too easy."

Julia did not move a muscle. She remained bent at the hips, waiting for the faceoff. Trisha laughed and casually crossed her stick over Julia's. Julia chopped on the shaft of Trisha's stick and it bounced on the ice.

"Okay. Could you two behave?" Cummings said.

"How about her tripping me?" Julia said.

Trisha smirked. "Can't we just play hockey? All this complaining . . ."

Charlie thought he heard Trisha mutter, "Miss Goody Two-Shoes," under her breath.

Cummings looked at both girls intently. She thumbed over her shoulder. "Charlie's line to the bench," she said. She grabbed Trisha's sweater as she skated by. "Do that again and you're off the team."

"What do you mean? . . . I didn't . . . I don't know what . . ." Trisha gave her head a shake, stormed off the ice, and sat in a huff on the bench. "Typical favouritism. Kick me off for setting up a goal. Makes sense to me."

Charlie wanted to be anywhere but sandwiched between two girls who hated each other and seemed to thoroughly dislike him too. He braced himself for the inevitable storm.

"Cummings is cracked," Trisha said to him. "Can you believe her?"

"I didn't really see what happened."

"What happened is Princess Julia chopped my stick in half, and I get in trouble."

"As if you're totally innocent," Alexandra said. "Julia doesn't lose her temper for nothing."

"Like at the ball hockey game?"

"Like . . . whatever."

"That was clever."

"Clever was our line getting kicked off the ice because of you."

Trisha elbowed Charlie. "She scores an empty-net goal and suddenly she's The Great One." She leaned forward. "A chair could have scored."

Alexandra leaned forward. "I'm getting off this line. No chance I'm playing with her."

"Whatever."

"Whatever."

Trisha wasn't done, though. "Alex, tell your bud Jules to work on her skating. She's falling all over the place." She elbowed Charlie again and chuckled.

Charlie suddenly thought back to their goal — and Julia sitting on the ice. Julia would never just fall. He glanced at Trisha, and she smiled back. Had she tripped Julia? It would explain why Trisha had been so wide open.

Matt got hold of the puck and made a sweet move at the blue line to gain the zone. Emily called for it in the slot. He slid it over and Emily blasted it in for a goal. Julia and her friends might not like those two girls, but boy could they play!

18

BRIGHT LIGHTS

The rain was coming down in buckets. Charlie had never seen so much water pour from the sky. It was raining so hard his mother let him borrow an umbrella, even though it was almost guaranteed never to make it back home again. Still he was soaked to the skin. Pudge shivered next to him, equally wet.

"Maybe we should call the skate-a-thon off," Pudge said. "Attendance is gonna suffer with this weather."

"We won't get a bus again, and we'll lose our deposit," Charlie replied. Pudge didn't answer, and who could blame him for wanting to go home. Not a single member of the committee had shown, apart from the ever-reliable Dalton. Charlie had sent one of the buses back, and this one was less than half full — a waste, as A.J. had predicted.

A fresh crack of thunder sounded, as if to punctuate his dire thoughts, which not even the arrival of Scott, Nick, Zachary and Matt could lighten. Ms Cummings tapped Charlie's umbrella with hers.

"Are we about ready to go?" she said. "It's a long drive to Humberside, especially with the rain. The driver told me he has to make another pickup after he drops us off, and he really would like to get a move on."

Charlie cast his eyes around. "May as well," he said.

She put her foot on the first step. "We can leave now," she said to the driver, and went into the bus.

Charlie took a final look around. The rain was skipping off the pavement, leaving a fine mist hovering, like a low-lying fog. It was actually kind of cool, and he allowed himself the luxury of watching, if only for a few seconds, to distract himself from what was happening. In the distance, he made out the form of two umbrellas, and as they got closer, he detected three people huddled underneath. One umbrella tilted up slightly.

"Sorry, Charlie," Julia said. "I had to haul these two out of bed."

Rebecca and Alexandra peered out from under a small umbrella.

"And I'm going to be thanking you for a long time," Alexandra grumbled.

"We're glad you made it, anyway," Charlie said. "You're lucky. We were just about to leave."

"I sure feel lucky," Alexandra said.

"We should get into the bus," Rebecca said.

"Good idea," Charlie said. "By any chance, did you bring your pledge sheets and permission forms?"

Rebecca and Alexandra handed him their permission forms. "What pledge sheets?" Alexandra said.

"You know . . . the pledges . . . the sheets."

"I told you guys," Julia said, handing hers over. "Didn't you get any pledges?"

"Sorry, Jules," Alexandra said. "I forgot. My bad."

"How could you forget?" Charlie said, his frustration rising to the surface. "Why do you think we're doing this?"

"I'm asking myself that same question," Alexandra shot back.

"We can get sponsors after," Rebecca suggested.

"That's probably okay," Julia said. "Right, Charlie?"

With only ten students participating he wasn't about to say no. "Fine. No problem. But we should get going." He noticed Julia scowl at her two friends as they got into the bus. Charlie wanted to ask Julia about the practice yesterday, but she went in before he had the chance. There would be time later, so he didn't sweat it. Charlie followed, and the driver closed the door. The three girls sat up front. Dalton was talking to Ms Cummings. The guys were at the back. He took a seat behind Pudge.

He tapped Pudge on the shoulder and said, "I think we should sneak by without losing money. Even if the other kids who registered didn't show, they might have still raised some money."

"Did we get enough pledges up front to pay for the ice time?"

Charlie held up a cheque. "I gave the money we've collected so far to my mom, and she wrote me this to cover it. I've already collected some money from you, Julia, Zachary, Matt and, believe it or not, Scott!"

"I guess pigs can fly," Pudge said.

"The rest will pay when they collect on their pledges. Oh, and Dalton scored big — he got two hundred fifty dollars in pledges. That dude is amazing."

"He might have got this wrong," Pudge said. "Our fellow students didn't exactly get too stoked about the skate-a-thon."

"I guess it wasn't the best idea," Charlie said.

"It was a good idea and it should've worked."

"But it's like no one cares."

"No one cares about what?" Scott said.

Charlie was taken aback. He must have said that louder than he wanted.

"We were just talking about the fundraising," Pudge said. "Charlie's right. Except for . . . I don't know . . . a handful of people . . . like the people on this bus, no one seems to care if the school closes."

"It's been one big epic fail," Charlie said, "and this skate-a-nightmare isn't going to set any fundraising records either."

For practically the first time since he'd met Scott, his friend leaned back in his seat without saying anything. Nick looked out the window. A depressing silence spread. Charlie felt helpless and angry at the same time. Why didn't people care? Why didn't they help out? They could raise the money if everyone tried. Instead, it seemed more cool to joke about the school closing, and uncool to do anything about it. It was hopeless. In a few weeks they'd all be at different schools — sooner if this storm destroyed the plastic sheeting. He looked out his window. They were on the ramp to the highway that went around the lake, which meant they still had a long way to go.

A huge thunderclap made him jump out of his seat.

"Is this the end of the world?" Scott said.

"That was like ten thunders all together, times two

— or one of Scott's burps," Nick said.

"Maybe it wasn't a burp," Scott said, crossing his legs and waving his hand in front of his nose.

"You didn't eat a burrito for breakfast, did you?" Nick said.

"Let me think. There was the bowl of cereal, a granola bar, toast, a banana, half a container of yogurt, another banana, and yes, a burrito from dinner two nights before. Can't expect me to skate a marathon when I'm half starved."

Nick began scratching at the window. "Great. A bus with windows that don't open."

"It's not my fault," Scott said. "Blame the beans."

That broke the boys up.

"So what's so amusing?" Alexandra said. She was kneeling on her seat peering over the top.

Charlie struggled to think of an explanation.

"I heard Scott's name linked to a burrito," she said. "This could be a long day." She turned back around.

"I'm glad I didn't mention the French toast," Scott whispered to his friends.

The sky lit up as a bolt of lighting illuminated the windows so brightly that Charlie wondered if the driver had turned on the lights. That was followed by yet another massive crash of thunder.

"I might have had two burritos," Scott said.

No one laughed. The storm was getting a bit scary.

Charlie saw something moving up ahead on the hill that bordered the highway. "That's kinda strange. Do you see that?" he said to Pudge.

Pudge strained his neck to look.

Charlie heard a loud rumbling.

CRASH!

The next thing he knew he'd been thrown out of his seat. The bus veered violently to the right. Charlie heard a high-pitched squeal, and then felt another crash against the side of the bus, even harder this time. Charlie and Pudge banged into each other, sending Charlie somersaulting over the arm of a chair across the aisle.

CRASH!

The wheels screeched, and then the noise stopped. For a second Charlie thought it was over. Then he felt the sensation of falling.

Pudge fell on him, and then flew off. Charlie spun over, landing on Scott and Nick. He heard Nick gasp for breath. Screams and moans mingled in the air, as Charlie struggled to untangle himself. Charlie looked down, too terrified to utter a sound. The windows were pressing into mud. He could make out bits of rock and tree branches.

It took a few seconds for his brain to catch up.

The bus had slid off the road and rolled.

19

BY A THREAD

"Are you guys okay?" Charlie said loudly.

"I'm good," Pudge said, sitting up.

"I don't believe I am seriously injured," Dalton said from a few rows up.

Then Charlie heard Nick moaning softly.

"Did you hurt something?" he asked urgently.

"My leg — it feels busted," Nick said between short breaths.

"Help me here, Pudge," Charlie said.

They turned Nick around as gently as possible so he could lie down. Scott was struggling to sit up, and Dalton went to help him. With the bus flipped on its side, Scott was actually sitting on the windows, leaning against the roof. His left arm dangled down his side. "I can't feel my arm," he whispered. "It's totally dead. I can't feel anything."

Charlie couldn't believe his eyes. Scott's arm had somehow grown several centimetres.

"You've dislocated it, for sure," Dalton said. "Hold it to your side."

Scott leaned back against the roof and grasped his arm with his other hand.

"Anyone else hurt?" Charlie called out.

"Bashed my knee up pretty good," Zachary said between clenched teeth.

A flash of lightning lit up the bus. Charlie looked around in horror. His friends had been tossed around like ping-pong balls. And now everyone was lying on the windows, and no one was moving at the front. A crack of thunder unnerved him, and he fought to stay calm.

"Matt's hurt too," Pudge told him. "He's bleeding real bad."

"I'll be okay," Matt said bravely. "It's only my nose that's bleeding."

Charlie's heart practically jumped out of his chest when he saw his friend. Blood covered the side of his face. There was a gash on his forehead, and blood was oozing out.

Charlie crawled a few metres towards the front. "Ms Cummings? Ms Cummings?" His voice quivered slightly. "Are you okay?"

"She's hurt," Julia answered. "Can you come over here?"

"Go ahead, Charlie," Pudge said. "Check it out."

Their eyes met. This was bad — scary bad.

"Call 9-1-1," Charlie said, "I'll be right back."

"I've got them on the line," Dalton answered. "The emergency vehicles are on their way."

Charlie began crawling across the windows to reach the girls. It was awkward, and his pants got soaking wet, but he was too freaked out to care. A second flash of lightning gave him a clear view. His teacher lay on her back clutching her leg, blood trickling down her temple.

"Ms Cummings, the bus fell off the road. We've been in an accident!" he said to her.

She opened her eyes and raised her head slightly. "Where are we?" she asked. Her head fell back.

Julia clambered across the windows and crouched beside Charlie. Her lower lip shook as she spoke. "We need to get out of here. We're falling into the lake. Water is coming in."

Charlie looked closely at her. "Are you okay? There's blood on your jacket."

"I'm fine. I'm fine. It's not my blood." She gripped Charlie's arm. "Alex and Becca are really hurt."

Charlie felt sick to his stomach.

"Who's not hurt?" she asked.

Her question snapped him out of his fog. "You, me, Pudge and Dalton."

She groaned. "We've gotta get out."

"Charlie. Julia," Dalton yelled. "The 9-1-1 dispatcher told me to try to get everyone off the bus."

"We're thinking the same. You and Pudge get the guys to the back, and we'll bring the girls," Charlie said.

He found Alexandra kneeling, swaying slightly, looking confused. Julia slipped in next to him.

"Becca's way worse than me, Jules," Alexandra said, half-crying.

"We'll take care of her," Julia reassured her.

Charlie and Julia both went to Rebecca. She was curled up on her side, her breathing very quick and shallow, and both arms were wrapped around her stomach, but she was calm.

"Where does it hurt?" asked Charlie.

"I think I broke some ribs when I fell," she gasped.

"I'm light-headed. I can't breathe right."

"Rebecca and Alexandra, listen to me. We're going to get you off the bus now," Charlie said, trying desperately to sound in control. "We'll help you to the back doors. Julia, you get Alexandra, and I'll help Rebecca."

The bus rocked a bit, and he and Julia exchanged a worried look. Alexandra was able to walk, but Rebecca was in so much pain she couldn't move. Charlie looked over Julia's shoulder. The water in the front of the bus seemed to be rising. Time was running out.

Charlie put his arm around Rebecca's neck and squeezed the other under her knees. It was too tight a space to just pick her up and he had to slide her up on his thighs first. By pushing against the roof he was able to slowly get to his feet. Bent over, he made his way towards the back, willing himself to ignore the strain in his knees and back. Rebecca closed her eyes the entire time, her only sound a single whimper when her foot hit the side of a chair.

Pudge saw him struggle and helped him the last bit. Alexandra was able to crawl by herself. Ms Cummings made it with Julia's help. Dalton was tending to the boys' injuries. They were sitting on the windows off to the side. Charlie opened the emergency exit. The wind practically ripped it out of his hands, and it smashed into the ground. He popped his head out, shielding his eyes so he could see. It was a frightening scene. It wasn't ground that the door had smashed into: it was mud. The hill had collapsed and mud and trees had smashed into the bus, sending it off the road. The back of the bus was still on shore; the rest was in the lake. A massive evergreen tree, its roots ripped right out of the ground, lay on its side about ten metres away, wedged in between two boulders. Mud was everywhere, littered with rocks, busted-up and splintered trees, and tons of branches. He looked up the hill, and in the distance on the highway he saw a few cars.

Charlie gestured to his friends. With the door open the storm was deafening, and he had to shout to be heard. "The ambulance is gonna take forever to get to us. There's too much mud. It's covered the highway. But there's a tree close by. We can hold onto that until help comes. We'll never be able to walk through the mud." He looked down. In crawling back and forth his pants were now completely drenched. "And we'd better do it quickly," he added grimly. "Most of the bus is already in the lake, and there's more water coming in."

The bus creaked, then bobbed up and down, sending Pudge first into Dalton, and then both of them crashing back into a seat. Charlie fell on Julia and they both went down as well.

Charlie struggled to his feet. He reached down and helped Julia up.

"Are you okay?" he said.

She nodded, but Charlie could see the fall had hurt.

"How about me and Pudge jump down and help people out," Charlie said.

"Let's just hurry," Julia pleaded.

They crawled out. Charlie immediately sank about a foot into the mud. Water drifted over top — and it was freezing cold. He gave his head a shake to focus. No time to worry about that. He leaned into the bus. Zachary was closest to him, holding his knee tightly.

"Zachary, how do you want to do this?" Charlie said.

"By magic carpet, preferably."

Only Zachary could be so cool at a time like this.

"I'm all out of those," Charlie said.

"Then how about I go backwards and you pull me out."

The injuries made things complicated and slow, especially with Nick and Rebecca. Both of them were in excruciating pain, and every movement was agony. Finally, Pudge and Charlie lowered Ms Cummings into the mud.

Charlie rested his hands on his knees for a second, struggling to catch his breath. The rain was still pelting down and it made his eyes sting. To make things worse, the bus had slid towards the lake while they helped people out, and he and Pudge had to pull their feet out of the mud to keep close to the door; it was incredibly tiring. He was beyond relieved when Dalton and Julia joined him.

"Almost done," Charlie gasped. "That tree looks solid. We'll be okay once we get there." But something began to bother him, a nagging feeling, as if he had forgotten something.

"There's no way Zachary, Nick or Rebecca can make it themselves," Pudge said to him quietly.

Charlie almost felt like laughing. It was getting to be too much. He couldn't feel his feet, and even standing up straight was an effort. When he saw his injured friends, however, he felt ashamed of himself. He was still way better off. "Let's do this," he growled, and he and Pudge punched fists.

Dalton trudged over to them. "I believe I can help Matt and Alexandra, and Julia should be able to assist Ms Cummings and Scott, since their legs are not hurt. Zachary, Nick and Rebecca will require two people, in my opinion. Perhaps we can get started, and you can carry one of them over. Then all four of us should be able to help the remaining two."

They all nodded agreement.

"We should take Rebecca first," Charlie said to Pudge. "She's the most hurt." She was also the lightest, and Charlie needed a rest. They picked her up, and she wrapped her arms around their necks. The mud wasn't as deep, and the tree wasn't that far, but it was still tough. The four helpers slowly made their way back, each of them fighting desperately for breath.

Dalton and Pudge picked up Nick and began the backbreaking walk to the tree.

Zachary began to laugh. "I don't think you can carry me, Julia."

Julia looked up at him with half-closed eyes. "I was kinda thinking the same thing."

Julia had been a warrior so far, but Zachary was simply too big for her. They would have to wait for Dalton and Pudge to help.

A gurgling sound caught his attention. The bus was sliding again, and the water underneath bubbled up. He hobbled over for one last look. Water was spilling into the bus with the door open, the rain adding to it. He guessed the front was filling up now, and the bus would sink pretty soon. He moved away. Off in the distance, he saw that several fire trucks had arrived, their lights flashing overhead, and he spotted a crew of firefighters struggling towards them. They were going to be on that tree for a while, he figured.

But that wasn't what bothered him. In the back of his mind, he knew something was wrong. He counted everyone. They were all there.

And then it hit him.

"The driver!" he yelled.

"We're so stupid," Julia said. "How did we . . . we've got to . . ." She stared into his eyes.

He clutched her shoulder. "You wait here and tell Pudge and Dalton to help Zachary. I'll check him out."

"But the bus is . . ." Julia left it unsaid.

"Be quick, dude," Zachary said. "Real quick."

Charlie hesitated for a moment, and then climbed back in. His legs could barely hold him, and after a few metres he found it easier to crawl. His knees were aching, and each step was brutally painful.

He kneeled down next to the driver. Water sloshed around the bus like in a giant bathtub. It went up to his knees. A wave of fear hit him.

They weren't going to make it.

20

GOING DOWN

Charlie shook the driver's shoulder. He didn't move. Charlie shook him harder. He slowly turned his head.

"Sir. We really have to go. Everyone else is out," Charlie said.

"Did you say you all got out?" the driver said weakly.

Charlie tugged on his shoulder again. "Yes. It's only you and me. It's not safe. The water . . . this bus is sinking. Come on."

"At least I won't have the kids on my conscience," he said.

"What was that?" Charlie said, not understanding.

The driver's face was full of sadness. "You get going, son. It's too dangerous. Go."

A loud creak was followed by a gurgling sound. Charlie pulled harder. "I'll help you. It's not that hard." He was exhausted, but he had to try.

The driver shook his head. "I can't move. It's my foot. The side of the bus got dented in and trapped it. Get out now. Don't worry about me."

Charlie desperately wanted to go, more than anything.

But the driver would drown! He couldn't just leave.

He reached down and pulled on the driver's pant leg. It wouldn't budge. He slipped both hands under the driver's knee and began tugging, and the bus driver reached down and pulled from his thigh.

"It's useless," the driver said, fighting for breath. "Please just go." He closed his eyes.

The bus shifted again. Charlie lurched forward and almost hit his head on the windshield.

A hand pulled him back to his feet. Had the driver pulled himself free?

"Charlie. Come on," Julia said. She pressed close. "It's going to sink," she whispered.

He shook his head frantically. "His foot is trapped. He can't move."

She put her hand to her mouth and her eyes went as big as saucers.

"Maybe the two of us can get him loose," he said.

Charlie grabbed the steering wheel and began pushing against the side of the bus with his foot, just above where the driver's foot was trapped. He pushed and pushed and pushed until his heart was about to burst.

"That should do it," he said, more hoping than really believing. He reached under the driver's leg.

Julia grabbed the driver around the waist.

"One . . . two . . . three," Charlie counted.

They began to pull.

Charlie lost the feeling in his hands; he had long since stopped feeling his feet. The water was so cold. But he continued to pull, and so did Julia, and so did the driver.

Charlie threw his head back and felt the leg move. "A little more," he grunted.

The driver let go. "I think you two need to leave. I can't bear . . . I can't have you hurt. You must go. The water is getting too high. Once the bus goes down, you won't be able to get out."

Julia looked into Charlie's eyes. He could see she was scared. But there was determination there, too. She wasn't going to leave, and neither was he.

"We're getting off this bus — together," Charlie said, through gritted teeth. He reached for the driver's leg again and pulled frantically. Julia and the driver began to pull as well.

It was quiet enough for Charlie to hear their breathing, the sloshing of the water, and the creaking of the bus as it tilted. Charlie braced himself and gave another mighty pull.

He and Julia went flying backwards. The frigid water took his breath away and he wiped his face with his hands so he could see.

"Are you hurt?" Julia said.

"I'm good," Charlie said. "Is the . . . ?"

The driver struggled to his knees. "I'm free. Hurry up. Hurry!"

Charlie began to crawl. His head was pounding, and he stopped. His feet and hands were totally numb, and he couldn't breathe. He had to rest.

But Julia kept pulling him and was yelling in his ear so much he gave in and followed her. She jumped out of the bus and spun around to face him. Pudge was next to her.

"Faster! Faster!" Julia screamed.

He felt himself sliding backwards. The bus was bobbing up and down. His mind froze. The bus was completely in the lake — and he was falling towards the front. He reached out and Pudge grabbed him by his wrists. At the same time he felt a hand grab him by the belt — the driver.

"Pull! Pull!"

He felt the bus slide out from under him, and then he flopped into the water. It felt like landing in a bathtub of ice.

"No time for swimming," Pudge gasped. Charlie heard his friend growl fiercely, and the next thing he knew he was being pulled through the mud.

"I've got you, Sir," Dalton said.

Charlie saw him pull the driver from the water. Still dazed, Charlie got to his knees. The rain was still falling, but this time it felt good, almost warm.

"You almost gave me a heart attack," Pudge said.

Charlie let his head slump to his chest.

Pudge put his arm on his back.

"You can fall asleep when you get to the tree, Major," Pudge said.

He was too tired to answer.

With Pudge's help, he half-walked and was half-dragged to the tree to join the others.

When he got there, Pudge hoisted him up. Julia fell in next to him. The branches poked into his back and sides, but he could not keep his eyes open. It was as if he was floating in air, and then everything went dark.

21

PAGE ONE

The nurse looked down at the muddy puddles that were forming at their feet. Charlie and Pudge rubbed the floor sheepishly with their shoes in a vain attempt to wipe away the mess.

"He's in Room 218," the nurse said tersely. "Go down that hall and it's near the end." She looked down at the floor again and shook her head.

Charlie said thanks and cuffed Pudge's arm.

"I think she was quite impressed with us," he said, as they were walking away.

"What were we doing leaving without an umbrella?" Pudge said. "Especially considering you were in the hospital for three days with hypothermia."

"And considering it's rained practically every day since school started I kind of wonder the same thing," Charlie said.

They found the room and Charlie knocked on the door.

"Enter — if you have food."

Charlie felt like he had walked into a war zone. There were casts everywhere. Scott sported one on his left arm, and Zachary, who greeted them with a wave of a crutch, had one on his right leg. Nick lay on the hospital bed, his right leg in a cast and suspended in the air by straps. Only Matt seemed to have emerged from the accident without having broken anything, although the wide bandage on his head showed how seriously he had been hurt.

Scott sat on the end of the bed. "Just because you saved everyone's life doesn't mean you can show up without snacks," he said.

"It looks like the operation went well," Charlie said to Nick.

"The doc said it did," he said. "They put a steel rod in my leg and had to straighten the bone and reattach it."

The guys all groaned.

"We're trying to eat," Scott said. "Gross."

"You don't have any food," Nick said.

"I said we were trying."

"Did the doctor say how long until you can play again?" Charlie said.

Nick shook his head. "I asked him and he laughed. I took that to mean a long time."

"So it's more than two weeks," Scott said.

Nick rolled his eyes. "What about you? How long are you going to hide behind a broken arm and a cracked collarbone?"

"For about six to eight weeks, maybe more," Scott said, "but I'm superhuman — so I figure about six to eight weeks, maybe more."

"How about you, Zachary?" Pudge said.

"Doctor wasn't too sure. I have to have an MRI. Right now they think I'll probably need surgery. Total pain."

"Matt's the wimp here," Scott said. "He has a concussion and a slight skull fracture, and he won't play. I mean really, my skull's been fractured for years and it never slowed me down."

"That explains a lot," Nick whispered.

Charlie ran his hands over his head. "The co-ed team is cooked. So much for winning the money — and what are the Rebels going to do?"

"You and Pudge will have to rag the puck until we get back," Scott said.

"At least Hilton was able to shift our next few games to later in the season," Pudge said. "Hopefully, we'll have some of you back by then."

"The Rebels could use the break," Matt said.

The Rebels fast start had faded recently, and they had lost their last three games. Charlie figured he and his friends were too preoccupied with their school problems, so maybe Matt had something there.

"I have some good news," Charlie said. "The rink manager gave us another date for the skate-a-thon. He heard what happened and he said he won't charge us for the time we missed."

"I ain't taking no bus to get there," Scott said.

That broke everyone up.

"Don't make me laugh," Nick pleaded. "It hurts."

The door opened and Julia, Alexandra and Rebecca came in. Julia waved a bouquet of flowers in the air. "The nurse said she'd bring a vase. We thought it would cheer the room up a bit."

"Much appreciated," Nick said. "It'll be nice to smell something other than these guys."

"How are your ribs?" Scott asked Rebecca.

Touching her side, she said, "I broke three right here. I'll be fine in a few weeks, apparently. It hurt so much on the bus I swear I thought I was going to stop breathing."

"You were pretty calm, though," Charlie said.

She blushed. "You guys were awesome."

Alexandra cleared her throat. "I wanted to thank you too, you and Pudge, and I've already thanked Julia about a million times. I have to hunt Dalton down as well. I don't remember much, only that I was so unbelievably scared. Anyway, you guys were truly heroic, and I can't believe what you did to save the bus driver."

"What did he do?" Scott said.

"No one told you?" Alexandra said. "It's the most amazing thing ever."

"Why am I always the last to hear about amazing things?" Scott said.

"Because you get all teary-eyed and it's embarrassing," Nick said.

"That's true," Scott said, wiping his eyes.

"Be quiet, you two," Alexandra said, pretending to scold them. "If you behave, I'll tell you how Charlie and Julia saved the bus driver from certain death."

"Our little Char-Char? For real?" Scott said, clasping his hands under his chin and sighing.

A knock on the door interrupted, and a tall, thin woman wearing blue jeans and a red sweatshirt entered. She flashed a toothy smile. "I hope I'm in the right room. Sorry for just barging in. Is there a Charlie Joyce here?"

He'd never seen her before. What could she want with him? He raised his hand slowly.

"Wonderful. I've been looking all over town for you." She reached out and shook his hand. "I'm Lorie Sherman, a reporter for *The Examiner*. I went by your house, and spoke to your grandmother and your very interesting and talkative sister, Danielle. Your grandmother directed me to your mom's café, and after a nice coffee and a delicious pastry, your mom told me you had come to the hospital to visit your friend, Nick." She pointed at his broken leg. "I assume you're Nick."

"You can if you want, ma'am."

She laughed, and as she looked around her eyes got almost as big as her round glasses. "Is it my imagination, or do I have all the kids from the bus, right here, right now?"

"Everyone except for Dalton," Charlie said.

She laughed again and clapped her hands. "This is too perfect. I spoke to the bus driver and his wife — such lovely people — and he told me the beginning and the end of the story, but he was trapped in his seat for the middle. I'm going to write a feature about the accident. Do you mind filling me in?"

"Not at all," Scott said. "What you need to keep in mind is the guys were pretty scared. I had to chill them out so they wouldn't lose it. They all look up to me — in hockey and in school, and, well, basically everything — on account of my athleticism and general grace under pressure . . . and . . . well . . . that's probably what you should write about."

Lorie took off her glasses. "And your name is . . . ?"

"You can call me Scott . . . or Murray . . . although Murray isn't my name so it wouldn't make as much sense."

Rebecca was holding her ribs, trying desperately not to laugh. Nick had a hand on his cast, trying to do the same. Lorie held up a camera. "How about we start with a group shot. Scott or Murray can be in it. I'm not fussy. Now where's Julia Chow?"

Julia raised her hand.

"And I also understand Pudge Moretti was part of the rescue?"

He raised his hand tentatively as well.

"Can I get the wounded around Nick on the bed, and Julia, Pudge and Charlie standing at the back."

They shuffled into position.

Lorie sighed. "Nick, do you have some extra shirts for your wet friends? I know the bus fell into the lake, but I think our readers will wonder why Charlie and Pudge are still soaking."

"We forgot an umbrella . . ." Charlie began, but the laughter cut him off.

"In fact, I do happen to have some snazzy shirts in that dresser over there," Nick said.

Charlie and Pudge went over to the dresser and took out a couple of T-shirts. They had to endure a few whistles and catcalls as they took their shirts off and put Nick's on.

"Fabulous," Lorie said, as they took their places again. "Don't forget to give me some big smiles. You'll want to look your best. This will be on the front page." She took several shots.

"Now, Charlie, can I start with you?" She put her camera on a table and took out a tape recorder from her pocket. "What do you remember about the accident? And don't leave anything out."

It was strange but he hadn't thought a lot about it. After the three days in hospital, he had gone home and slept the next couple of days away. Now, sitting amongst all his friends, all at once it came back to him, the sudden thud of the mud smashing into the bus, the feeling of falling, the splash . . . the screaming, and the shock of seeing his friends so badly hurt . . . He remembered Pudge's toughness and calm — and he felt a surge of pride knowing they were best friends. He thought of Dalton's leadership and especially his willingness to return to the bus to help the driver. And of course he remembered Julia coming back to help. The terror of it flooded back to him.

All his friends had been brave. Those that were hurt never complained. He was unbelievably proud of all of them, and of himself.

"There was a huge sound of thunder," he began, "and Scott made a joke about it . . ."

22

GO TERRIERS

Charlie leaned on his left knee with his hand and carved around the end boards, slowing so he wouldn't bang into anyone. The new skates felt great. The Rebels' sponsor had donated new ones to the kids who had lost theirs when the bus sank. Charlie's old ones had been getting tight. But that wasn't the only good thing to happen since the accident. The rink was completely packed; it was hard to do anything more than shuffle along.

The sight of so many kids at the skate-a-thon made his heart swell. What a difference! He had collected over 150 pledge sheets. Julia had done a quick estimate and thought they might make about $15,000. Lorie, the journalist who had interviewed him in the hospital, had come to take pictures.

Charlie could have done without the attention, but he was grateful to Lorie. It seemed everyone in Terrence Falls had read her article, and it made people want to help, from the students and parents, to local businesses and the general community.

The next pancake breakfast had sold out in forty-five minutes and ended with A.J. blaming the committee for not giving her enough money to buy more stock. Donations from the parents flooded in; practically every parent gave something. Business owners kept calling the school with offers of money. It almost made the accident worth it! Almost.

Ms Cummings had suffered a serious concussion, two broken ribs and a badly bruised arm. Without a coach, and with so many players hurt, the tournament team was done. That was a potential $25,000 lost. Charlie doubted they could hit their target without it.

He spotted Dalton in the players' bench. He was pouring cups of hot chocolate.

"Hey, dude. How's this for a skate-a-thon?" he said.

"It is gratifying to see such support for the school," Dalton said. "This past week has been nothing short of remarkable."

Charlie would never get used to how he talked, but since the accident, he didn't find it odd anymore — that was just Dalton being Dalton.

"Does the committee know how much money we've raised so far?"

"It is hard to say exactly. I have not had the opportunity to speak with the treasurer, and Mr. Hilton is handling most of the corporate donations. But the latest ballpark figures I heard at our update meeting yesterday were nearing one hundred thousand, and not all the parent donations were counted. In other words, we haven't hit our target yet, but there is hope."

Charlie thought of the tournament team. "If only we could have fielded a hockey team," he said. "That would have been huge."

Julia stopped in front of Charlie. He looked down at the snow that had shot halfway up his leg.

"Was that really necessary?" he asked.

"I felt it was."

"Dalton was telling me the fundraising is getting close. A tournament win could have been the difference," Charlie said.

Julia pouted. "I admit I was looking forward to it, just to play — for fun. We had a good team."

Before the accident the tournament was the last thing he wanted to do for fun, what with Alexandra and Trisha as his wingers and a simmering feud between the girls. Now that it was over he agreed with her. It would have been fun.

"Just the people we wanted to talk to." Trisha trailed her left foot behind her and slowed to a stop next to Charlie. Emily came over also.

"Me and Em were talking about the team," Trisha said. "Even though so many players got hurt, when you think about it, we could still put out a good team."

"We'd have two boys, who'd be on every second shift," Emily said, "and the rest of us girls can kick the butts of the girls on any other team."

"I asked Jake and Liam and Thomas if they'd play," Trisha said. Charlie's stomach tightened. "But they turned out to be total jerks and just started dissing everyone and . . . I told them to forget it."

Charlie liked the sound of that.

"What do you think?" Emily said. "Why not?"

"I don't know . . . It seems almost disrespectful, after the accident, and with Ms Cummings hurt . . ." Charlie began.

As he listened to himself, he realized those reasons didn't hold any water. The truth was he simply assumed he wouldn't play because his friends weren't playing.

"We don't need a coach. It's only a three-game round robin," Emily said.

"Three wins, and that's twenty-five grand. We have to play," Trisha said.

"It would be a substantial contribution to the roof fund," Dalton said.

Charlie was not going to make this decision himself. He looked at Julia. "What do you think?"

She shuffled her skates. "I never really thought about it," she said.

"I can understand if you don't want to," Emily said.

"I'd be totally freaked out by that bus crash, and if you don't want to play that's cool with us," Trisha said. "But I know Li wants to play and Sophie and Sandra and Cassie. And with you two, and Pudge and Michelle, then we have ourselves a team."

Julia did not say anything.

"Please? For TFH?" Trisha said. She tapped Charlie's skate. "I want to play on your line," she said. "We'll be awesome together."

"You'll be unstoppable together," Emily said.

Charlie was tempted. Maybe it was worth the try. "It might not hurt to give it a go," he said. "I mean, if we actually win it . . ."

Trisha put her arm around his shoulders. "Sweet. I knew you'd come through, Charlie Joyce. You're awesome. Isn't he awesome, Em?"

"Definitely," Emily said.

He hadn't actually agreed to play, had he?

"I guess . . . if Charlie will play . . . I'll play too," Julia said.

"I'll talk to Pudge, and see what he thinks," Charlie said. An idea popped into his head — a familiar one. "And I'll ask Hilton if he'll coach us. He might do it considering what happened."

"Has he coached before?" Trisha said.

Charlie laughed. "I forgive you, since you're new to TFH, but the answer is yes."

Trisha slapped him on the back. "Then I like him already."

"This is an excellent idea," Dalton said. He handed them each a hot chocolate. "Let's toast your success in the tournament."

Charlie picked up another cup and handed it to Dalton. "We're toasting *our* success," he said, "because you're going to be the manager."

Dalton coloured slightly. "I've never done something like that, and I'm not sure you really need me."

"We do," Julia said. "Tournament teams need an organizer."

"And Hilton will be more likely to coach if he knows there's a manager to help," Charlie said.

Dalton pulled his shoulders back and held up his cup. "Then a toast to the Terrence Falls Terriers."

"I didn't know that was our team name," Charlie said. "How could I not know that?"

They all laughed, Trisha loudest of all. "You really are funny, Charlie Joyce."

Charlie thought he saw Julia's eyes narrow momentarily, but he couldn't be sure.

"To the Terriers, then," Charlie said, and they clinked cups.

Charlie took a sip, and it burned his tongue slightly. Trisha was right. They should play. Why not? And if they won — then he could actually let himself think the unthinkable.

23

BATTLE STATIONS

The dressing room was quiet, completely quiet, which was weird because it was usually anything but. The boys had finished dressing in the other room and were sitting with the girls in their room waiting to be called onto the ice for the first game of the Bee-Bees tournament. It was a large space, and with only ten players they were spread out. Trisha, Emily and Li were together, with Cassie, Sandra and Sophie huddled nearby. Julia and Michelle were at the opposite corner. He and Pudge were in the middle.

Dalton came in and leaned a small whiteboard against the wall. "Apparently, there is a delay of about ten minutes because of the Zamboni. I'll keep you informed. Mr. Hilton has asked me to tell you he will address the team in four to five minutes." He picked up the whiteboard and gave it a wipe with a cloth. "The arena is filled to the brim with students from Terrence Falls. Practically the entire school is in attendance. It's really quite exciting."

He smiled and left.

The players mostly just continued looking at the floor or fussing with their equipment. Only Trisha and

Emily spoke to each other in whispers. The quiet was driving Charlie crazy. It was wrong. The team was flat — no energy. He knew you couldn't win hockey games like that, and this tournament was too important for him to just let it go. Before the accident, the team had been about Julia's and Charlie's friends. Now he realized it was about a bunch of people who had not played much together. Five minutes was not enough time to unite a team through friendship. But they had something else in common, and Charlie decided to go with it.

"It's kinda cool, all the kids in the stands," Charlie said to Pudge, but in a loud enough voice to get everyone's attention. "Since the crash the entire school has gotten completely stoked."

"It's different, for sure," Pudge said.

Out of the corner of his eye he noticed Trisha and Emily were watching them.

"Not sure I told you, but Dalton thinks we're close to a hundred grand. With this tournament, we could basically be there."

Pudge nodded.

Charlie went on. "The accident got everyone's attention, and we all woke up and realized Terrence Falls was important to us." He pretended to be surprised that everyone was listening to their conversation.

All the girls continued to look at him.

It was working. Charlie decided to go for it.

"Me and Pudge were talking last night and, the rest of the crew agreed, that . . . well . . . that we should apologize to you."

Julia's eyes grew wide. Trisha was looking at him intently. Emily looked serious.

"I . . . I mean we . . . did not come into this with the right attitude. Actually, we didn't even want to play. We play with bodychecking, and I guess we thought it was a waste of time to play non-contact, and, I'm sorry, but maybe a part of it was we thought playing with girls would cramp our style."

The room was dead quiet.

Pudge nodded.

"I don't think I purposely thought that, but in the back of my mind, it was there. I acted dumb when Alexandra and Trisha beat me in a drill, and worse when Emily bumped into me."

"That was my fault," Emily jumped in, "and I've been feeling bad about it. It was a cheap shot, and I knew you weren't ready for it. Sorry."

That surprised him. "No worries. Girls and boys playing hockey together — it can be complicated." Everybody laughed.

Trisha broke in. "I should apologize to some of you too." Charlie wondered why. "I was a bit hyper coming into this. I can be so competitive, it's pathetic sometimes; and then Em and I were new to the school, and we came on a bit strong. I dissed a few of you, and that's not me. I was just nervous and I said some stupid things." She bit her lower lip. Her cornrows were tied in a ponytail, so her hair was off her face. She was a good-looking girl. It was as if Charlie was seeing her for the first time. "And what I feel worst about is the ball hockey game, and how we acted, and even being on that team with those guys. I didn't know what they were like, and they asked me and Em to play and we did. Sorry, Julia."

"I'm sorry too," Emily said.

Julia didn't say anything. She seemed to be thinking hard about something. Without smiling she said, "It's cool. Forget about it. I'm sorry for losing my temper like that." Then she smiled, and with a twinkle in her eye added, "Now you should apologize for winning the ball hockey tournament."

That broke the tension. "Those boys are jerks, but they sure can play," Trisha said.

Charlie could attest to that. It was one of Jake's most annoying traits.

The door opened and Hilton came in, followed by Dalton, Scott and Zachary. Scott held the door open as Matt pushed Nick through in his wheelchair. The dressing room instantly became a noisy place.

"Let me know when you need me to use my mind control powers," Scott said. "I'm particularly effective at getting refs to call penalties on the other team."

"Can you use those powers to say something intelligent?" Nick said.

Scott's shoulders slumped. "I wish. It's very depressing."

"Don't forget pathetic, too," Nick said.

"I don't have to. You always remind me."

"That's what friends do."

"I thought friends were kind and supportive."

Nick shook his head. "The better the friend, the worse they treat you. That's how you know."

Scott grinned and patted Nick gently on the shoulder. "You must be my best friend 'cause you treat me worse than anyone."

"Okay, you two," Hilton said. "I like the team to be

loose, but there's a limit." He faced the team. Charlie leaned back against the wall. It was one of his favourite moments in hockey, a few minutes before the game, butterflies in his stomach, and the best coach he's ever had about to give a pep talk.

"We are going to win this tournament," Hilton said. "We have too much to lose. But don't get me wrong. It's not about putting pressure on yourselves. Forget about winning. Forget about the roof, and all that. When you hit the ice, I want everything to be about effort. We will work the other teams to death. They won't be taking this as seriously as we are. Remember that in this tournament you get one point for each period you win, and then one more point for winning the game, so we can't take any time off, not even one shift.

"In this game I want you to overwhelm the other team from the start. I want the game over by the end of the first period. Unfortunately, we only have nine players and one goalie, and we have three games to play today. We will have to conserve our energy at times, so a quick start is crucial."

He nodded and the players nodded back. "I know you are experienced players, so there's no need to complicate things. Defencemen, up the boards and out with quick first passes. Wingers, work hard to set up for the outlet. Centres, for the first period go for the goals. I'm willing to take that chance. Then we'll switch it up and you can focus on your defensive assignments. Got it?"

"Got it," the players responded.

"Dalton has managed to do some statistical work," Hilton said. "Dalton, what do you have for us?"

Dalton unfolded a paper. "We're playing a team

called Winona High. They are not well known for athletics, having won only one significant trophy in the last ten years — in girls' cross-country."

"If they come out in shorts and T-shirts we're cooked," Scott joked.

Dalton continued. "They have three boys that play A-level hockey, and one that plays Double-A. They also have two girls that play A-level hockey. That should give us a talent advantage, at least on paper." He pointed at a cooler he had placed by the door. "By the way, I have purchased a wide array of foods and drinks to replenish depleted vitamins and minerals. We have very little time between this game and the next one against Northern, so I have prepared some appropriate snacks."

"I'm often depleted by cheering," Scott said.

"Sorry," Dalton replied, placing one foot on the cooler.

Scott pouted. "Fine. I'll starve to death with the two sandwiches and the bag of chips and the apple I brought."

"I believe the biggest challenge, Mr. Hilton, will be our final game against Chelsea," Dalton added.

"What?" Charlie exclaimed. "Chelsea is in the tournament?"

"They are a last-minute entry," Dalton said. "There are now five teams in the tournament. Each team plays three games, although one team has to play an extra game; fortunately, not us. Chelsea has some very good players, apparently. Especially . . ." he looked at his paper, "Savard and Burnett. They are Triple-A players, I believe."

Hilton checked his watch. "Okay, Terrence Falls.

We won't worry about Chelsea just yet. Put this game away, fast, and break their spirit. We don't want Winona to even consider the possibility of winning a period, let alone the game. Are we ready?"

The players roared back, "Yes!"

"That reminds me. I wrote a team cheer," Scott announced, as the players got up. "If you lose energy, just give me the sign and I'll unleash it."

"Please tell me you're joking," Nick said.

"I'll do something better. I'll debut it right now." He clenched a fist. "Terrence Falls? Yes! Terrence Falls? Yes! Terrence Falls? Yes! Yes! Yes!"

"That's the best cheer I've ever heard," Nick said. "I think you should stand up in front of the entire school and scream that at the top of your lungs."

"Nick, you're a genius. Why keep this to myself? So let's hear it, people."

"Terrence Falls?" Scott yelled.

"Yes!" they chanted back between fits of laughter.

Scott kept the chant going as he led them to the ice. Charlie hung back with Pudge.

"We needed Chelsea like a hole in the head," Charlie said. "They're going to be tough to beat with only ten players — not to mention Savard and Burnett." They were both great players, and Charlie had gone up against those two enough times to know that Hilton's strategy of overwhelming them in the first period would not work against Chelsea.

"Isn't there a saying, 'One game at a time'?" Pudge said. "We'll worry about Chelsea after we've won the first two."

Charlie tilted his head to one side and cuffed Pudge

on the helmet. "Wise words, Sergeant. Let's kick some Winona butt."

"Right behind you, Major," Pudge said.

Charlie walked out and down the corridor to the ice. Despite Pudge's good advice, Charlie couldn't get Chelsea out of his mind. It was yet another giant roadblock placed in front of them.

He hopped onto the ice and immediately raced across the blue line. The ice was hard and his skates made a loud scraping sound as he curved towards the back boards. He continued behind the net and then stopped at the bench for a quick sip of water.

Scott and Nick had stationed themselves by the boards next to the Terrence Falls bench.

"Terrence Falls?" Scott screamed.

"Yes!" a bunch of students screamed back.

The students were on their feet chanting Scott's ridiculous cheer. Charlie's heart pounded. Everything had seemed so dark when Principal Holmes had announced the school closing. It had gotten darker when the fundraising was going nowhere, and seemed completely doomed when the bus was hit by the mudslide. And now the whole school was behind the team.

Julia stopped beside him and reached for her water bottle.

"Is Charlie Joyce ready to play?"

"After the bus accident, this'll be a piece of cake," he said.

But he knew it wasn't going to be easy at all.

24

HIGH HOPES

Charlie wheeled with the puck in his own end looking for an opening. Hilton had put him with Julia and Trisha. The second line was Emily at centre flanked by Sandra and Sophie. Pudge, Li and Michelle were on defence. The game had barely started and Charlie's legs were still tight. It felt good to skate hard.

Julia cut across the slot, taking Charlie's place as centre. It was a quick, short pass and she would get out of their end no problem. He was on the verge of passing when he noticed Trisha barrelling across the red line, angled slightly towards Winona's end. He didn't hesitate. Hilton had told them to go for it, so he rifled a pass about ten centimetres off the ice up the middle.

The defencemen were caught watching. The puck went right between them and onto Trisha's stick. She had to spin quickly to stay onside, but once over the blue line she took a direct line at the goalie, feinting right, then left, before shifting right to the glove side and shoving the puck past the outstretched goalie pad.

The game was barely thirty seconds old, and they had scored. Talk about listening to your coach! Charlie leapt up and punched the air. He skated over to Julia and slapped her back. "Terrence Falls? Yes!" he shouted.

Julia smiled back. "Yes! Yes! Yes!" she chanted.

He tapped her on the shin pads and headed to congratulate Trisha, who was slapping gloves at their bench. She skidded to a stop in front of him and tapped his shin pads with her stick. "I knew you'd see me. I told you we'd be unstoppable together." Her eyes were blazing with energy. "It's your turn next, and then Julia, and this game is ours."

She sure came to play, he thought. He tapped her shin pads and set up for the faceoff.

Trisha lined up on the right wing. He nodded to her and flicked his head towards the boards. She nodded back almost imperceptibly. The ref dropped the puck and Charlie whacked it with a forehand. Trisha anticipated him winning the faceoff and had left the circle early. She gathered the puck against the wall and scooted up the wing, the Winona defenceman backing up nervously. Charlie followed up the middle, flanked by Julia on the left.

At the blue line, he swerved behind her. Trisha faked an inside move, which made the defenceman take one step that way, and then she bounced it outside. Charlie thought she might get around the corner, but at the hash marks she slowed and banked the puck off the wall back to the blue line.

It was a perfect pass. Charlie took it on his backhand, and cut hard on the outside edge of his left skate. Julia meanwhile had not slowed at all and had beaten the right defenceman to the net. He took two steps forward and wristed a hard pass towards the far post. Fortunately, the goalie had stayed back in her crease.

Julia threw herself at the puck fearlessly, storming across the front of the net and then backhanding it over the goalie's shoulder and in.

Charlie punched the air for the second time. The game plan was most definitely working. Julia curled in Winona's end, stick over her head, and she headed to Charlie. He put his arm around her shoulder.

"Terrence Falls?" he said.

"Yes! Yes! Yes!" she shouted again.

Trisha came over and threw her arms around them both. "Like taking candy from a baby," she said. "We should have time for another one this shift."

Hilton had another idea, however. Emily's line was waiting at centre.

"Hold that thought," Charlie said. The three line-mates headed to the bench. Emily held her glove up and they all gave her a high five.

Charlie took a seat on the bench and reached for some water.

"Joyce. Do something. You're letting the girls do all the hard work."

Charlie recognized Scott's voice. Then his cheer began again.

The place was an absolute madhouse. Charlie had never played in a game with such a wild atmosphere. It sounded like a pro game. The crowd kept it up practically the entire time — and so did the TFH players. It was 5–0 after the end of the first, and 9–0 after the second. There were eight minutes left in the third period, and Emily had just scored to make it 12–0.

Hilton stopped Charlie's line before they went out for the faceoff.

"I think you'll agree that we've scored enough, and we'll win all three periods. Let's not score again unless you absolutely have to," he said.

Charlie had expected that. His coach hated his players showing off, and now that they had the four points wrapped up, there was no need to keep pressing.

Trisha followed him out. "I don't agree," she said to him as they drifted to the faceoff. Trisha had never played for Hilton, and, as she had said herself in the dressing room — and shown during the game — she was ultra-competitive and never let up. "Winning the tournament could come down to most goals if there's a tie for points, and other teams will kill these guys too."

It occurred to him that Trisha might have a point. But there was no way he would disobey a direct order from his coach, at least not a coach like Hilton.

"If we win all three games, we won't have to worry about goals," Charlie said. "It's 12–0. I'm feeling guilty already. I think we should ease up."

Trisha bit her lower lip, and then her face lit up with a smile. "Okay, Charlie Joyce. We'll do it your way." She tapped his shin pads and took her spot at right wing.

The ref blew her whistle and glared at him. "Come on, number eight. Line it up."

Charlie rushed over, and the ref dropped it before he got his stick down.

"What's with that?" he said.

"Play the game," the ref said.

Charlie gave his head a shake and watched Trisha pressure the left defenceman, although she didn't go in too hard. The puck moved to the centre, and he set off up ice. Charlie could have stripped him of the puck, but he let him cross the red line and fire it deep into Terrence Falls' end. Cassie had not had much action, and she came out to trap the puck behind the net, leaving it there for Michelle.

The Winona left winger skated at her. Michelle waited until she had committed herself and then took the puck out the other side. For a second Charlie was tempted to goal suck and look for the stretch pass. Trisha was hovering at the red line too, obviously with the same idea. Julia had hustled back, and Michelle passed to her.

Charlie immediately felt ashamed. Not ten seconds after telling Trisha to back off, there he was, looking to score. Julia was the only one who had listened. He skated back and branched off near the blue line. Julia snapped a pass over. Trisha had come across and Charlie gave it to her near the red line. Trisha took it over the line, and then lofted a lazy wrist shot on goal. Her forecheck was equally laid back, and Winona got the puck out easily this time.

The rest of the game followed the same pattern. Terrence Falls was too good to give up a goal, and under Hilton's orders, not interested in scoring. Time after time they sent the puck spinning into Winona's end content to defend and get the puck out. Cassie got a few more shots in the last minutes of the game.

It ended 12–0. At the buzzer, a dejected Winona team gathered around their net, in stark contrast to Terrence Falls. Stoked by the easy win, there were high-fives all around and lots of laughter.

"I admire you for controlling yourself and not

scoring," Charlie said to Trisha, as they headed to centre to shake hands.

She laughed. "Don't think I didn't notice you inching your way to centre looking for the breakaway."

"I admit my natural instincts took over for a second."

"I like your instincts," she said.

The conversation felt a bit weird all of a sudden. For some reason he actually felt more relaxed around her when she was mean to him. Nice Trisha was hard to read. Now that he thought about it, it was a bit like how he felt around Julia sometimes.

Charlie finished shaking hands with the Winona players, and then curled slowly back to his bench. Zachary, Scott and Rebecca had come down to offer what Scott called "injury high-fives." He spotted Nick and Matt in the stands talking to some kids from school. Hilton and Dalton were standing together, and Dalton was laughing at something their coach had said.

It was a nice scene — and if they could do this two more times, they'd get the money — and maybe save their school!

25

NORTHERN EXPOSURE

The puck hit a leg in front and bounced into the corner. Charlie raced to get it. He faked a move behind the net and whirled the other way along the board. Two Northern defenders pressured. Charlie slid it to Michelle at the point, who fired it without hesitation across the blue line to Pudge. That was dangerous, as the Northern centre extended his stick and just missed intercepting. As soon as Pudge had the puck, Charlie stormed the net for a rebound, arriving just as Pudge fired a slapshot. The front of the net was so congested the puck hit another leg and then banged off Julia's skate — right to Charlie. He slapped at it, but so did a defenceman, and Charlie didn't get much wood on it. The puck hit the goalie's blocker and dropped to her right, about a metre and a half from the post.

"Get it, Trisha," Charlie yelled.

Trisha lunged and knocked it to the corner, racing after it. Charlie gambled and went behind the net. If she lost it, they would both be out of the play. But it was 4–all, and less than a minute to play. They had won the first two periods, but Northern had come back to tie it up.

Trisha got the puck, hesitated a moment, and then sent it around the wall on her forehand. Charlie pressed against the boards to knock the puck down, and immediately took it out the far side, looking for an opportunity to pass.

Pudge came down low, but the right winger stayed with him. Julia was in front battling for position. There was a defenceman on her, and he was pushing her away. He was too big, and Charlie doubted she could get free. So he backed up with the puck on his forehand towards the wall. Pudge stopped abruptly and got back to the point. The right winger did not know whether she should pressure Charlie or stay with Pudge. Charlie took advantage and slid a pass to Pudge and then went a couple of metres backwards to the corner. Pudge one-timed a pass back to him. Charlie held it, drawing the right winger ever closer to him. He passed it to Pudge, and jumped past a Northern defenceman to get close to the net.

This time Pudge got the puck through. The athletic Northern goalie was equal to the challenge, and kicked it out with a right pad save. Again, the puck came to Charlie. A defenceman charged at him. He snapped a shot at the net, not really aiming, and not really seeing it.

PING!

The puck ricocheted off the post and into the corner. He watched the defenceman track the puck down and head up ice. No one bothered to stop her. There were only five seconds on the clock. She flicked it towards Terrence Falls' end, and turned back to her net. The buzzer rang to end the game.

"That was brutal. A post?" Charlie said.

"Do you know what happens now?" Julia asked him.

He shook his head.

A referee skated by.

"Hey ref," he called out. "Do we have overtime?"

She shook her head. "We go right to a shootout. I'll explain it to your coach. Back to your benches, please."

Charlie pushed off twice with his left skate and glided the rest of the way on his right.

"Almost had one there," Pudge said to him.

"I rushed it," Charlie said, a bit angry at himself. He'd had time, and did not have to one-time it. Dumb mistake. He'd had a good game, though: two goals and one assist. Trisha had potted a goal and had an assist, and Julia had gotten a goal and two assists.

"OMG," Julia groaned at the bench. "I hate shootouts."

"You'll need to learn to love them, and quickly," Hilton said. "It's an NHL-style shootout — three shooters, and two have to be girls. Most goals wins. If it's still tied after three shooters, it becomes sudden death." In a louder voice he announced, "The first three shooters are Charlie, Trisha and Julia, in that order. The rest of you come to the bench."

Charlie was across from Emily, and for the briefest of seconds he saw her grimace. He understood she would want to shoot. She was a good player, and had done well on what was probably the weaker line. To her credit she did not complain and always offered encouragement.

"You own this goalie, Trish," she said. "Smoke it past her."

They made their way to centre to wait for the

shootout to begin. Trisha waved the other two towards her.

"This goalie is quick on her feet," she said quietly, "and she's good on the deke. I think we should shoot if she stays back in her crease. She'll play for the deke, I know it."

Charlie did not know how to take that. He was not used to being told what to do on a breakaway, unless it was by Hilton. Or was the problem that it was Trisha giving him pointers? Her advice made sense, though. The goalie had been back in her crease all game. He'd been thinking shot too.

The shooters from Northern interrupted before he could answer.

"Look," a tall girl said, pointing her stick at Julia. "That's the best they can do."

"It's cute, in a pathetic way," a girl with a red helmet said.

"Maybe you're just pathetic — in a pathetic way," Julia shot back.

The tall girl rolled her eyes. "Listen to the tough girl. Did any of you even touch the puck this game?" she said, to her friend's great amusement.

Julia laughed. "You might have noticed me putting the puck in your net; and you'll see me do it again in the shootout."

"In your dreams, girl."

"Good luck in the shootout," Trisha said, "and while you're missing the net, we'll discuss whether any of you girls have washed your hair in the past week."

The referee blew her whistle. "Give me the first shooters," she said.

The Northern players huddled up.

"That was fairly intense," Charlie said.

Trisha and Julia were laughing.

"That was fun, dude," Trisha said. "Now I'm gonna roof a backhander just to show her who's boss."

Julia gave Charlie's shoulder a punch. "They're just messing with us. Go get us a lead."

Charlie skated to centre.

Scott's voice boomed over the crowd noise. "I command you to score, Joyce." then a chant went up from the TFH students: "Char-lie! Char-lie! Char-lie!"

He felt his nerves kick in. The noise level rose higher and higher, until the cheers echoed throughout the arena.

"When I blow the whistle you both go at the same time," the referee said.

Charlie took a deep breath to refocus.

The ref blew her whistle.

The crowd roared, and Charlie set off at a slow pace. Unfortunately, the goalie did the exact opposite of what he wanted. She came way out to challenge, a full metre above the crease line. If she stayed that far out he would have to go with the deke. At the blue line, he picked up speed to try to shake her up, cutting right to his forehand, and then swinging it to his backhand at the top of the circle. She had not budged. Alarm bells sounded in his head. The shot would not work. She had the angle. But changing your mind at the last second was about the worst thing you could do on a penalty shot. She was so far out, though. He had to deke.

The goalie suddenly backed up until she was in the middle of the crease area. He had waited too long.

Charlie felt sick. Without thinking he took one more stride, dragged the puck with his right foot forward, and let it fly from about three metres. His chest constricted. The goalie dropped to her left knee and flung out her blocker. She had misjudged it slightly and the puck went just over the blocker, hit the shaft of her stick, and bounced off her shoulder.

She fell backwards, swimming her arms over her head, and in doing so the thick part of her stick hit the puck and it sneaked inside the right post, spinning on its edge. The Terrence Falls supporters went crazy. It was a goal — a lucky one.

He looked back to his end. The Northern shooter was high-fiving his teammates. He had scored also. At least the pressure was off him now. Trisha and Julia greeted him with an outstretched glove.

"Thanks for the heart attack," Trisha said.

"It went in," Julia said. "Who cares how?"

Charlie looked up at the ceiling. "At the last second I changed my mind and was about to deke. That was a fluke. She fooled me by collapsing to the goal line at the last second."

"I'm still going shot," Trisha said. "She'll try the same stunt with me."

Charlie was about to offer some advice, but she left for centre before he could. She sure is confident, he thought.

"I hope she's right," Charlie said.

"She better be," Julia said. "She told me ten times how she never misses on a shootout."

"Shooters who have gone must go to the bench," a referee said to him.

Charlie patted Julia's shin pads with his stick. "I'd either shoot or deke," he said. "Otherwise, I have no clue."

She rolled her eyes. "Thanks for that."

Pudge opened the door and held out his glove. They punched, and then he gave Charlie a healthy whack on the helmet.

"I never doubted that would go in for a second," Pudge said.

Charlie took a deep breath. "That was living way to close to the edge," he said.

"Nick, I believe it is time to use our natural wizard powers," Scott announced.

They were next to the bench by the boards. Nick was propped up on some pillows so he could see the play better from his wheelchair.

Scott stood and put his hand on his heart, while Nick held his arms up over his head and flickered his fingers.

"Ipsy, Apsy, Ticksy, Bisha," they chanted. "I see a goal, and it's scored by Trisha."

Scott paused and then yelled to the bench, "Tell Dalton to get more powerful wizards for the Chelsea game."

The whistle blew and Trisha took off like a house on fire and, as before, the goalie came out. Trisha did not hesitate. At the hash marks she snapped a wrister, glove side, to the top corner. She made a big curl deep in the corner, stick raised over her head. She had done it.

"Awesome shot," Charlie said, pounding Pudge on the helmet.

"I didn't know you were such a Northern fan," Pudge said, and he shook his head.

Charlie glanced over in time to see the Northern shooter with her stick held high. He banged the top of the boards. Still tied!

"I hate both shooters going at once," Charlie said. "I don't know who to watch."

Trisha came to the bench with a big grin on her face. She hopped the boards and stood next to Emily. The two friends punched gloves very softly, as if the goal had been no big deal. Charlie had to hand it to them. Those two were calm under pressure, and that was a big-time shot.

"Peanuts, toffee, toast and pie, Julia will score, and that's no lie," Scott and Nick chanted this time.

The noise got even louder, which Charlie hadn't thought was possible. "I can't look," Pudge said. "Tell me when it's over."

The whistle blew and suddenly the arena grew quiet, as if everyone watching had taken a collective breath.

Julia went in fast, like Trisha; and again, the goalie was out of her crease. Two metres from the hash marks Julia pulled the puck back. The goalie held firm. Julia brought the puck forward.

Charlie leaned forward, barely able to watch. There wasn't much to shoot at. The goalie was still way out.

Julia snapped her wrists, and the goalie dropped to her butterfly.

Charlie gasped.

The crowd roared.

Pudge was hugging him, and the Terrence Falls players were jumping up on the bench and screaming and yelling.

At the last possible moment, Julia had faked the shot, taken the puck wide left on her forehand and swept past the helpless goalie to stuff it in the wide-open net.

The Northern shooter skated back to her bench, her stick across her knees, her head down.

Charlie hopped over the boards, and he was not the first one. Michelle, Li and Sandra jumped into Julia's arms and they began hopping up and down. That broke up quickly and they raced down to Cassie, who waited with arms extended. Soon all the girls were in a group hug, pounding each other on the helmet.

Charlie and Pudge stood to the side. Something didn't feel right about joining in.

Julia noticed them first. "The boys are all lonely," she said. Michelle, Sandra and she came over and gave them hugs, and soon all the girls were celebrating with Charlie and Pudge. Charlie felt slightly embarrassed — and at the same time it was fun.

They lined up to shake hands with Northern. He braced himself for a diss when he came to the tall girl.

"Good luck against Chelsea," she said.

Her friend added, "And good luck with the fundraising."

Charlie finished shaking hands, and as he skated off caught up with Julia.

"I'll rank that up with the greatest goals of all time," Charlie said to Julia.

"We haven't won yet," she said.

He could tell she was stoked, though. "You got us closer," he said. "I could barely watch."

She hopped off the ice, as did he, and they walked

together to the dressing room.

"I was so nervous I thought I'd be sick," she confessed. "Then that crazy goalie came so far out of her net and I didn't know what to do. I changed my mind at the last second, and I was praying, 'Please don't poke check me. Please don't poke check me.'"

"I was saying, 'Please score. Please score.'"

She laughed and pushed open the dressing room door. Charlie followed her in. She turned and put a hand up to his chest.

"This is kind of the girls' dressing room, Charlie."

Michelle and Li were giggling at him from the corner. He felt beyond dumb.

"Um . . . I'll go find Pudge," he said.

But as he opened the door, the rest of the girls piled in and he had to step aside.

"Can we help you, Charlie Joyce?" Emily said.

"Are you afraid to get undressed in your own room?" Trisha teased.

Charlie knew he was beet red. There was no way out of this but leave — and quickly. "I just wanted to say great game, ladies. You won it for us. Awesome. We take this effort level into the Chelsea game and we've won that money."

"Charlie Joyce came in to give us a victory speech," Trisha said. "How cute is that, girls?"

Emily laughed. "Very cute, Charlie Joyce."

"Thanks, Charlie Joyce," the girls chorused, giggling.

"Right. Yeah. Thanks. Bye."

He retreated to his dressing room. Pudge was unwrapping the tape from his shin pads. Zachary, Scott and Matt were sitting across from him on the opposite bench, and Nick was in his wheelchair in the middle of the room.

"It's the Ladies' Man," Scott announced.

Charlie took off his helmet and slumped next to Pudge. "I really do stupid things sometimes," he said.

"You also state the obvious a lot," Nick said.

"And was there a reason you decided to almost not score in the shootout?" Scott said, with pretended curiosity. "In hockey you try to put the puck *past* the other team's goalie."

"How would you know?" Nick said. "Have you *ever* scored?"

"No," Scott said, "but I knew a guy who knew a guy who had a cousin who once scored a goal in practice."

"My mistake," Nick said, holding his hands up in the air. "I didn't realize you were an expert."

"Chelsea is playing next," Zachary said. "We should check them out. Maybe Savard and Burnett didn't join."

"They won their first game 14–2," Pudge said, tossing a tape ball into the garbage. "I'm pretty sure they're here."

"Then we better play every period like it's overtime," Charlie said.

It had all come down to one game, and with the four boys across from him unable to play, Terrence Falls was seriously undermanned — literally. They had barely beat Northern in a shootout. Would it be enough against the Chelsea powerhouse?

It had better be.

26

REVERSAL OF FORTUNE

Charlie heaved a huge sigh and skated to the faceoff circle to Cassie's left. He glanced at the clock — 2:25 to play and the score tied at three apiece. Chelsea had just missed an open net. Their winger took a fraction of a second too long to shoot and Pudge had been able to drive across the line and stop the puck. Cassie had then scrambled over and fallen on the puck to get a stoppage in play.

Savard was already in the circle to Cassie's left. Hilton had made sure Charlie was almost always out against him, and on the few shifts he could not be, Emily had stepped up big time. Savard had scored two goals, but all things considered, Charlie thought that was a major victory. Even better was that while Chelsea had scored two in the first period, which gave them the first point, Terrence Falls had rallied for two in the next period to snag the second. They had traded markers in the third; and with so little time left, the next goal would almost certainly win it.

Charlie adopted a reverse grip and approached the faceoff. The ref held the puck over the dot and hesitated. That hesitation made Charlie flinch and he pulled his stick back. The ref straightened out and pointed.

"New centre for Terrence Falls," she said.

Charlie put his stick across his knees and looked up at the ref. "I barely moved my stick," he said.

She pointed again.

"You're supposed to drop the puck when you hold it out," he said.

The look on her face suggested he'd better keep his mouth shut if he didn't want a penalty. He left the circle. Trisha brushed by him. Julia had taken a step towards the dot, but seeing Trisha already set up, she slowly drifted back to the hash marks. Charlie took Trisha's spot, behind Emily.

Charlie looked to the point. Burnett had switched sides with the other defenceman, standing three metres inside the blue line close to the top of the circle. He had a deadly slapshot.

Emily looked over her shoulder. "You got him?"

"No problem," Charlie said.

Charlie took a step away from the Chelsea left winger to make sure he had a clear path to Burnett.

Savard slapped Trisha's stick; then the ref dropped the puck. It was child's play for Savard to backhand the puck with a reverse grip towards Burnett. Charlie's heart skipped a beat. He rushed towards Burnett, who had already begun his backswing. In horror Charlie felt himself tumble to the ice. He had tripped over the extended left foot of Chelsea's left winger, but he had no time to consider if the trip was deliberate. Burnett was winding up right in front of him. He put a glove over his face and braced himself.

He didn't feel anything. A roar went up from the

crowd. Charlie looked up and then let his head sink back to the ice. Burnett had his stick over his head. No surprise there — it was too good a chance for Burnett to miss.

Trisha was screaming at the ref. "He hit my freakin' stick," she fumed. "What's wrong with you. Are you blind? Are you stupid?"

"Button it, number 10, or you'll get an unsportsmanlike," the ref said.

"You threw our centre out for nothing, and then their centre whacks my stick before the draw and you drop the puck. Do you want Chelsea to win? Do you teach there or something?"

Julia stepped in between them and pushed Trisha away. "Forget it," she said.

"But he totally hit my stick," she screamed, looking at the ref.

"Trisha, you'll get a penalty. We'll get it back."

Trisha growled and stomped her skate blade on the ice before letting Julia lead her away. Charlie stood, dejected, by the blue line.

One of the refs passed him.

"Didn't you see their winger trip me?" Charlie said to him.

The ref shrugged. "Not my call. Ask the other ref," he said, looking away.

Charlie sat next to Trisha.

"I got tripped on the play by the left winger," he said. "She totally stuck out her foot. The refs are sleeping."

Trisha didn't respond.

"I . . . um . . . I said, I got tripped . . ." he began again.

"I heard you," Trisha said. "Don't worry about it." She stood up as Emily gathered the puck at the blue line. "Go for it, Em. Coast to coast," she called.

Emily dipsy-doodled her way past a forechecker and cut up ice into Chelsea's half of the neutral zone. Burnett was still out there and he swerved towards her, sweeping his stick at the puck. Emily was a hair quicker and fired it into their end, side-stepping Burnett and charging after it. Charlie admired her hustle. The girl never stopped skating.

The Chelsea goalie scooted to the corner to corral the puck, leaving it there for her defenceman. She took it on her forehand. The sight of Emily bearing down on her must have set her nerves off because rather than play it safe and rifle the puck behind the net she panicked and sent it up the middle. Sandra was there first, and moved in on goal.

The ref blew the play down.

The Terrence Falls students rose and cheered. Burnett had hooked her from behind, and the ref had called a penalty. Burnett was shaking his head and laughing, as if it was a bad call. Charlie wondered if it shouldn't have been a penalty shot. Trisha obviously felt the same, and she made sure the refs heard her opinion.

"She was on a breakaway," she yelled. "That's an obvious penalty shot. Come on. Get in the game. That's two lame calls. You're so bogus it hurts."

She was going too far. The ref would give them a bench penalty if she kept it up. "Trisha. We got the man advantage. We can't afford to even it up," he said.

Trisha stared at him, enraged. "Did you see it? Did you? She was on a breakaway." She banged the top of the boards. "The ref is giving them the game."

Charlie sat back. She wasn't going to listen to him.

Julia said softly, "Trisha, you're going to get a penalty. We need you for the last shift. You can't go to the box. You're right, but the refs aren't going to change their minds."

Trisha turned to her sharply, and then without a word sat back down. Hunched over, she rocked and continued to shake her head. "Unbelievable," she muttered several times. She stood up suddenly and sought Hilton's attention.

"Should we switch it up, Coach?" she said.

"They just got out there," Hilton answered.

"We should pull the goalie now and have a two-man advantage," Trisha said.

Hilton pursed his lips. "There's still too much time on the clock for my liking. Give them another thirty seconds." He waved at Cassie and then the clock, holding up one finger. "I'm going to leave Emily out there. Trisha and Julia shift for Sandra and Sophie. Charlie, you'll go on for Cassie when she comes off. Get the puck under control, and set Pudge up at the point for a shot. Okay?"

"Got it," Charlie said.

Julia nodded.

Trisha grabbed his shoulder. "We have to get on the ice," she said.

He understood how she felt. He'd been there. She just wanted to win so badly it was hard for her to control her feelings.

"Get ready," he said to her. "We're going to tie this up."

He held out his glove and they punched.

"Bring it back, Em," Trisha screamed.

Emily couldn't possibly hear, not with the noise the crowd was making. Somehow Nick and Scott had found drums for this game, and the Terrence Falls fans were clapping to the beat. Still, Charlie began to urge Emily on, as well.

The ref dropped the puck and Emily knocked it to the corner. The Chelsea defender and Sandra fought for control. The puck squibbed up the wall to the point and Pudge punched it back deep. The scene repeated itself, only this time, the Chelsea winger was able to chip it out off the boards. Michelle raced across, gathered the puck on her forehand, and skated across the neutral zone to the far boards. The Chelsea left winger pressured her before she could cross the red line, however, forcing Michelle to pass to Sophie about two metres outside the blue line. Chelsea's left defenceman was there to challenge, and Sophie could not get it in. Savard swooped over, and with three powerful strides got the puck to centre and sent it deep into Terrence Falls' end.

Charlie sat back down. There was a minute and thirty seconds left. Lots of time if they could get it back down the ice quickly. He took a sip of water and readied himself. Cassie would follow the play and come off with the rush. Pudge had the puck behind the net. He faked to his right and came around the left side, about three metres from the boards. A forechecker moved in. Pudge waited for her to commit, and then sent a sweet pass to Emily breaking across the top of the circle.

"Get out of the way, ref!" Trisha screamed. She smashed her stick on the boards.

Charlie couldn't blame her. The puck deflected off the ref's skate and spun crazily to the wall near the blue line. Savard was first to it, and he jammed it back into their zone, killing valuable seconds off the clock.

Hilton had his foot on the boards. "Wingers, change 'em up! Change 'em up!"

Sophie and Sandra turned to the bench. Emily looked over and Hilton waved her back. She immediately set off to help on the rush. Michelle raced to get the puck, and wasted no time heading up ice. Julia and Trisha hopped the boards and joined in. A forechecker lunged at Michelle, but she swept past her, gained the line and passed across the zone to Trisha. Trisha cradled the puck, and then lofted a high wrist shot to the opposite corner in Chelsea's end. The timing was perfect. Julia hit the blue line at full speed and beat the right defender to the puck. It was another beautiful play by his wingers.

"Charlie. Get out there."

Hilton lifted Charlie off the bench. He had been so busy watching, he had forgotten Cassie was coming off for the extra attacker. Charlie threw himself over the boards and skated hard to get in the play. Julia had continued behind their net and had the puck at the midboards, close to the wall. Trisha was wide left, moving slowly towards their net. Charlie figured she would either cut to the net if Julia passed it to her, or go behind it. He slowed to see what she would do.

Trisha took off and at the last second veered around the net. Julia banked the puck off the back wall to her. Charlie put it into high gear and stormed into the slot. Savard tried to pick him up, but he was like a mad bull and there was no way he would be stopped. Trisha saucered the puck and Charlie stepped into it with all his strength.

All six TFH players banged their sticks on the ice.

The goalie sat with her legs stretched out in front of her, holding the puck on top of her glove to the ref.

Charlie cruised to the right faceoff with his stick across his knees and his head down. He had shot the puck right into her glove. It was the perfect chance. He'd blown it.

"Charlie, let me take the draw. You set up at the top of the circle. We need your shot." Trisha peered at him, her intense eyes wide open. "I can beat this guy. I know it."

Charlie straightened out. He had taken dozens of draws against Savard. He was a faceoff master, and Charlie had trouble beating him. If they lost the draw, and Chelsea got the puck out, the game would be over. But she had come through before. He decided to trust her.

"He usually relies on the reverse grip and his timing. You need to tie him up first," Charlie said.

She set up for the draw.

Trisha was not the listening type. Charlie doubted she would follow his advice. He lined up behind her and raised his stick slightly.

"I'm going in front of the net," Pudge said to him.

That was good thinking. His buddy was strong and practically impossible to move. If they won the draw, he would set up a good screen.

Trisha stepped back from the circle. "Charlie, over to the left a bit."

It was painful, being ordered around. He had to do it, just to get it over with.

Trisha waved her glove at him. "No. More. Here." She came over and banged the tip of her stick on the ice half a metre away.

Charlie couldn't help himself and he rolled his eyes. "Just win the draw already."

"Line it up, number 10," the ref said. She blew her whistle.

The crowd grew quiet in anticipation. The ref held the puck out. Trisha moved early, pivoting with her left foot, and spun into Savard as the puck fell. Savard was blocked off, and Trisha muscled the puck back to Charlie, directly onto his stick. Pudge turned to face him. He was in front of the goalie.

This time it was Charlie's turn for shooting practice. He reared back, took one quick look, and fired at the top corner, stick side.

The crowd roared.

Trisha wrapped her arms around him, jumping up and down. "You did it! I knew it. You're awesome. Awesome. What a shot. I knew it."

Julia threw herself on them, screaming Scott's cheer at the top of her lungs. "Terrence Falls? Yes! Terrence Falls? Yes!"

Emily was jumping like mad also, too excited to speak.

Pudge came over with a huge grin and he wrapped his arms around the four of them.

"I was just praying you wouldn't hit me," he said.

"It was tempting, but . . ." Charlie said.

As a group they made their way to the bench and

high-fived their teammates. Scott and Nick were banging on their drums and chanting the school name, along with everyone else. It was a magical moment, and Charlie didn't want it to end. The ref's whistle reminded him that it would have to, though. This game wasn't over, and the prize money wasn't theirs yet.

Cassie was skating backwards to her net, banging the ice with her big stick.

"Charlie's line, I want you to stay out there," Hilton said. "Don't be afraid to go for the goal if you can, but nothing crazy. I like our chances in the shootout."

Burnett had left the penalty box, and he and Savard were talking at the blue line. As Charlie came for the faceoff, Savard pushed off on one foot and glided to a stop a metre from the circle.

"Did you really have to score that goal?" Savard said. "I felt like going home."

"We need that money to fix our roof," Charlie said. "Otherwise, we're going to have to invade your school for a few months."

"It's almost worth losing to put a stop to that," Savard said. He paused and said, "But we'll win because Chelsea never loses to Terrence Falls."

The referee held the puck over the dot, and the two rivals bent over. Their sticks clashed and the puck bounced off Charlie's skate. Savard took a swipe at it, and sent the puck to the right boards. Trisha got to it first and backhanded it to Michelle. She whisked it to Pudge. Charlie set up a metre inside the red line, hoping for a quick pass. Trisha had other ideas.

She had sneaked up the right wall and burst into

the middle holding her stick up high. Pudge fired it. Trisha reached for it; so did Burnett. They both got to the puck at the same time, and Trisha fell hard to the ice. A hush came over the arena. She wasn't moving. Charlie rushed over. Burnett was kneeling next to her.

"Are you okay?" Burnett said. "I'm sorry. I didn't mean to run into you."

Charlie could hear the concern in his voice. He knew Burnett was a clean player and would never body-check in non-contact, let alone a girl. He had only gone for the puck.

Charlie dropped to his knees. "Hey, Trisha. Can you talk? Are you good?"

"Move aside, boys. Let me take a look." The ref knelt down. "How are you feeling, young lady?" she said.

"A bit winded," Trisha answered.

Charlie was relieved to hear her voice. She'd be okay. She was too tough to go down in a situation like this.

Trisha raised her head, and then got to her hands and knees. The two refs hooked their hands under her arms and lifted her up.

"I'm real sorry," Burnett repeated.

"Not your fault," Trisha said. "It's just hockey. I'm fine." She unhooked her arms from the refs'. Charlie helped her to the bench, and Julia came over too.

"Did you hit your head?" Charlie asked.

"His shoulder got me in the chest," she said, gasping. "I'm winded more than anything else. He's like a concrete wall."

"He's at least twice your size," Charlie said.

Hilton had the door open, and he reached out to help her.

Trisha looked back. "Go score a goal or something."

"You be ready for the shootout," Charlie said, laughing.

That was the Trisha he had come to know. He looked at the clock. There were only fifteen seconds left. The players were content to let the clock run down, and after some scrappy play in the neutral zone, the buzzer sounded to end it.

Charlie and Julia stopped at centre.

"We've had some practice at this," Charlie said. "This game is ours."

"I'll score if you do," Julia said.

"Deal."

He held out his glove and she gave it a punch.

"Line up and shake hands," a ref said to them.

"But what about the shootout?" Charlie said.

She shook her head. "There's no time for that. The next game is starting in five minutes and we need to flood the ice."

"We have to finish the game, though," Charlie said, skating after her. "It's all tied up. We need a winner."

"Chelsea won," she said. "They had two more goals overall in the tournament."

That hit him like a slap in the face and he stopped in his tracks. He saw the ref talking to Hilton. His coach was arguing, but the ref waved him off and skated away. A few Chelsea players raised their sticks and some high-fived, but it was half-hearted. They obviously were not proud of the way it had ended.

Charlie's head began to swim, and he looked around in a daze. No shootout. Two more goals?

Julia stood before him. There were tears in her eyes.

He had no words to make her feel better. He wanted to cry himself.

They had lost. It was so unfair.

27

THE WALKING DEAD

Dalton hit the Return key.

"I think that should do it," Dalton said. "I just had to change some settings."

"Dalton, you're a genius," Pudge said. "I couldn't get the stupid thing to work."

Dalton's cheeks turned red. "Glad to help." He clicked the mouse a few times. "You simply need to click on this icon and the movie will start," he said. "I believe Mr. Hilton will be making an announcement first, however. I think it will be interesting . . . for sure, interesting." He looked around. "I should speak to Melissa and A.J. about setting up a second beverage centre on the other side of the cafeteria. Students would appreciate the convenience. Excuse me for a moment, gentlemen."

Julia came over. "Are we ready to go?" she said. "The crowd is getting restless."

"Apparently, Hilton's going to make some announcements and we can start after that," Charlie said.

Alexandra and Rebecca joined them.

"I like the cotton candy machine; at a buck a bag you can't afford not to pig out," Alexandra said, stuffing a hunk into her mouth. "Want some?"

Julia took a handful and shared it with Charlie and Pudge.

"It's good to see you guys at school," Charlie said to Alexandra and Rebecca. "How are you feeling?"

"The doctor said I can come back to school next week," Alexandra said. Suddenly, her eyes welled up. "Sorry. I know I'm being lame," she said, wiping the tears away. "But I can't believe we won't actually be here much longer."

"I heard the roof work might not even get done in time for the start of school next year," Rebecca said. "This really could be it."

"Are you trying to cheer us up?" Julia said.

"Sorry, Jules," Rebecca said. "After the accident . . . well, I thought that everything would be okay, that fate was on our side." She shook her head slowly. "But I guess life isn't a fairy tale, and there isn't always a happy ending."

Julia put her hand on Rebecca's shoulder. "I've cried enough. You lighten up this minute or I'm sending you home."

Rebecca laughed. "I promise I'll be obnoxiously cheerful from now on."

Scott came over, followed by Nick in his wheelchair. Scott had three bags of popcorn and a half-eaten bag of cotton candy.

"Thanks for getting everyone snacks, Slatsky," Alexandra said.

Scott's eyes darted nervously. "Um, I was thinking these were for me . . . and I'm really hungry . . . and I'd share, but I have to eat all this myself or I might faint . . .

which will be bad for movie night, and . . ." His voice trailed off, and he stuffed a big hunk of cotton candy in his mouth.

Charlie noticed a few more latecomers straggle in. The place was packed, with sleeping bags spread out all over the floor. Lots of kids had even come in their pyjamas, and everyone was joking and goofing around. "At least movie night's a success. We should raise at least five thousand in ticket sales, and with concessions it could be over seventy-five hundred," he said.

Charlie looked up at the stage. Hilton was setting up a microphone. "Can I have your attention?" he said. The students quieted down. "I won't be long, and I definitely do not want to delay the first TFH double feature movie night." Some of the students clapped politely. "Some of you may not know that I am the teacher rep for the Fundraising Committee." A louder cheer went up. "Thanks," he said, smiling. "I know. It's a great honour. Anyway, I have a few announcements in connection with that. First, through the hard work of your committee and your fellow students, we managed to raise, including what we make tonight, approximately twenty-four thousand dollars!"

A few students clapped.

"And we must also thank the parents, who donated another fifty-eight thousand dollars, which is really something."

That news was met with silence. Charlie crossed his arms and leaned against the wall. There it was. Now everyone knew. They had not come close.

"But there's more," Hilton carried on. "Our business community became energized this past week, impressed by all your efforts to keep TFH open; and with their help, we were able to raise another eighteen thousand dollars."

That was cool of them to try to help, thought Charlie.

"Have you been keeping track?" he asked Pudge.

"An even hundred thousand," Pudge said.

Charlie gave a low whistle. He wondered what they would do with that money. Give it back?

"Now I would like to introduce your committee president, Melissa, and two very special guests, Andrea Ferreira and J.C. Savard."

"This is bizarre. What's he doing here?" Charlie said to Pudge.

Andrea accepted the microphone from Hilton. "Hi, Terrence Falls. I'm the president of Chelsea High student council. First off, let me tell you I think this movie night is a great idea; and you've had tons of great ideas for fundraising. I'm not too proud to admit we could use some of your school spirit and energy."

"No chance," someone yelled from the crowd, followed by some laughter.

Andrea didn't let it faze her. She laughed and said, "You might be right. But anyway, if TFH has to shut down we are happy to have some of you come to Chelsea — and find out why Chelsea's the most awesome school there is . . ."

A bunch of kids booed, and Andrea laughed again. "I'm just kidding. I know we're rivals, but — and don't let this get around — we also have a lot of respect for you guys, and we especially respect how hard you've worked on the fundraising. To raise this much money is awesome, really; and we want to help out. J.C.'s going to make an announcement about that."

"Is he going to admit finally that Chelsea cheats at hockey?" Scott whispered.

"It's time their trickery was exposed," Nick agreed.

"Some of you might know that there was a co-ed hockey tournament this past weekend," J.C. began, which set off another round of cheering, "and as usual, it was Chelsea and Terrence Falls in the finals. You guys only had nine players, and I admit I thought we'd win easily. But it ended in a tie, and we were awarded the win because we had two more goals in the other games.

"Like Andrea said, me and some of my teammates admire what you're trying to do. We all read about the bus accident and how you've come together to try and save your school year. As nice as it would have been to have the prize money from the hockey tournament, we think you could use it more. So we're here to donate the twenty-five thousand dollars to the Terrence Falls High Roof Fund."

The announcement was met with stunned silence.

Then Scott and Nick started chanting, "Chel-sea! Chel-sea! Chel-sea!" and soon everyone had joined in.

Andrea handed a cheque to Melissa, who waved it over her head.

Pudge pulled on Charlie's sleeve. "That brings it to one hundred and twenty-five thousand."

Charlie started to get excited. They had not raised all the money, but surely they could do something. Maybe there was a chance. This must have been what Dalton was talking about.

"I wonder if the repair could get started while we

keep fundraising," Charlie said to Pudge.

Hilton took the microphone back. "Thanks, Andrea and J.C. That generosity is really inspiring, and please tell everyone at Chelsea how much we appreciate this — but don't get too confident, because we all know that next year Terrence Falls will be winning the Champions Cup."

"Ter-rence Falls! Ter-rence Falls! Ter-rence Falls!"

Hilton held his hand up and the chanting petered out. "We have one final announcement. Please give a warm Terrence Falls welcome to Heather Wright, the founder and President of Bee-Bees Boutique, and the sponsor of the co-ed hockey tournament."

She walked onto the stage and waved, taking the microphone from Hilton. "This is so heartwarming and fun. I almost wish I was back in high school . . . almost."

The kids laughed.

"I first learned about Terrence Falls when two students came and asked one of our managers, Joanne Bettencourt, if we would allow them to use the prize money from the hockey tournament for their roof fundraiser. Ms Bettencourt asked me, and I thought that under the circumstances we should allow it. I also want to say how impressed I am by the generosity of the kids at Chelsea. So good work, guys." She extended a thumbs-up to J.C. and Andrea.

"Ms Bettencourt also sent me a newspaper article about the bus crash. Maybe it was a coincidence, but the same two kids who came to ask about the prize money were on that bus; and more amazing is that they, along with others, risked their own lives to save the lives of the other passengers and the bus driver. I got in touch with Mr. Hilton, and inquired about the fundraising. He told me how hard you've all worked, and how close you are to hitting your target."

It was so quiet you could hear a pin drop.

She held up a piece of paper. "I have a cheque here from Bee-Bees Boutique payable to Terrence Falls High School Roof Fund in the amount of twenty-five thousand dollars, which I believe —"

She never got the chance to finish.

The kids went crazy.

Pandemonium. Chaos. Insanity.

The school was staying open!

Charlie barely remembered the next five minutes. He and Pudge were high-fiving like maniacs, and hugging and screaming, along with everyone else. Zachary hobbled over on his crutches, Nick wheeling behind him, along with Scott and Matt. Julia, Alexandra and Rebecca joined them also, and everyone got a hug. Scott then got up on a chair.

"Terrence Falls?" he yelled.

"Yes!"

"Terrence Falls?"

"Yes!"

"Terrence Falls?"

"Yes! Yes! Yes!"

Charlie ended up next to Julia somehow.

She brushed her hair from her face. "You know, Charlie, you were really brave. I stayed because of you. I was so scared I could've cried."

Charlie was about to say something tough. But the truth was he had been totally scared, and it was really seeing her determination that made him stay.

He leaned over. "Don't blow my cover, but I was beyond terrified. I'd need a new word to describe it."

"Scarified?" she offered.

"Petriscared?" he said.

"Okay — scared will do," she laughed.

"I might have left if you weren't there," he said, seriously now. He had wanted to tell her that for a long time, and it felt good to finally say it.

She tucked her hair behind her ears. "Charlie Joyce doesn't run away from things," she said.

He didn't know what got into him, but he gave her a hug, and for a moment he forgot about all the celebrating and the noise.

"How about we get movie night started?" Hilton said into the mic.

For once the students didn't listen to him. Everyone was still too stoked, and they wandered around slapping hands, hugging and talking about it. Eventually, they made their way back to their spots on the floor. Hilton didn't seem to mind, and he waited patiently. When he saw that most of them had settled back in, he announced, "Roll 'em, guys!"

Charlie and Pudge went back to the computer to start the movie.

Dalton came over. "Tremendous news, don't you think? Sorry I couldn't tell you beforehand. I was under strict orders. You guys should sit with your friends. I have this."

Charlie loved that idea. He was tired of organizing stuff and wanted to relax and have fun. He saw J.C. sitting with the rest of his buds and he wanted to talk to the Chelsea star and catch up. Apart from their brief banter on the ice, he had not spoken to him since hockey camp this past summer. But something didn't feel right, and then he suddenly realized that Dalton was not simply being helpful. Dalton didn't have friends to sit with — and after everything he had done, that was plain wrong.

"Start the movie, Dalton," Charlie ordered.

Dalton saluted, and with a click of the mouse, the movie popped onto the big screen. Charlie put an arm around Dalton's shoulders. "And you come with me," he said, half-dragging him along.

"Hey, Rebels," he said, kneeling down, "Listen up. I got an idea. We need a manager, and it occurred to me that the greatest manager in the world is right here. What do you say?"

Scott sat up and put a hand against his cheek and gasped. "Joyce! I don't think you've ever had an idea in your life, and now you have the most genius idea of all time."

Nick's leg was propped up on some pillows. He reached over and shook Dalton's hand. "One thing to remember: Scott has a very small brain and he needs lots of help. Be patient."

"Welcome to the crew," Zachary said, lying on his back with his hands behind his head.

"I . . . um . . . I do enjoy the game of hockey," Dalton stammered. "Thanks. It's quite an honour."

They all laughed.

"You're so funny," Alexandra said. "These guys are so disorganized they're desperate. They should be paying you."

"I couldn't ask for money," Dalton said so sincerely they laughed harder.

"*Shhh!*" came from all around.

"And sit down!" another kid added.

Charlie pushed down on Dalton's shoulder. "The computer will work fine. The Rebels stick together," he said.

J.C. held out his hand, grinning from ear to ear, and Charlie shook it.

"We'll catch up after the first flick," J.C. said. "I want to hear about that crazy accident."

"It's a long story," Charlie said.

J.C. gave him a thumbs-up and turned to watch the film.

A zombie appeared over a hill, dragging one leg behind. He moved slowly across the screen, blood dripping down his cheek.

"That looks like Scott at breakfast time," Nick said.

"I'm a mess before I have my coffee," Scott said.

"*Shhh!*"

They did their best to not laugh, but it was no use, they couldn't stop.

An avalanche of Shhhs came their way.

Charlie settled back to watch. It was cool to think movie night was his idea, and now there were hundreds of kids hanging out together. So what if they were missing the Champions Cup? TFH was staying open, which meant they had won the biggest game of all.

He could not wait for school to start tomorrow — and how often does a guy say that!

ABOUT THE AUTHOR

David Skuy spent most of his childhood playing one sport or another — hockey, soccer, football, rugby. Now he is a writer and lawyer who lives in Toronto, Ontario with his wife and two kids. He still plays hockey once a week and remains a die-hard Leafs fan.

He began writing the Game Time series to try to capture the competition, the challenges, the friendships and the rivalries that make sports so much fun.